IW

VIZ GRAPHIC NOVEL

Descendants of Darkness™

Yami no Matsuei

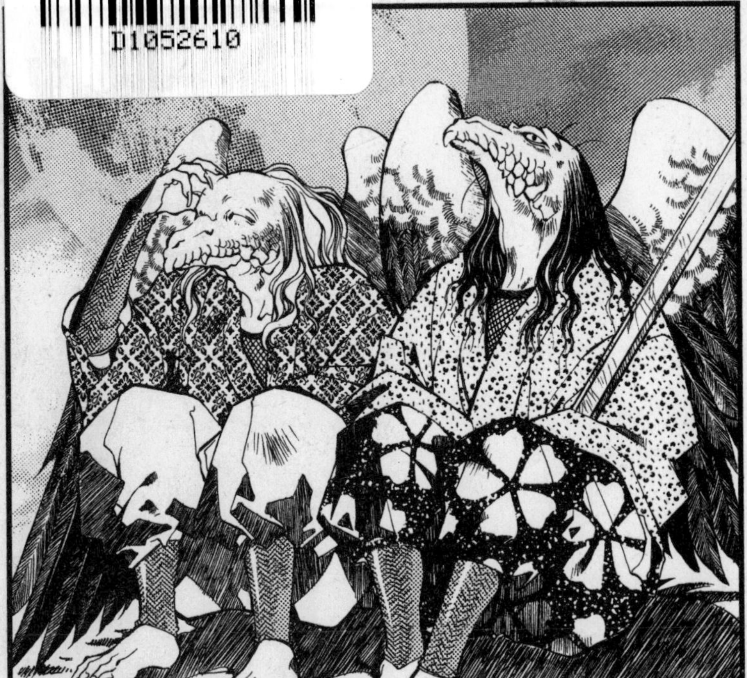

9

Story & Art by Yoko Matsushita

Descendants of Darkness
Yami no Matsuei
Vol. 9
Shôjo Edition

Story & Art by
Yoko Matsushita

English Adaptation/Lance Caselman
Translation/David Ury
Touch-Up & Lettering/Gia Cam Luc
Graphics & Cover Design/Courtney Utt
Editor/Nancy Thistlethwaite

Managing Editor/Annette Roman
Director of Production/Noboru Watanabe
VP of Publishing/Alvin Lu
Sr. Director of Acquisitions/Rika Inouye
VP of Sales & Marketing/Liza Coppola
Publisher/Hyoe Narita

Yami no Matsuei by Yoko Matsushita © Yoko Matsushita 1999. All rights reserved. First published in Japan in 2000 by HAKUSENSHA, Inc., Tokyo. English language translation rights in America and Canada arranged with HAKUSENSHA, Inc., Tokyo. New and adapted artwork and text © 2005 VIZ Media, LLC. THE DESCENDANTS OF DARKNESS logo is a trademark of VIZ Media, LLC. The stories, characters and incidents mentioned in this publication are entirely fictional.

Published by VIZ Media, LLC
P.O. Box 77064
San Francisco, CA 94107

Shôjo Edition
10 9 8 7 6 5 4 3 2 1
First printing, December 2005

For advertising rates or media kit, e-mail advertising@viz.com

www.viz.com   store.viz.com

Table of Contents

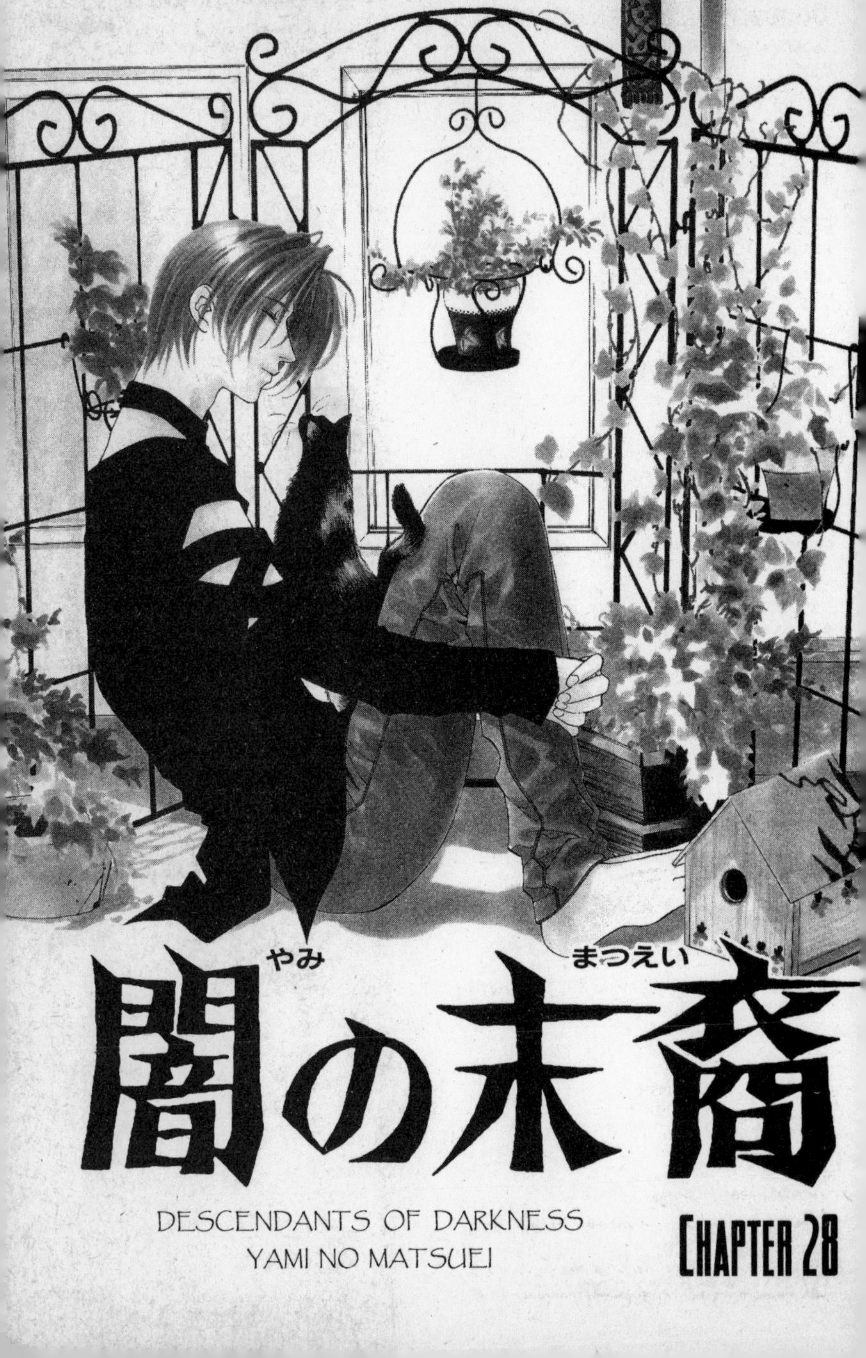

闇(やみ)の末裔(まつえい)

DESCENDANTS OF DARKNESS
YAMI NO MATSUEI

CHAPTER 28

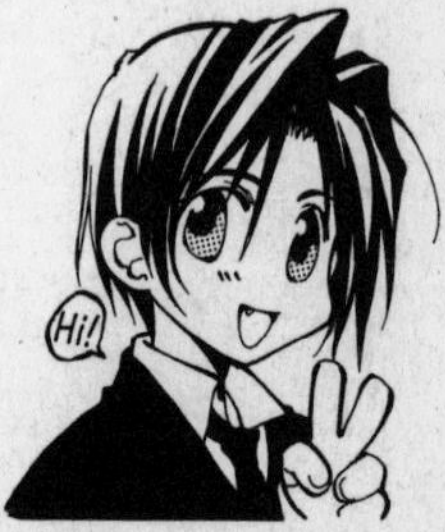
Hi!

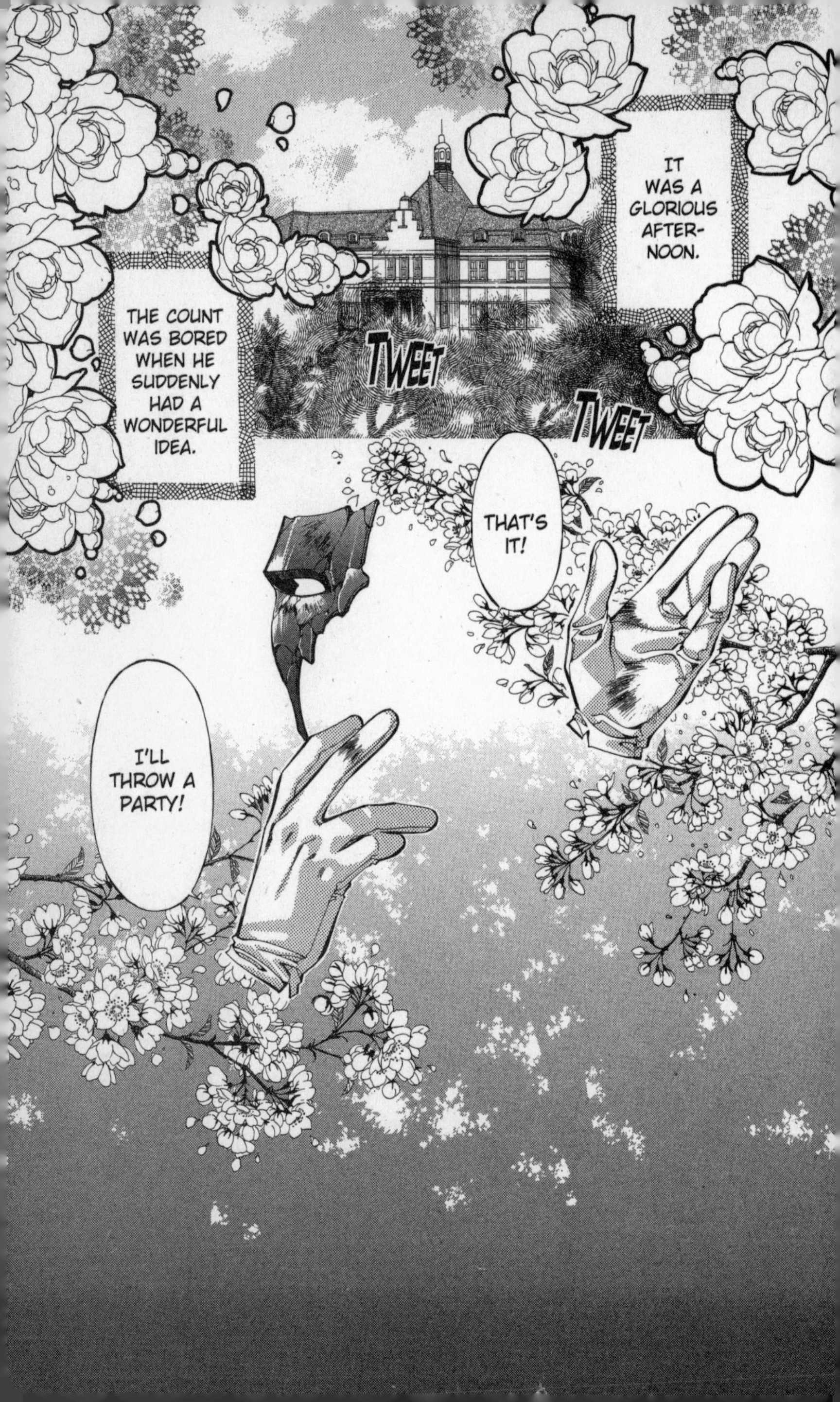
IT WAS A GLORIOUS AFTER-NOON.
TWEET
TWEET
THE COUNT WAS BORED WHEN HE SUDDENLY HAD A WONDERFUL IDEA.
THAT'S IT!
I'LL THROW A PARTY!

The Ministry of Hades, Area Five:
The Judgment Bureau

A COSTUME PARTY TO COMMEMORATE THE RECONSTRUCTION?

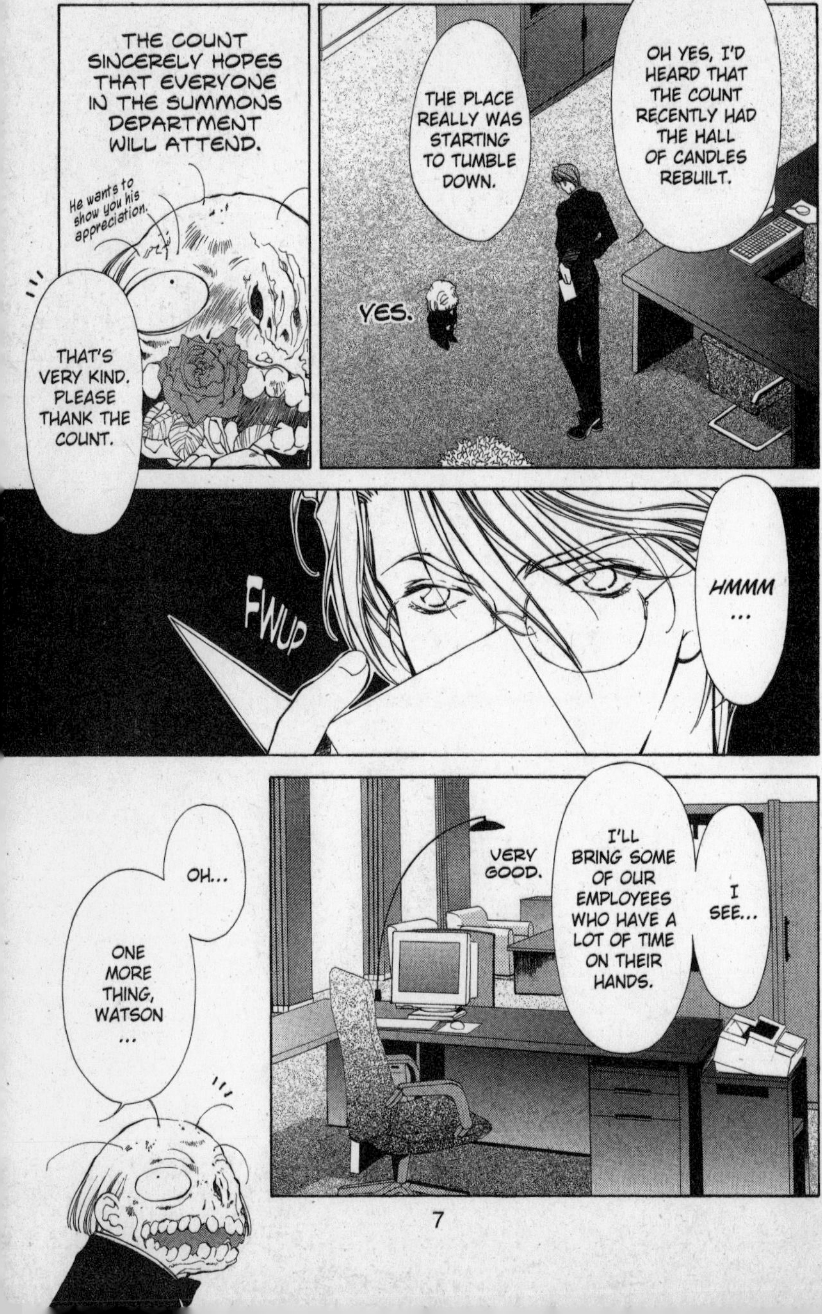
OH YES, I'D HEARD THAT THE COUNT RECENTLY HAD THE HALL OF CANDLES REBUILT.
THE PLACE REALLY WAS STARTING TO TUMBLE DOWN.
YES.
THE COUNT SINCERELY HOPES THAT EVERYONE IN THE SUMMONS DEPARTMENT WILL ATTEND.
He wants to show you his appreciation.
THAT'S VERY KIND. PLEASE THANK THE COUNT.
HMMM ...
FWUP
I SEE...
I'LL BRING SOME OF OUR EMPLOYEES WHO HAVE A LOT OF TIME ON THEIR HANDS.
VERY GOOD.
OH...
ONE MORE THING, WATSON ...

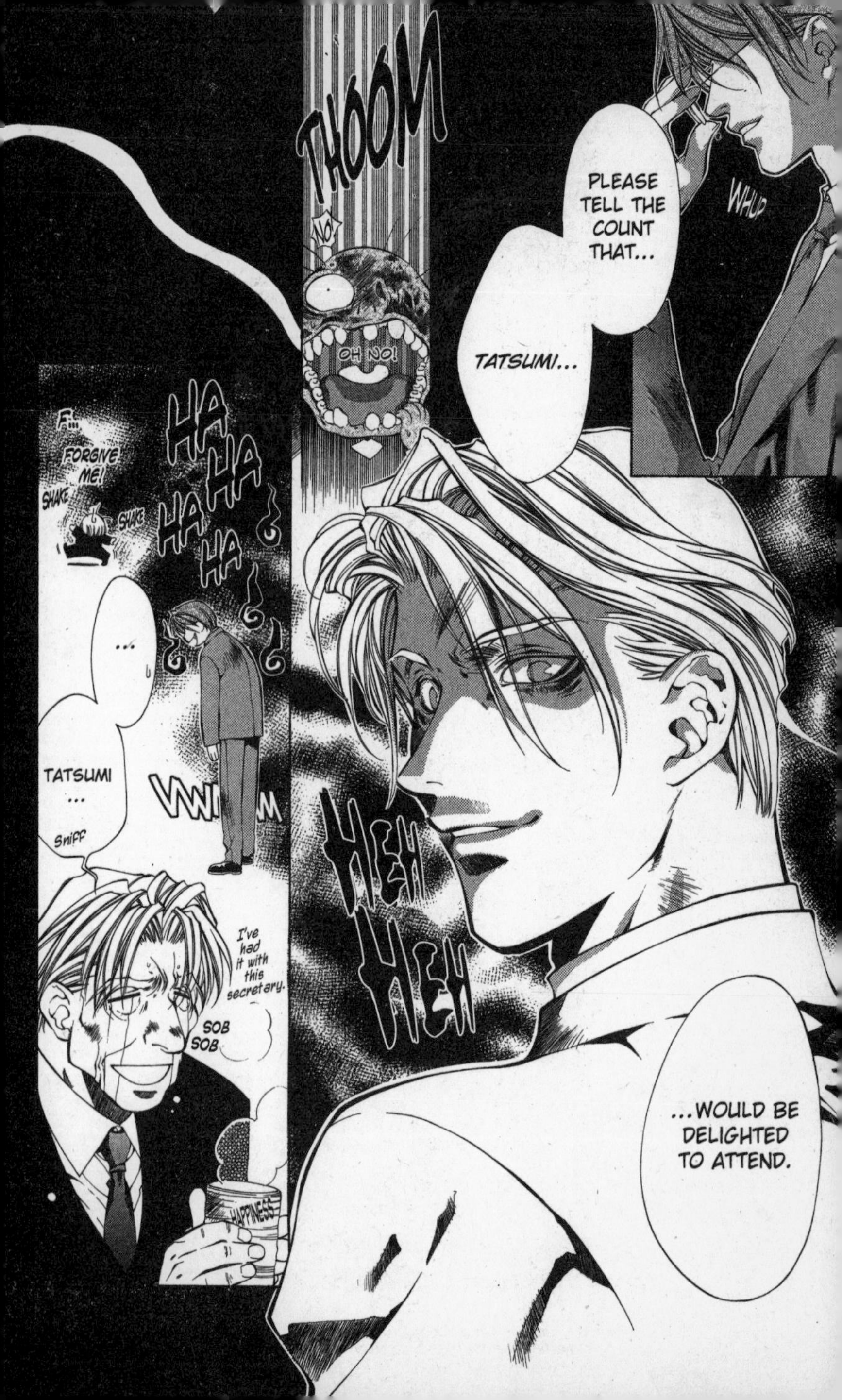
PLEASE TELL THE COUNT THAT...
WHUP
TATSUMI...
HEH HEH
...WOULD BE DELIGHTED TO ATTEND.
THOOM
NO!
OH NO!
F... FORGIVE ME!
SHAKE
SHAKE
HA HA HA HA HA
...
TATSUMI ...
Sniff
I've had it with this secretary.
SOB SOB
HAPPINESS

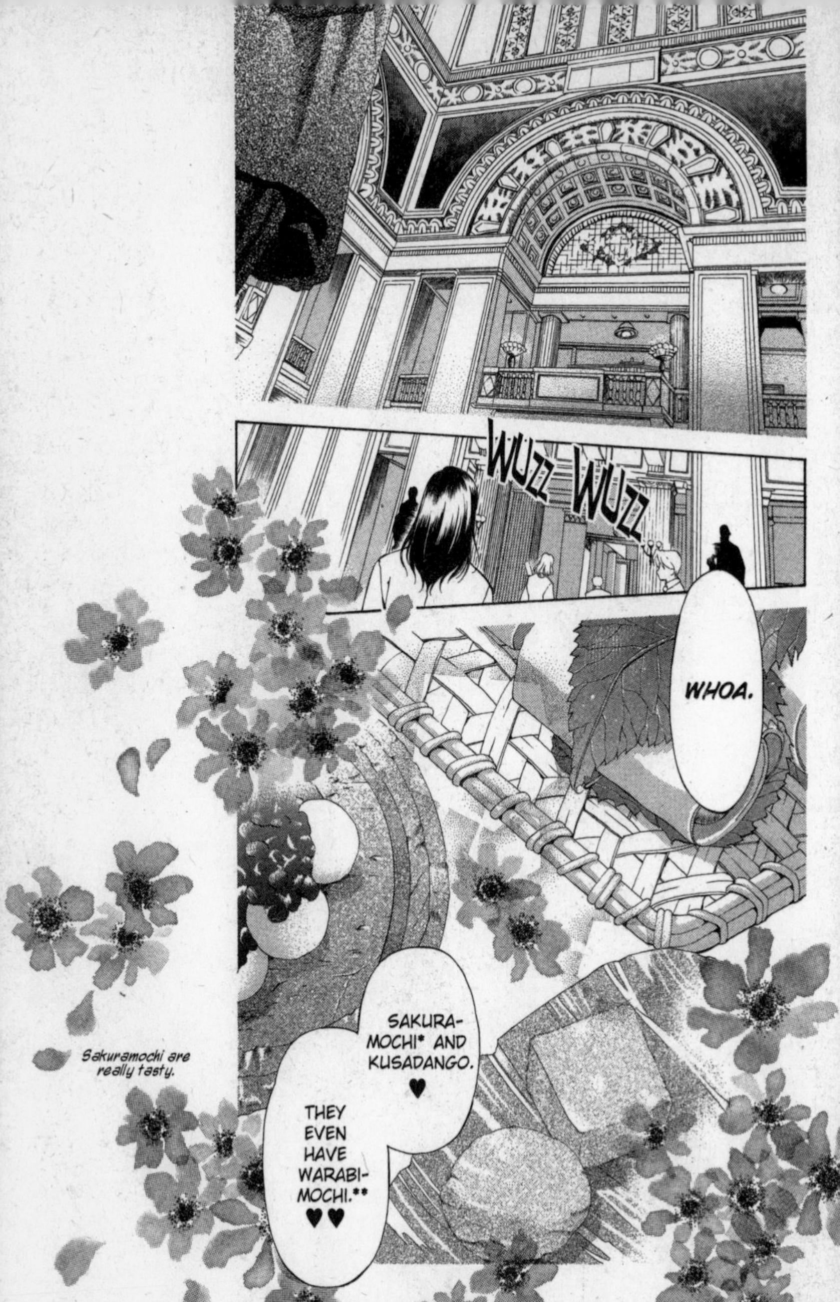
WUZZ WUZZ
WHOA.
SAKURA-MOCHI* AND KUSADANGO. ♥
THEY EVEN HAVE WARABI-MOCHI.** ♥♥
Sakuramochi are really tasty.

*Sakuramochi is rice and beans wrapped in a cherry leaf. Kusadango is a green rice ball.
**A rice ball coated with soybean powder.

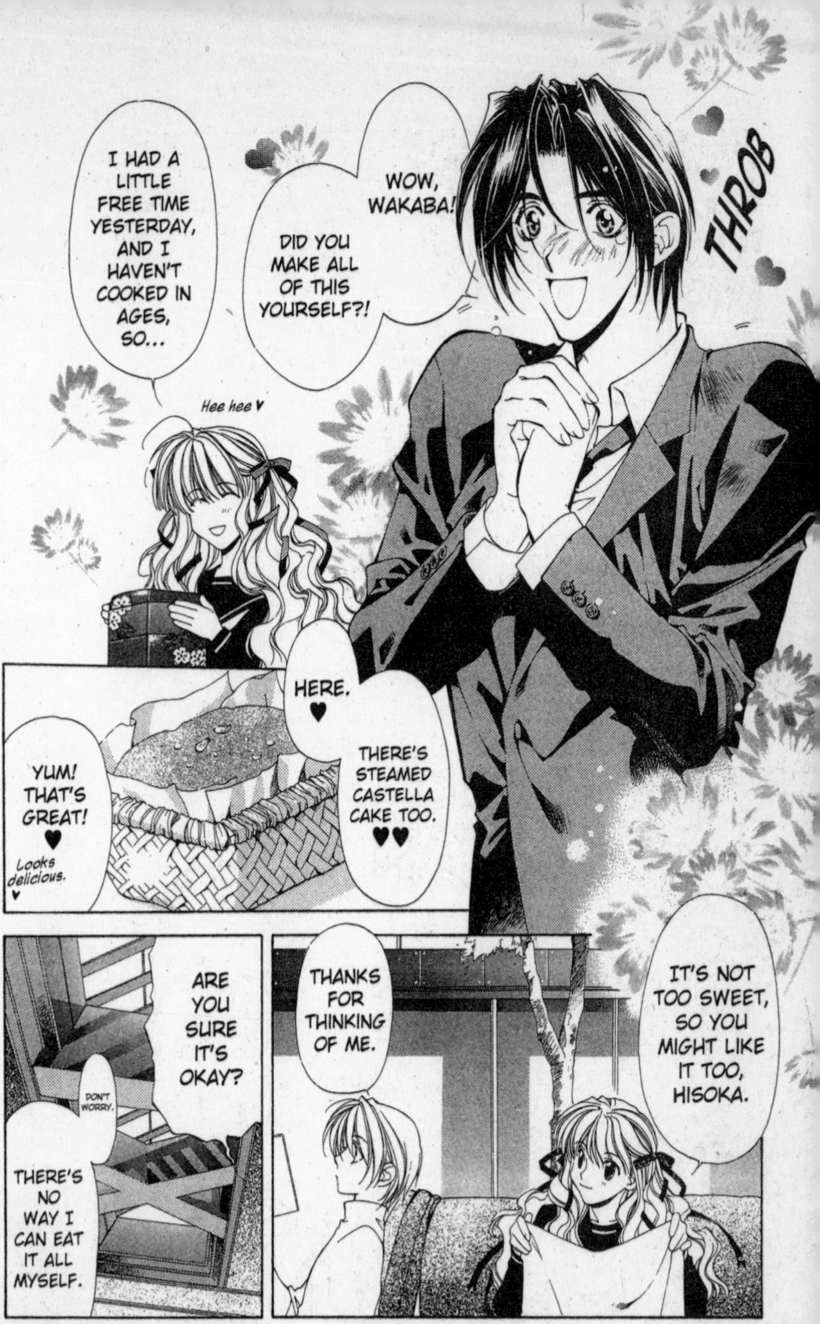
THROB
WOW, WAKABA!
DID YOU MAKE ALL OF THIS YOURSELF?!
I HAD A LITTLE FREE TIME YESTERDAY, AND I HAVEN'T COOKED IN AGES, SO...
Hee hee ♥
HERE. ♥
THERE'S STEAMED CASTELLA CAKE TOO. ♥♥
YUM! THAT'S GREAT! ♥
Looks delicious. ♥
IT'S NOT TOO SWEET, SO YOU MIGHT LIKE IT TOO, HISOKA.
THANKS FOR THINKING OF ME.
ARE YOU SURE IT'S OKAY?
DON'T WORRY.
THERE'S NO WAY I CAN EAT IT ALL MYSELF.

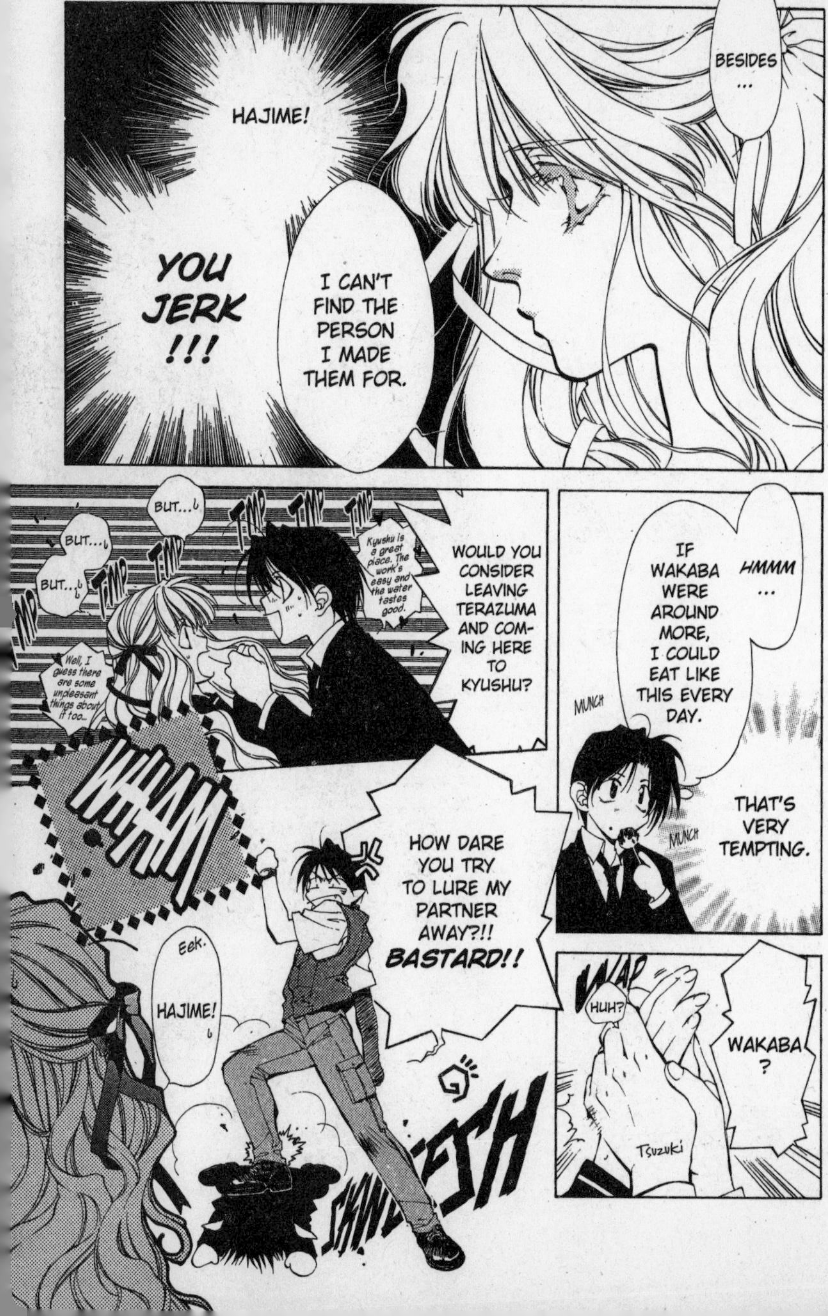
BESIDES ...
I CAN'T FIND THE PERSON I MADE THEM FOR.
HAJIME!
YOU JERK !!!
HMMM ...
IF WAKABA WERE AROUND MORE, I COULD EAT LIKE THIS EVERY DAY.
MUNCH
MUNCH
THAT'S VERY TEMPTING.
WOULD YOU CONSIDER LEAVING TERAZUMA AND COM-ING HERE TO KYUSHU?
Kyushu is a great place. The work's easy and the water tastes good.
TMP TMP TMP TMP TMP TMP TMP
BUT...
BUT...
BUT...
Well, I guess there are some unpleasant things about it too...
WHAM
HOW DARE YOU TRY TO LURE MY PARTNER AWAY?!! BASTARD!!
Eek.
HAJIME!
SHWISH
WAP
HUH?
WAKABA ?
Tsuzuki

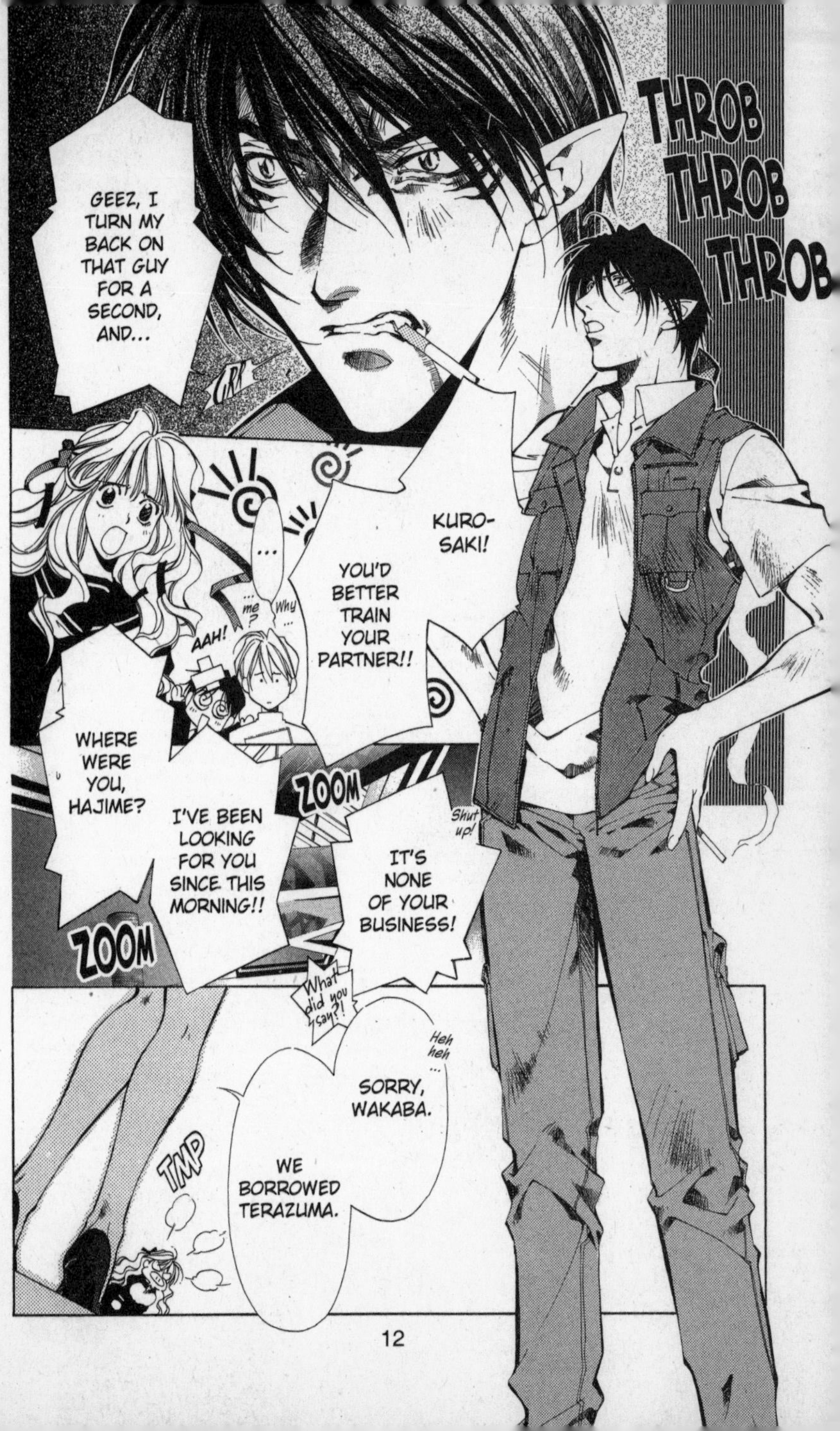
THROB THROB THROB
GEEZ, I TURN MY BACK ON THAT GUY FOR A SECOND, AND...
KURO-SAKI!
YOU'D BETTER TRAIN YOUR PARTNER!!
...
Why ...
... me?
AAH!
IT'S NONE OF YOUR BUSINESS!
Shut up!
ZOOM
I'VE BEEN LOOKING FOR YOU SINCE THIS MORNING!!
WHERE WERE YOU, HAJIME?
ZOOM
What did you say?!
Heh heh ...
SORRY, WAKABA.
WE BORROWED TERAZUMA.
TMP

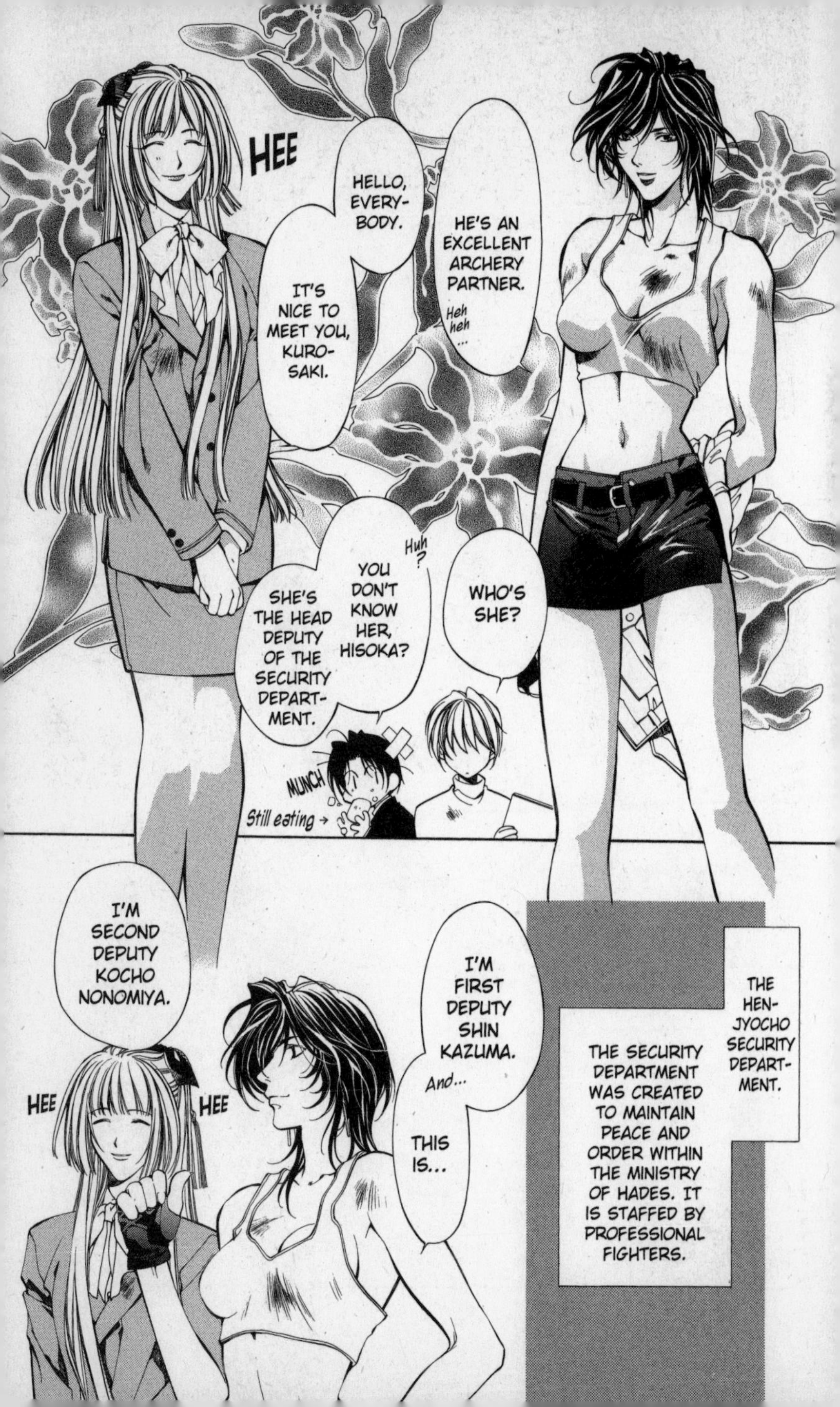
HE'S AN EXCELLENT ARCHERY PARTNER.
Heh heh ...
HELLO, EVERY-BODY.
IT'S NICE TO MEET YOU, KURO-SAKI.
HEE
WHO'S SHE?
Huh?
YOU DON'T KNOW HER, HISOKA?
SHE'S THE HEAD DEPUTY OF THE SECURITY DEPART-MENT.
MUNCH
Still eating →
THE HEN-JYOCHO SECURITY DEPART-MENT.
THE SECURITY DEPARTMENT WAS CREATED TO MAINTAIN PEACE AND ORDER WITHIN THE MINISTRY OF HADES. IT IS STAFFED BY PROFESSIONAL FIGHTERS.
I'M FIRST DEPUTY SHIN KAZUMA.
And...
THIS IS...
I'M SECOND DEPUTY KOCHO NONOMIYA.
HEE
HEE

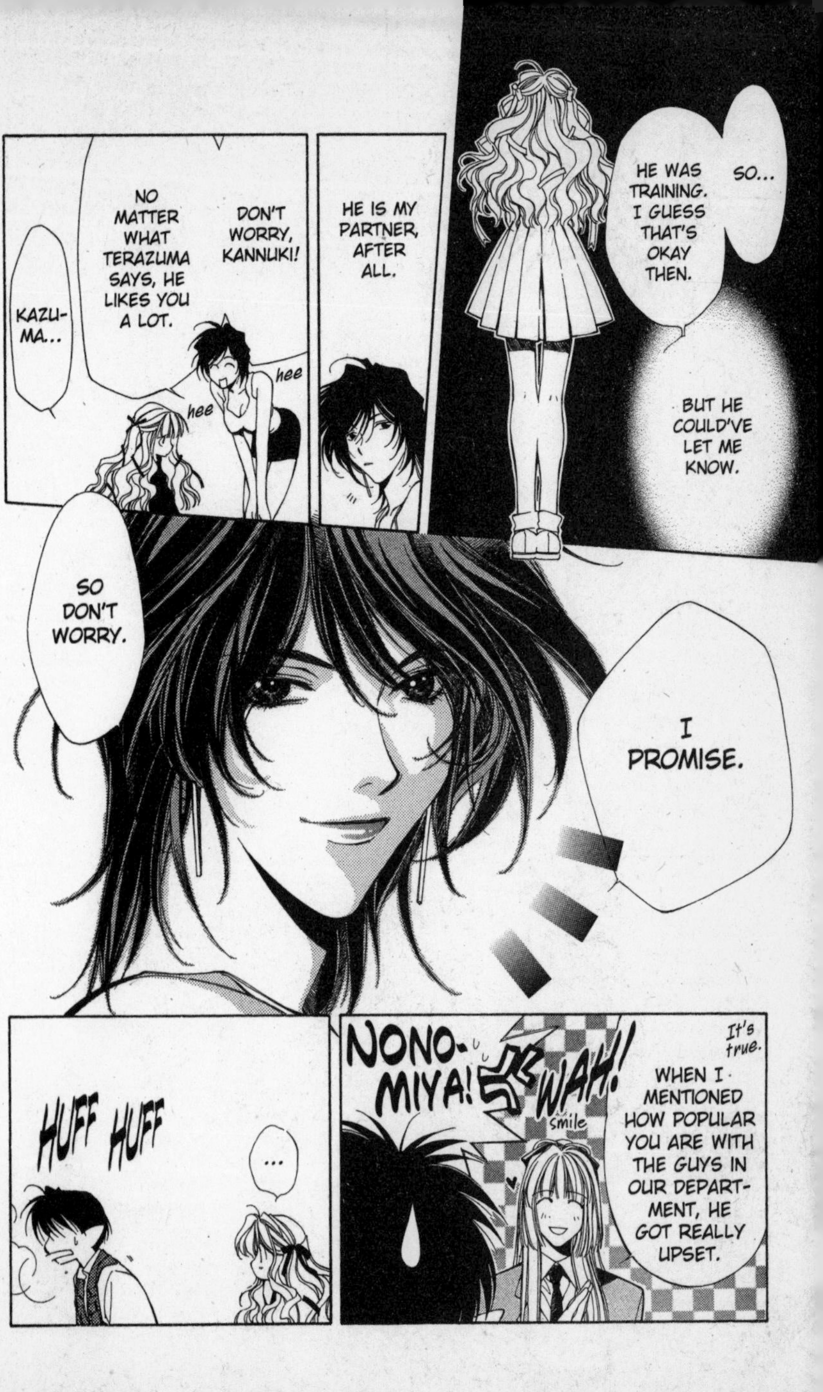
SO...
HE WAS TRAINING. I GUESS THAT'S OKAY THEN.
BUT HE COULD'VE LET ME KNOW.
HE IS MY PARTNER, AFTER ALL.
DON'T WORRY, KANNUKI!
NO MATTER WHAT TERAZUMA SAYS, HE LIKES YOU A LOT.
hee
hee
KAZUMA...
SO DON'T WORRY.
I PROMISE.
It's true.
WHEN I MENTIONED HOW POPULAR YOU ARE WITH THE GUYS IN OUR DEPARTMENT, HE GOT REALLY UPSET.
NONO-MIYA!
WAH!
smile
HUFF HUFF
...

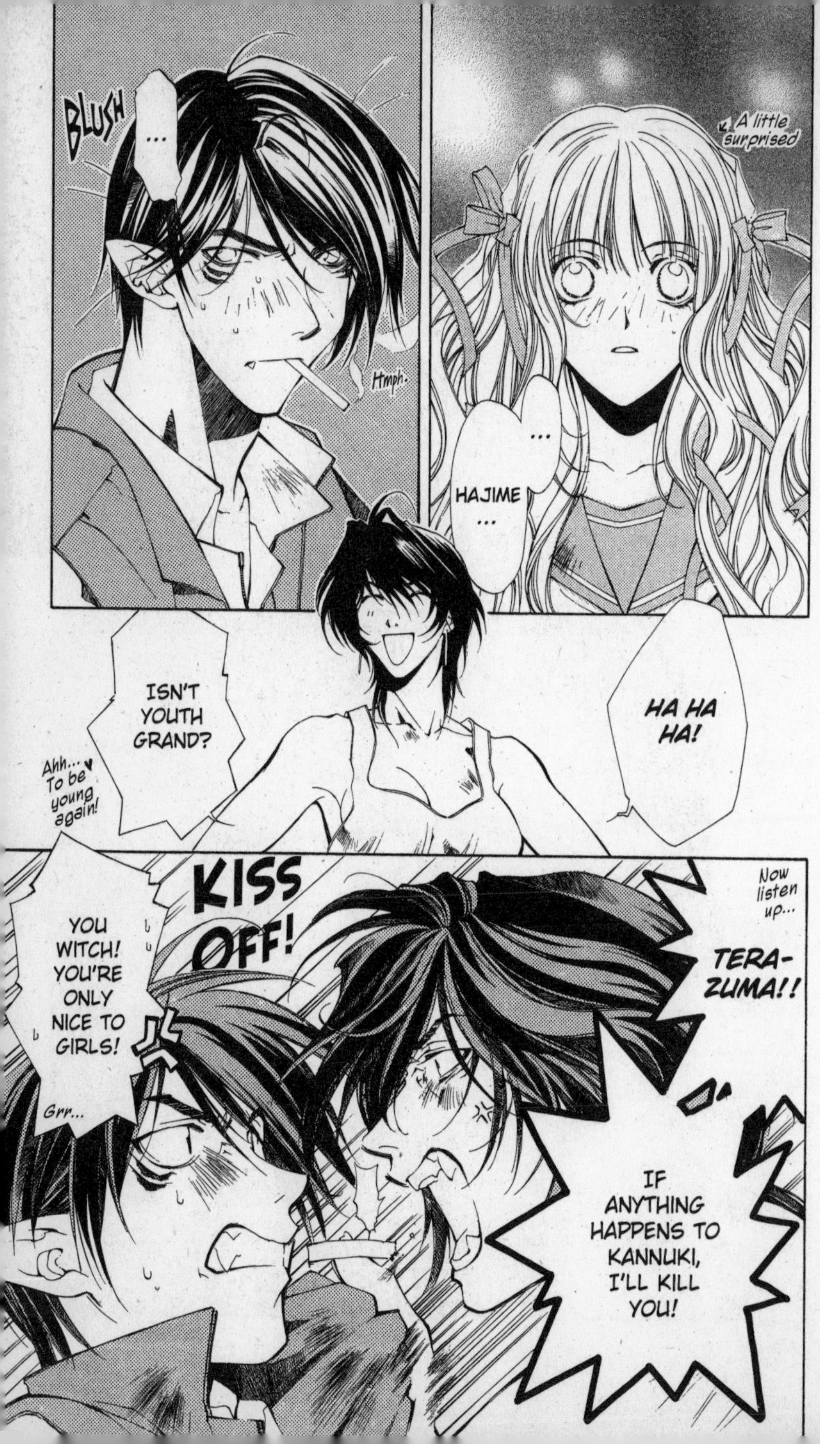
A little surprised
...
HAJIME ...
BLUSH
...
Hmph.
HA HA HA!
ISN'T YOUTH GRAND?
Ahh... To be young again!
Now listen up...
TERA-ZUMA!!
IF ANYTHING HAPPENS TO KANNUKI, I'LL KILL YOU!
KISS OFF!
YOU WITCH! YOU'RE ONLY NICE TO GIRLS!
Grr...

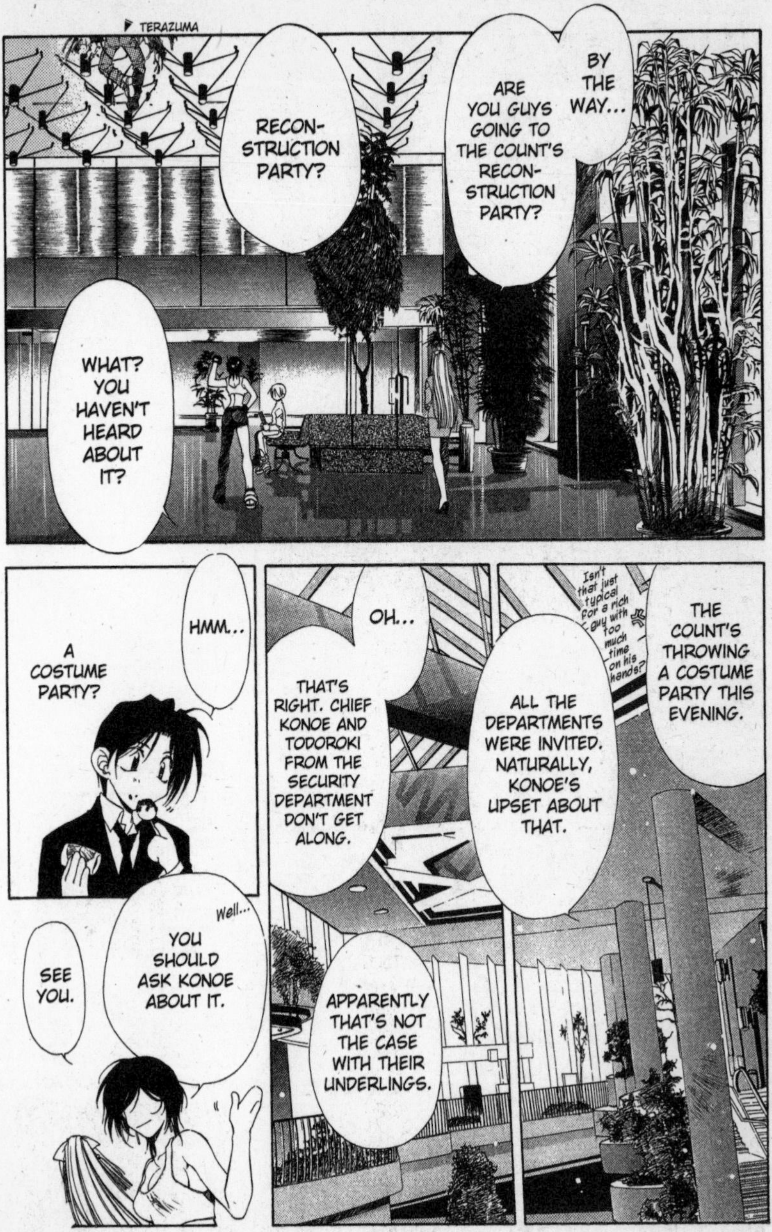
TERAZUMA
BY THE WAY...
ARE YOU GUYS GOING TO THE COUNT'S RECON-STRUCTION PARTY?
RECON-STRUCTION PARTY?
WHAT? YOU HAVEN'T HEARD ABOUT IT?
THE COUNT'S THROWING A COSTUME PARTY THIS EVENING.
Isn't that just typical for a rich guy with too much time on his hands?
ALL THE DEPARTMENTS WERE INVITED. NATURALLY, KONOE'S UPSET ABOUT THAT.
OH...
THAT'S RIGHT. CHIEF KONOE AND TODOROKI FROM THE SECURITY DEPARTMENT DON'T GET ALONG.
APPARENTLY THAT'S NOT THE CASE WITH THEIR UNDERLINGS.
HMM...
A COSTUME PARTY?
Well...
YOU SHOULD ASK KONOE ABOUT IT.
SEE YOU.

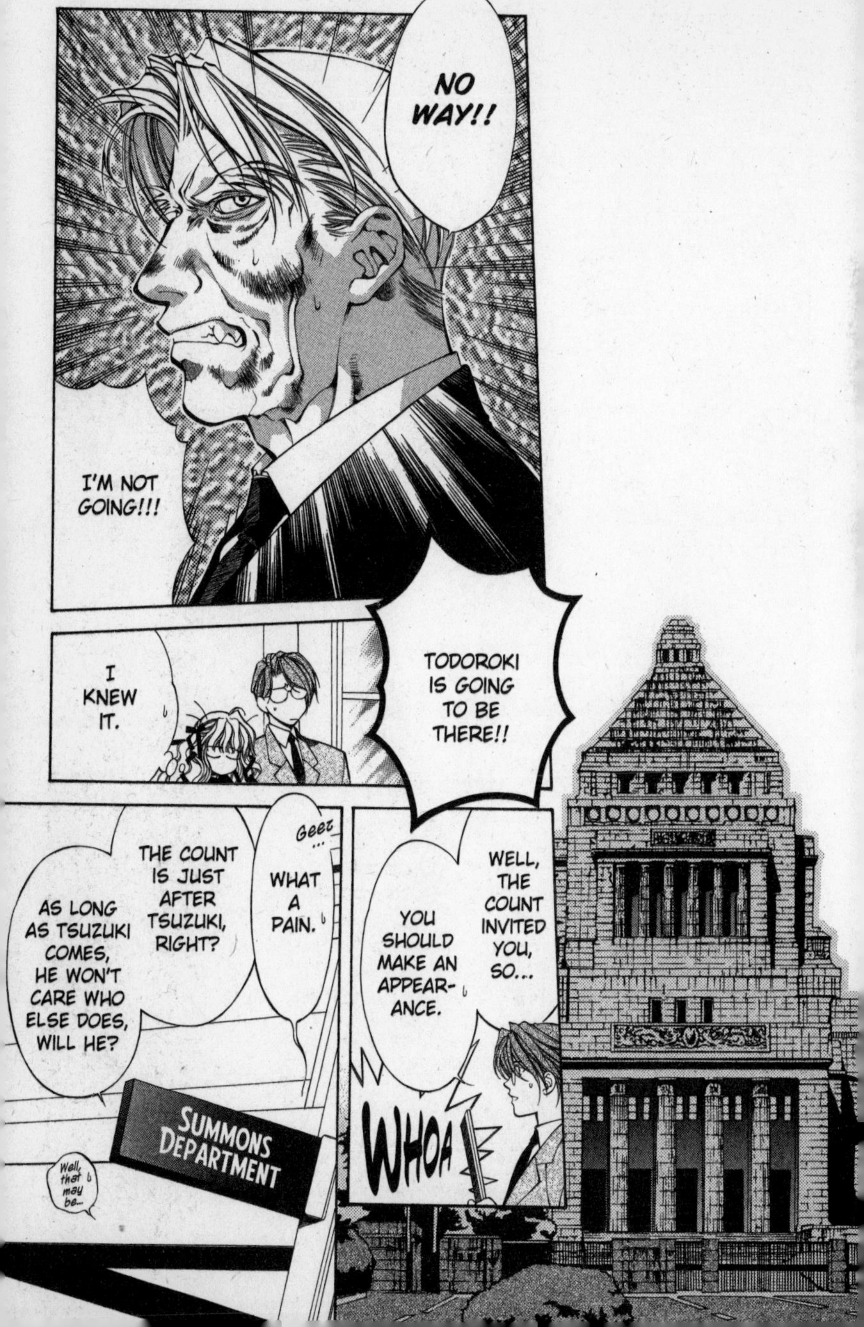
NO WAY!!
I'M NOT GOING!!!
TODOROKI IS GOING TO BE THERE!!
I KNEW IT.
WELL, THE COUNT INVITED YOU, SO...
YOU SHOULD MAKE AN APPEAR-ANCE.
WHOA
Geez...
WHAT A PAIN.
THE COUNT IS JUST AFTER TSUZUKI, RIGHT?
AS LONG AS TSUZUKI COMES, HE WON'T CARE WHO ELSE DOES, WILL HE?
SUMMONS DEPARTMENT
Well, that may be...

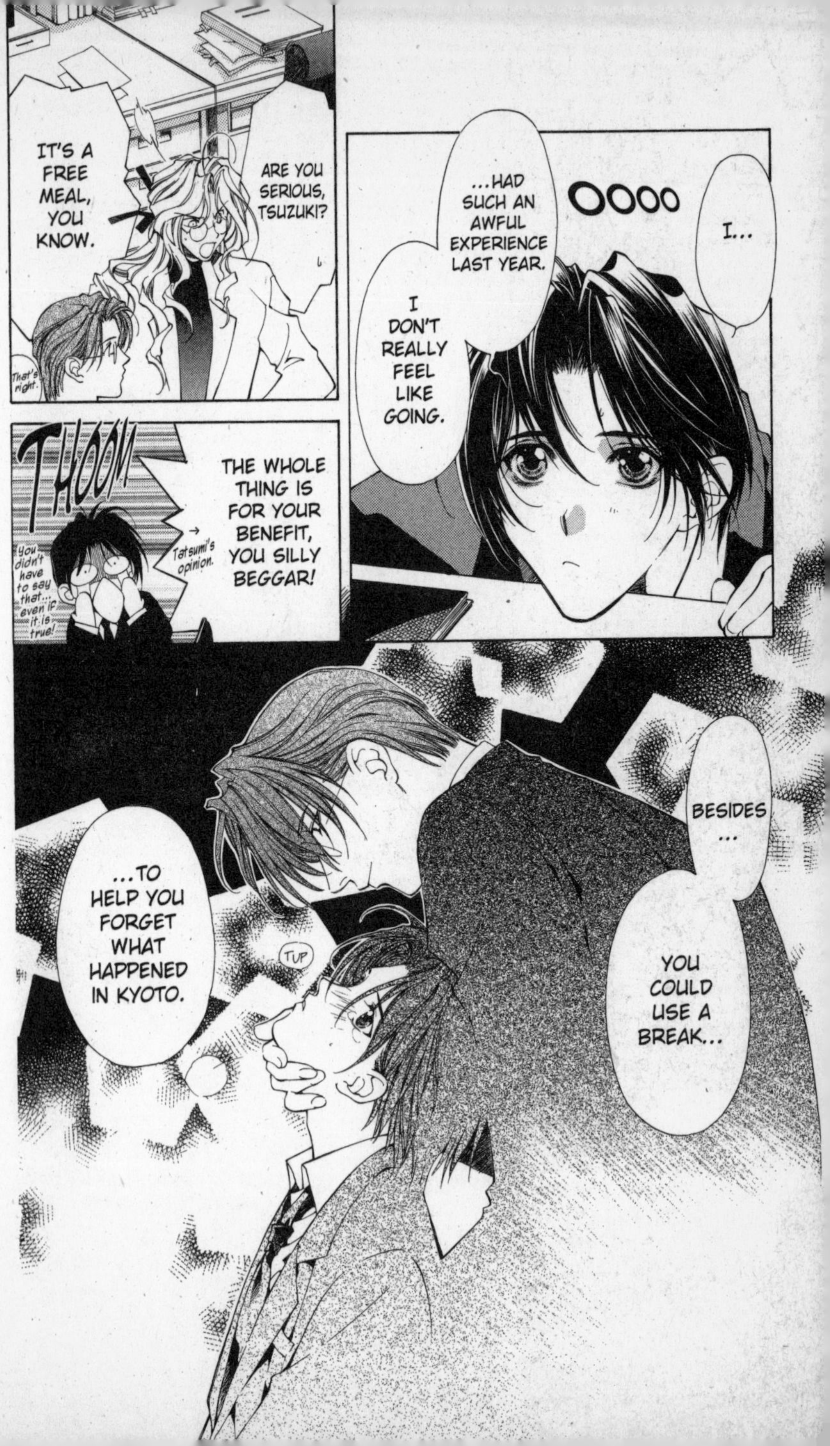
I...
OOOO
...HAD SUCH AN AWFUL EXPERIENCE LAST YEAR.
I DON'T REALLY FEEL LIKE GOING.
ARE YOU SERIOUS, TSUZUKI?
IT'S A FREE MEAL, YOU KNOW.
That's right.
THE WHOLE THING IS FOR YOUR BENEFIT, YOU SILLY BEGGAR!
→ Tatsumi's opinion.
THOOM
You didn't have to say that... even if it is true!
BESIDES...
YOU COULD USE A BREAK...
TUP
...TO HELP YOU FORGET WHAT HAPPENED IN KYOTO.

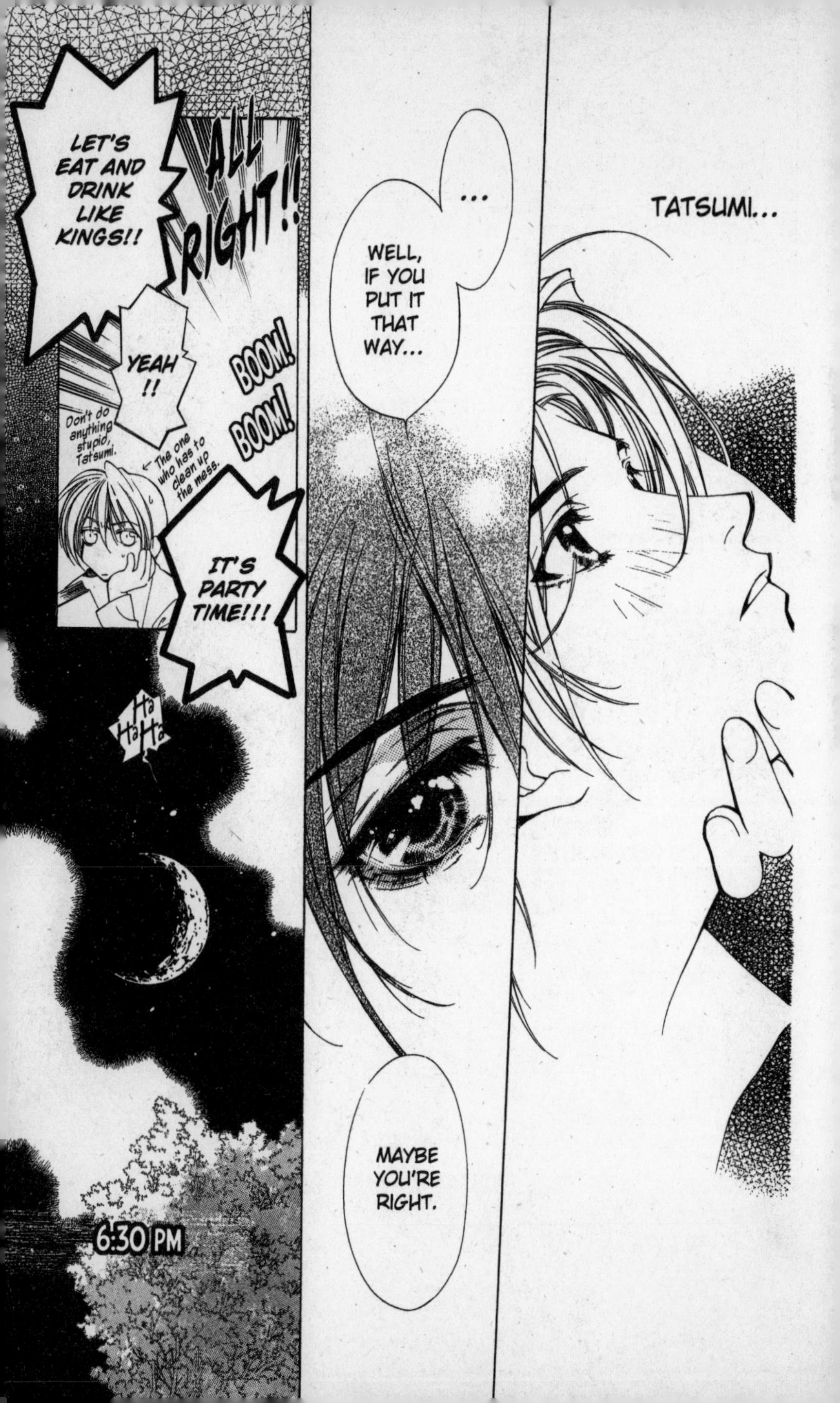
TATSUMI...
...
WELL, IF YOU PUT IT THAT WAY...
MAYBE YOU'RE RIGHT.
ALL RIGHT!!
LET'S EAT AND DRINK LIKE KINGS!!
BOOM! BOOM!
YEAH!!
Don't do anything stupid, Tatsumi.
← The one who has to clean up the mess.
IT'S PARTY TIME!!!
HaHaHa
6:30 PM

THE HALL OF CANDLES COSTUME PARTY...

...WILL SOON BEGIN.

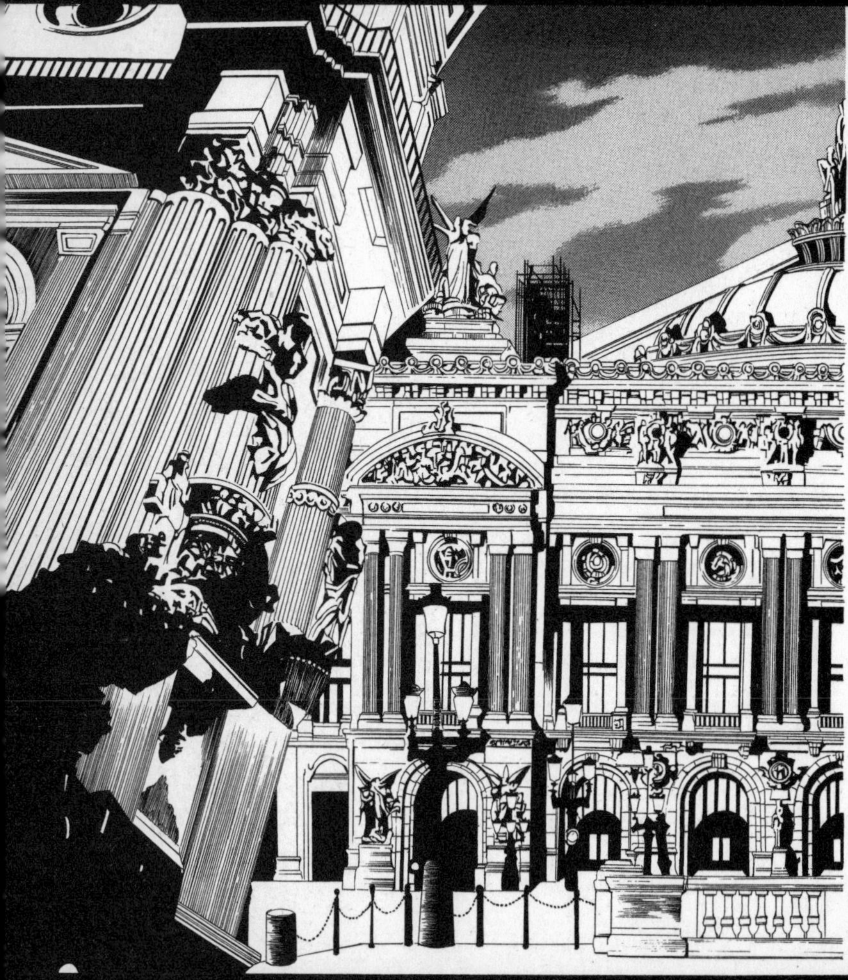

—

CHAPTER 29

GOO
GOO

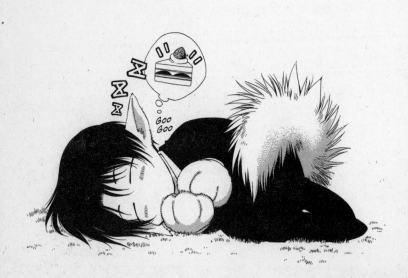

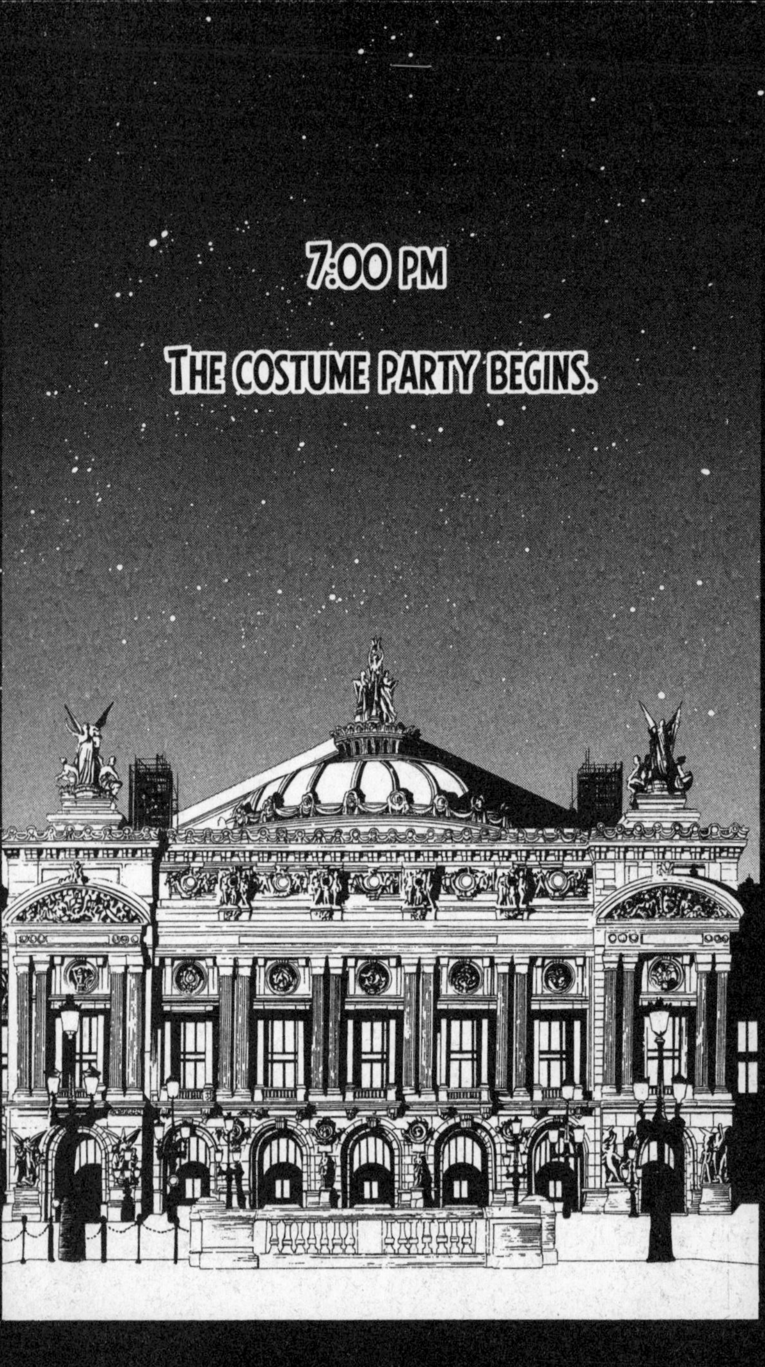
7:00 PM
THE COSTUME PARTY BEGINS.

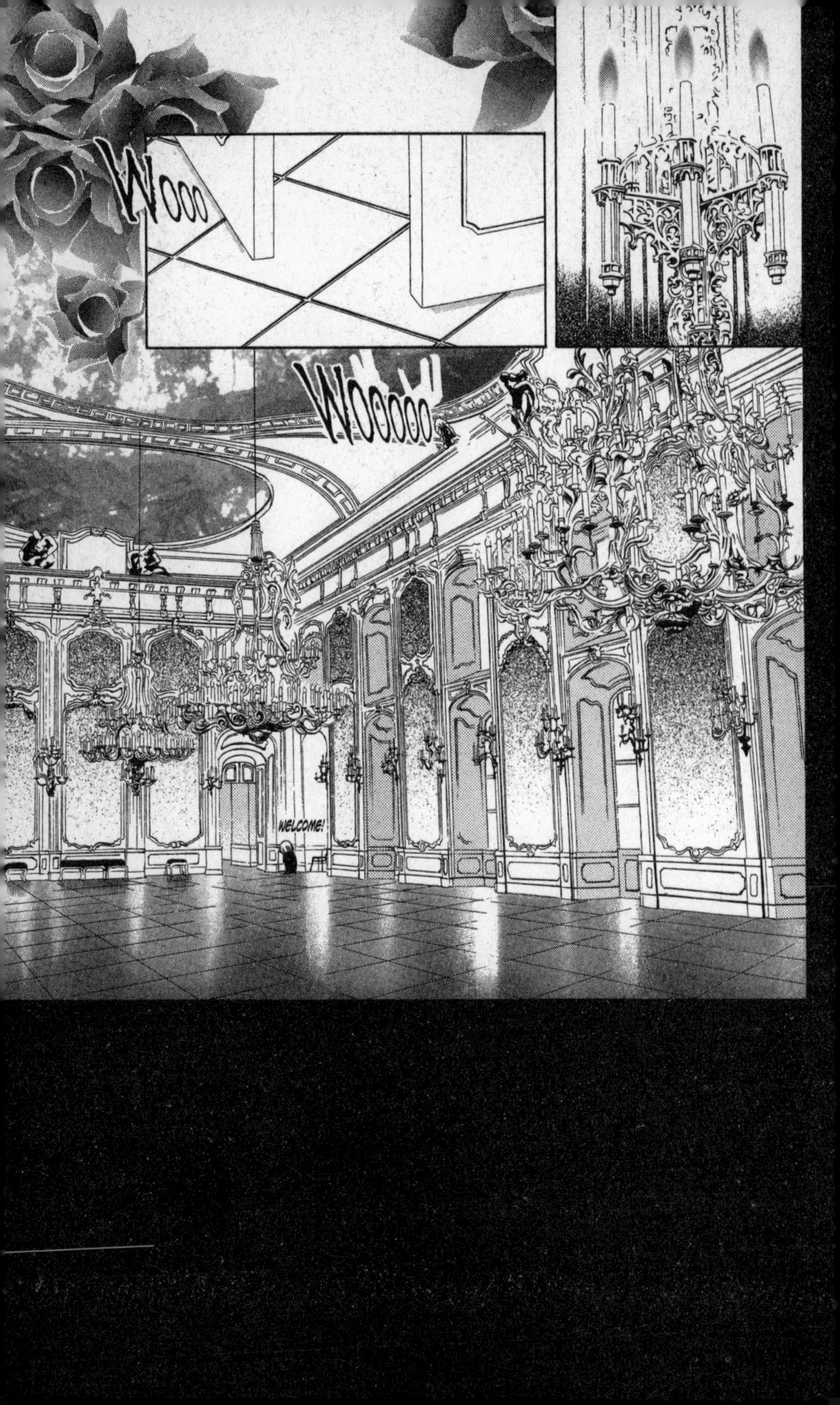
Wooo
Woooo
WELCOME!

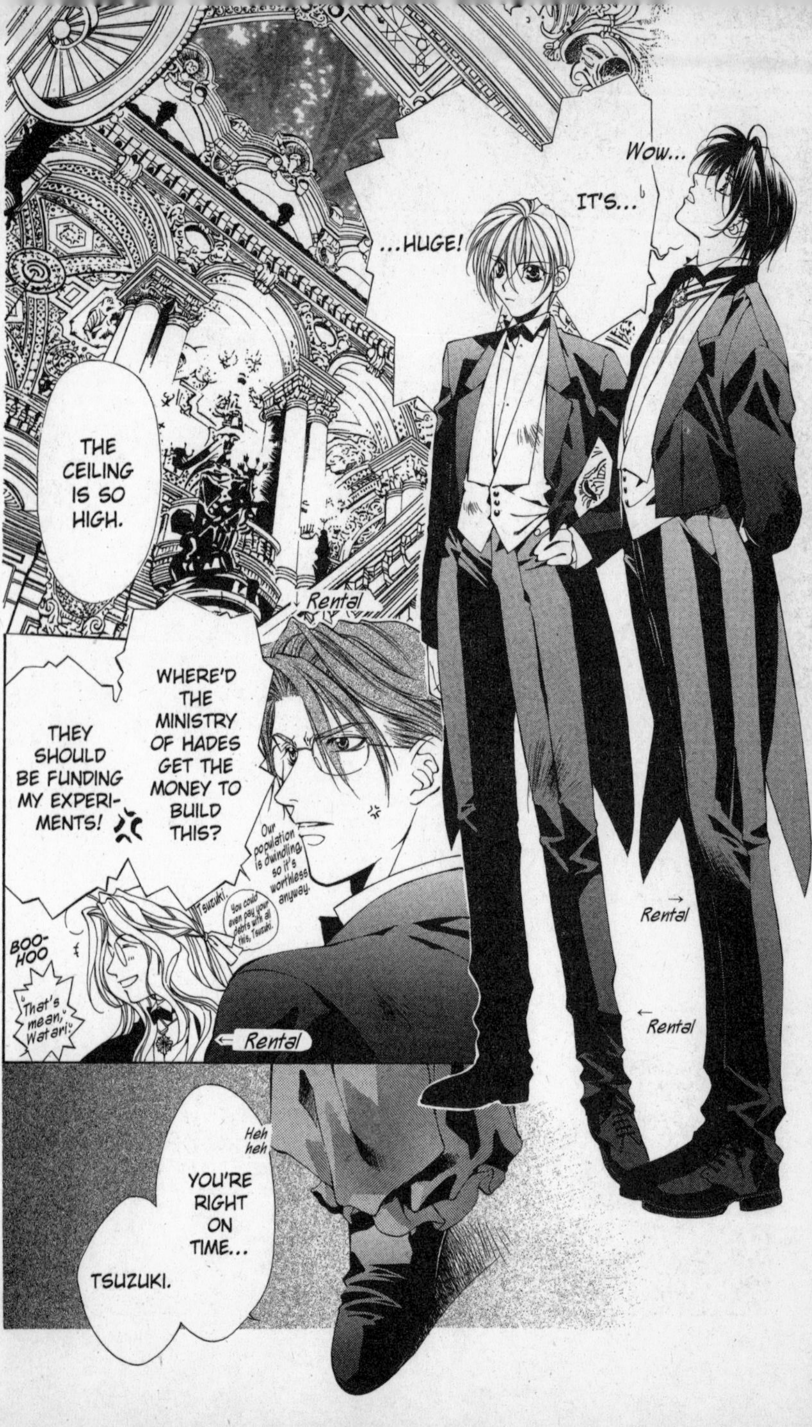
Wow...
IT'S...
...HUGE!
THE CEILING IS SO HIGH.
Rental
Rental
Rental
WHERE'D THE MINISTRY OF HADES GET THE MONEY TO BUILD THIS?
THEY SHOULD BE FUNDING MY EXPERIMENTS!
Our population is dwindling, so it's worthless anyway.
Tsuzuki.
You could even pay your debts with all this, Tsuzuki.
BOO-HOO
That's mean, Watari!
Rental
Heh heh
YOU'RE RIGHT ON TIME...
TSUZUKI.

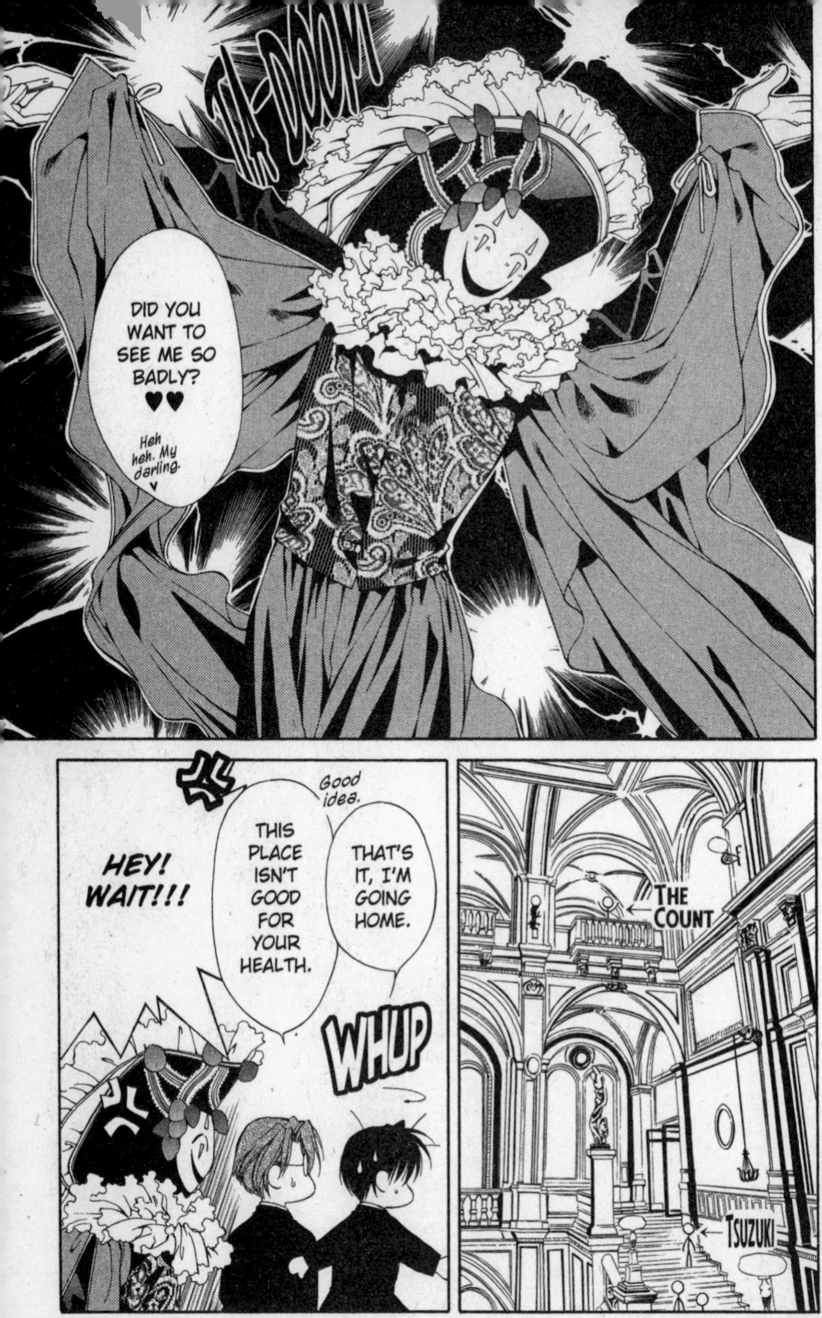
TA-DOOM
DID YOU WANT TO SEE ME SO BADLY? ♥♥
Heh heh. My darling. ♥
THE COUNT
TSUZUKI
And the others
THAT'S IT, I'M GOING HOME.
Good idea.
THIS PLACE ISN'T GOOD FOR YOUR HEALTH.
HEY! WAIT!!!
WHUP

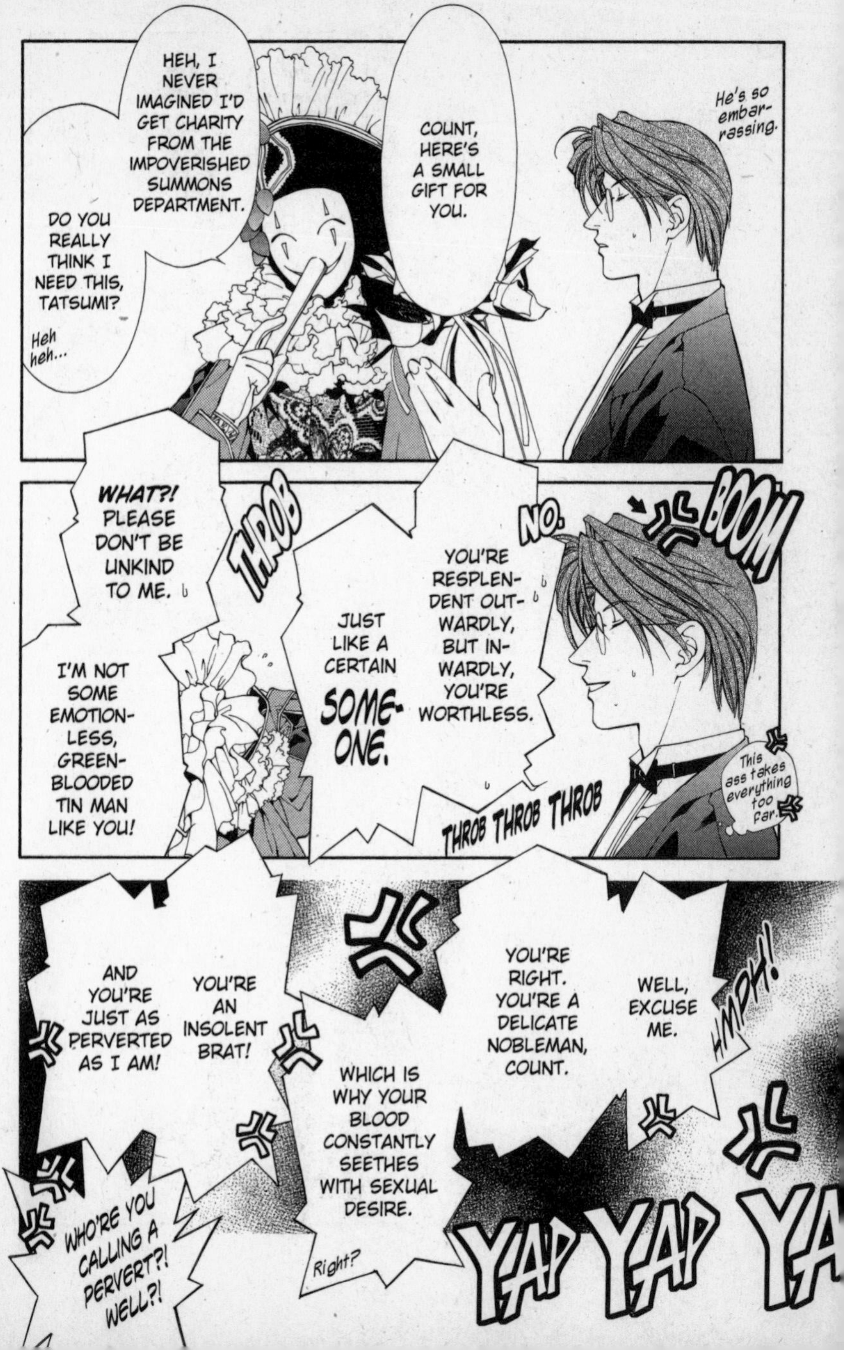
He's so embar-rassing.
COUNT, HERE'S A SMALL GIFT FOR YOU.
HEH, I NEVER IMAGINED I'D GET CHARITY FROM THE IMPOVERISHED SUMMONS DEPARTMENT.
DO YOU REALLY THINK I NEED THIS, TATSUMI?
Heh heh...
BOOM
NO.
YOU'RE RESPLEN-DENT OUT-WARDLY, BUT IN-WARDLY, YOU'RE WORTHLESS.
JUST LIKE A CERTAIN SOME-ONE.
THROB
WHAT?! PLEASE DON'T BE UNKIND TO ME.
I'M NOT SOME EMOTION-LESS, GREEN-BLOODED TIN MAN LIKE YOU!
THROB THROB THROB
This ass takes everything too far.
HMPH!
WELL, EXCUSE ME.
YOU'RE RIGHT. YOU'RE A DELICATE NOBLEMAN, COUNT.
WHICH IS WHY YOUR BLOOD CONSTANTLY SEETHES WITH SEXUAL DESIRE.
Right?
YOU'RE AN INSOLENT BRAT!
AND YOU'RE JUST AS PERVERTED AS I AM!
WHO'RE YOU CALLING A PERVERT?! WELL?!
YAP YAP YA

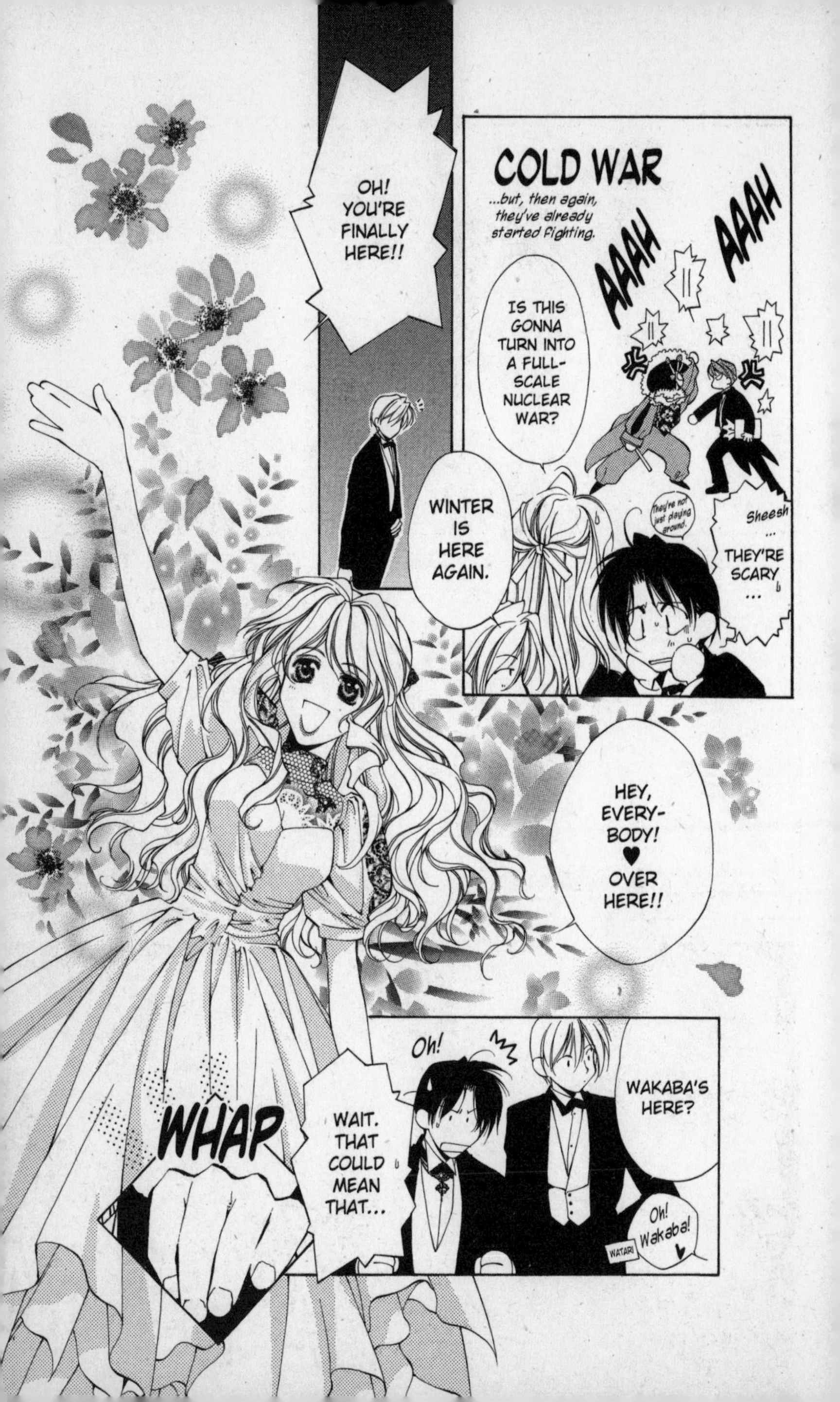
COLD WAR
...but, then again, they've already started fighting.
AAAH
AAAH
IS THIS GONNA TURN INTO A FULL-SCALE NUCLEAR WAR?
Sheesh... THEY'RE SCARY...
They're not just playing around.
WINTER IS HERE AGAIN.
OH! YOU'RE FINALLY HERE!!
HEY, EVERY-BODY! ♥ OVER HERE!!
WAKABA'S HERE?
Oh!
WAIT. THAT COULD MEAN THAT...
Oh! Wakaba! ♥
WATARI
WHAP

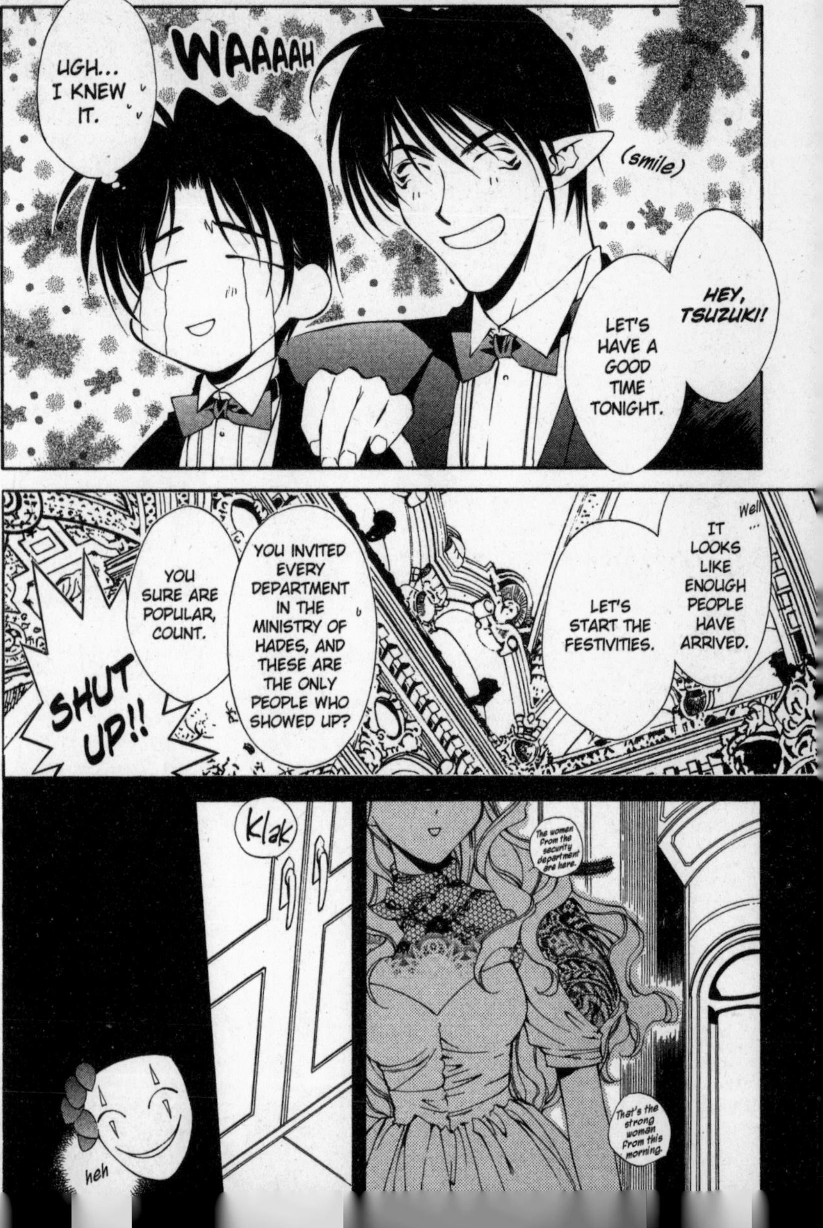
HEY, TSUZUKI!
LET'S HAVE A GOOD TIME TONIGHT.
(smile)
WAAAAH
UGH... I KNEW IT.
Well...
IT LOOKS LIKE ENOUGH PEOPLE HAVE ARRIVED.
LET'S START THE FESTIVITIES.
YOU INVITED EVERY DEPARTMENT IN THE MINISTRY OF HADES, AND THESE ARE THE ONLY PEOPLE WHO SHOWED UP?
YOU SURE ARE POPULAR, COUNT.
SHUT UP!!
The women from the security department are here.
That's the strong woman from this morning.
Klak
heh

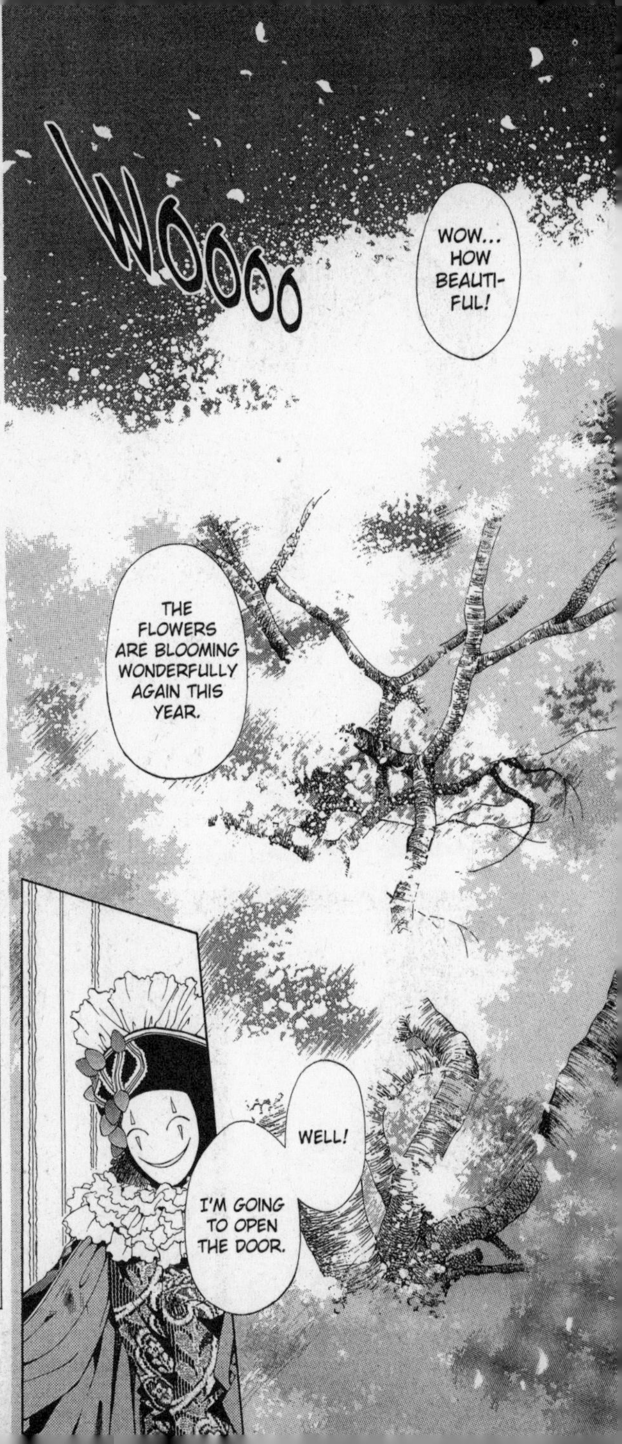
WOOOO
WOW... HOW BEAUTIFUL!
THE FLOWERS ARE BLOOMING WONDERFULLY AGAIN THIS YEAR.
WELL!
I'M GOING TO OPEN THE DOOR.

Almost up to double digits.

That was fast.

I suffered through vol. 9!!! (Ha!)

There were lots of corrections I wanted to make to volume 9, but I didn't have time.

It almost killed Me! Heh Heh!!

I know, I know, don't start pointing out that there aren't many differences between this volume and the original comics from the magazine. I just had too much stuff to do. And time sure flies. This is already volume 9. I'm so close to my dream of reaching double digits! Volume 10 will come out this year... I hope. (Ha!) The company has ordered me to finish it, so from now on my stomach is going to hurt. If only money could buy time, then it wouldn't be so hard. If only there were 50 hours in a day, I could get everything done. (sob)

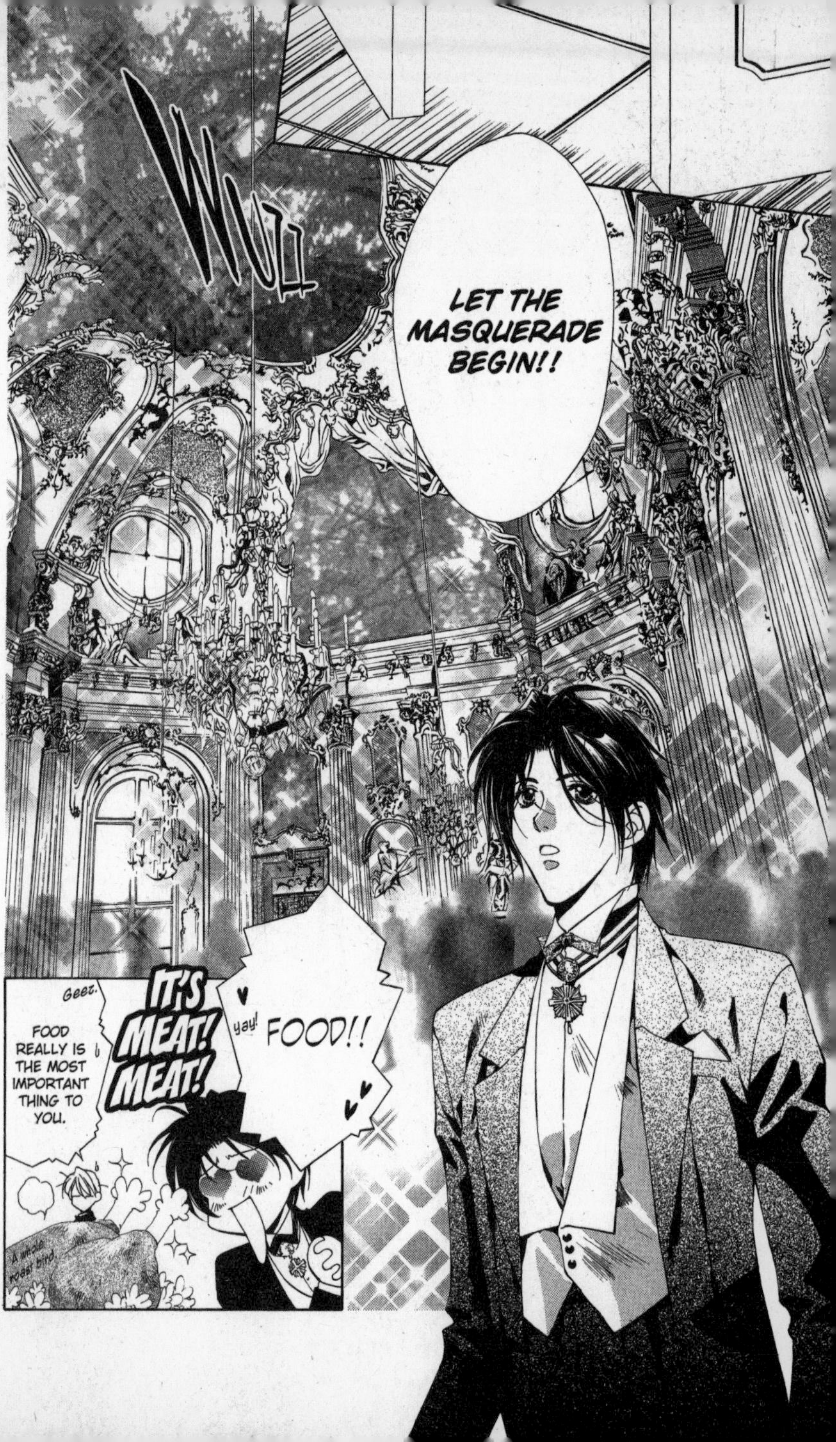
LET THE MASQUERADE BEGIN!!
yay! FOOD!!
IT'S MEAT! MEAT!
Geez.
FOOD REALLY IS THE MOST IMPORTANT THING TO YOU.
A whole roast bird.

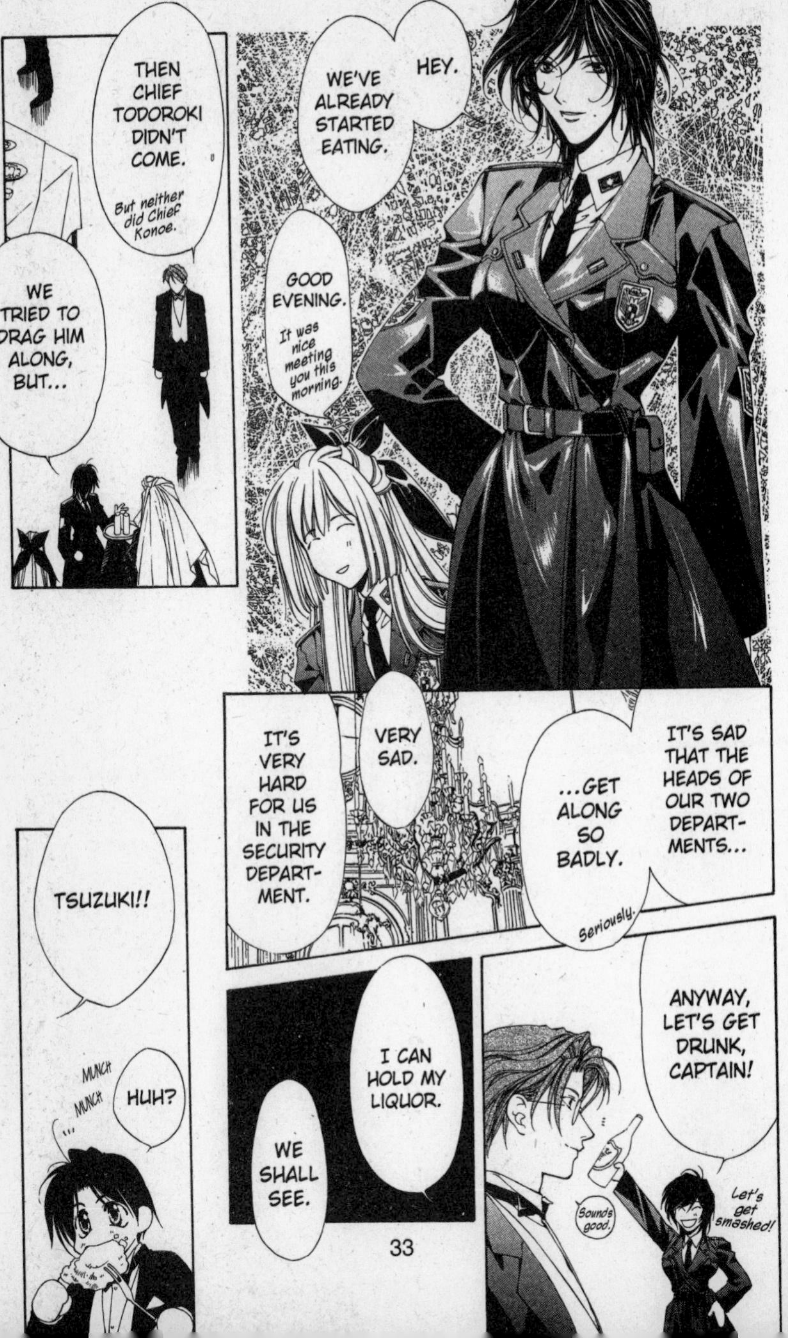
HEY.
WE'VE ALREADY STARTED EATING.
GOOD EVENING.
It was nice meeting you this morning.
THEN CHIEF TODOROKI DIDN'T COME.
But neither did Chief Konoe.
WE TRIED TO DRAG HIM ALONG, BUT...
IT'S SAD THAT THE HEADS OF OUR TWO DEPART-MENTS...
...GET ALONG SO BADLY.
Seriously.
VERY SAD.
IT'S VERY HARD FOR US IN THE SECURITY DEPART-MENT.
ANYWAY, LET'S GET DRUNK, CAPTAIN!
Let's get smashed!
Sounds good.
I CAN HOLD MY LIQUOR.
WE SHALL SEE.
TSUZUKI!!
MUNCH MUNCH
HUH?
...

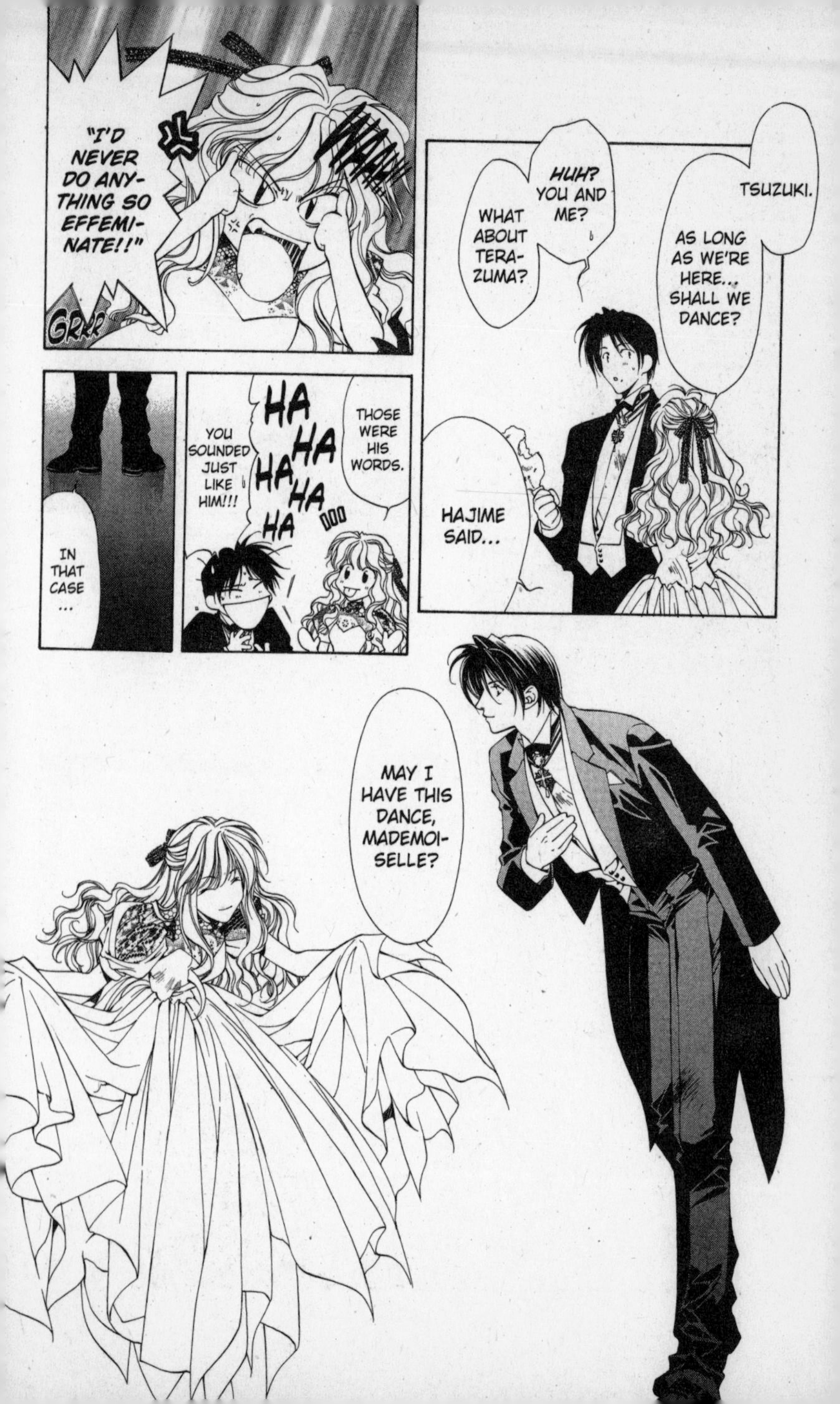
TSUZUKI.
AS LONG AS WE'RE HERE... SHALL WE DANCE?
HUH? YOU AND ME?
WHAT ABOUT TERA-ZUMA?
HAJIME SAID...
"I'D NEVER DO ANY-THING SO EFFEMI-NATE!!"
GRRR
THOSE WERE HIS WORDS.
HA HA HA HA HA
YOU SOUNDED JUST LIKE HIM!!!
IN THAT CASE ...
MAY I HAVE THIS DANCE, MADEMOI-SELLE?

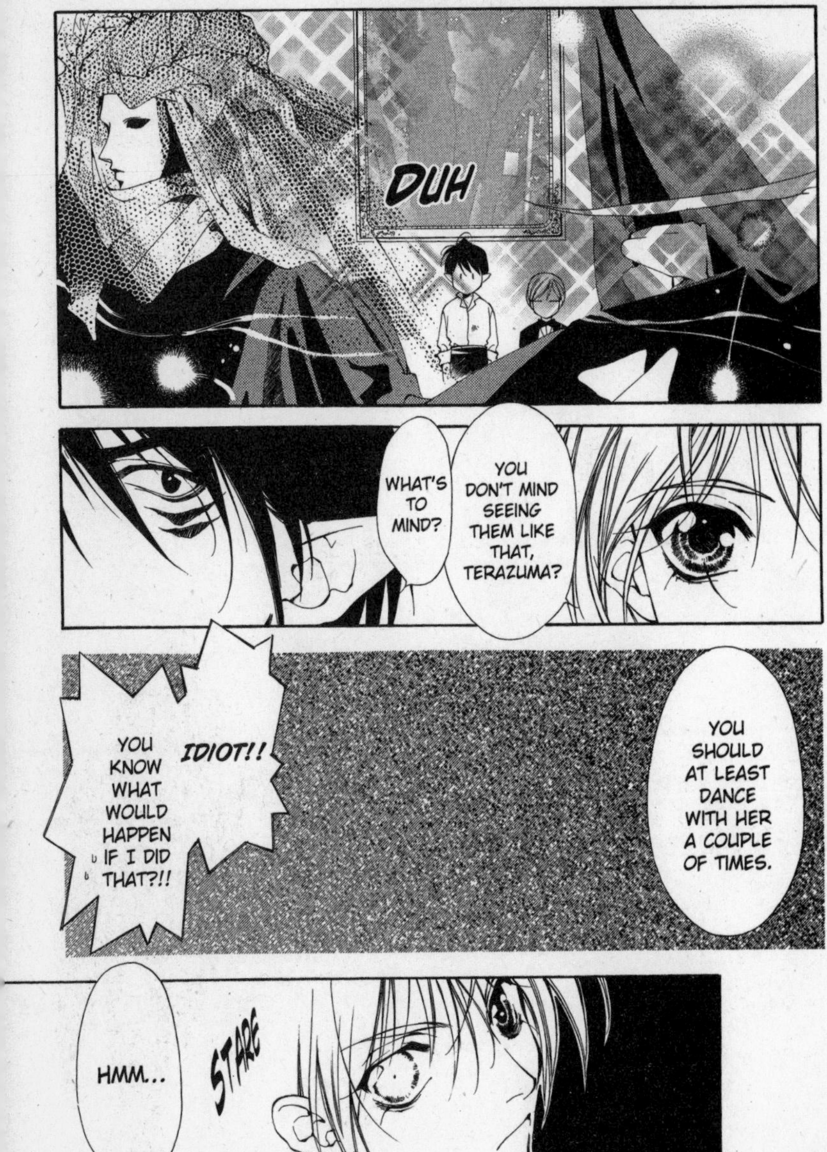
DUH
YOU DON'T MIND SEEING THEM LIKE THAT, TERAZUMA?
WHAT'S TO MIND?
YOU SHOULD AT LEAST DANCE WITH HER A COUPLE OF TIMES.
IDIOT!!
YOU KNOW WHAT WOULD HAPPEN IF I DID THAT?!!
STARE
HMM...

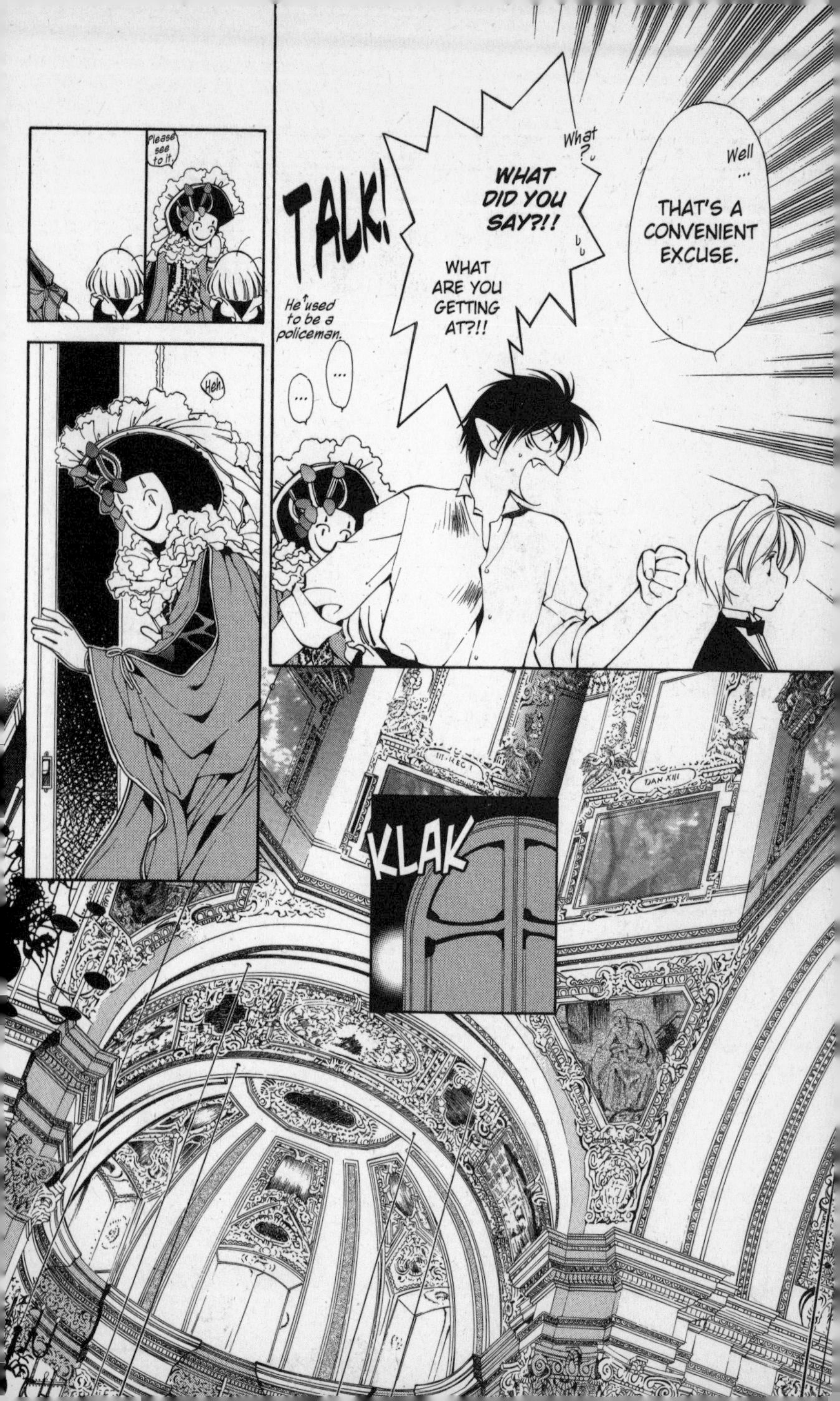
Well ...
THAT'S A CONVENIENT EXCUSE.
What?
WHAT DID YOU SAY?!!
WHAT ARE YOU GETTING AT?!!
TALK!
He used to be a policeman.
...
...
Please see to it.
KLAK
Heh.

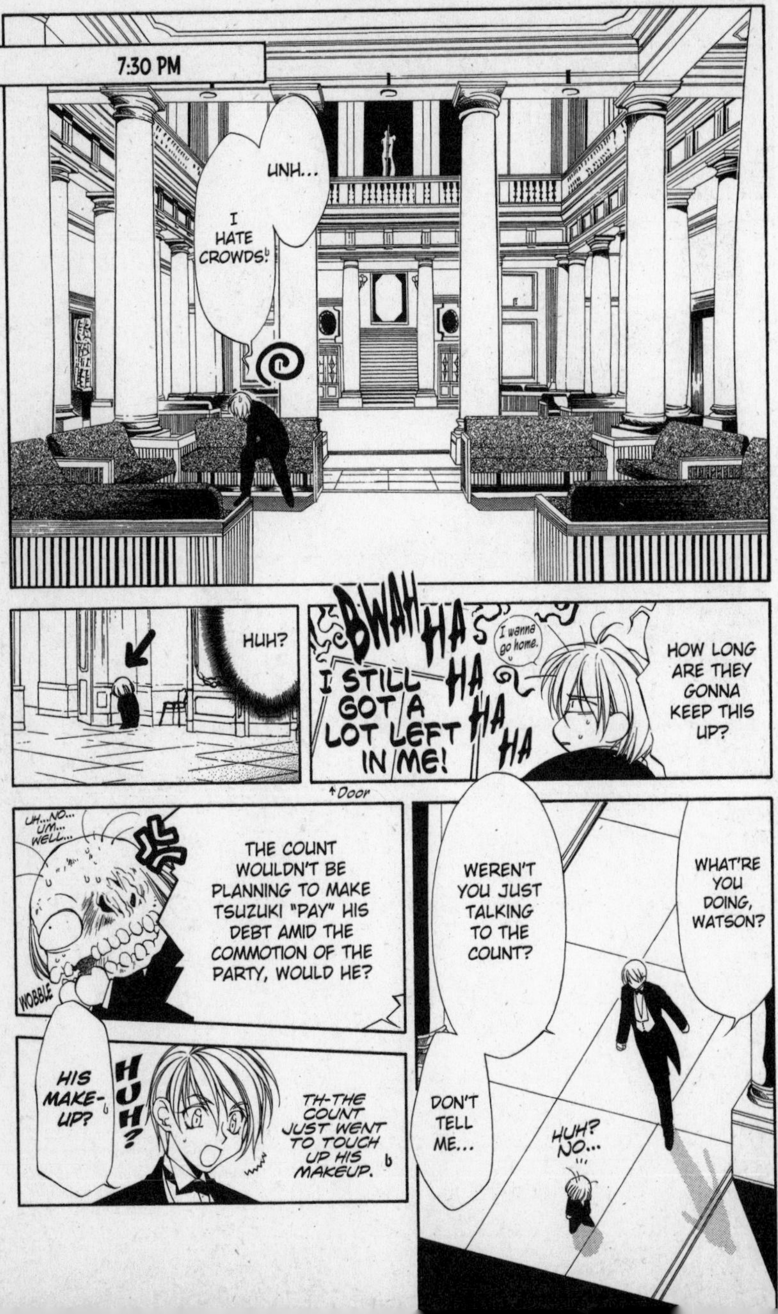
7:30 PM
UNH...
I HATE CROWDS!
HOW LONG ARE THEY GONNA KEEP THIS UP?
I wanna go home.
BWAH HA HA HA HA
I STILL GOT A LOT LEFT IN ME!
HUH?
↑Door
WHAT'RE YOU DOING, WATSON?
WEREN'T YOU JUST TALKING TO THE COUNT?
HUH? NO...
DON'T TELL ME...
THE COUNT WOULDN'T BE PLANNING TO MAKE TSUZUKI "PAY" HIS DEBT AMID THE COMMOTION OF THE PARTY, WOULD HE?
UH...NO... UM... WELL...
WOBBLE
TH-THE COUNT JUST WENT TO TOUCH UP HIS MAKEUP.
HUH?
HIS MAKE-UP?

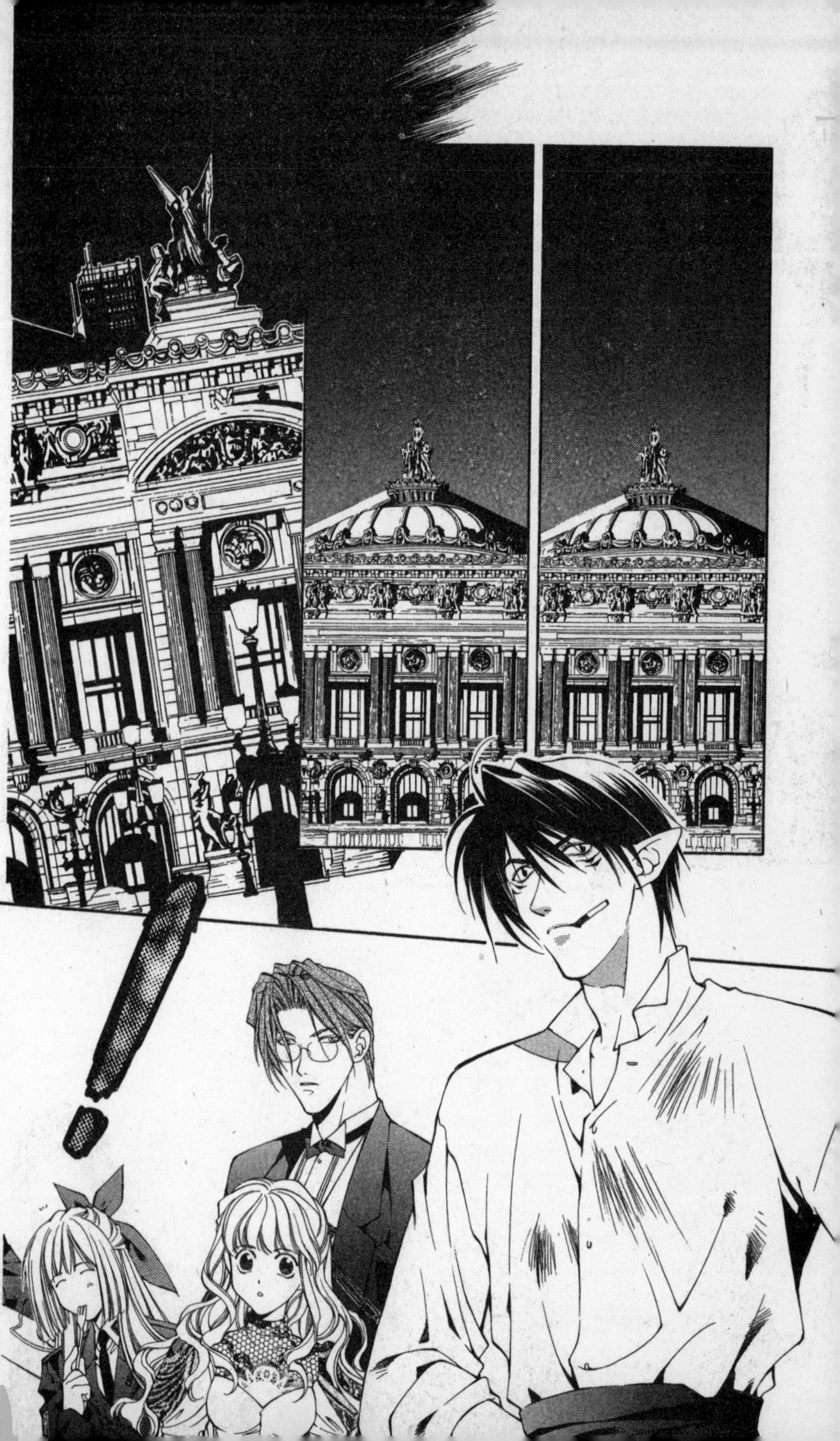

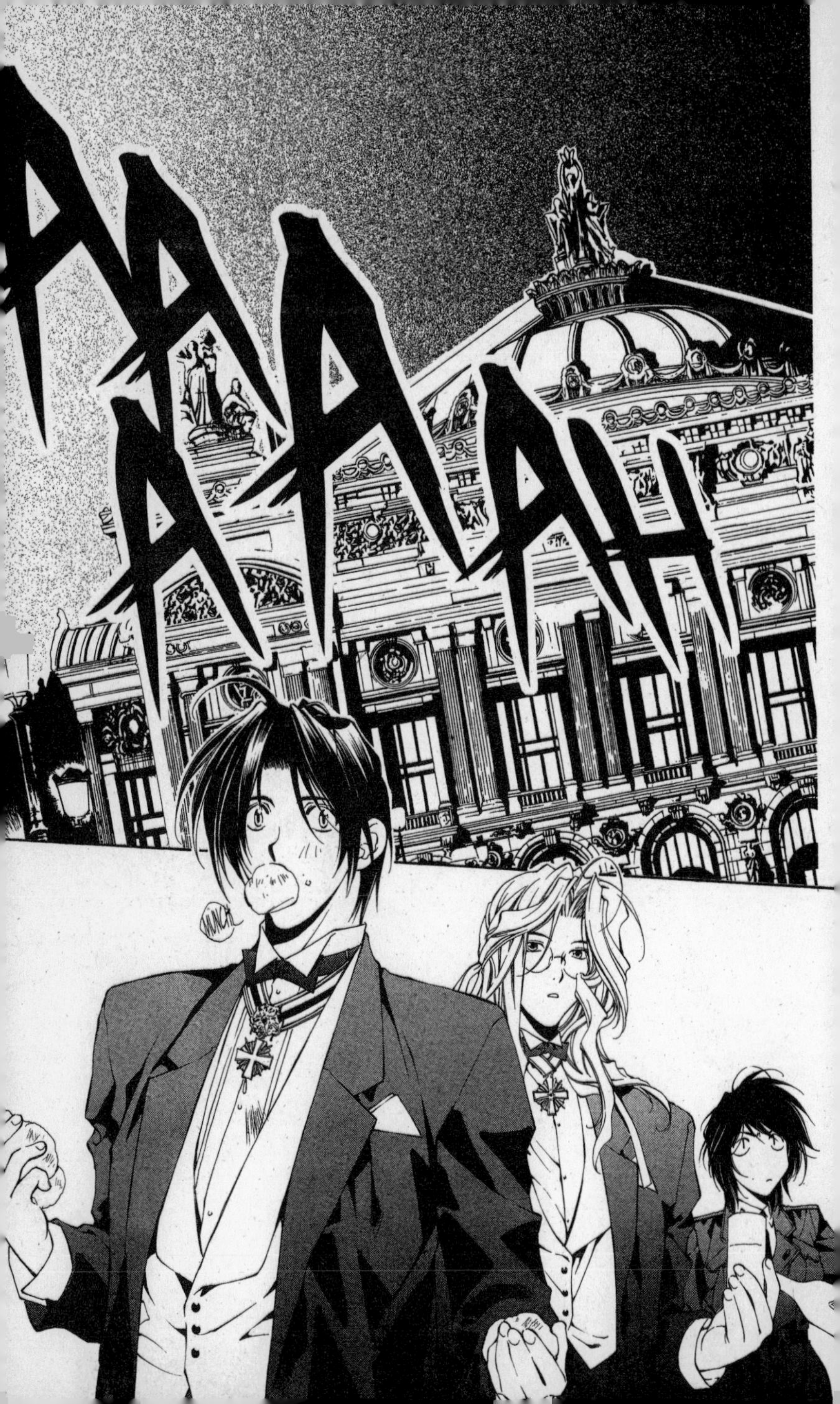
AAAAAH
MUNCH

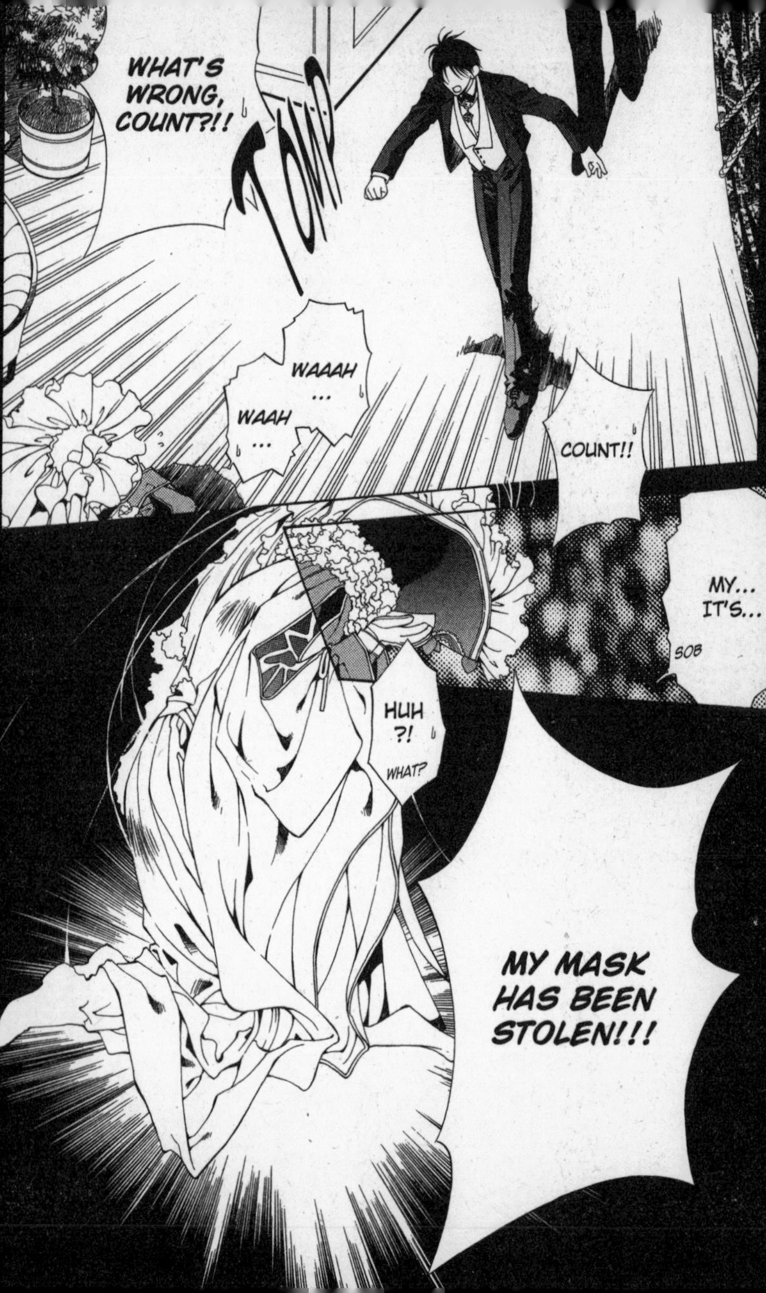
TOMP
COUNT!!
WHAT'S WRONG, COUNT?!!
WAAAH ...
WAAH ...
MY... IT'S...
SOB
HUH ?!
WHAT?
MY MASK HAS BEEN STOLEN!!!

CHAPTER 30

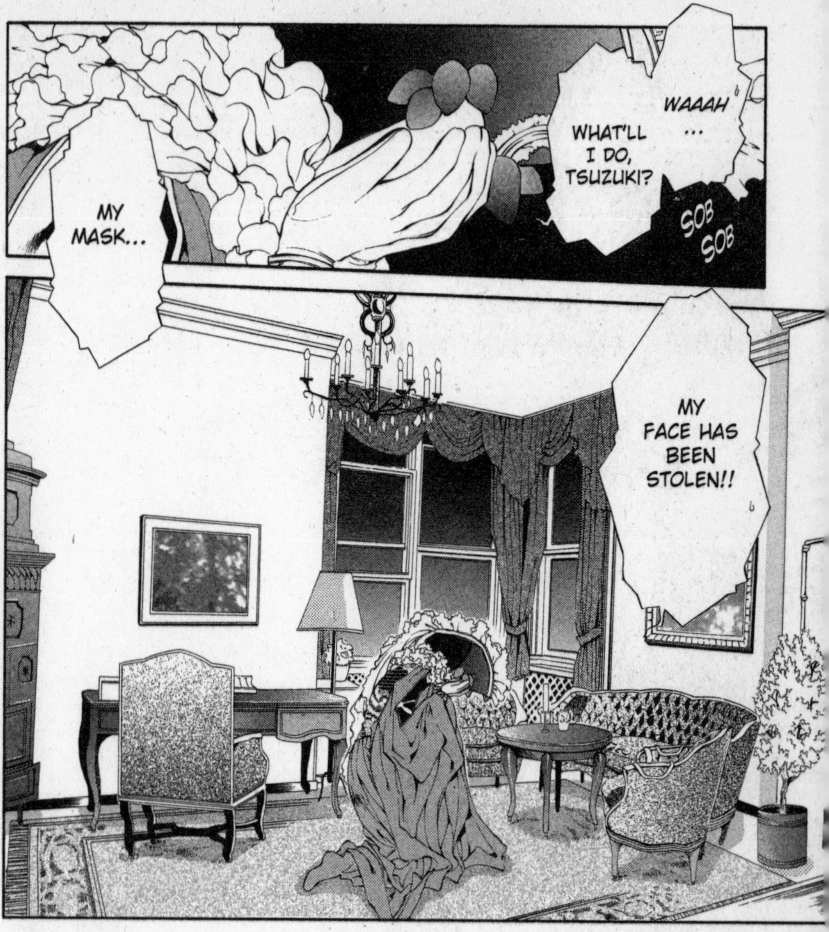
WAAAH ...
WHAT'LL I DO, TSUZUKI?
SOB SOB
MY MASK...
MY FACE HAS BEEN STOLEN!!

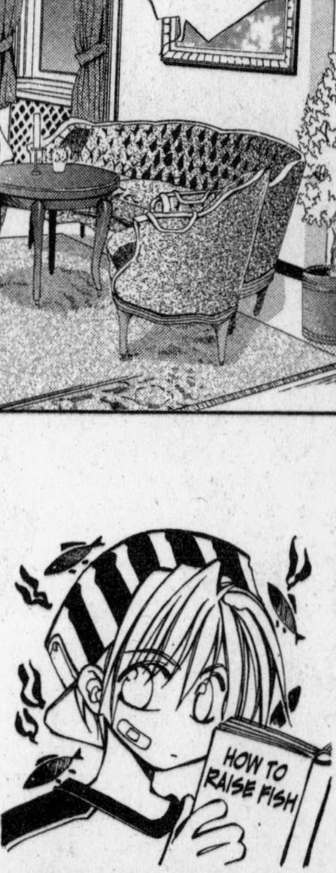
HOW TO RAISE FISH

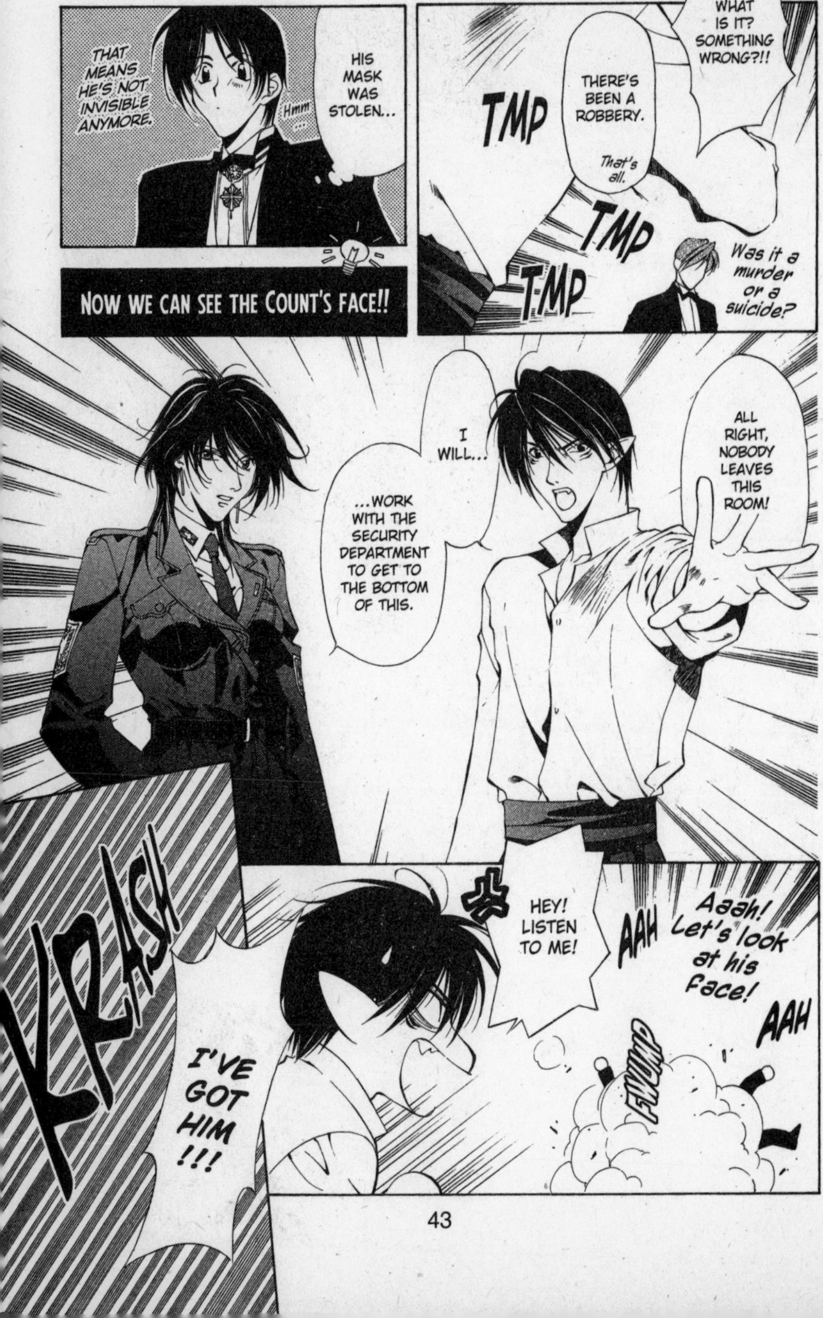
WHAT IS IT? SOMETHING WRONG?!!
THERE'S BEEN A ROBBERY.
That's all.
TMP
TMP
TMP
Was it a murder or a suicide?
HIS MASK WAS STOLEN...
Hmm...
THAT MEANS HE'S NOT INVISIBLE ANYMORE.
NOW WE CAN SEE THE COUNT'S FACE!!
ALL RIGHT, NOBODY LEAVES THIS ROOM!
I WILL...
...WORK WITH THE SECURITY DEPARTMENT TO GET TO THE BOTTOM OF THIS.
Aaah! Let's look at his face!
AAH
AAH
HEY! LISTEN TO ME!
FWUMP
I'VE GOT HIM!!!
KRASH

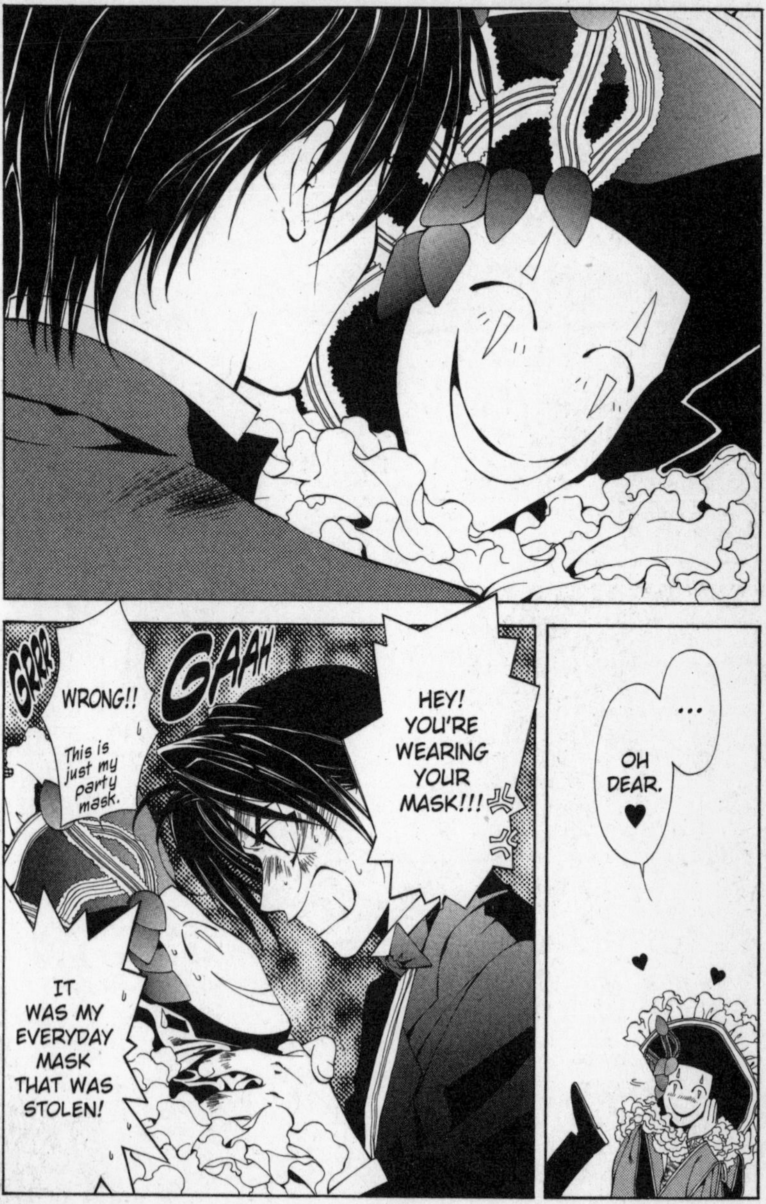
...
OH DEAR. ♥
HEY! YOU'RE WEARING YOUR MASK!!!
GAAH
WRONG!!
This is just my party mask.
GRRR
IT WAS MY EVERYDAY MASK THAT WAS STOLEN!

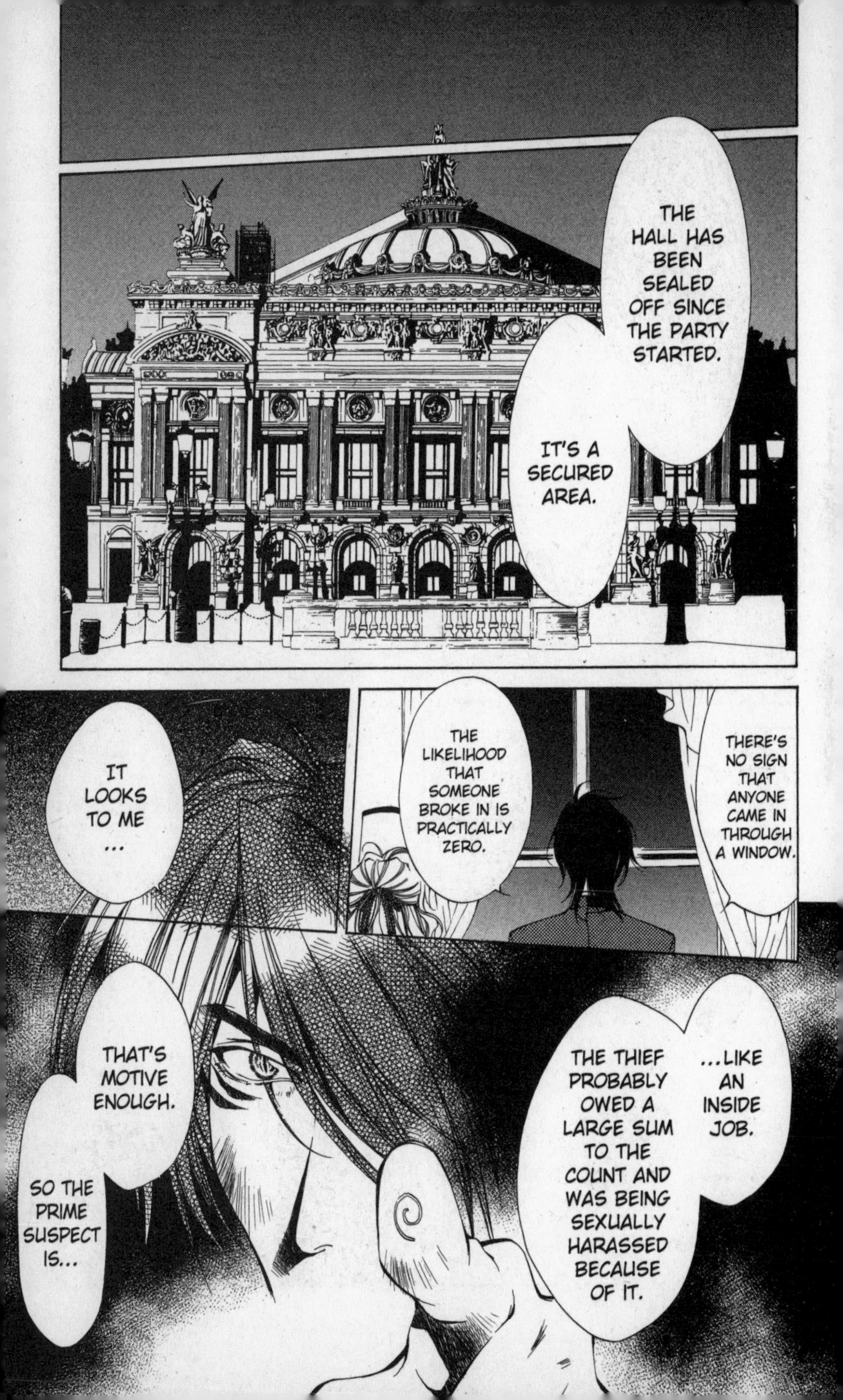
THE HALL HAS BEEN SEALED OFF SINCE THE PARTY STARTED.
IT'S A SECURED AREA.
THERE'S NO SIGN THAT ANYONE CAME IN THROUGH A WINDOW.
THE LIKELIHOOD THAT SOMEONE BROKE IN IS PRACTICALLY ZERO.
IT LOOKS TO ME ...
...LIKE AN INSIDE JOB.
THE THIEF PROBABLY OWED A LARGE SUM TO THE COUNT AND WAS BEING SEXUALLY HARASSED BECAUSE OF IT.
THAT'S MOTIVE ENOUGH.
SO THE PRIME SUSPECT IS...

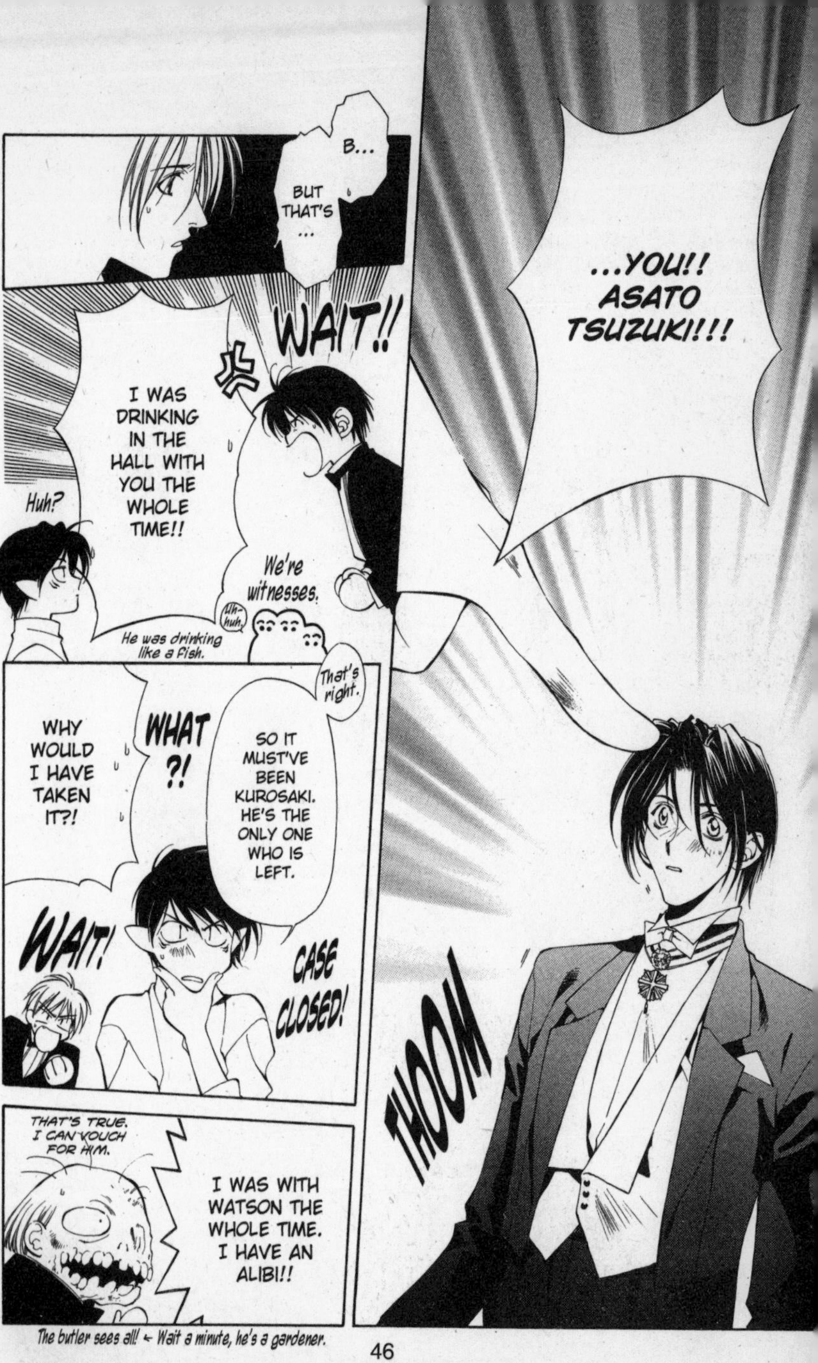

...YOU!! ASATO TSUZUKI!!!
THOOM
B...
BUT THAT'S ...
WAIT!!
I WAS DRINKING IN THE HALL WITH YOU THE WHOLE TIME!!
We're witnesses.
Uh-huh.
Huh?
He was drinking like a fish.
That's right.
SO IT MUST'VE BEEN KUROSAKI. HE'S THE ONLY ONE WHO IS LEFT.
WHAT ?!
WHY WOULD I HAVE TAKEN IT?!
CASE CLOSED!
WAIT!
I WAS WITH WATSON THE WHOLE TIME. I HAVE AN ALIBI!!
THAT'S TRUE. I CAN VOUCH FOR HIM.

The butler sees all! ← Wait a minute, he's a gardener.

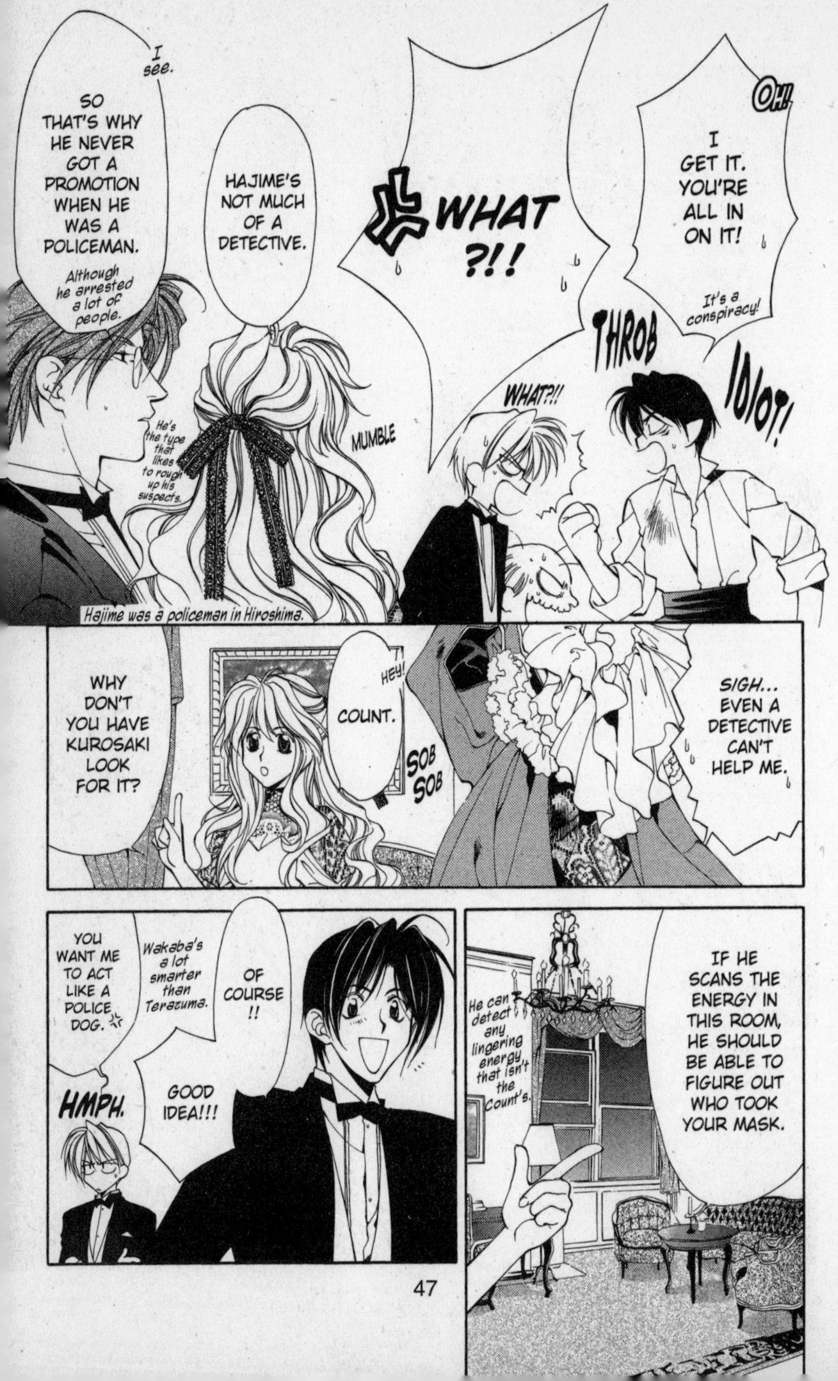
OH!
I GET IT. YOU'RE ALL IN ON IT!
It's a conspiracy!
IDIOT!
THROB
WHAT?!!
WHAT ?!!
HAJIME'S NOT MUCH OF A DETECTIVE.
MUMBLE
He's the type that likes to rough up his suspects.
I see.
SO THAT'S WHY HE NEVER GOT A PROMOTION WHEN HE WAS A POLICEMAN.
Although he arrested a lot of people.
Hajime was a policeman in Hiroshima.
SIGH... EVEN A DETECTIVE CAN'T HELP ME.
SOB SOB
HEY!
COUNT.
WHY DON'T YOU HAVE KUROSAKI LOOK FOR IT?
IF HE SCANS THE ENERGY IN THIS ROOM, HE SHOULD BE ABLE TO FIGURE OUT WHO TOOK YOUR MASK.
He can detect any lingering energy that isn't the Count's.
OF COURSE !!
Wakaba's a lot smarter than Terazuma.
YOU WANT ME TO ACT LIKE A POLICE DOG.
GOOD IDEA!!!
HMPH.

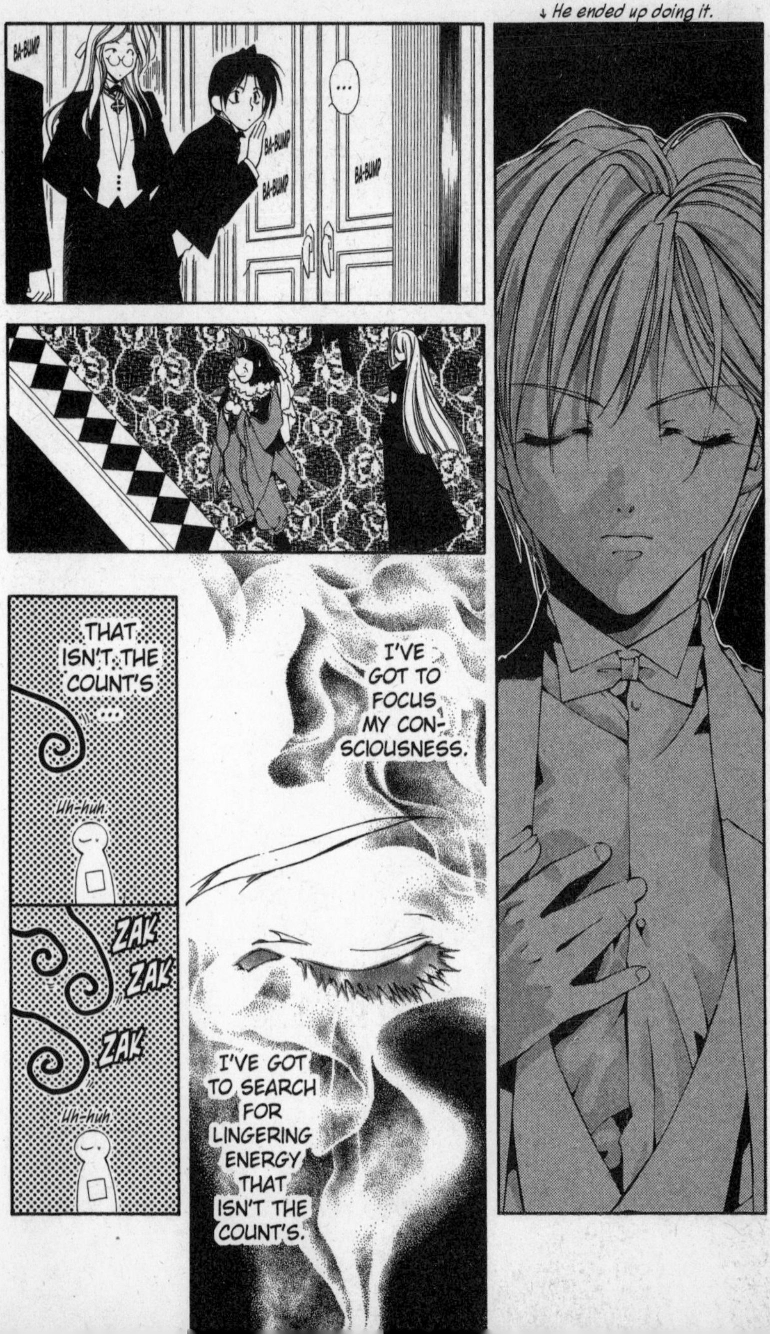
↓ He ended up doing it.
...
BA-BUMP
BA-BUMP
BA-BUMP
BA-BUMP
I'VE GOT TO FOCUS MY CON-SCIOUSNESS.
I'VE GOT TO SEARCH FOR LINGERING ENERGY THAT ISN'T THE COUNT'S.
THAT ISN'T THE COUNT'S ...
Uh-huh.
ZAK
ZAK
ZAK
Uh-huh.

▼ The Count's Imagination

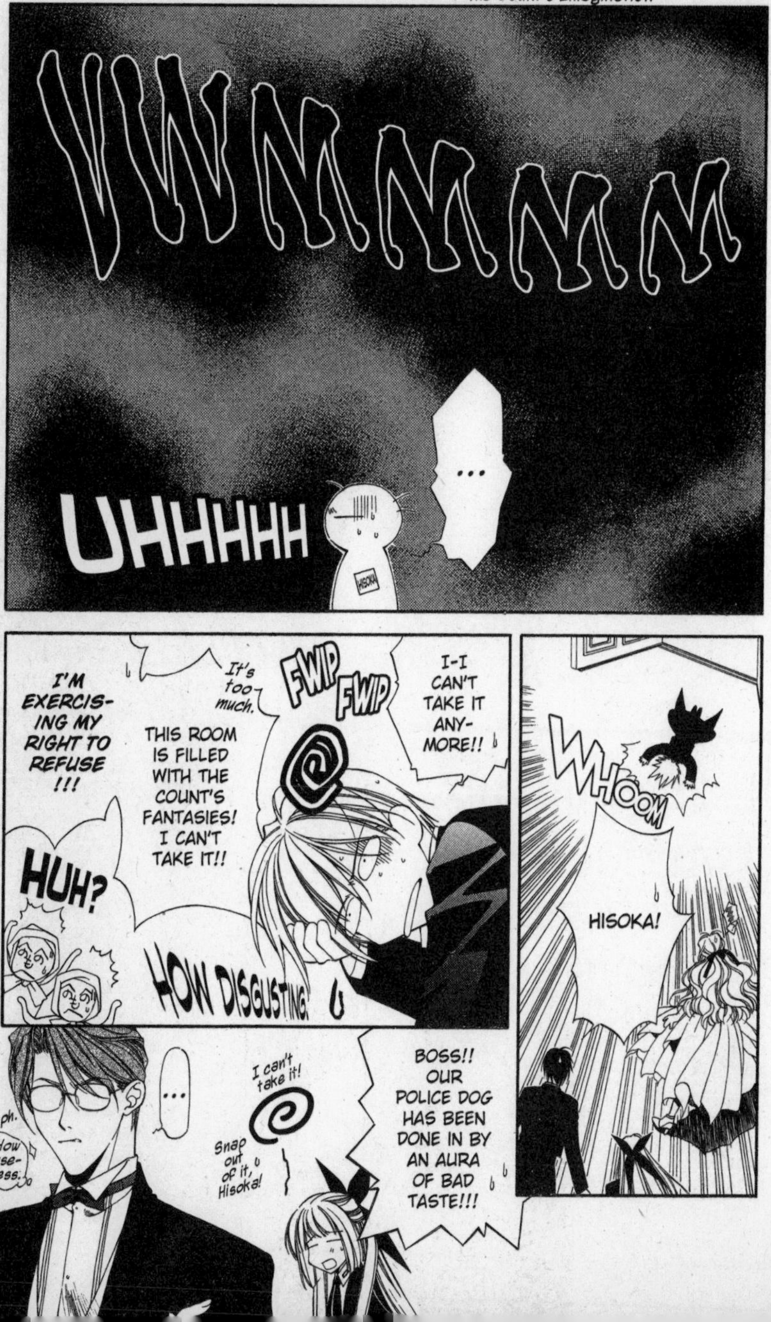

VWNMMMM
...
UHHHHH
WHOOM
HISOKA!
I-I CAN'T TAKE IT ANYMORE!!
FWIP FWIP
It's too-much.
THIS ROOM IS FILLED WITH THE COUNT'S FANTASIES! I CAN'T TAKE IT!!
I'M EXERCISING MY RIGHT TO REFUSE !!!
HUH?
HOW DISGUSTING.
BOSS!! OUR POLICE DOG HAS BEEN DONE IN BY AN AURA OF BAD TASTE!!!
I can't take it!
Snap out of it, Hisoka!
...
Hmph.
How useless.

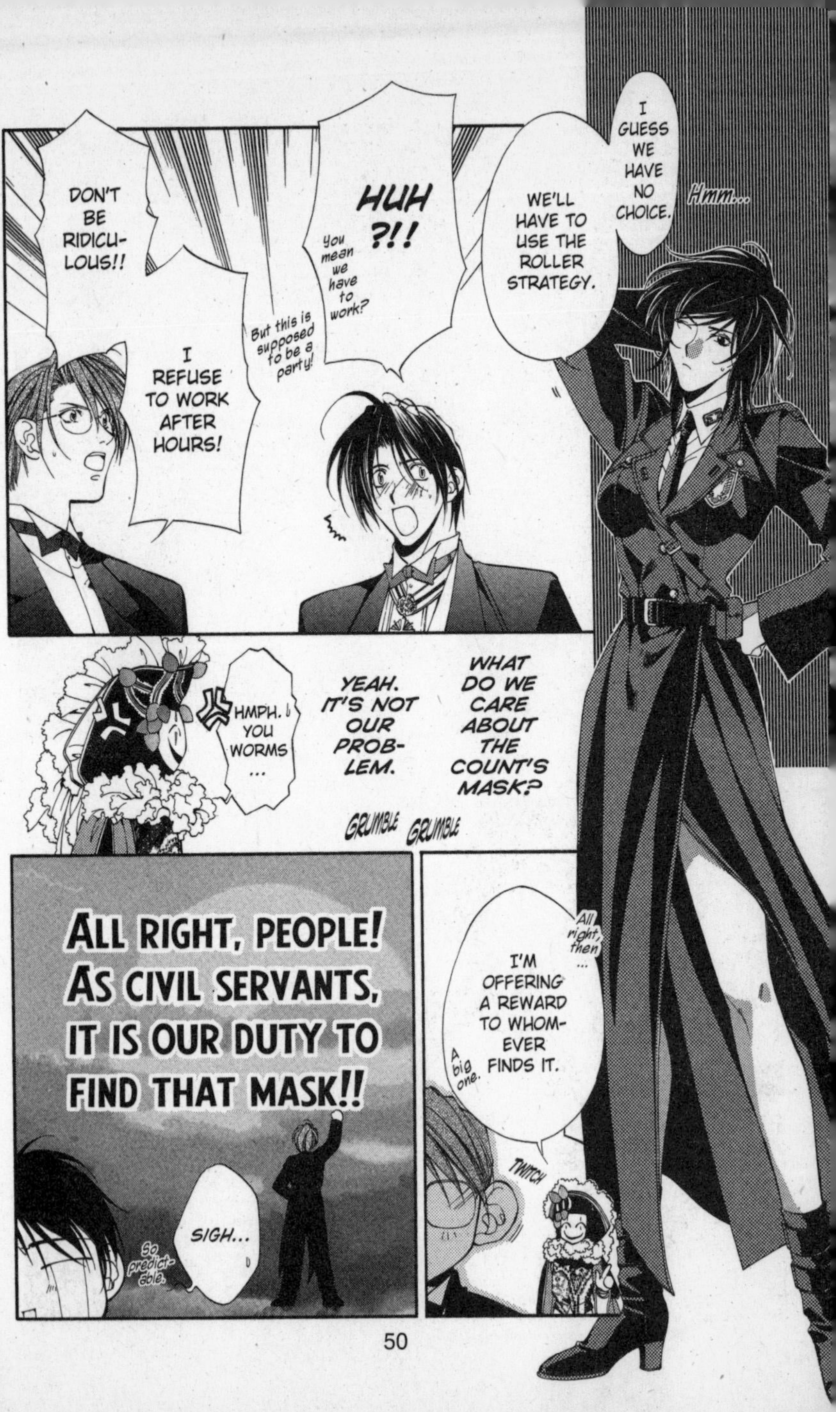

Hmm...
I GUESS WE HAVE NO CHOICE.
WE'LL HAVE TO USE THE ROLLER STRATEGY.
HUH?!!
You mean we have to work?
But this is supposed to be a party!
DON'T BE RIDICULOUS!!
I REFUSE TO WORK AFTER HOURS!
WHAT DO WE CARE ABOUT THE COUNT'S MASK?
YEAH. IT'S NOT OUR PROBLEM.
HMPH. YOU WORMS...
GRUMBLE GRUMBLE
All right, then...
I'M OFFERING A REWARD TO WHOMEVER FINDS IT.
A big one.
TWITCH
ALL RIGHT, PEOPLE! AS CIVIL SERVANTS, IT IS OUR DUTY TO FIND THAT MASK!!
SIGH...
So predictable.

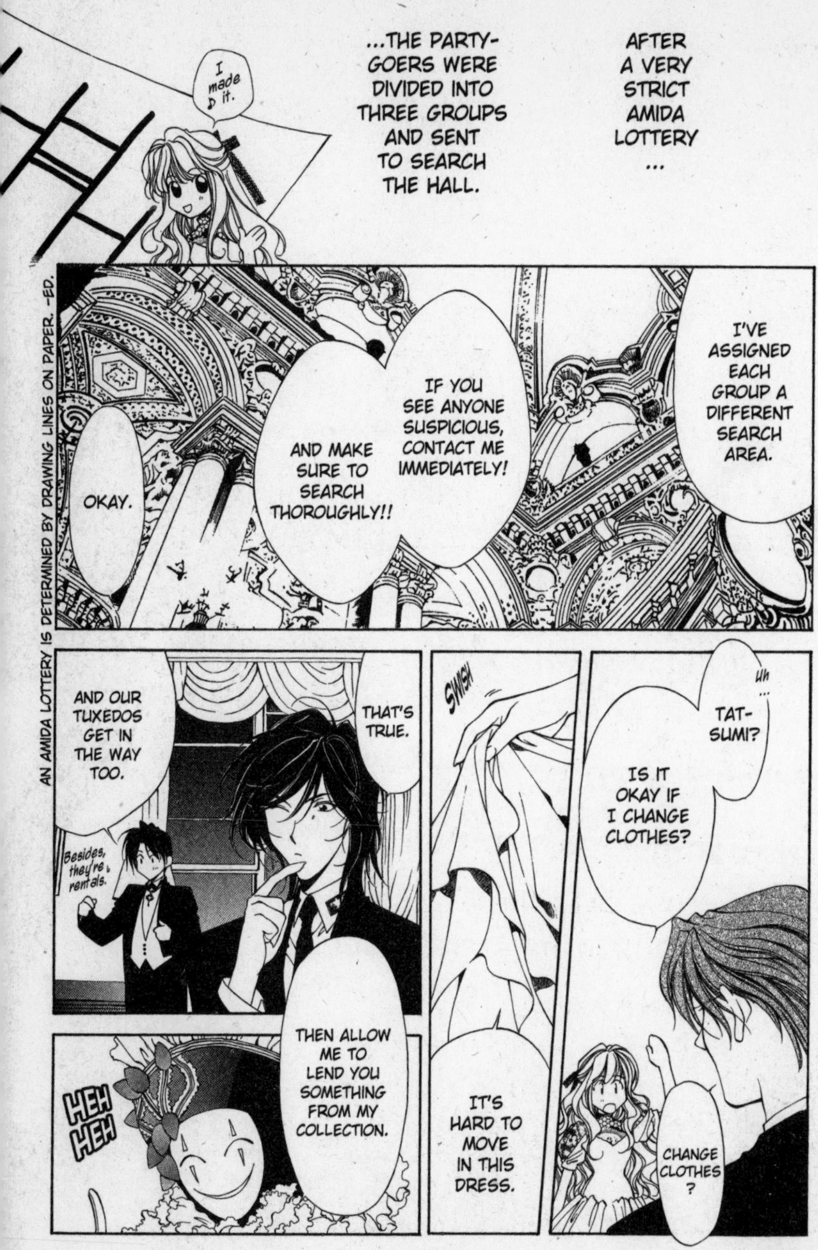
AFTER A VERY STRICT AMIDA LOTTERY...
...THE PARTY-GOERS WERE DIVIDED INTO THREE GROUPS AND SENT TO SEARCH THE HALL.
I made it ♪
I'VE ASSIGNED EACH GROUP A DIFFERENT SEARCH AREA.
IF YOU SEE ANYONE SUSPICIOUS, CONTACT ME IMMEDIATELY!
AND MAKE SURE TO SEARCH THOROUGHLY!!
OKAY.
uh...
TAT-SUMI?
IS IT OKAY IF I CHANGE CLOTHES?
CHANGE CLOTHES?
SWISH
IT'S HARD TO MOVE IN THIS DRESS.
THAT'S TRUE.
AND OUR TUXEDOS GET IN THE WAY TOO.
Besides, they're rentals.
THEN ALLOW ME TO LEND YOU SOMETHING FROM MY COLLECTION.
HEH HEH

AN AMIDA LOTTERY IS DETERMINED BY DRAWING LINES ON PAPER. -ED.

THERE'S MORE INSIDE THE DRESSER TOO.

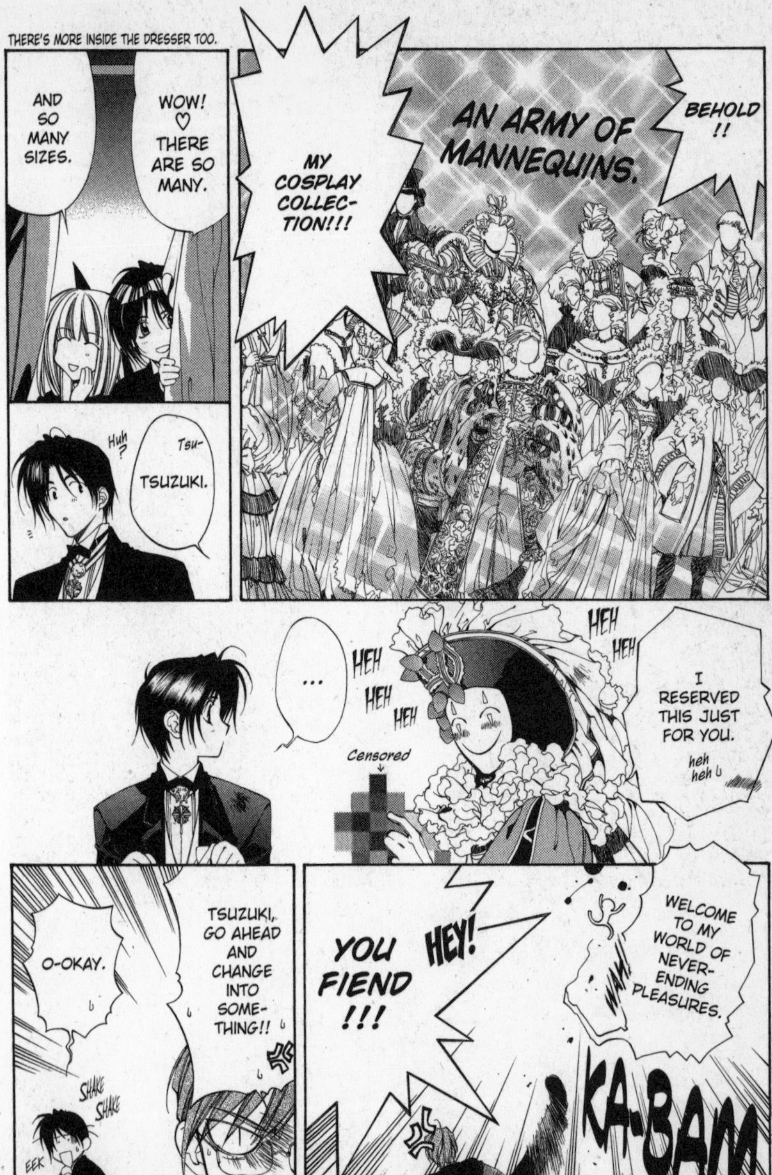
BEHOLD!!
AN ARMY OF MANNEQUINS.
MY COSPLAY COLLECTION!!!
WOW! ♡ THERE ARE SO MANY.
AND SO MANY SIZES.
Tsu- TSUZUKI.
Huh?
HEH HEH
I RESERVED THIS JUST FOR YOU. heh heh
Censored
HEH HEH HEH
...
WELCOME TO MY WORLD OF NEVER-ENDING PLEASURES.
HEY!
YOU FIEND!!!
KA-BAM
TSUZUKI, GO AHEAD AND CHANGE INTO SOME-THING!!
O-OKAY.
SHAKE SHAKE
EEK

WHY DOES THE COUNT HAVE GIRL'S CLOTHES?

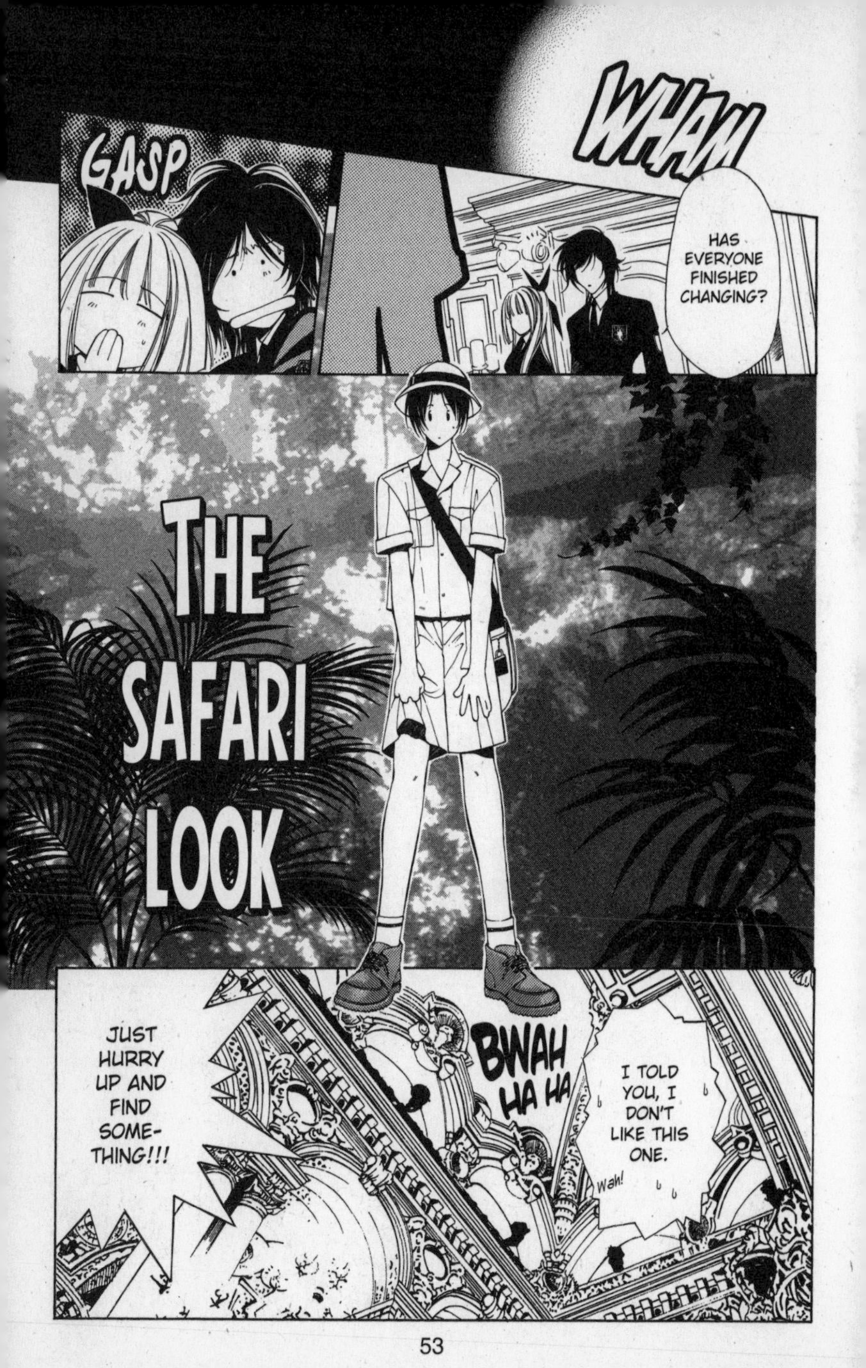
WHAM
HAS EVERYONE FINISHED CHANGING?
GASP
THE SAFARI LOOK
I TOLD YOU, I DON'T LIKE THIS ONE.
Wah!
BWAH HA HA
JUST HURRY UP AND FIND SOME-THING!!!

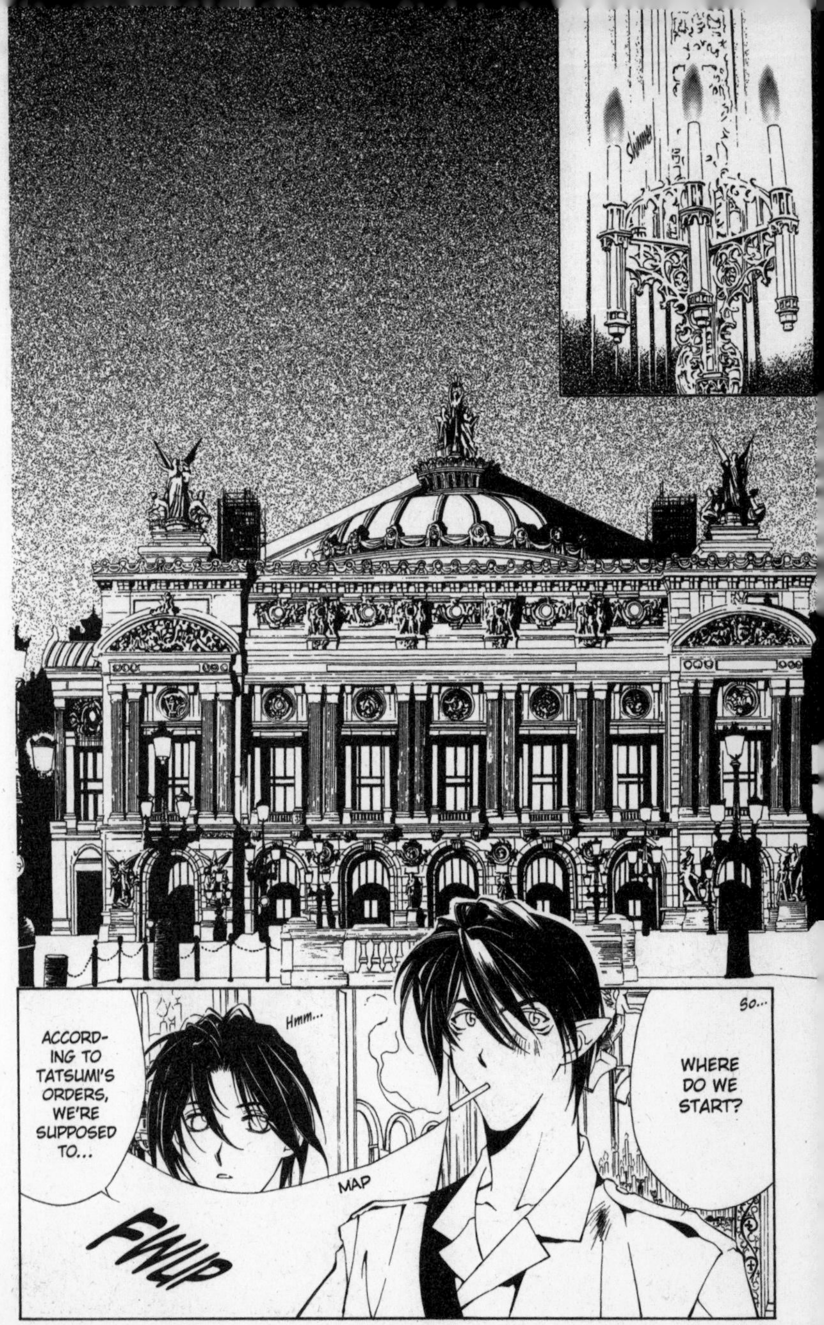
Shimmer
So...
WHERE DO WE START?
Hmm...
ACCORD-ING TO TATSUMI'S ORDERS, WE'RE SUPPOSED TO...
MAP
FWUP

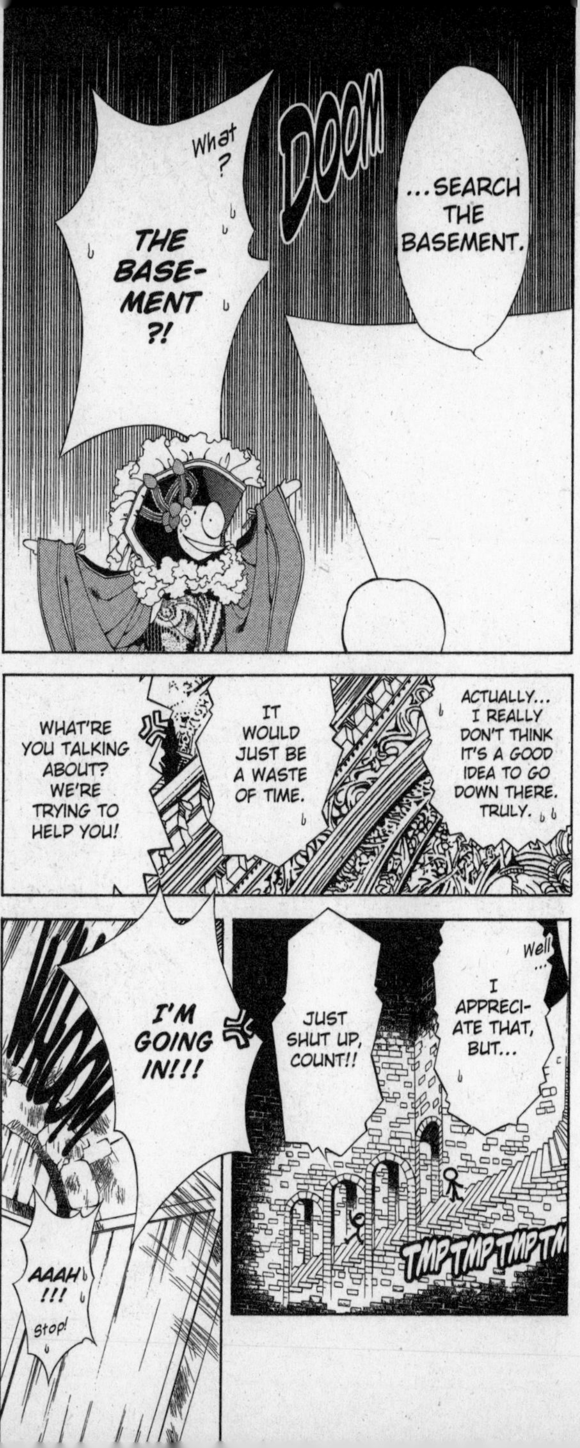
...SEARCH THE BASEMENT.
DOOM
What ?
THE BASE-MENT ?!
ACTUALLY... I REALLY DON'T THINK IT'S A GOOD IDEA TO GO DOWN THERE. TRULY.
IT WOULD JUST BE A WASTE OF TIME.
WHAT'RE YOU TALKING ABOUT? WE'RE TRYING TO HELP YOU!
Well... I APPRECI-ATE THAT, BUT...
JUST SHUT UP, COUNT!!
TMP TMP TMP TM
I'M GOING IN!!!
AAAH !!!
Stop!

AS USUAL... I HAVE NOTHING TO SAY!

Ha. Because I had fewer pages of manga for this book, I'm left with more quarter-page panels to fill. Oh no! It's tough when you have nothing to write about. I was told that if I don't have anything to say, I should just write about my hobbies. But my only hobby is video games, and I think it would be boring for girls to read about that. There just aren't as many female gamers out there. On top of that, I only play RPG and SLG games.

HA!

Sometimes I play ADV games too, but not very often. When you've got a job like this, it's impossible to have other hobbies.

I NEED SOMETHING TO TALK ABOUT!

I GUESS I COULD JUST DRAW SOMETHING.

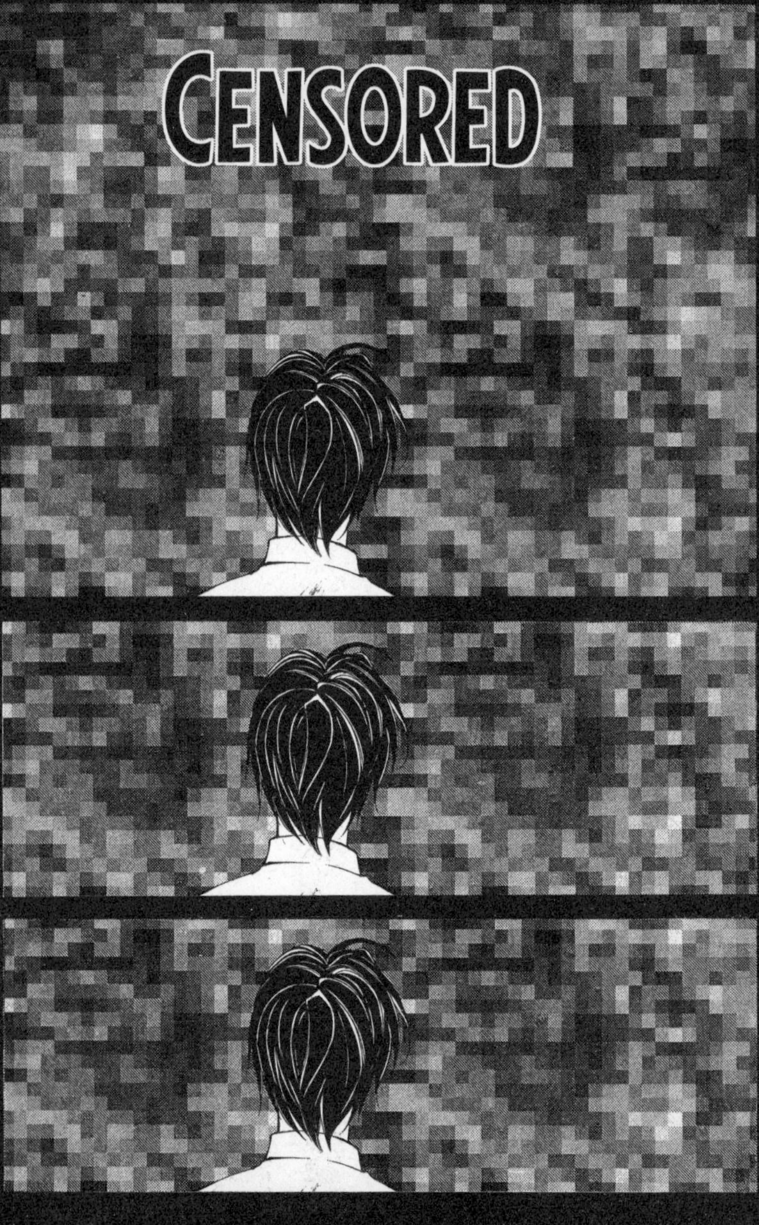
CENSORED

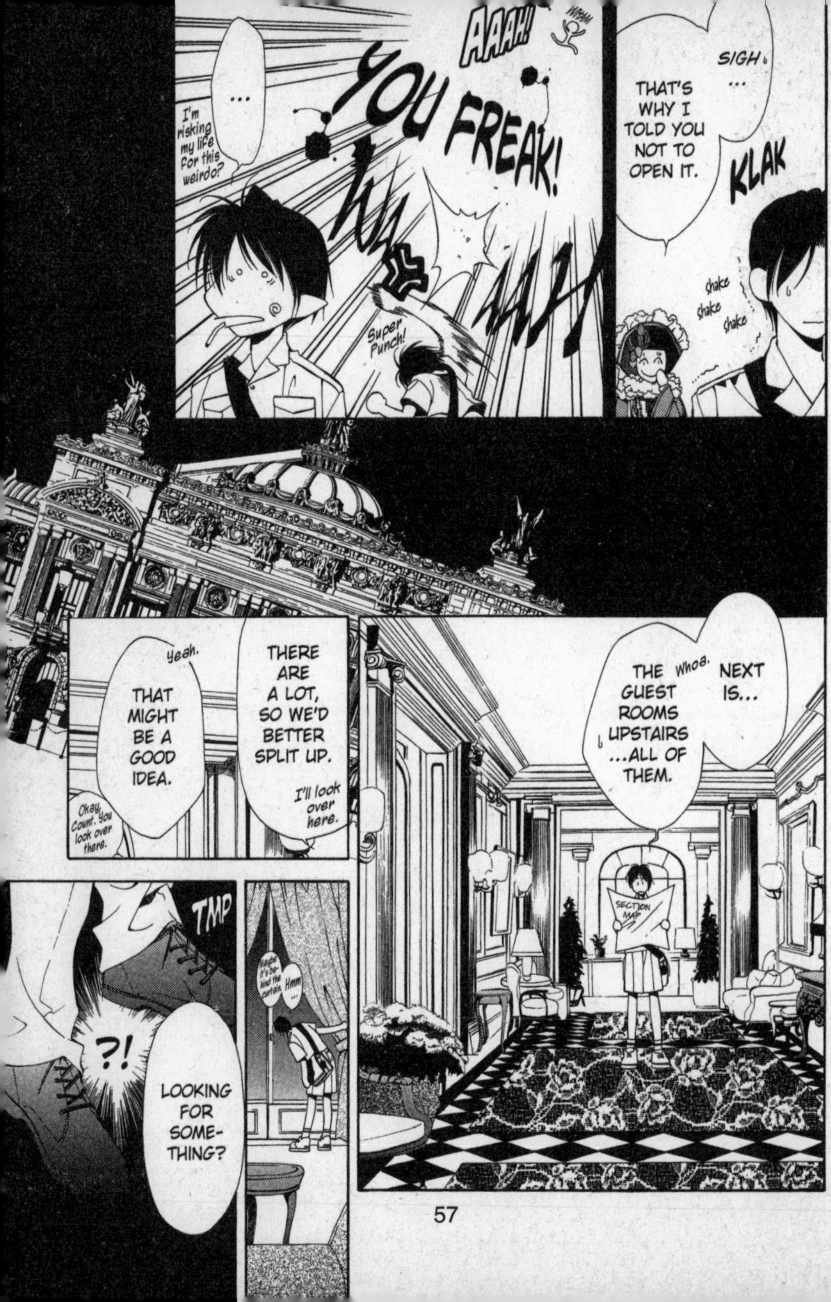
SIGH...
THAT'S WHY I TOLD YOU NOT TO OPEN IT.
KLAK
shake shake shake
AAAH!
YOU FREAK!
...
I'm risking my life for this weirdo?
Super Punch!
NEXT IS...
THE GUEST ROOMS UPSTAIRS ...ALL OF THEM.
Whoa.
SECTION MAP
THERE ARE A LOT, SO WE'D BETTER SPLIT UP.
I'll look over here.
Yeah.
THAT MIGHT BE A GOOD IDEA.
Okay, Count. You look over there.
Maybe it's behind the curtain.
Hmm...
TMP
?!
LOOKING FOR SOMETHING?

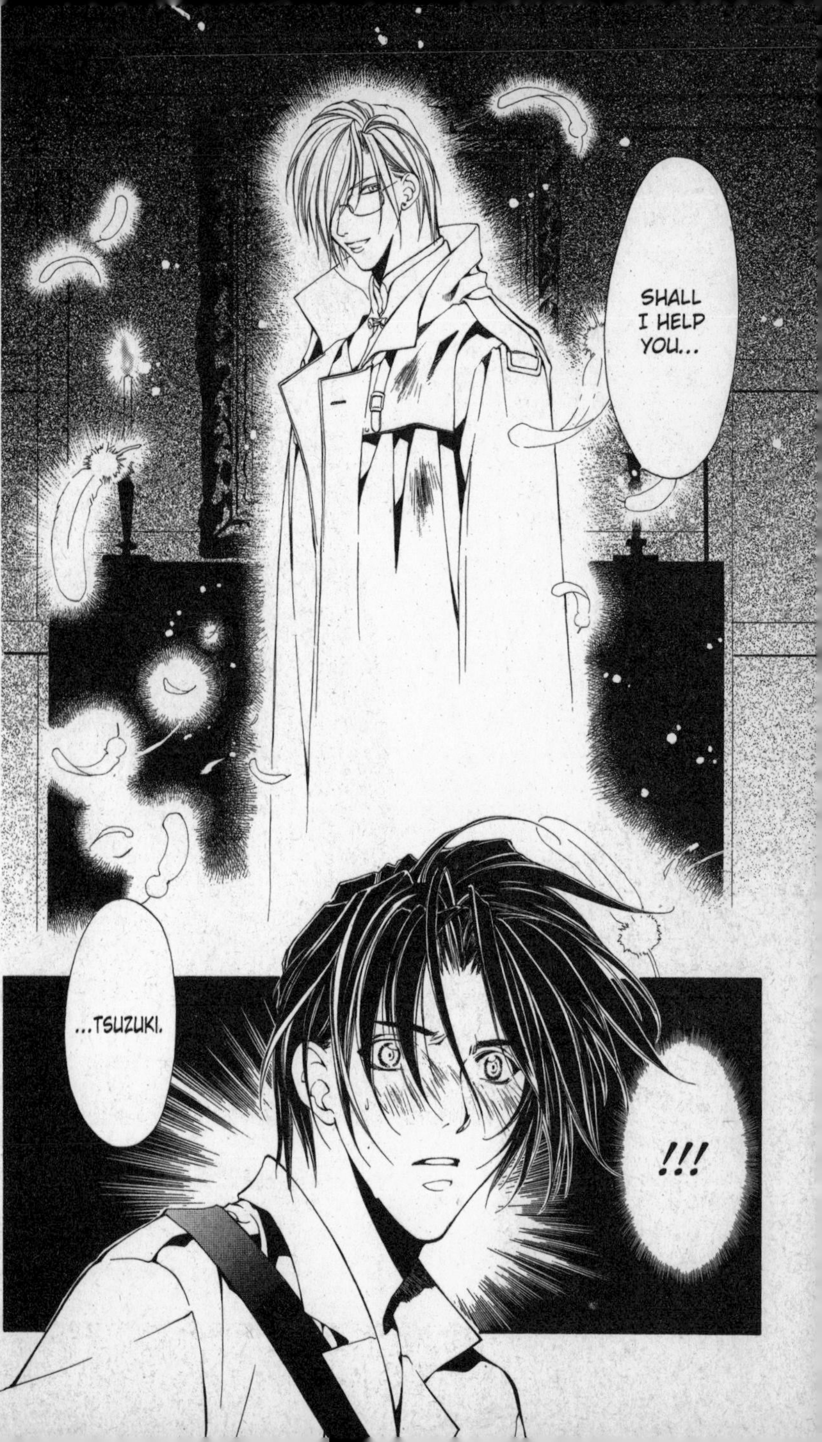
SHALL I HELP YOU...
!!!
...TSUZUKI.

[CHAPTER 3]

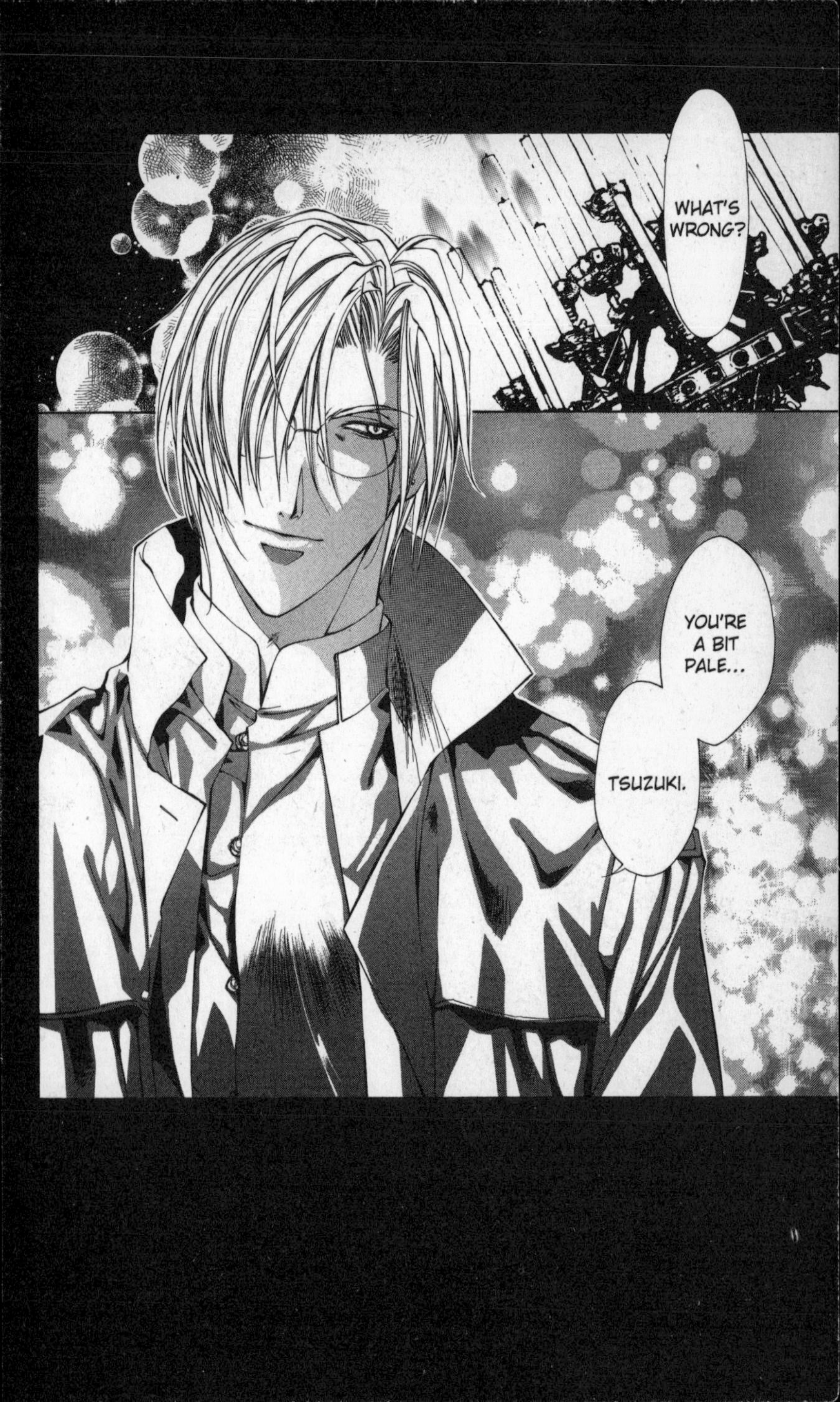
WHAT'S WRONG?
YOU'RE A BIT PALE...
TSUZUKI.

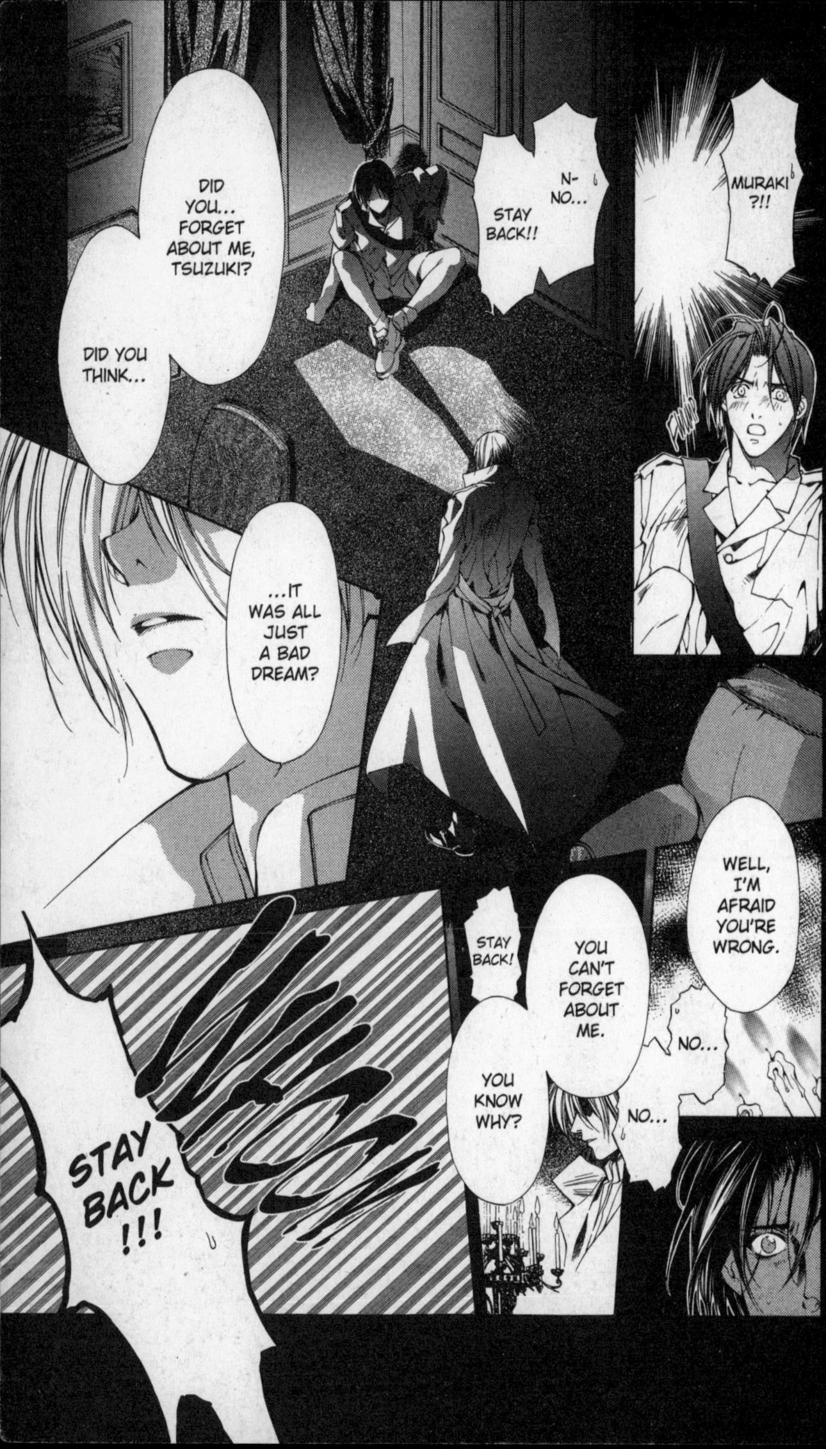
MURAKI ?!!
N- NO...
STAY BACK!!
DID YOU... FORGET ABOUT ME, TSUZUKI?
DID YOU THINK...
...IT WAS ALL JUST A BAD DREAM?
WELL, I'M AFRAID YOU'RE WRONG.
NO...
NO...
YOU CAN'T FORGET ABOUT ME.
STAY BACK!
YOU KNOW WHY?
STAY BACK !!!

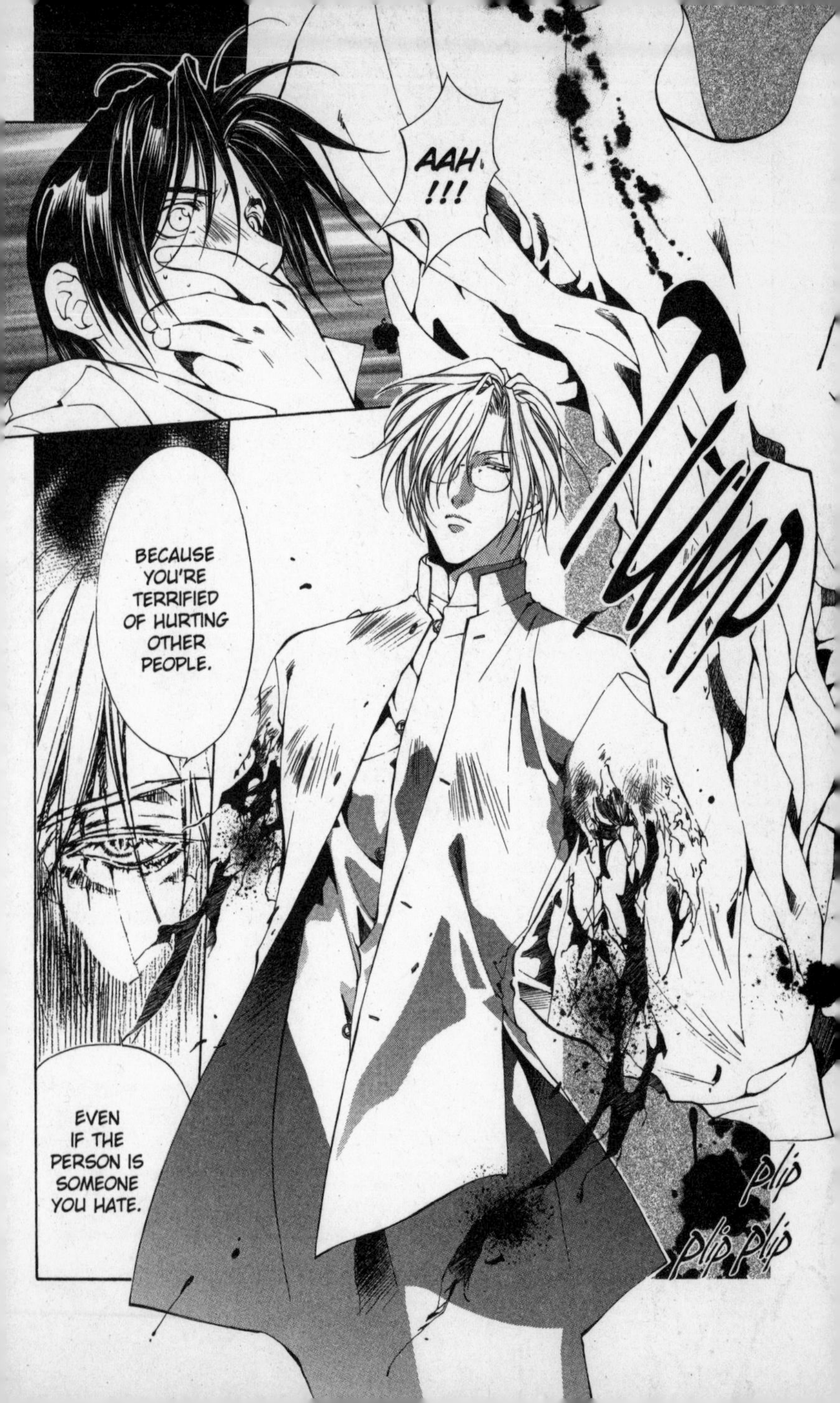
AAH !!!
THUMP
BECAUSE YOU'RE TERRIFIED OF HURTING OTHER PEOPLE.
plip plip plip
EVEN IF THE PERSON IS SOMEONE YOU HATE.

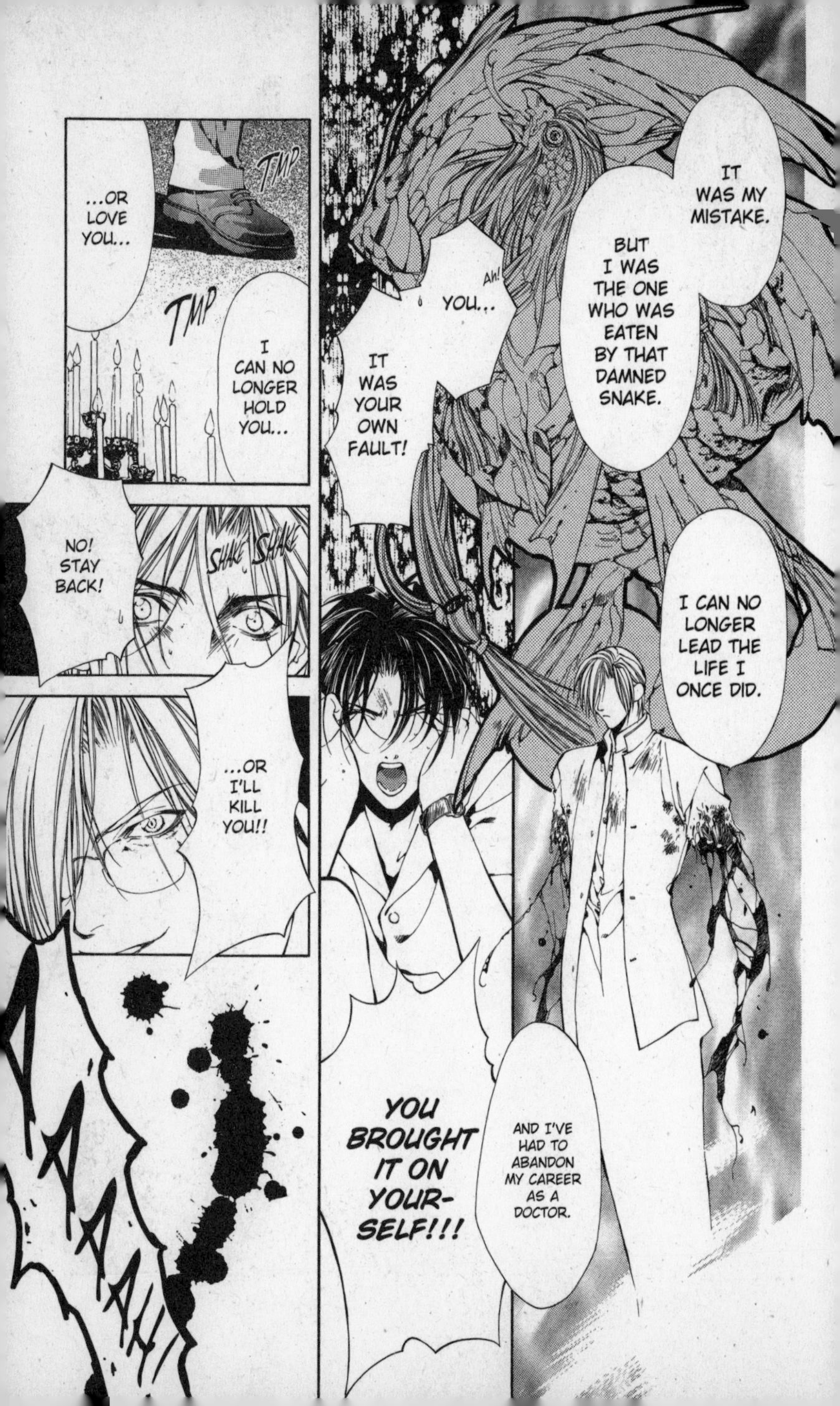
IT WAS MY MISTAKE.
BUT I WAS THE ONE WHO WAS EATEN BY THAT DAMNED SNAKE.
I CAN NO LONGER LEAD THE LIFE I ONCE DID.
AND I'VE HAD TO ABANDON MY CAREER AS A DOCTOR.
Ah! YOU...
IT WAS YOUR OWN FAULT!
YOU BROUGHT IT ON YOUR-SELF!!!
TMP
I CAN NO LONGER HOLD YOU...
...OR LOVE YOU...
TMP
SHAKE SHAKE
NO! STAY BACK!
...OR I'LL KILL YOU!!
AAAAH!

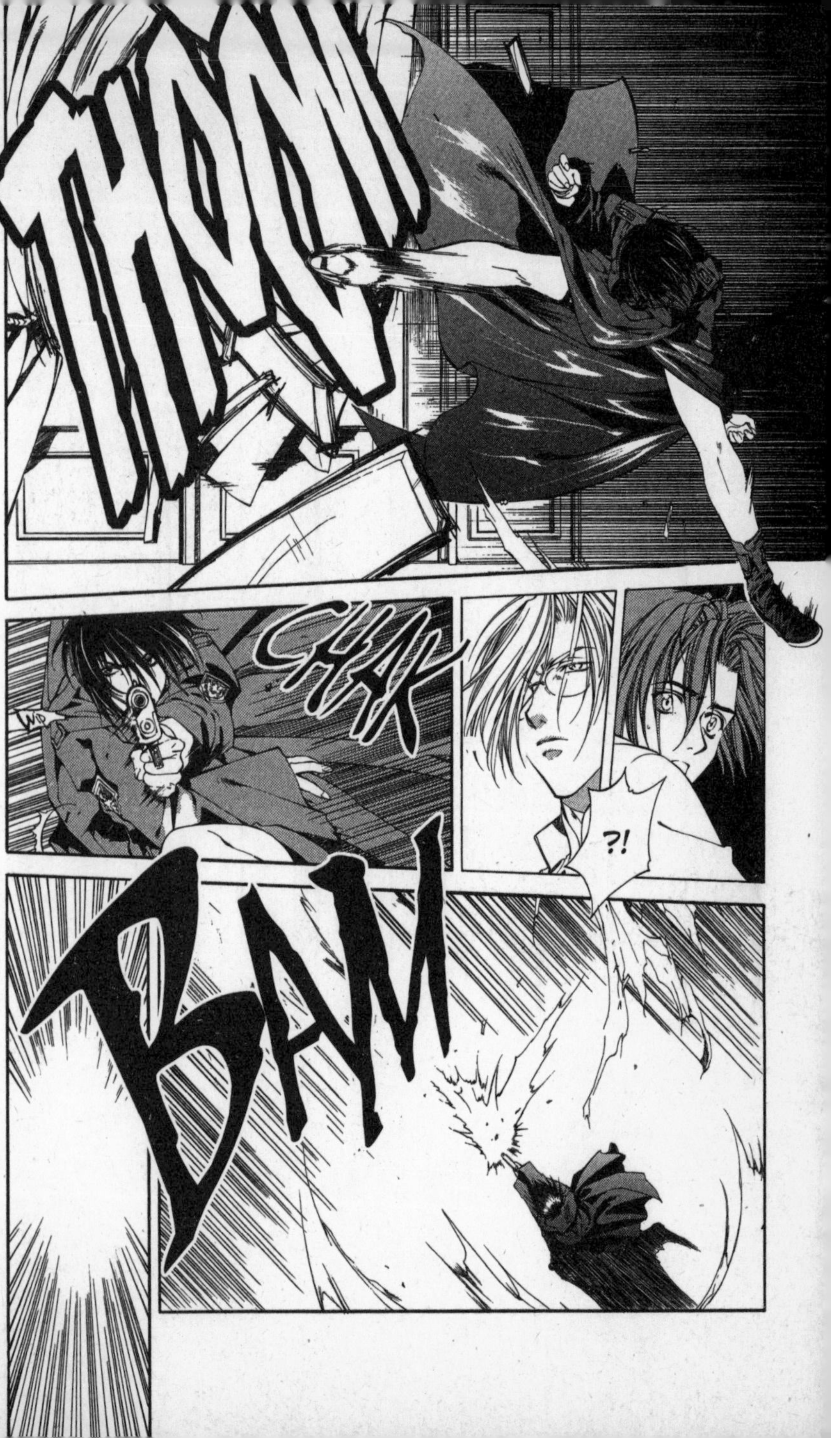
THOMM
?!
CHAK
BAM

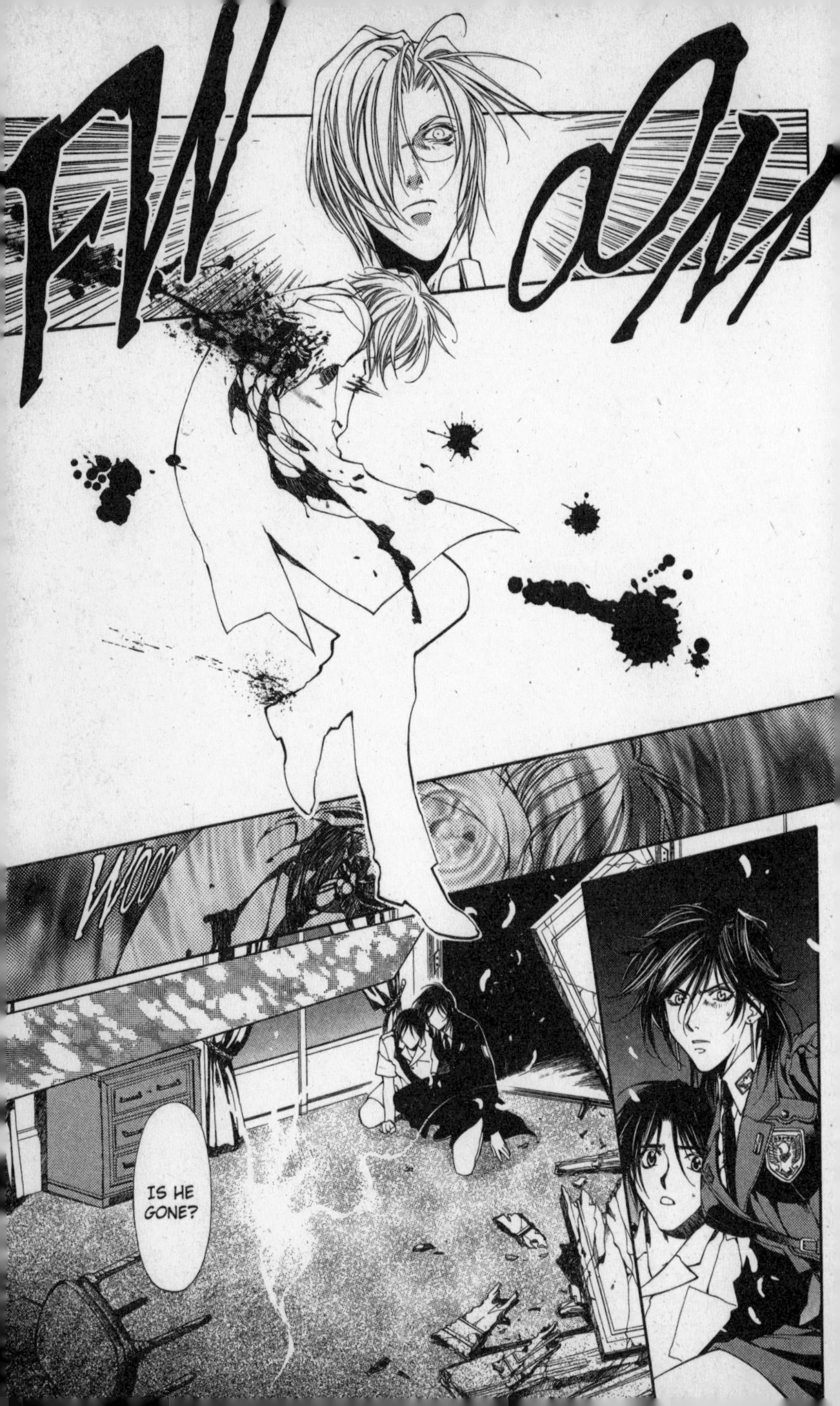
IS HE GONE?

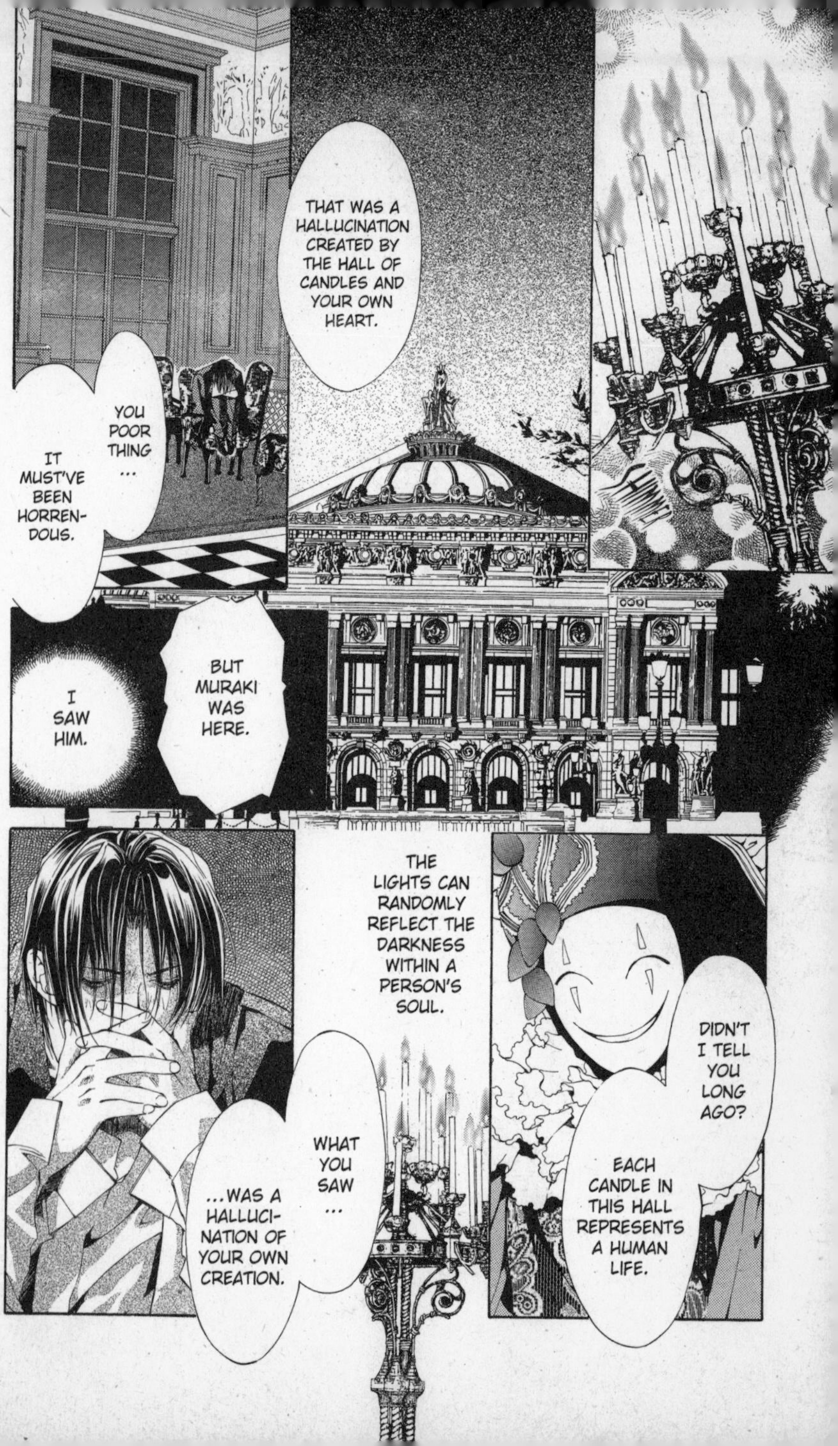
THAT WAS A HALLUCINATION CREATED BY THE HALL OF CANDLES AND YOUR OWN HEART.
YOU POOR THING...
IT MUST'VE BEEN HORREN-DOUS.
BUT MURAKI WAS HERE.
I SAW HIM.
DIDN'T I TELL YOU LONG AGO?
EACH CANDLE IN THIS HALL REPRESENTS A HUMAN LIFE.
THE LIGHTS CAN RANDOMLY REFLECT THE DARKNESS WITHIN A PERSON'S SOUL.
WHAT YOU SAW...
...WAS A HALLUCI-NATION OF YOUR OWN CREATION.

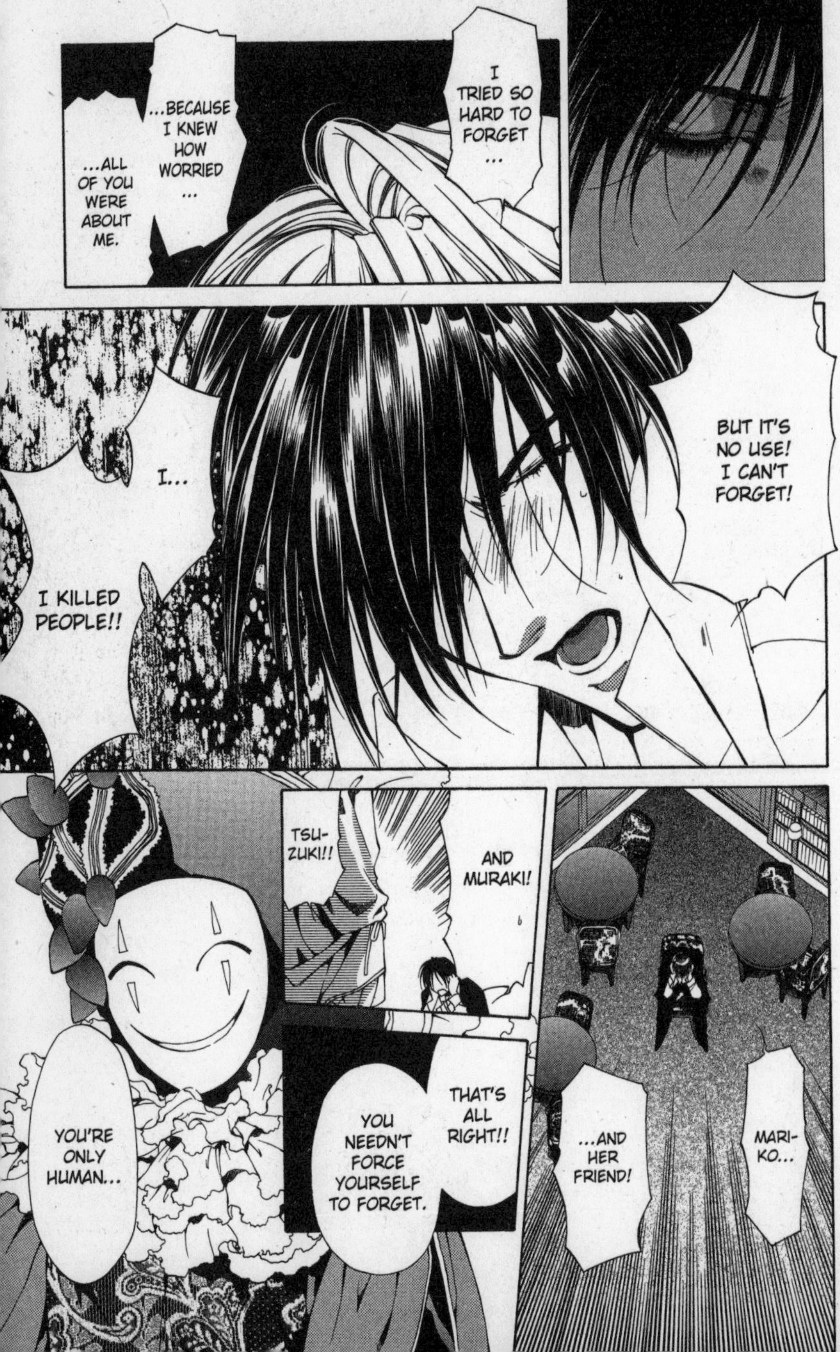
I TRIED SO HARD TO FORGET ...
...BECAUSE I KNEW HOW WORRIED ...
...ALL OF YOU WERE ABOUT ME.
BUT IT'S NO USE! I CAN'T FORGET!
I...
I KILLED PEOPLE!!
MARI-KO...
...AND HER FRIEND!
AND MURAKI!
TSU-ZUKI!!
THAT'S ALL RIGHT!!
YOU NEEDN'T FORCE YOURSELF TO FORGET.
YOU'RE ONLY HUMAN...

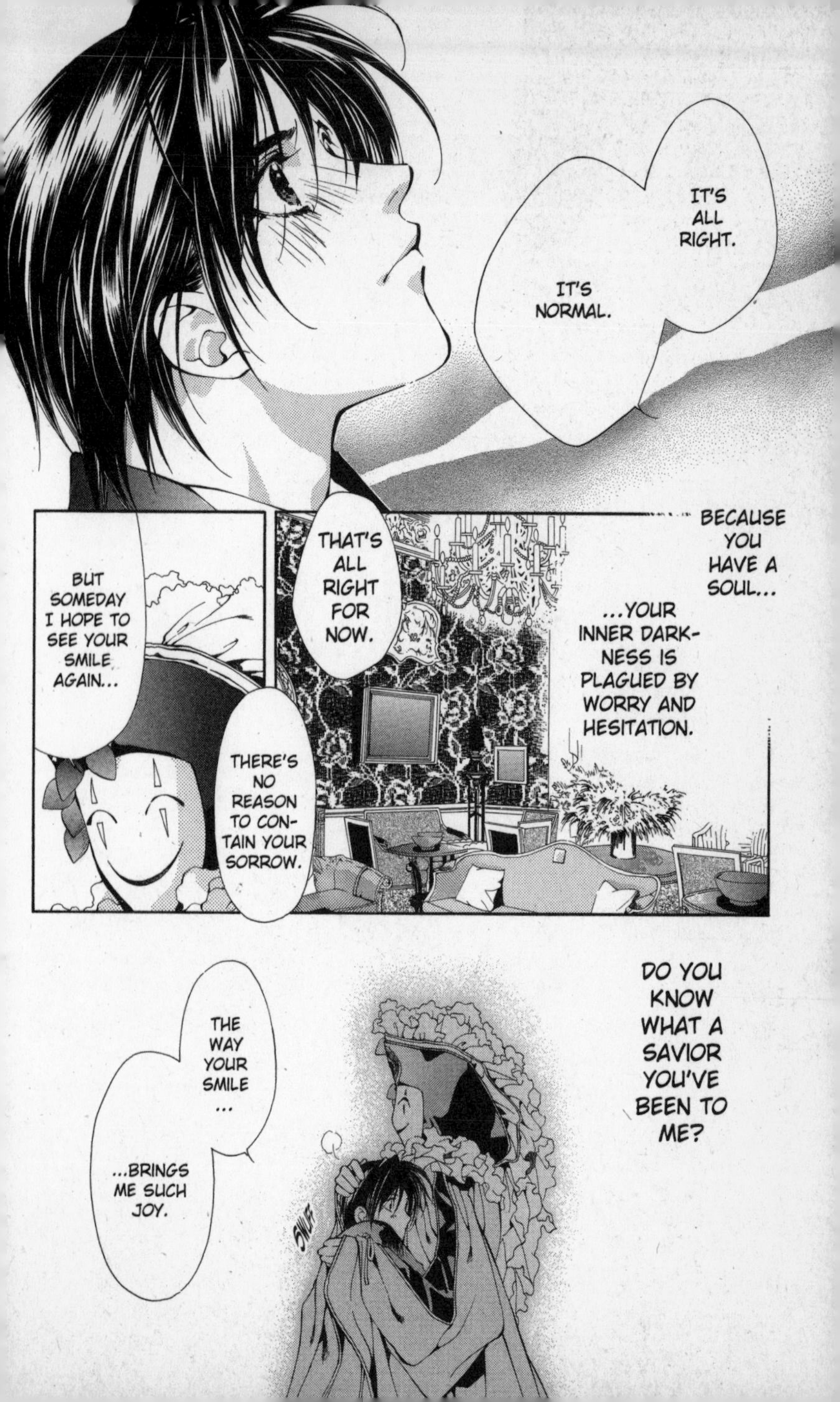
IT'S ALL RIGHT.
IT'S NORMAL.
BECAUSE YOU HAVE A SOUL...
...YOUR INNER DARK-NESS IS PLAGUED BY WORRY AND HESITATION.
THAT'S ALL RIGHT FOR NOW.
THERE'S NO REASON TO CON-TAIN YOUR SORROW.
BUT SOMEDAY I HOPE TO SEE YOUR SMILE AGAIN...
DO YOU KNOW WHAT A SAVIOR YOU'VE BEEN TO ME?
THE WAY YOUR SMILE ...
...BRINGS ME SUCH JOY.
SNUFF

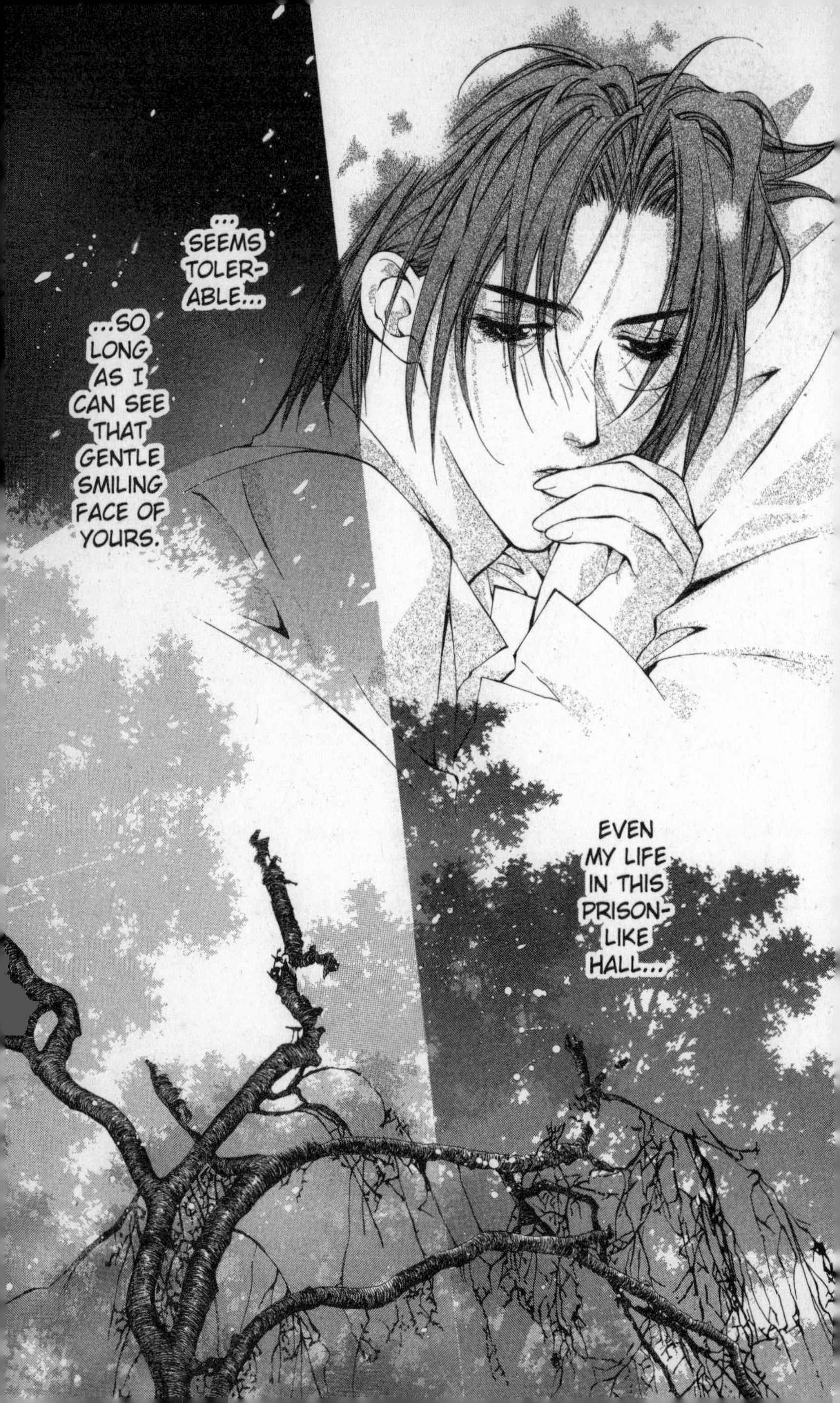
EVEN MY LIFE IN THIS PRISON-LIKE HALL...
...SEEMS TOLERABLE...
...SO LONG AS I CAN SEE THAT GENTLE SMILING FACE OF YOURS.

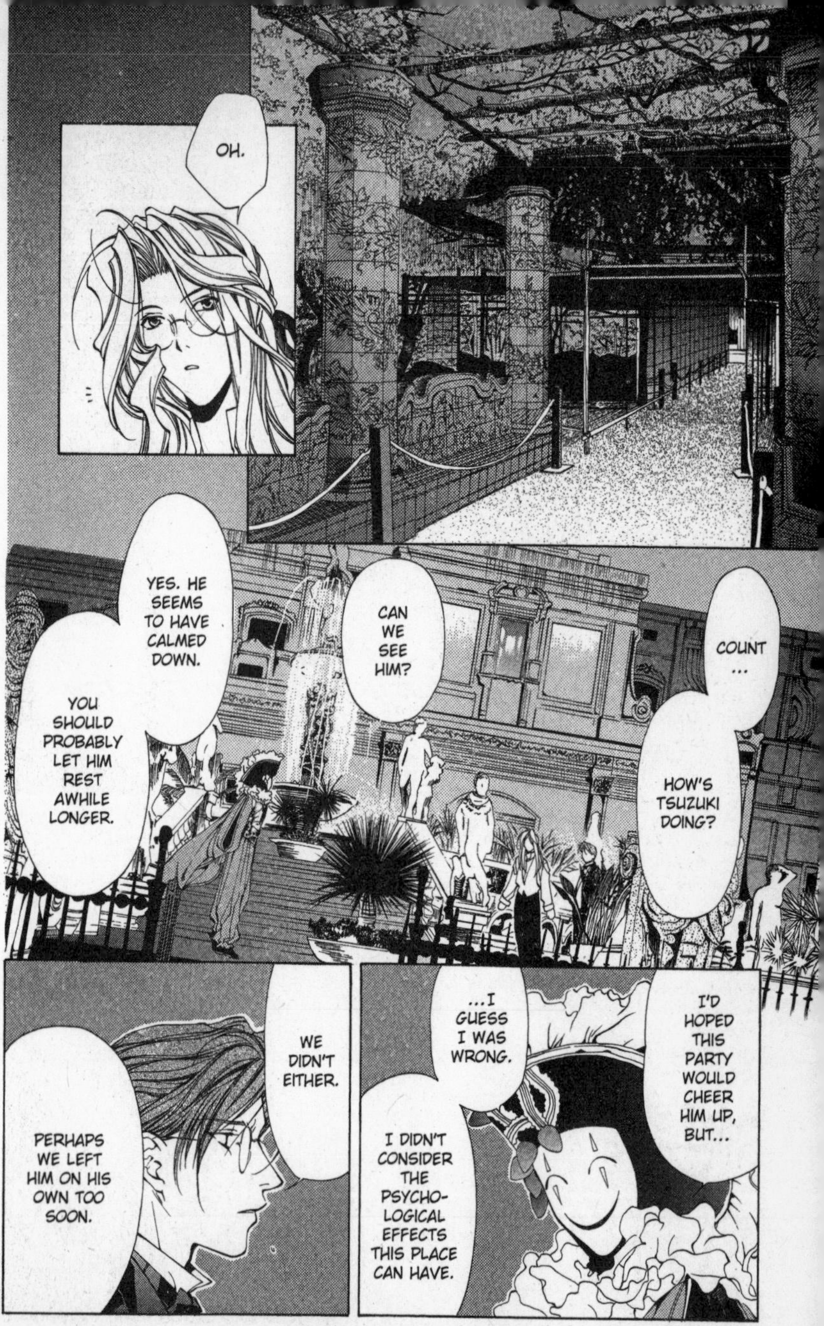
OH.
COUNT ...
HOW'S TSUZUKI DOING?
CAN WE SEE HIM?
YES. HE SEEMS TO HAVE CALMED DOWN.
YOU SHOULD PROBABLY LET HIM REST AWHILE LONGER.
I'D HOPED THIS PARTY WOULD CHEER HIM UP, BUT...
...I GUESS I WAS WRONG.
I DIDN'T CONSIDER THE PSYCHO-LOGICAL EFFECTS THIS PLACE CAN HAVE.
WE DIDN'T EITHER.
PERHAPS WE LEFT HIM ON HIS OWN TOO SOON.

He's pretty vulgar for an aristocrat.

Am I the only one who thinks so?

THE COUNT IS A GREAT GUY...

...at least that was my intention when I first drew him, but he's turned out to be pretty average. On top of that, he's a total pervert. (The difference between the Count and Muraki is that Muraki is more direct with his sexual harassment.) He's just a dirty old man...and I really don't understand his sense of style. I guess he's a charming, wealthy man. Poor Tsuzuki... he's surrounded by perverts.

I modeled the Count on a man from an educational math show. But now they've replaced him with a younger man. That's kind of sad. Well, that show has been around since I was a kid, so I guess it's only natural that it would change. Still, it's sad. I'd like to see him one more time.

Hello!
Simple math
A FAKE !!!
!!! TARU-PU.

▲ Not the actual model

...
I HAVE A FAVOR TO ASK ALL OF YOU...
IT'S DIFFICULT FOR ME TO LEAVE THE HALL OF CANDLES.
I CAN'T BE BY HIS SIDE TO EASE HIS SUFFERING.
SO, PLEASE...
WHENEVER HE'S IN PAIN... WHENEVER HE'S GOING THROUGH SOMETHING TERRIBLE...
I WANT YOU TO BE THERE FOR HIM.
HE IS VERY DEAR TO ME.

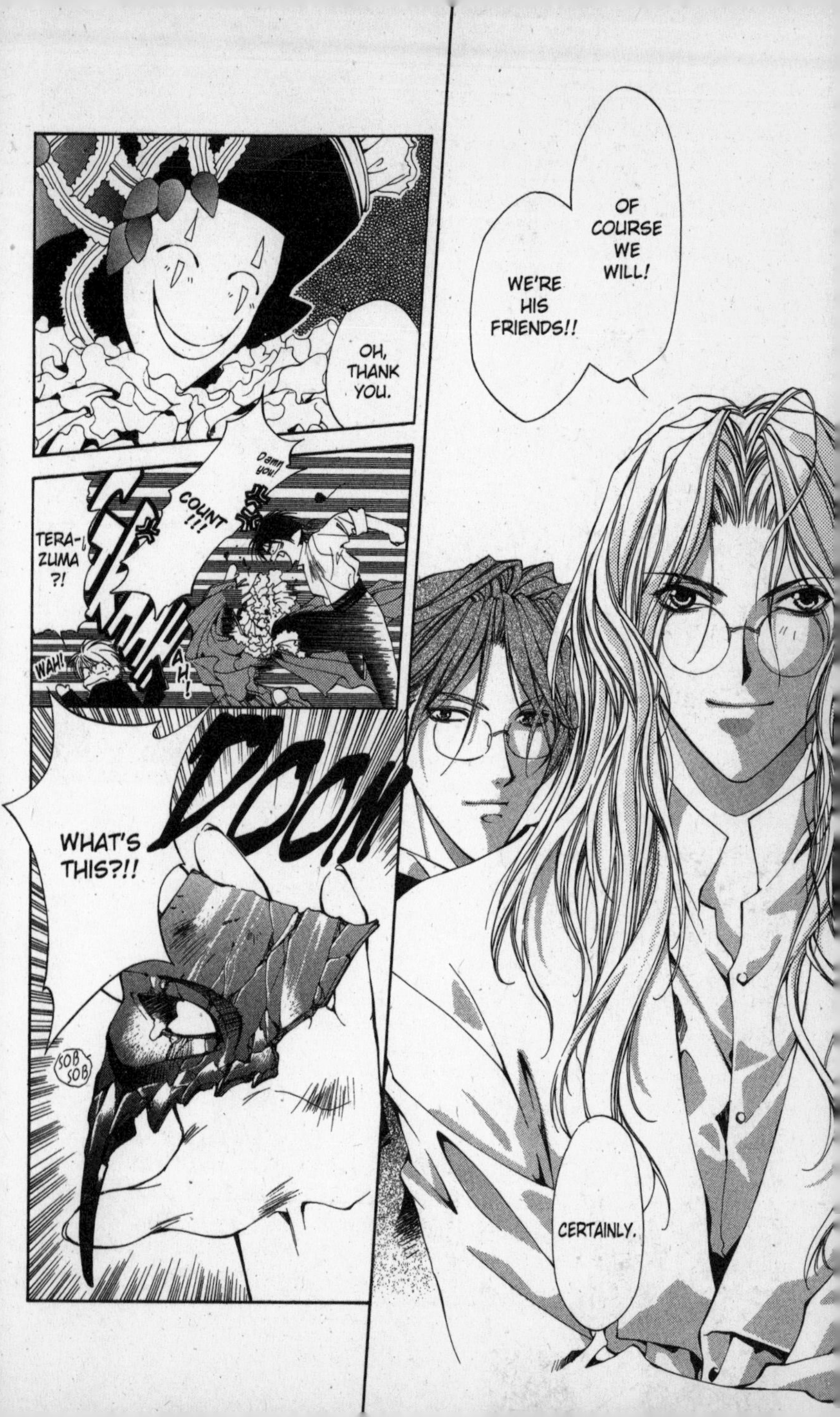
OF COURSE WE WILL!
WE'RE HIS FRIENDS!!
CERTAINLY.
OH, THANK YOU.
Damn you!
COUNT!!!
TERA-ZUMA?!
AH!
WAH!
DOOM
WHAT'S THIS?!!
SOB SOB

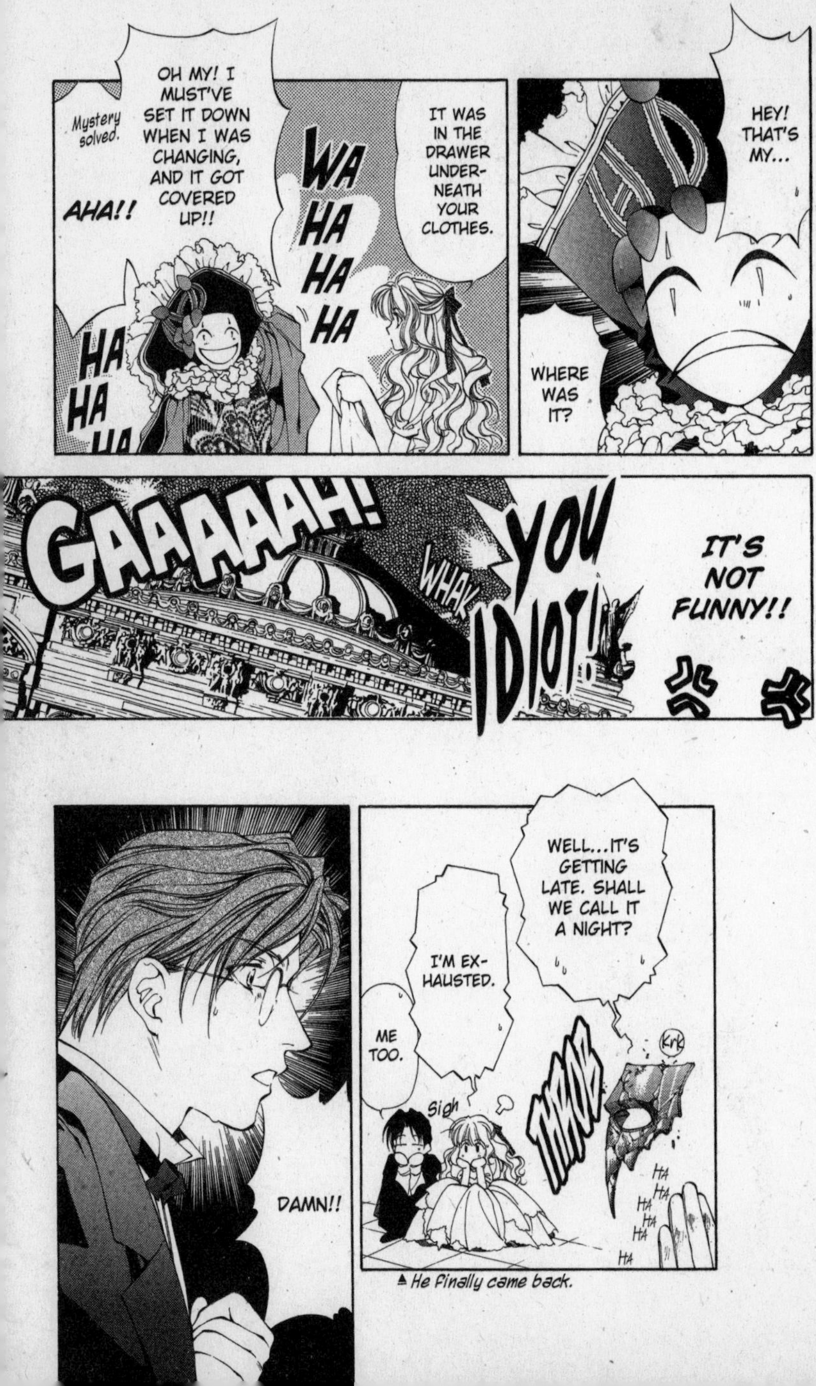
HEY! THAT'S MY...
WHERE WAS IT?
IT WAS IN THE DRAWER UNDERNEATH YOUR CLOTHES.
WA HA HA HA
OH MY! I MUST'VE SET IT DOWN WHEN I WAS CHANGING, AND IT GOT COVERED UP!!
Mystery solved.
AHA!!
HA HA
IT'S NOT FUNNY!!
YOU IDIOT!
WHAK
GAAAAAH!
WELL...IT'S GETTING LATE. SHALL WE CALL IT A NIGHT?
I'M EX-HAUSTED.
ME TOO.
Sigh
THROB
Krk
HA HA HA HA HA HA HA
▲He finally came back.
DAMN!!

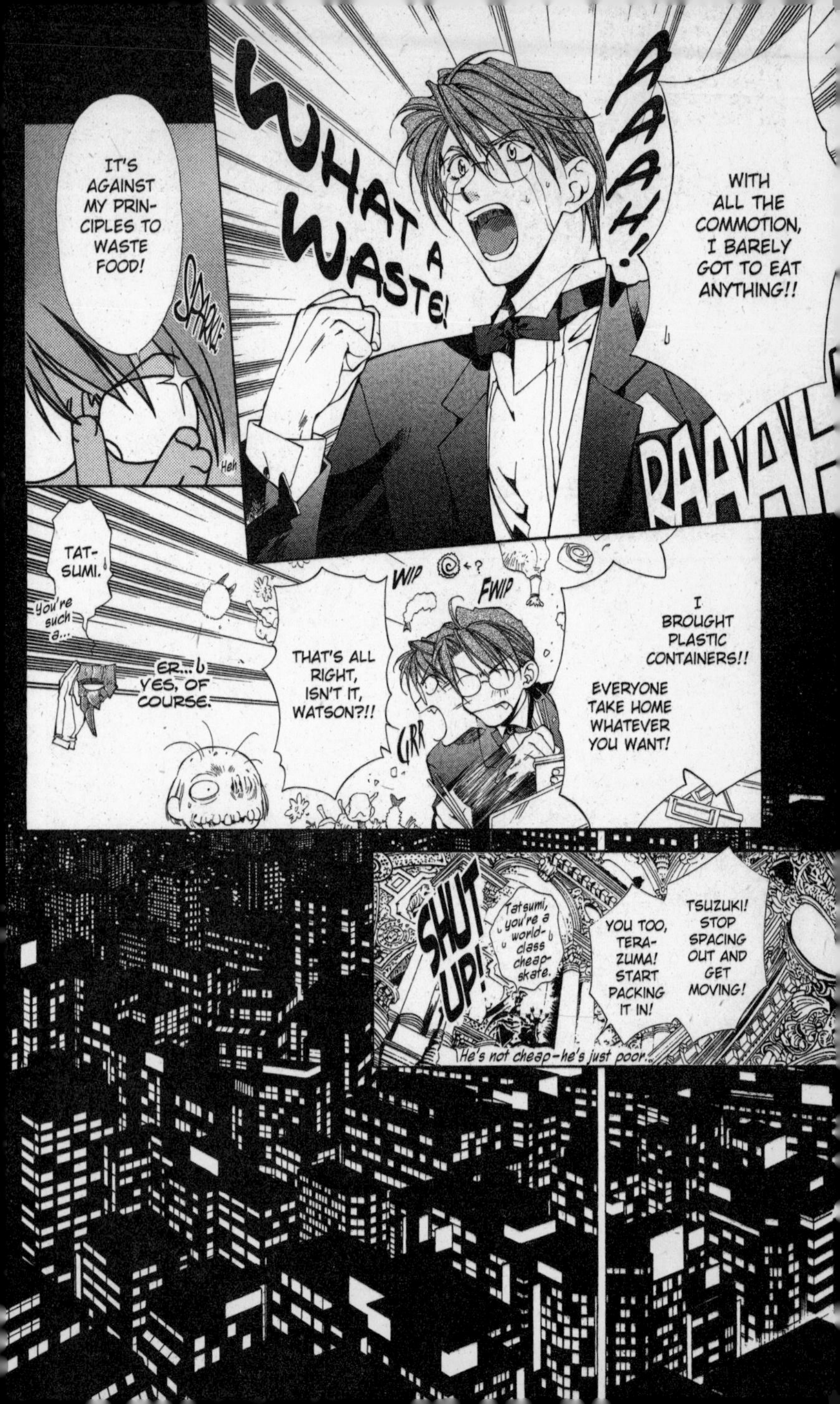

WITH ALL THE COMMOTION, I BARELY GOT TO EAT ANYTHING!!
AAAAH!!
WHAT A WASTE!
RAAAAH
IT'S AGAINST MY PRIN-CIPLES TO WASTE FOOD!
SPARKLE
Heh
I BROUGHT PLASTIC CONTAINERS!!
EVERYONE TAKE HOME WHATEVER YOU WANT!
WIP
FWIP
GRR
THAT'S ALL RIGHT, ISN'T IT, WATSON?!!
TAT-SUMI.
You're such a...
ER... YES, OF COURSE.
TSUZUKI! STOP SPACING OUT AND GET MOVING!
YOU TOO, TERA-ZUMA! START PACKING IT IN!
Tatsumi, you're a world-class cheap-skate.
SHUT UP!
He's not cheap—he's just poor...

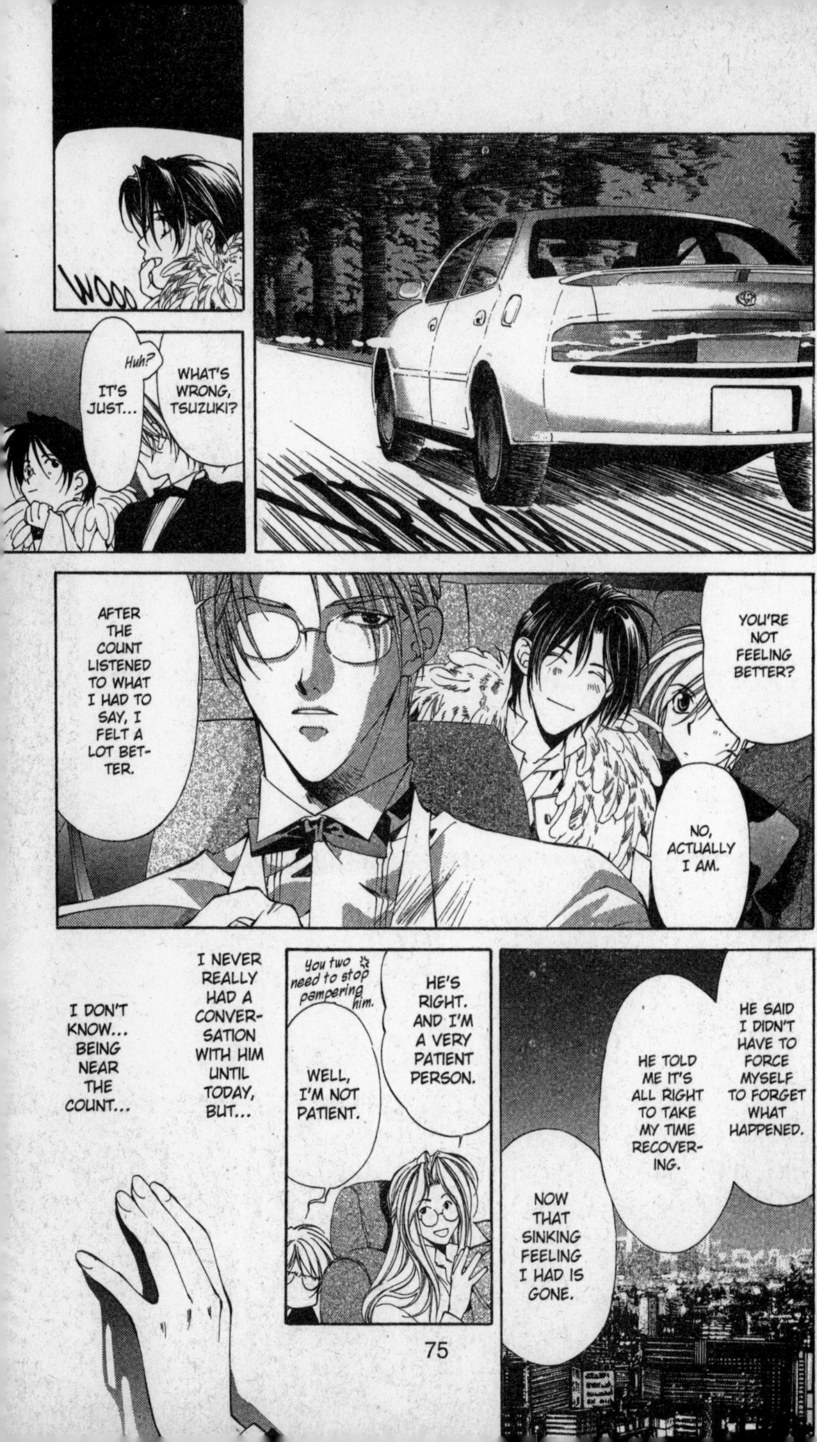
WOOO
WHAT'S WRONG, TSUZUKI?
Huh?
IT'S JUST...
YOU'RE NOT FEELING BETTER?
NO, ACTUALLY I AM.
AFTER THE COUNT LISTENED TO WHAT I HAD TO SAY, I FELT A LOT BET-TER.
HE SAID I DIDN'T HAVE TO FORCE MYSELF TO FORGET WHAT HAPPENED.
HE TOLD ME IT'S ALL RIGHT TO TAKE MY TIME RECOVER-ING.
NOW THAT SINKING FEELING I HAD IS GONE.
HE'S RIGHT. AND I'M A VERY PATIENT PERSON.
You two need to stop pampering him.
WELL, I'M NOT PATIENT.
I NEVER REALLY HAD A CONVER-SATION WITH HIM UNTIL TODAY, BUT...
I DON'T KNOW... BEING NEAR THE COUNT...

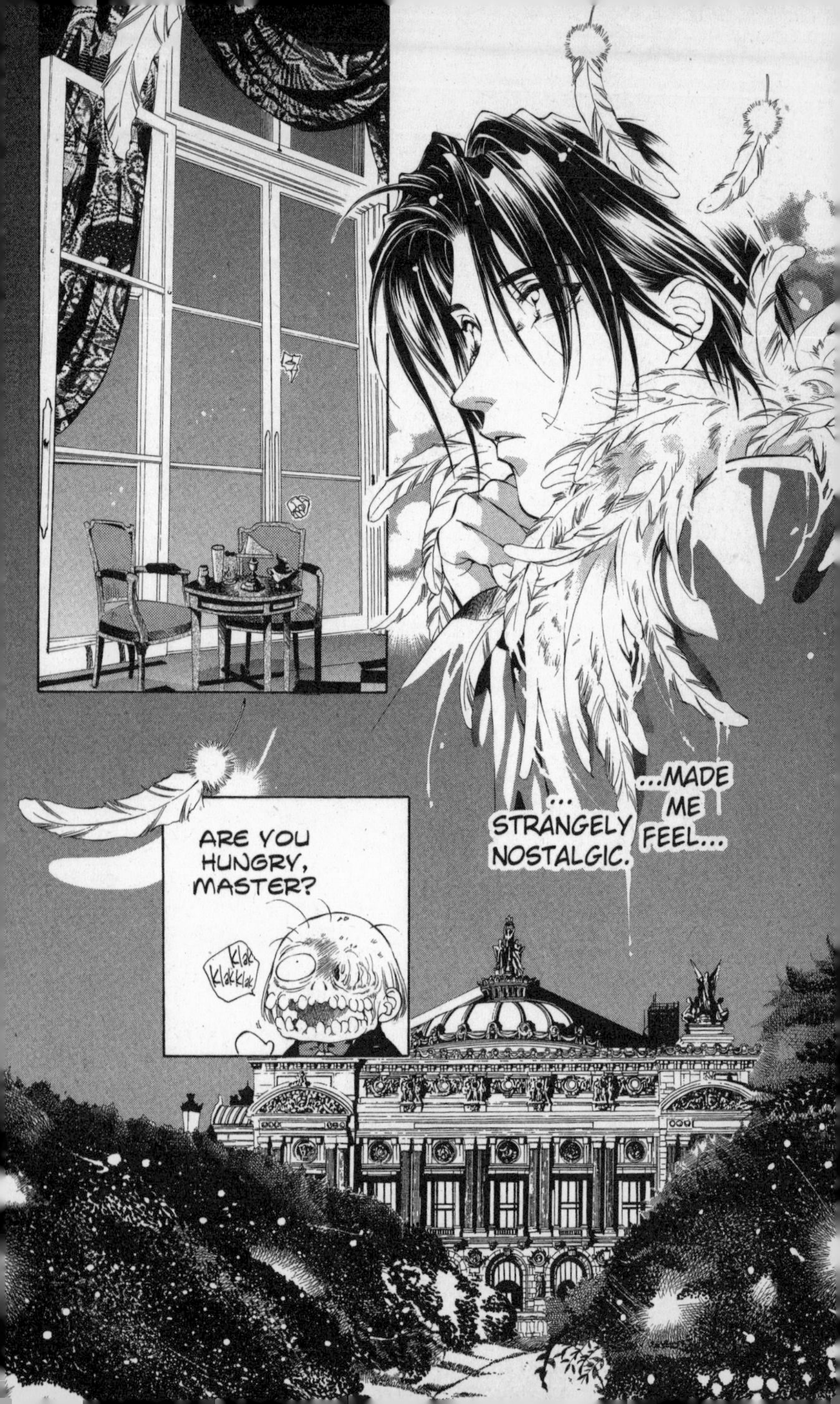
...MADE ME FEEL...
...STRANGELY NOSTALGIC.
ARE YOU HUNGRY, MASTER?
Klak Klakklak

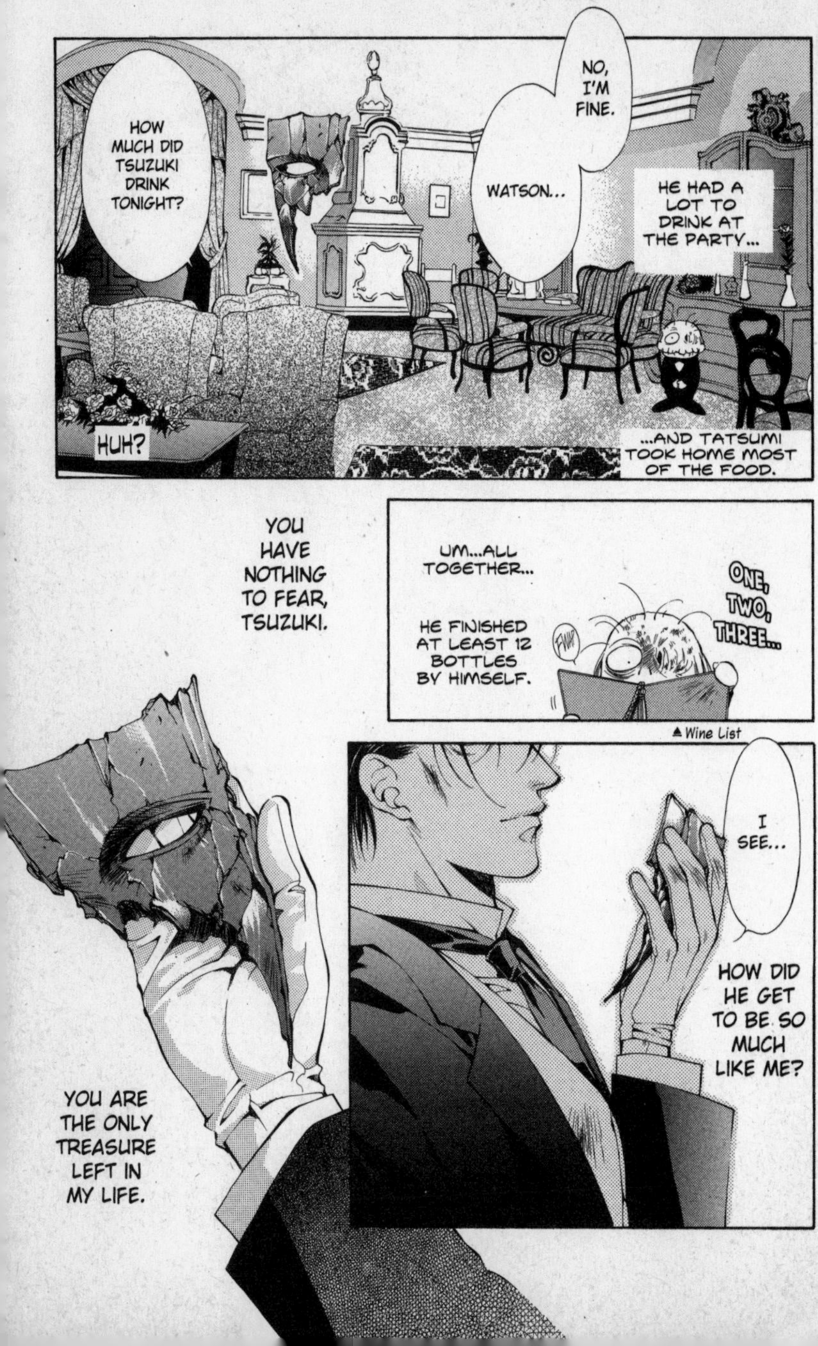
NO, I'M FINE.
HE HAD A LOT TO DRINK AT THE PARTY...
WATSON...
HOW MUCH DID TSUZUKI DRINK TONIGHT?
...AND TATSUMI TOOK HOME MOST OF THE FOOD.
HUH?
ONE, TWO, THREE...
UM...ALL TOGETHER...
HE FINISHED AT LEAST 12 BOTTLES BY HIMSELF.
FWAP
YOU HAVE NOTHING TO FEAR, TSUZUKI.
▲Wine List
I SEE...
HOW DID HE GET TO BE SO MUCH LIKE ME?
YOU ARE THE ONLY TREASURE LEFT IN MY LIFE.

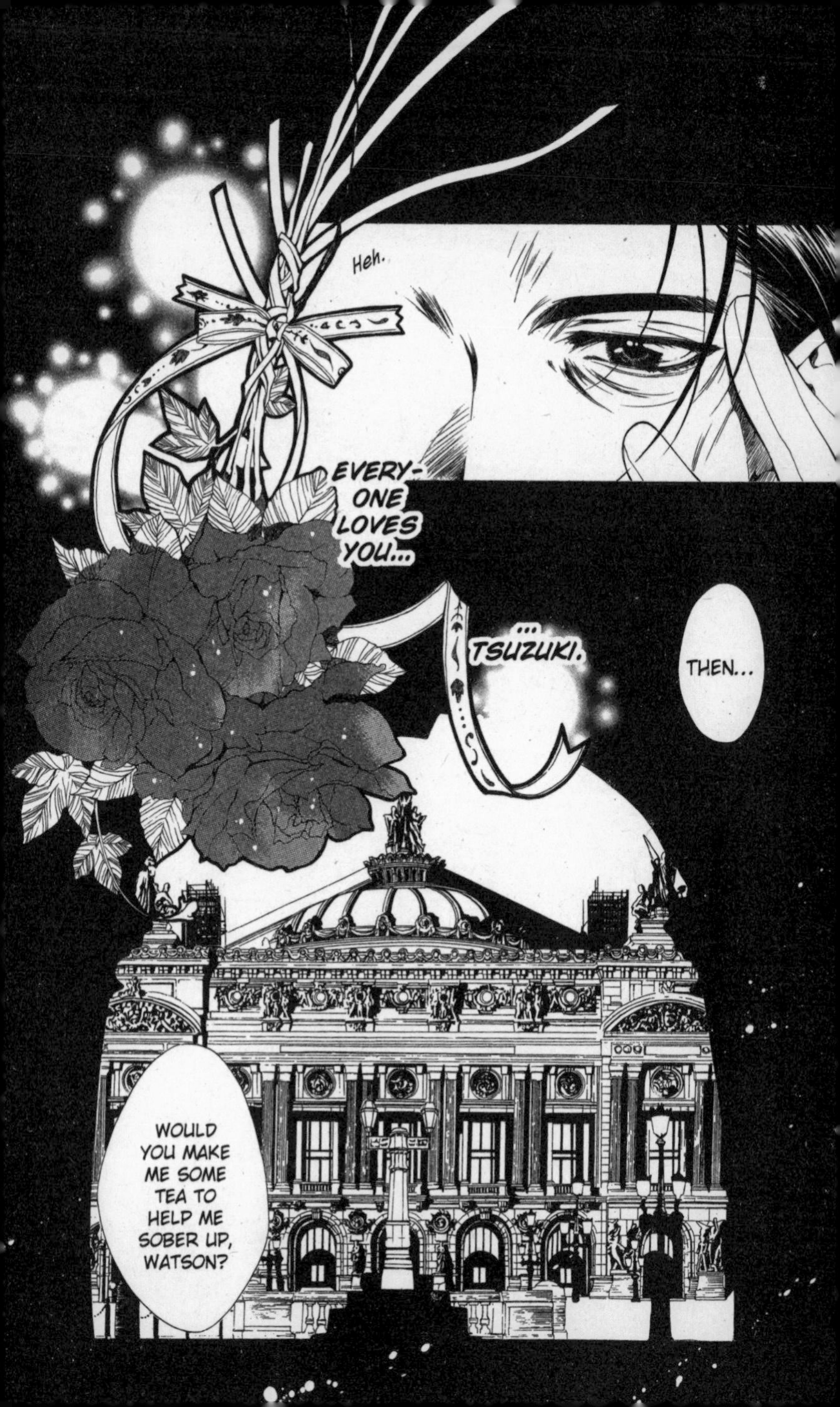
Heh.
EVERY-ONE LOVES YOU...
... TSUZUKI.
THEN...
WOULD YOU MAKE ME SOME TEA TO HELP ME SOBER UP, WATSON?

MMM.

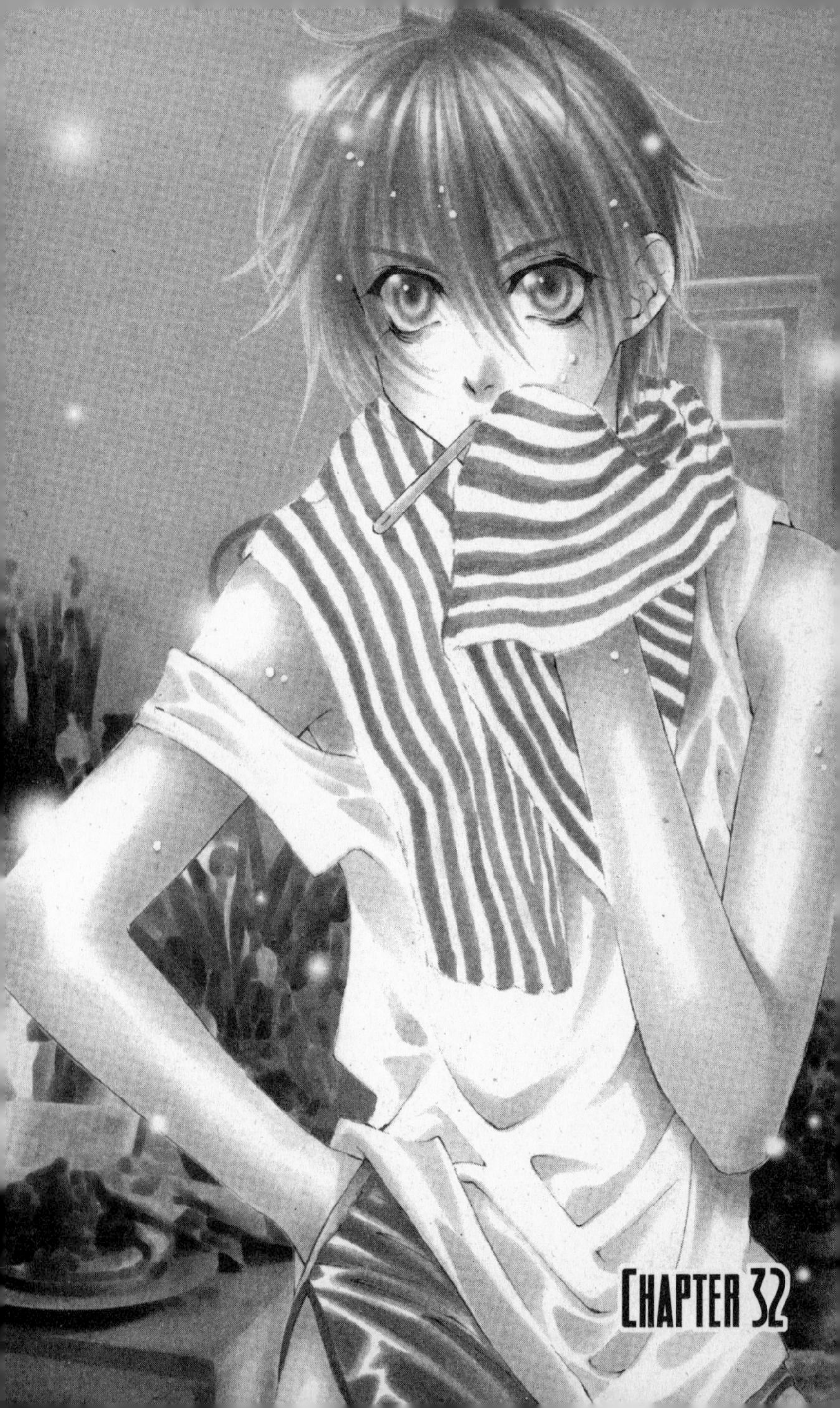
Chapter 32

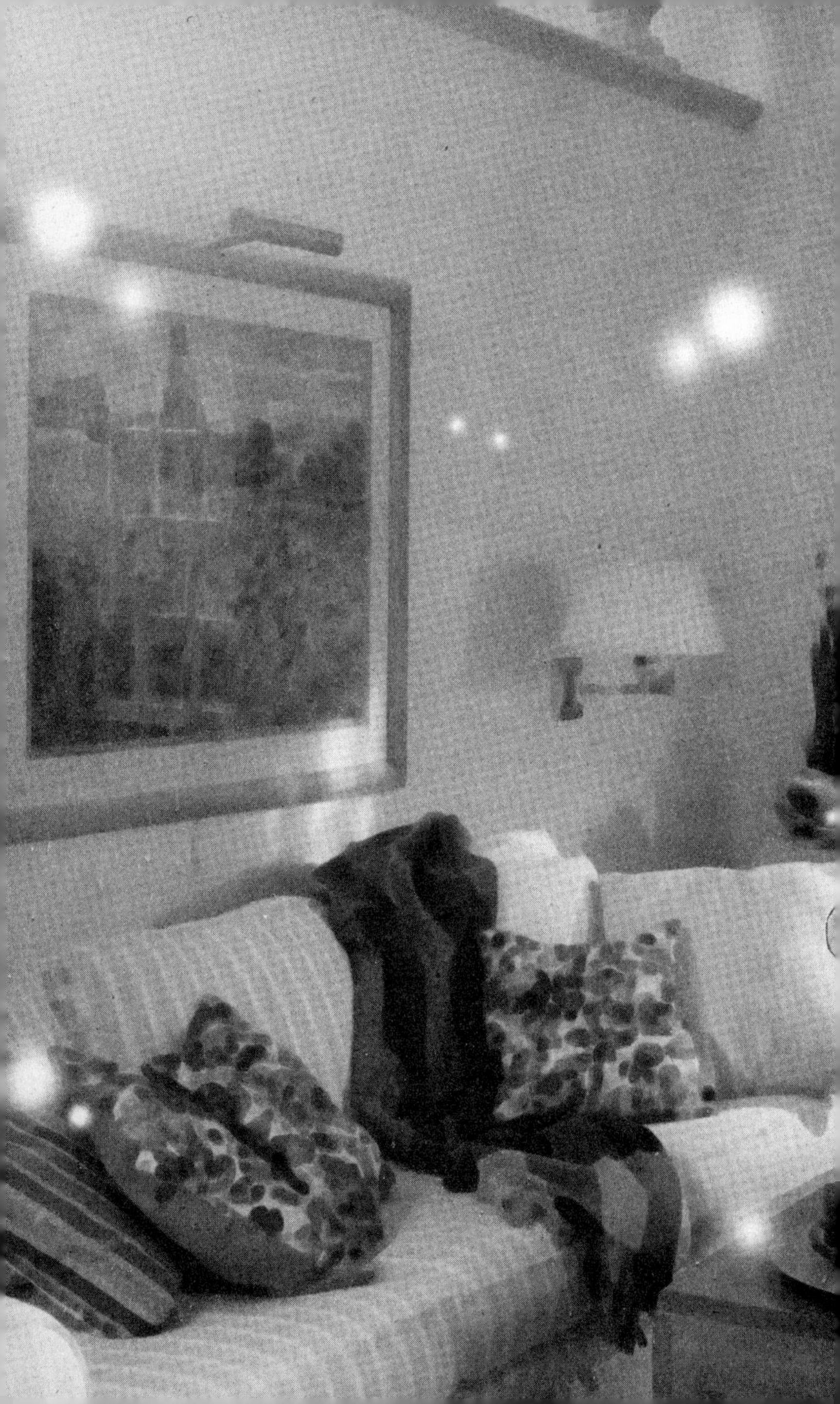

KAGOME, KAGOME,
WHEN WILL THE BIRD COME OUT OF ITS CAGE?
THE TURTLE AND THE CRANE SLIPPED OUT AT DAWN.
WHO'S THAT BEHIND YOU?

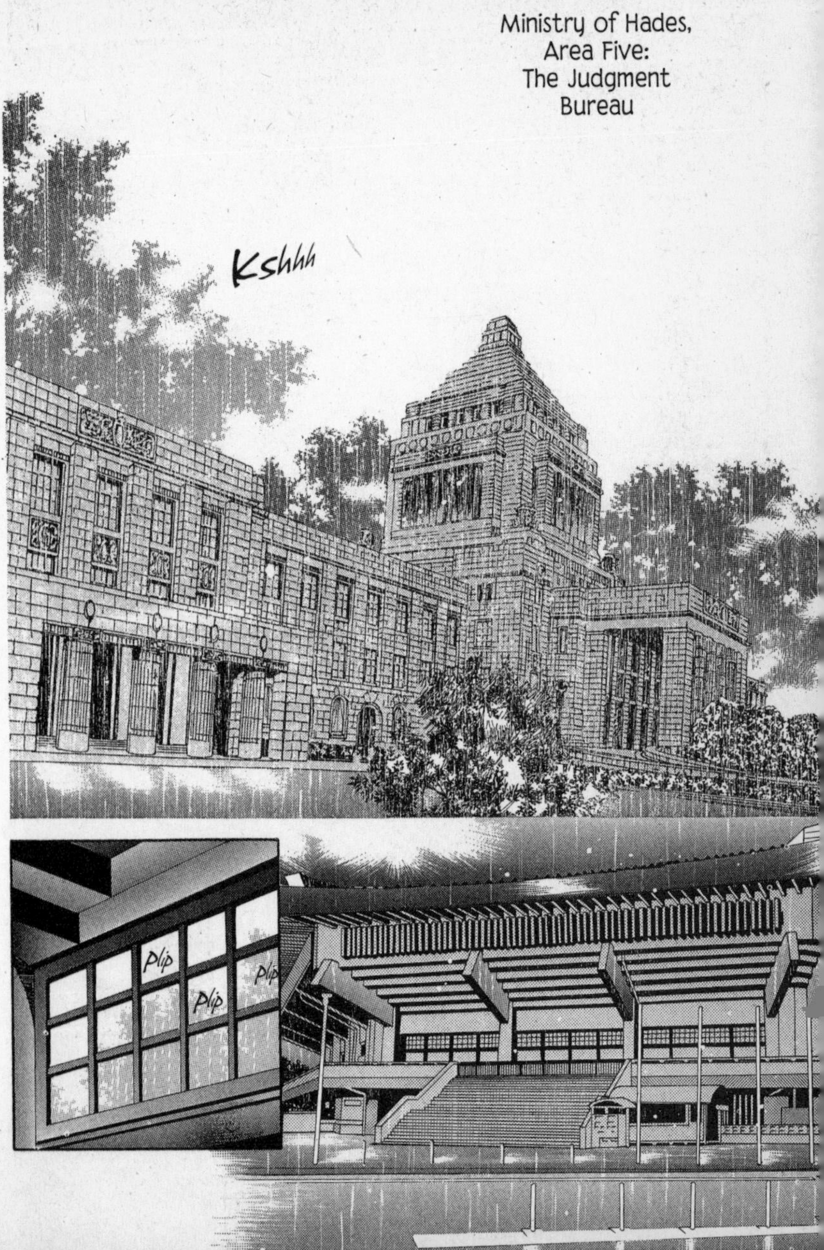
Ministry of Hades, Area Five: The Judgment Bureau
Kshhh
Plip
Plip
Plip

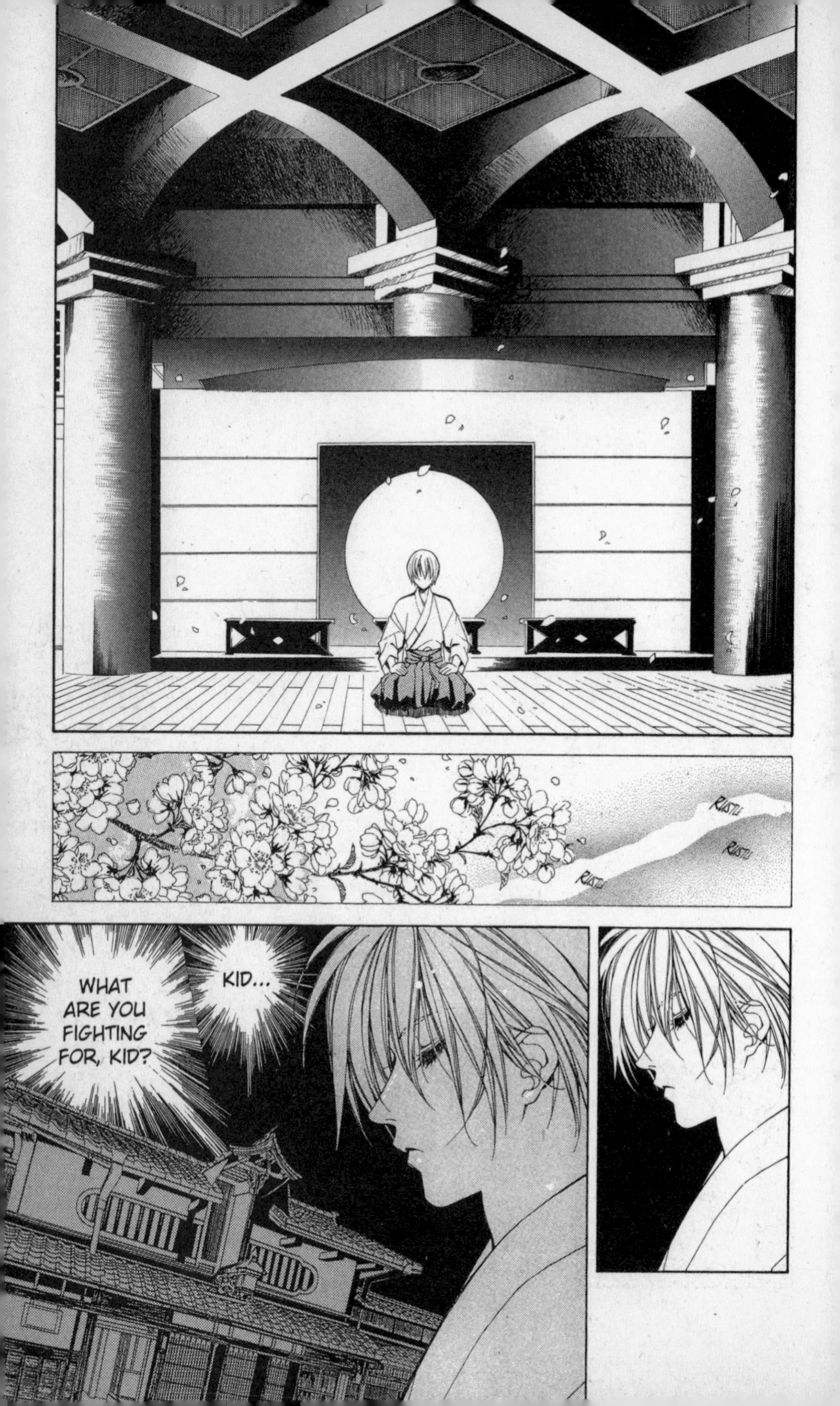
RUSTLE
RUSTLE
RUSTLE
KID...
WHAT ARE YOU FIGHTING FOR, KID?

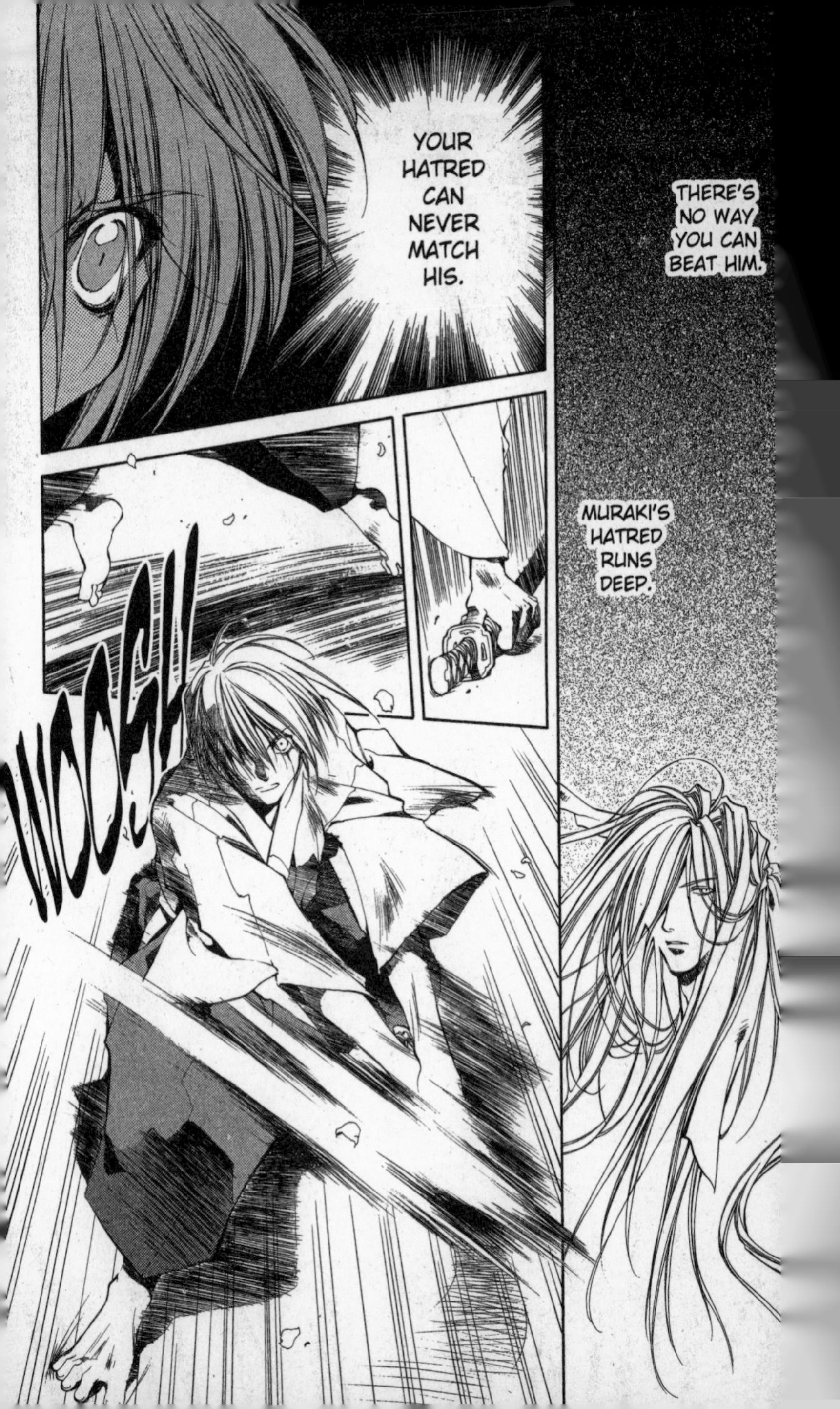
THERE'S NO WAY YOU CAN BEAT HIM.
MURAKI'S HATRED RUNS DEEP.
YOUR HATRED CAN NEVER MATCH HIS.
WOOSH!

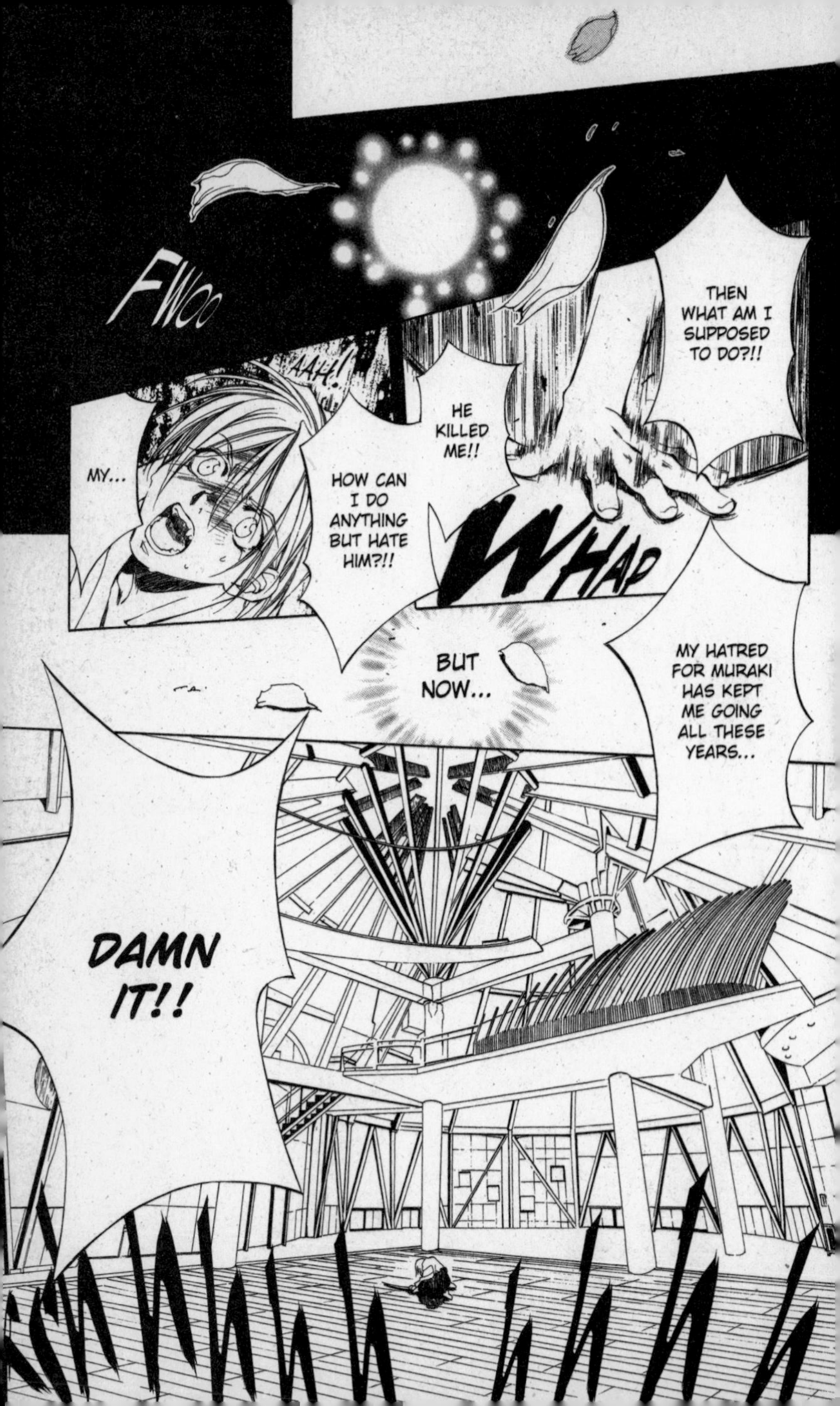
THEN WHAT AM I SUPPOSED TO DO?!!
FWOO
WHAP
HE KILLED ME!!
HOW CAN I DO ANYTHING BUT HATE HIM?!!
AAH!
MY...
MY HATRED FOR MURAKI HAS KEPT ME GOING ALL THESE YEARS...
BUT NOW...
DAMN IT!!

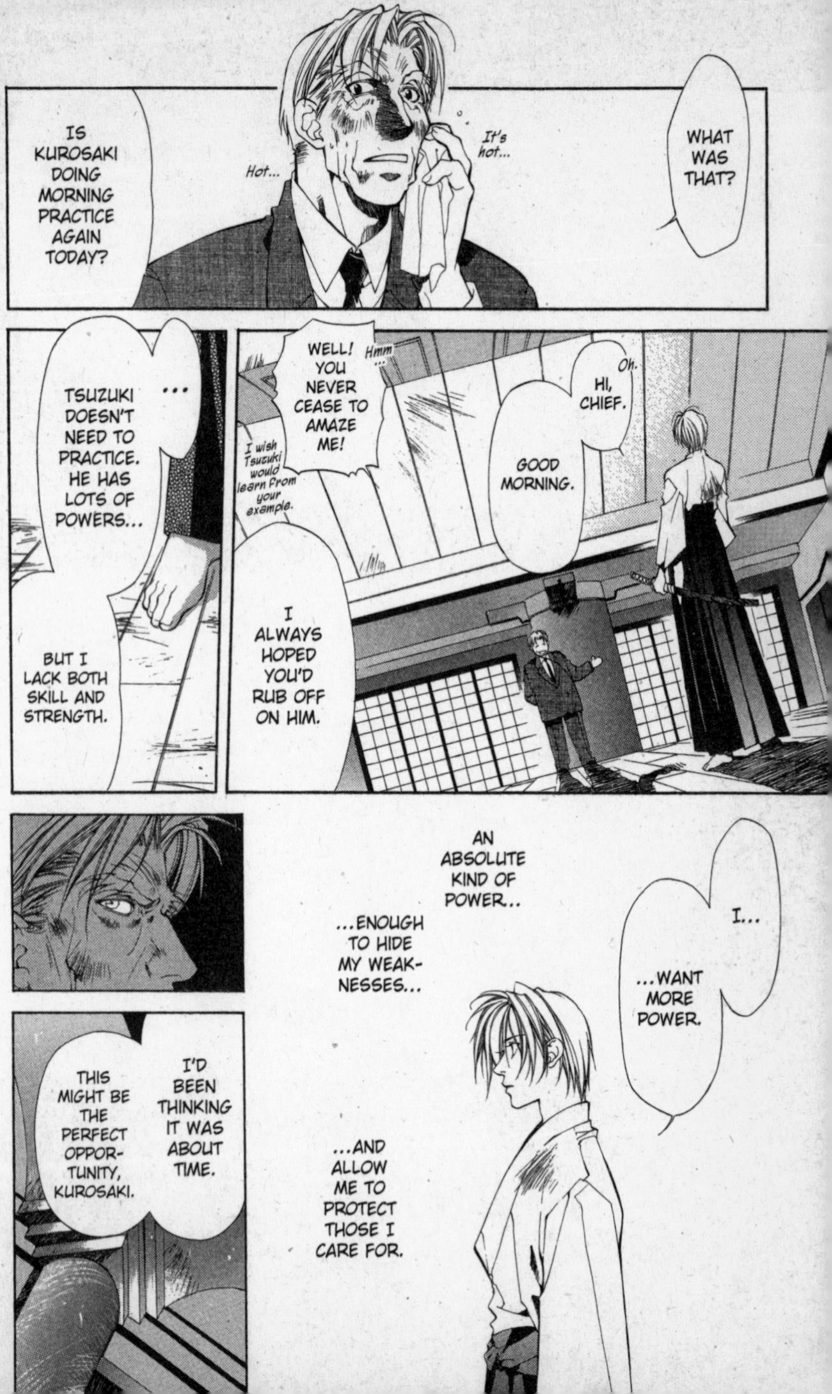
WHAT WAS THAT?
It's hot...
Hot...
IS KUROSAKI DOING MORNING PRACTICE AGAIN TODAY?
Oh.
HI, CHIEF.
GOOD MORNING.
Hmm...
WELL! YOU NEVER CEASE TO AMAZE ME!
I wish Tsuzuki would learn from your example.
I ALWAYS HOPED YOU'D RUB OFF ON HIM.
...
TSUZUKI DOESN'T NEED TO PRACTICE. HE HAS LOTS OF POWERS...
BUT I LACK BOTH SKILL AND STRENGTH.
I...
...WANT MORE POWER.
AN ABSOLUTE KIND OF POWER...
...ENOUGH TO HIDE MY WEAKNESSES...
...AND ALLOW ME TO PROTECT THOSE I CARE FOR.
I'D BEEN THINKING IT WAS ABOUT TIME.
THIS MIGHT BE THE PERFECT OPPORTUNITY, KUROSAKI.

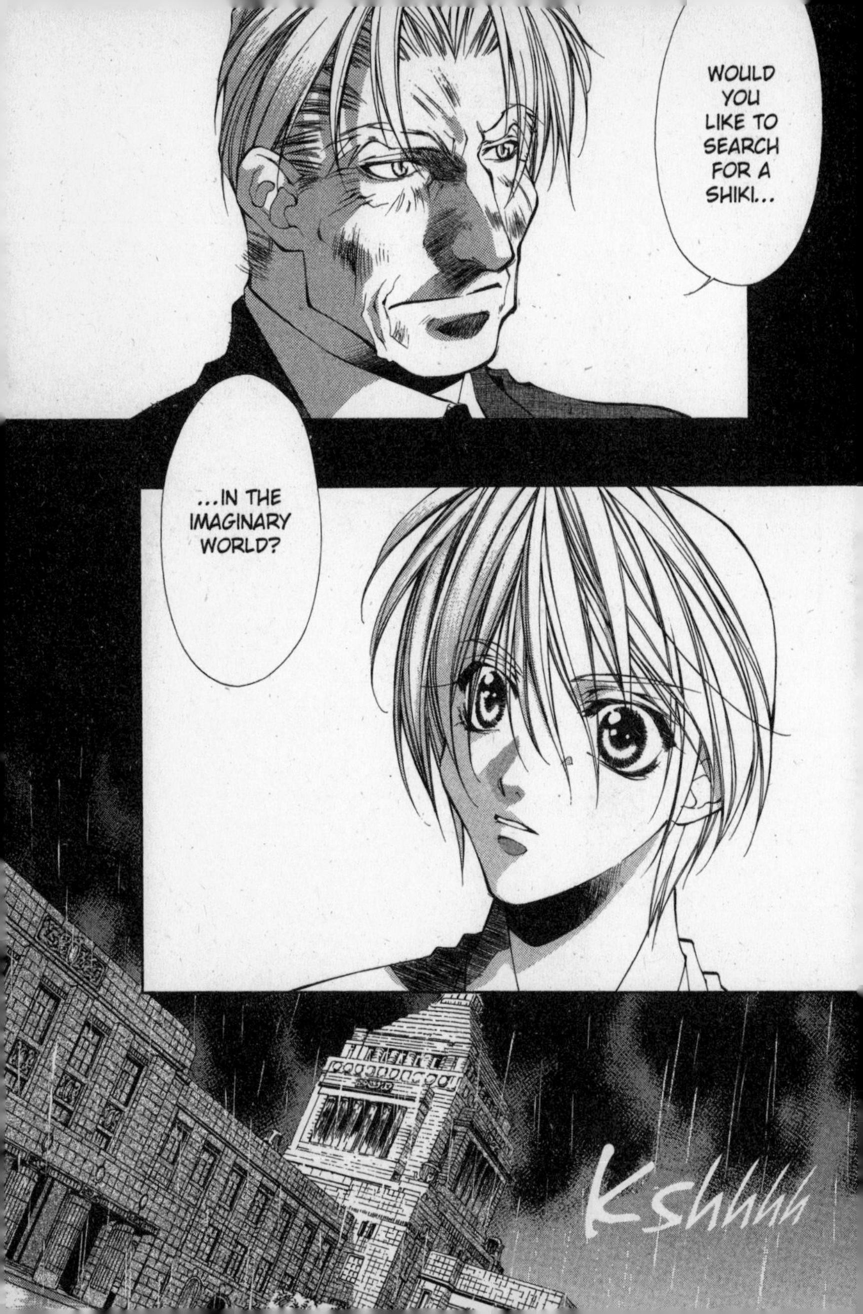

WOULD YOU LIKE TO SEARCH FOR A SHIKI...
...IN THE IMAGINARY WORLD?
Kshhhh

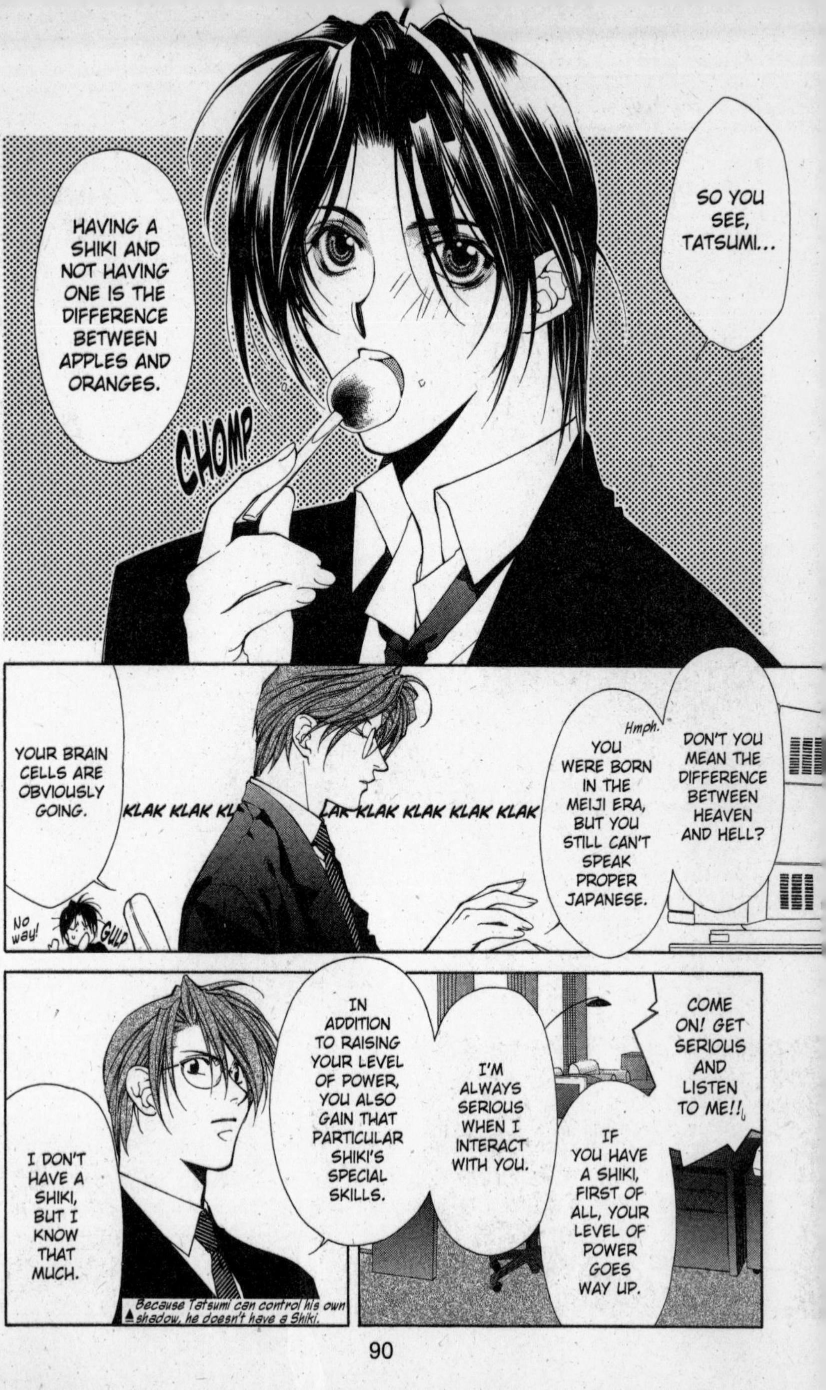
SO YOU SEE, TATSUMI...
HAVING A SHIKI AND NOT HAVING ONE IS THE DIFFERENCE BETWEEN APPLES AND ORANGES.
CHOMP
DON'T YOU MEAN THE DIFFERENCE BETWEEN HEAVEN AND HELL?
Hmph.
YOU WERE BORN IN THE MEIJI ERA, BUT YOU STILL CAN'T SPEAK PROPER JAPANESE.
KLAK KLAK KLAK KLAK KLAK KLAK
YOUR BRAIN CELLS ARE OBVIOUSLY GOING.
No way!
GULP
COME ON! GET SERIOUS AND LISTEN TO ME!!
I'M ALWAYS SERIOUS WHEN I INTERACT WITH YOU.
IF YOU HAVE A SHIKI, FIRST OF ALL, YOUR LEVEL OF POWER GOES WAY UP.
IN ADDITION TO RAISING YOUR LEVEL OF POWER, YOU ALSO GAIN THAT PARTICULAR SHIKI'S SPECIAL SKILLS.
I DON'T HAVE A SHIKI, BUT I KNOW THAT MUCH.
▲Because Tatsumi can control his own shadow, he doesn't have a Shiki.

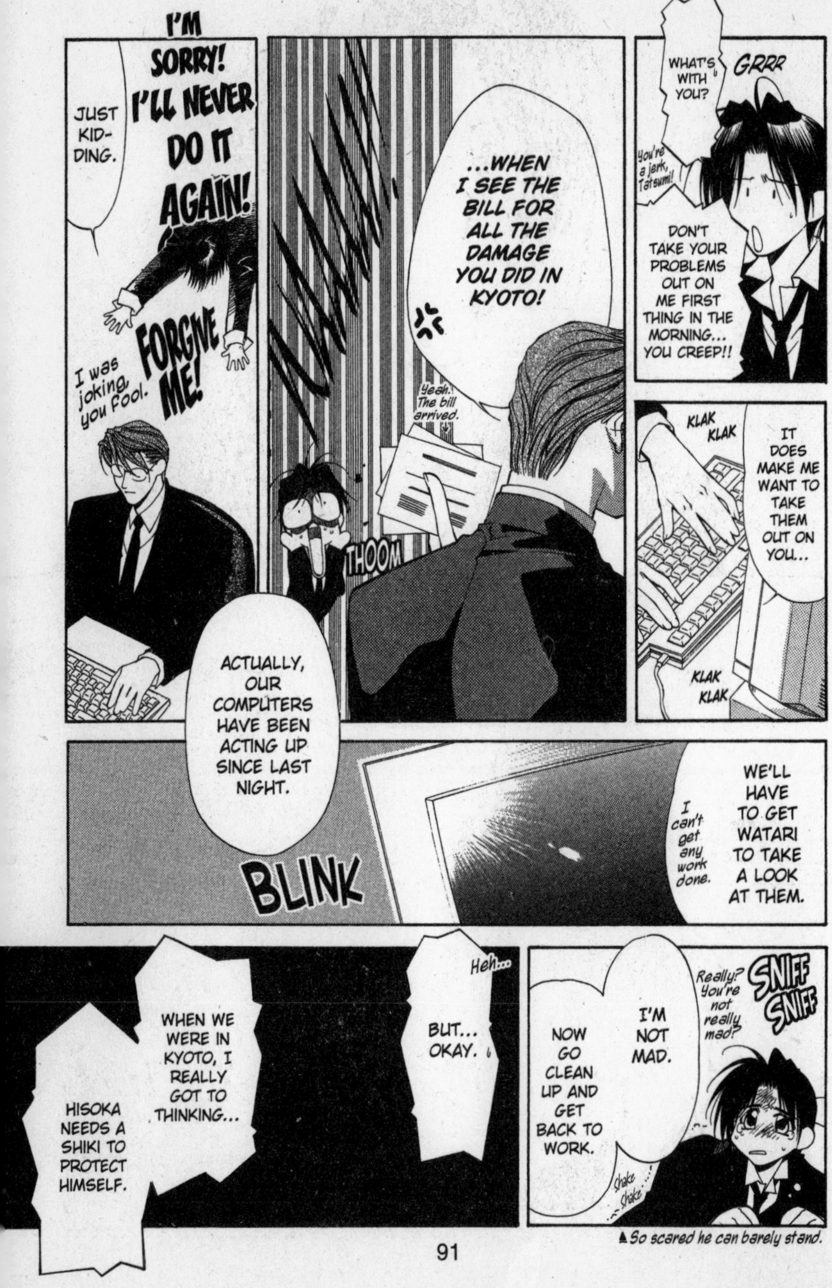
WHAT'S WITH YOU?
GRRR
You're a jerk, Tatsumi!
DON'T TAKE YOUR PROBLEMS OUT ON ME FIRST THING IN THE MORNING... YOU CREEP!!
KLAK KLAK
IT DOES MAKE ME WANT TO TAKE THEM OUT ON YOU...
KLAK KLAK
...WHEN I SEE THE BILL FOR ALL THE DAMAGE YOU DID IN KYOTO!
Yeah. The bill arrived.
THOOM
I'M SORRY! I'LL NEVER DO IT AGAIN!
JUST KID-DING.
FORGIVE ME!
I was joking, you fool.
ACTUALLY, OUR COMPUTERS HAVE BEEN ACTING UP SINCE LAST NIGHT.
WE'LL HAVE TO GET WATARI TO TAKE A LOOK AT THEM.
I can't get any work done.
BLINK
Really? You're not really mad?
SNIFF SNIFF
I'M NOT MAD.
NOW GO CLEAN UP AND GET BACK TO WORK.
Shake Shake
Heh...
BUT... OKAY.
WHEN WE WERE IN KYOTO, I REALLY GOT TO THINKING...
HISOKA NEEDS A SHIKI TO PROTECT HIMSELF.
▲So scared he can barely stand.

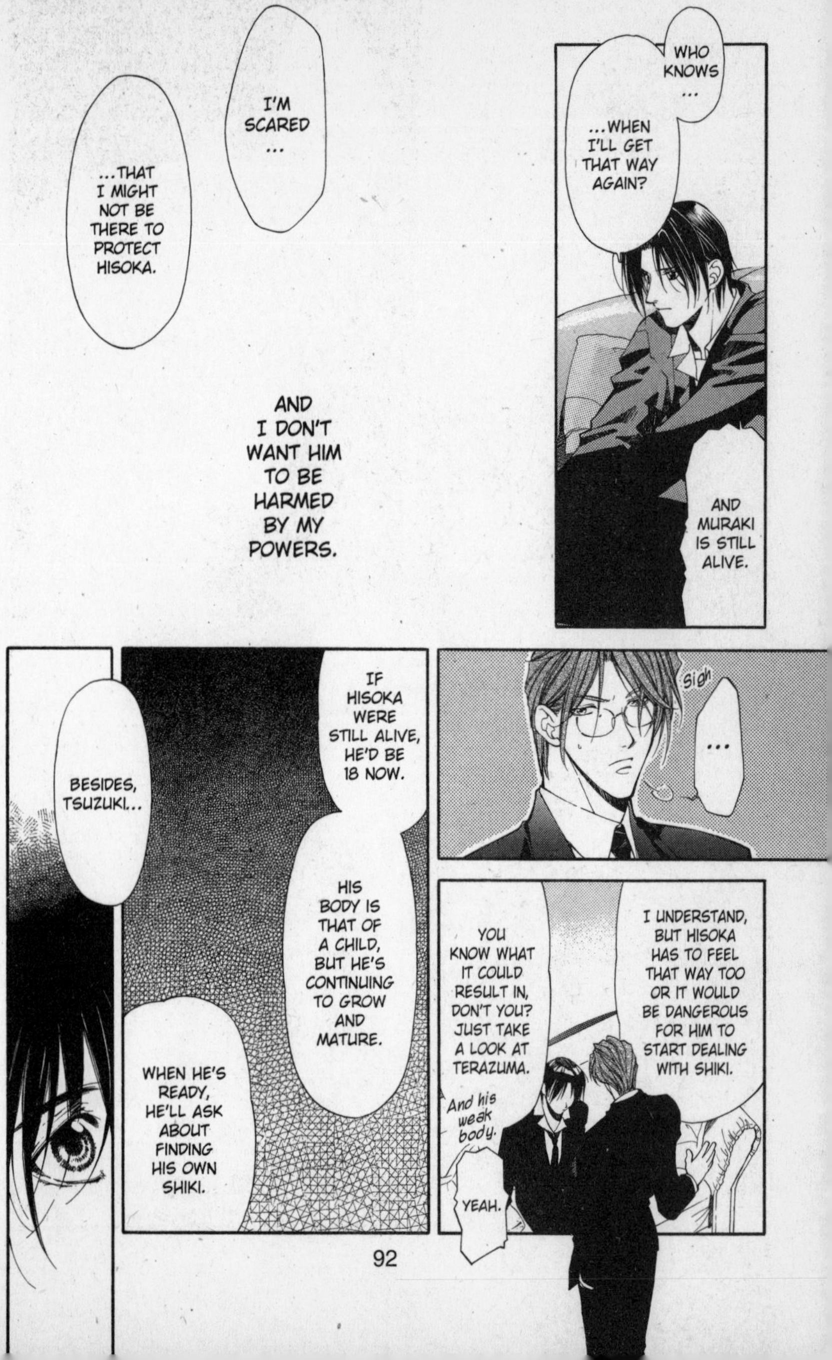
WHO KNOWS ...
...WHEN I'LL GET THAT WAY AGAIN?
AND MURAKI IS STILL ALIVE.
I'M SCARED ...
...THAT I MIGHT NOT BE THERE TO PROTECT HISOKA.
AND I DON'T WANT HIM TO BE HARMED BY MY POWERS.
Sigh
...
I UNDERSTAND, BUT HISOKA HAS TO FEEL THAT WAY TOO OR IT WOULD BE DANGEROUS FOR HIM TO START DEALING WITH SHIKI.
YOU KNOW WHAT IT COULD RESULT IN, DON'T YOU? JUST TAKE A LOOK AT TERAZUMA.
And his weak body.
YEAH.
IF HISOKA WERE STILL ALIVE, HE'D BE 18 NOW.
HIS BODY IS THAT OF A CHILD, BUT HE'S CONTINUING TO GROW AND MATURE.
WHEN HE'S READY, HE'LL ASK ABOUT FINDING HIS OWN SHIKI.
BESIDES, TSUZUKI...

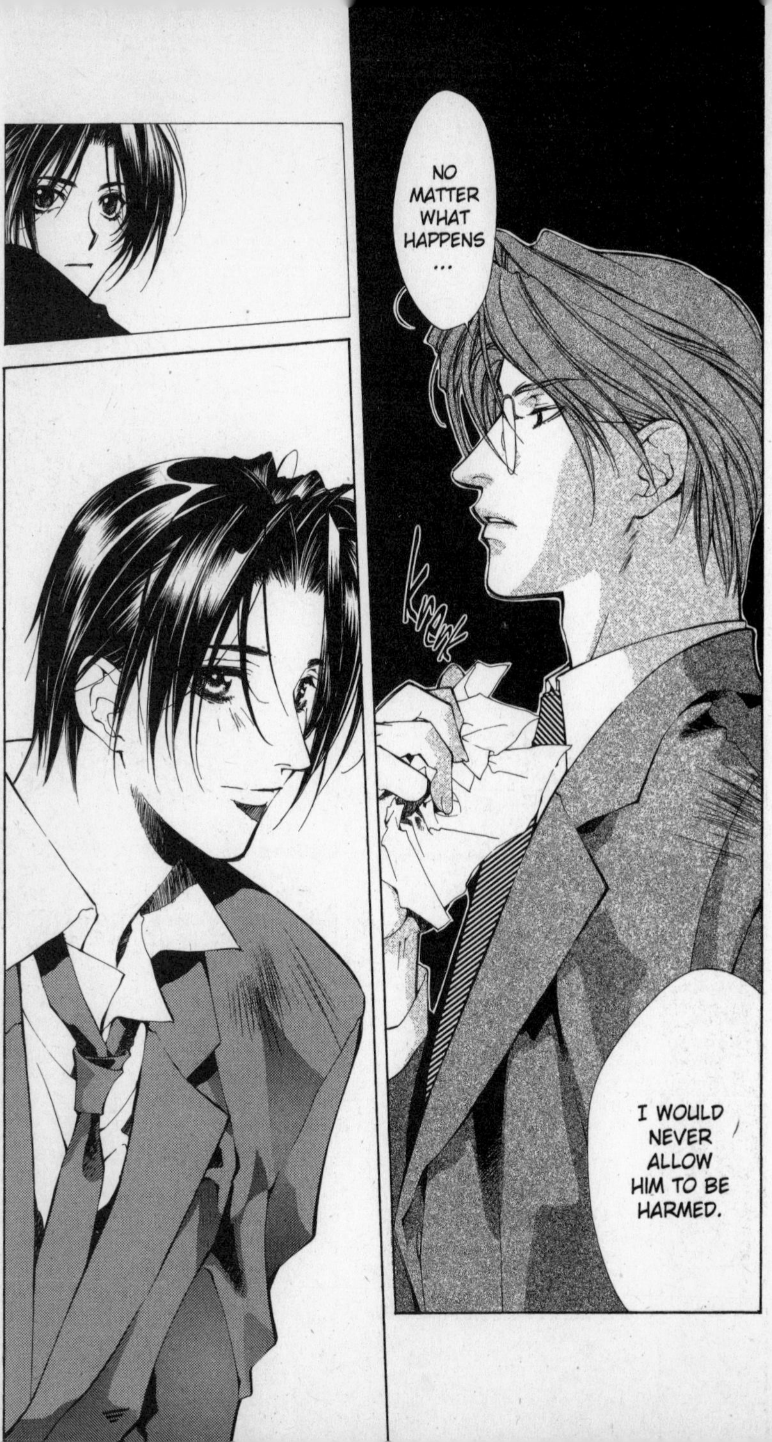
NO MATTER WHAT HAPPENS ...
Krenk
I WOULD NEVER ALLOW HIM TO BE HARMED.

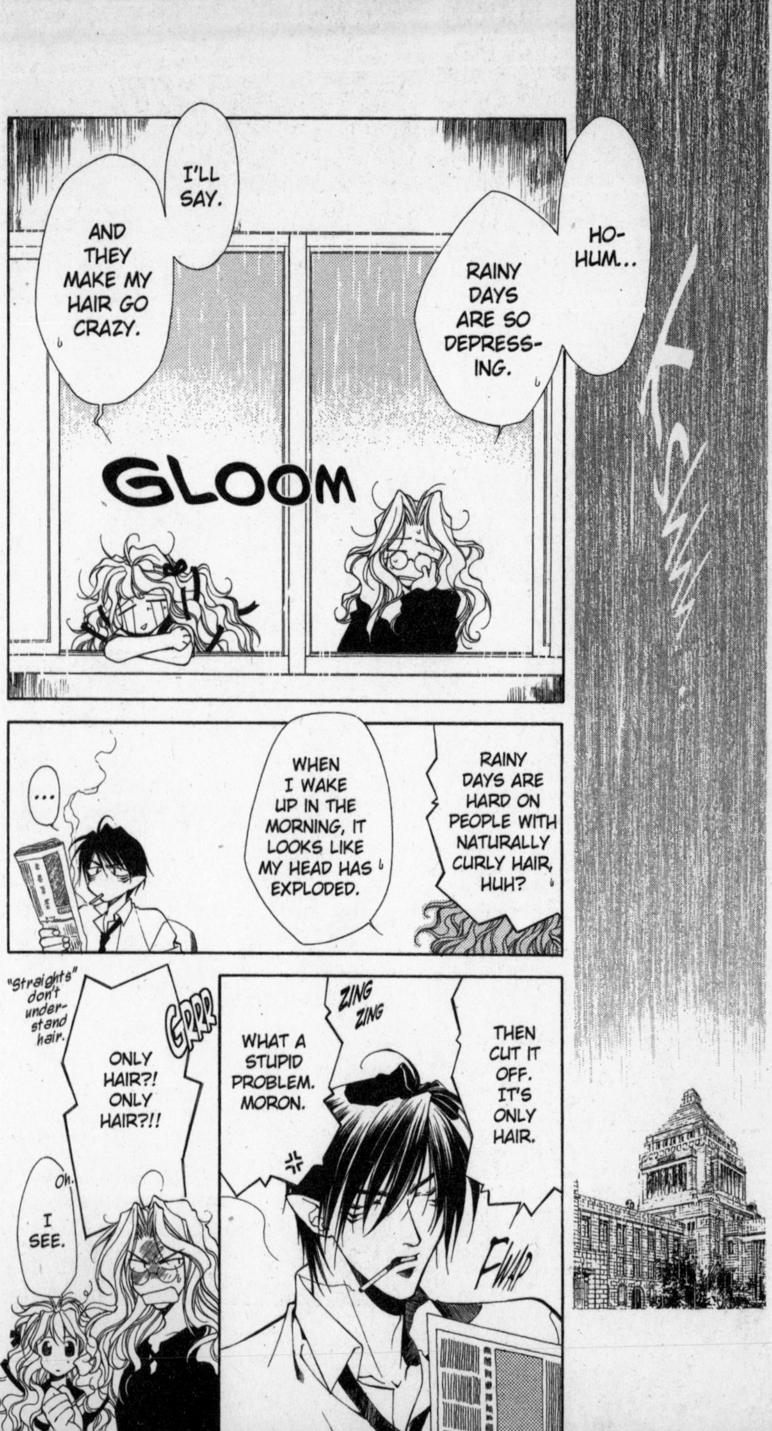
SWISH...
HO-HUM..
RAINY DAYS ARE SO DEPRESSING.
I'LL SAY.
AND THEY MAKE MY HAIR GO CRAZY.
GLOOM
RAINY DAYS ARE HARD ON PEOPLE WITH NATURALLY CURLY HAIR, HUH?
WHEN I WAKE UP IN THE MORNING, IT LOOKS LIKE MY HEAD HAS EXPLODED.
...
ZING ZING
THEN CUT IT OFF. IT'S ONLY HAIR.
WHAT A STUPID PROBLEM. MORON.
FWAP
GRRR
"Straights" don't understand hair.
ONLY HAIR?! ONLY HAIR?!!
Oh. I SEE.

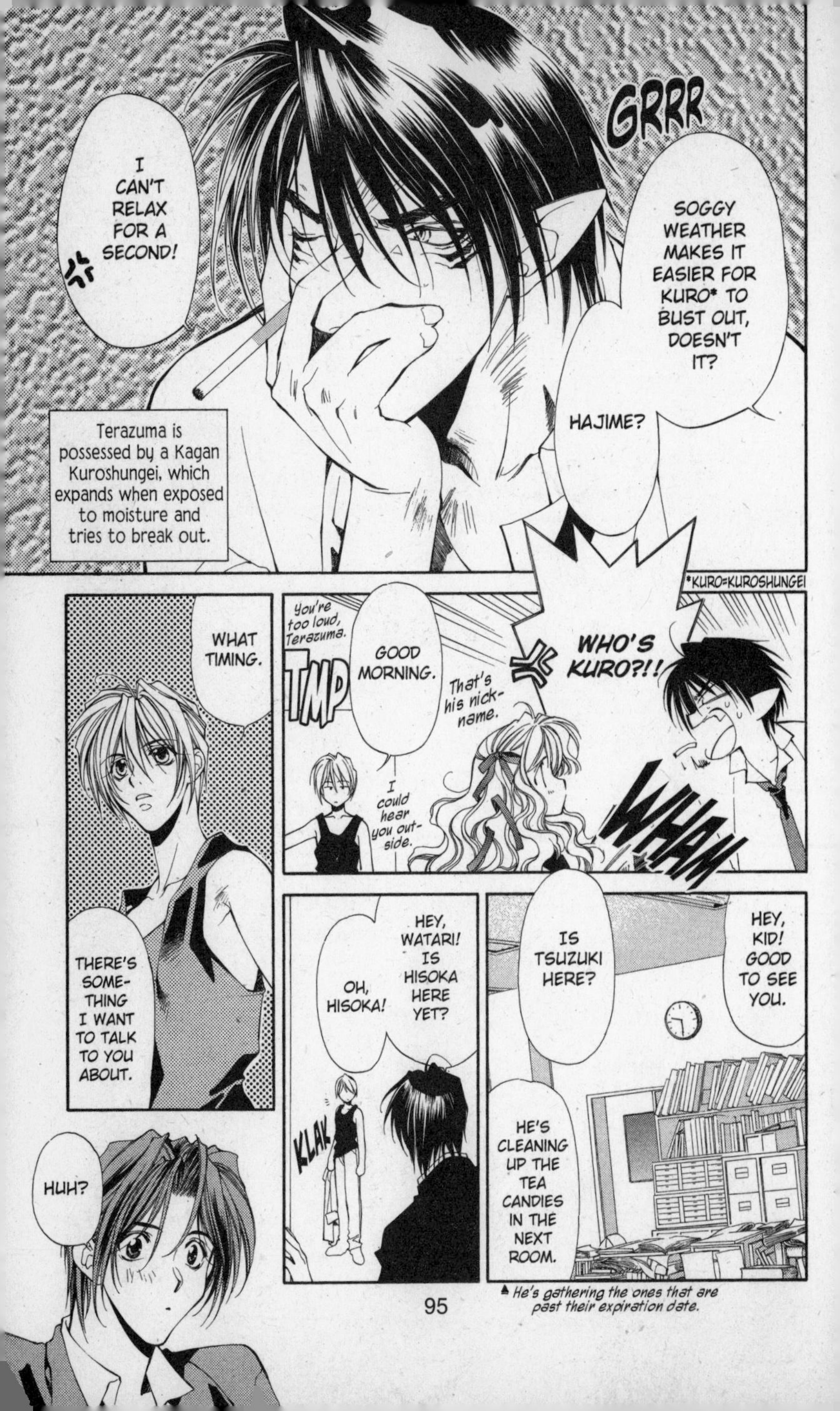
GRRR
SOGGY WEATHER MAKES IT EASIER FOR KURO* TO BUST OUT, DOESN'T IT?
HAJIME?
I CAN'T RELAX FOR A SECOND!
Terazuma is possessed by a Kagan Kuroshungei, which expands when exposed to moisture and tries to break out.
*KURO=KUROSHUNGEI
WHO'S KURO?!!
WHAM
That's his nick-name.
GOOD MORNING.
TMP
You're too loud, Terazuma.
I could hear you out-side.
HEY, KID! GOOD TO SEE YOU.
IS TSUZUKI HERE?
HE'S CLEANING UP THE TEA CANDIES IN THE NEXT ROOM.
▲ He's gathering the ones that are past their expiration date.
HEY, WATARI! IS HISOKA HERE YET?
OH, HISOKA!
KLAK
WHAT TIMING.
THERE'S SOME-THING I WANT TO TALK TO YOU ABOUT.
HUH?

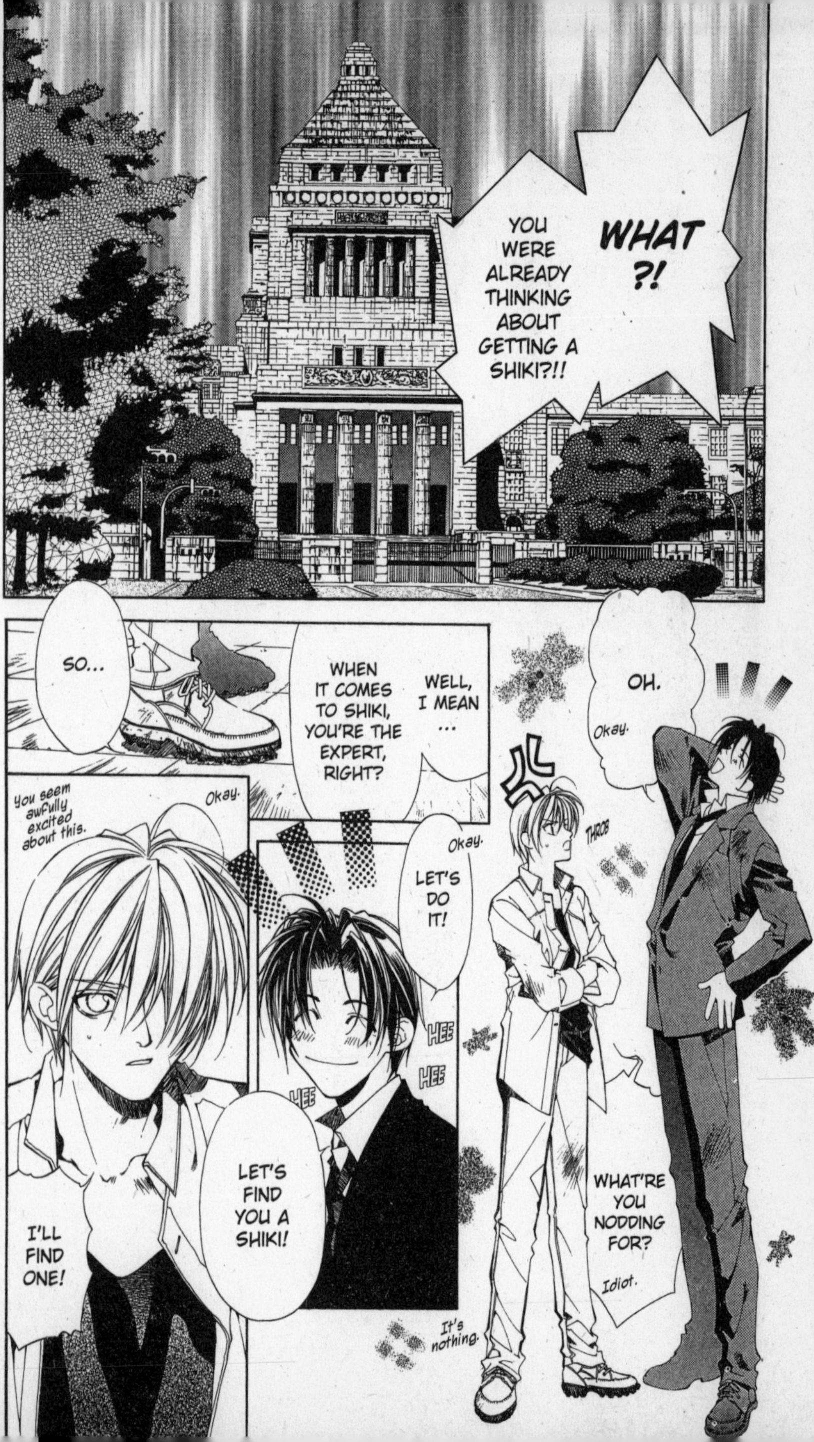
WHAT ?!
YOU WERE ALREADY THINKING ABOUT GETTING A SHIKI?!!
OH.
Okay.
THROB
WHAT'RE YOU NODDING FOR?
Idiot.
It's nothing.
WELL, I MEAN ...
WHEN IT COMES TO SHIKI, YOU'RE THE EXPERT, RIGHT?
SO...
Okay.
LET'S DO IT!
HEE
HEE
HEE
LET'S FIND YOU A SHIKI!
Okay.
You seem awfully excited about this.
I'LL FIND ONE!

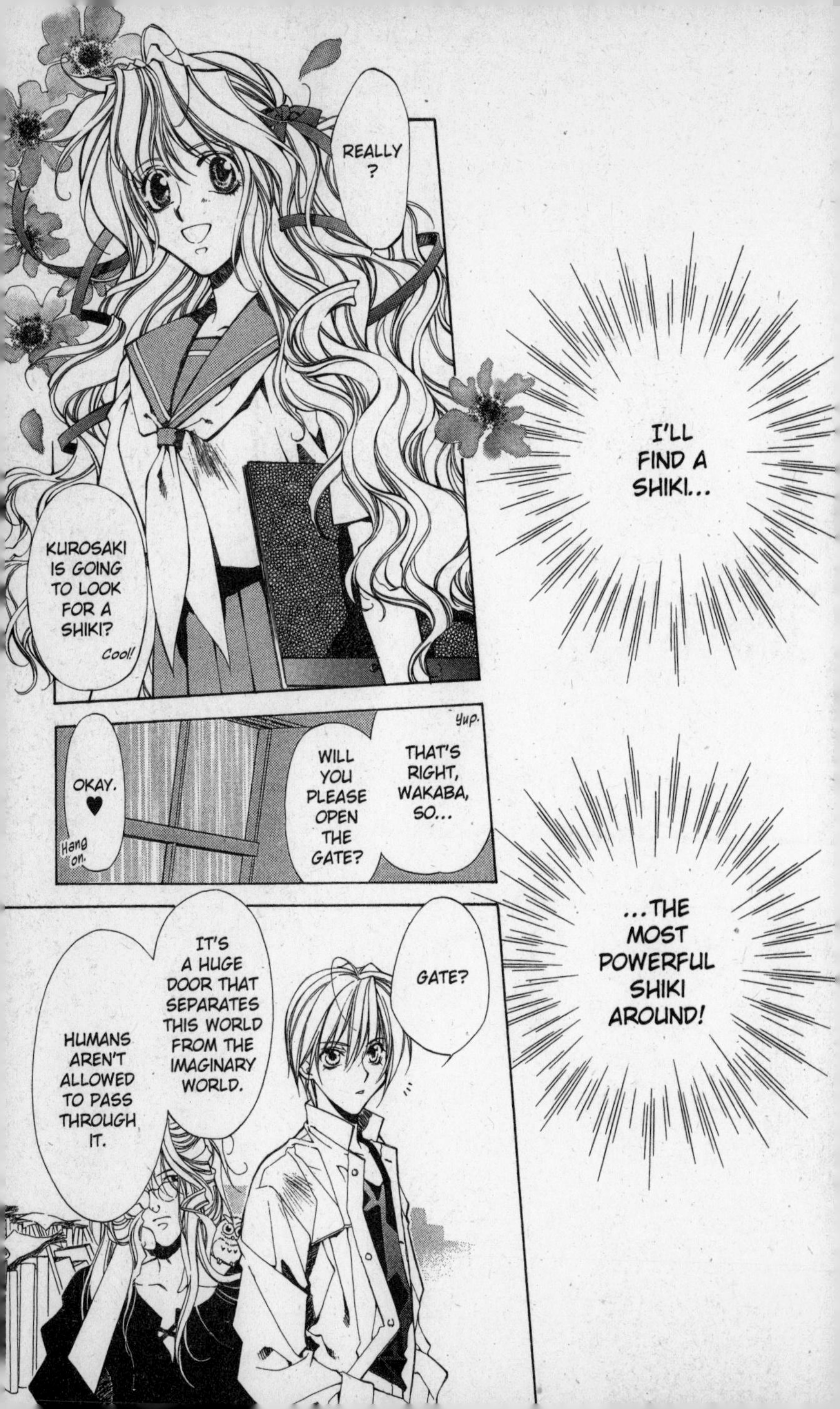
I'LL FIND A SHIKI...
...THE MOST POWERFUL SHIKI AROUND!
REALLY?
KUROSAKI IS GOING TO LOOK FOR A SHIKI?
Cool!
Yup.
THAT'S RIGHT, WAKABA, SO...
WILL YOU PLEASE OPEN THE GATE?
OKAY. ♥
Hang on.
GATE?
IT'S A HUGE DOOR THAT SEPARATES THIS WORLD FROM THE IMAGINARY WORLD.
HUMANS AREN'T ALLOWED TO PASS THROUGH IT.

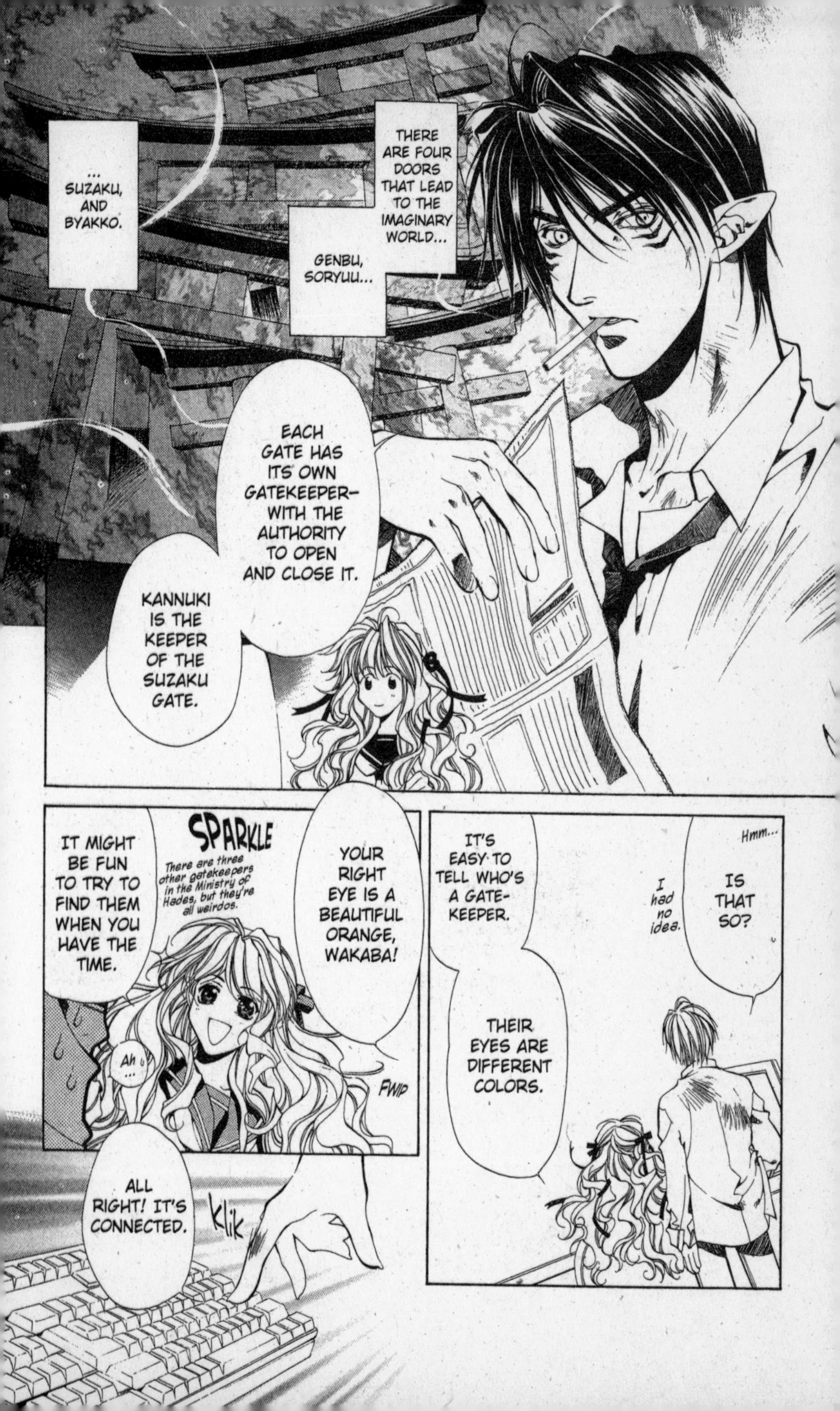
THERE ARE FOUR DOORS THAT LEAD TO THE IMAGINARY WORLD...
GENBU, SORYUU...
... SUZAKU, AND BYAKKO.
EACH GATE HAS ITS OWN GATEKEEPER— WITH THE AUTHORITY TO OPEN AND CLOSE IT.
KANNUKI IS THE KEEPER OF THE SUZAKU GATE.
Hmm...
IS THAT SO?
I had no idea.
IT'S EASY TO TELL WHO'S A GATE-KEEPER.
THEIR EYES ARE DIFFERENT COLORS.
YOUR RIGHT EYE IS A BEAUTIFUL ORANGE, WAKABA!
FWIP
SPARKLE
IT MIGHT BE FUN TO TRY TO FIND THEM WHEN YOU HAVE THE TIME.
There are three other gatekeepers in the Ministry of Hades, but they're all weirdos.
Ah ...
ALL RIGHT! IT'S CONNECTED.
klik

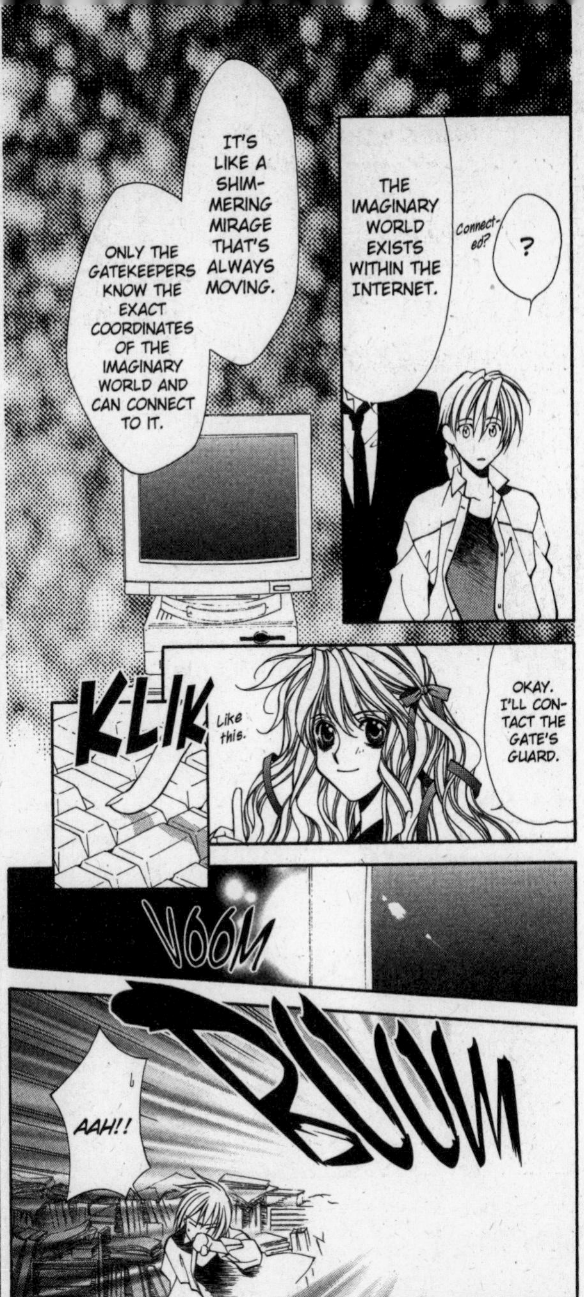
THE IMAGINARY WORLD EXISTS WITHIN THE INTERNET.
?
IT'S LIKE A SHIMMERING MIRAGE THAT'S ALWAYS MOVING.
ONLY THE GATEKEEPERS KNOW THE EXACT COORDINATES OF THE IMAGINARY WORLD AND CAN CONNECT TO IT.
Connect-ed?
OKAY. I'LL CONTACT THE GATE'S GUARD.
Like this.
KLIK
VOOM
AAH!!

I actually love the Swedish cartoon "Mumin." (Laugh) I love the puffy drawings and the beautiful colors too. Sometimes I go to novelty shops (I never go just for this--I tag along with a friend or go looking for a gift) and I always end up buying Mumin merchandise. (Laugh) It's really not like me. I even have a Mumin calendar for this year. The photo frame on my desk doesn't have a photograph in it, rather a drawing of Mumin. (I put in a postcard that's the perfect size. Sometimes I change it.) There isn't a particular Mumin character that I like, but... I am fond of Nyoro Nyoro. (Laugh) And the page for June has a drawing of Snafkin on it. It's really cool. June rain is falling and Snafkin is under a leaf trying to escape it. (Isn't that great?) The illustration is so green and pretty. Doesn't it kind of make you happy when the illustration of your birthday month is pretty? Or is it just me? (Laugh) On top of that, the calendar is designed so that you can tear the illustrations out and use them as postcards. Very convenient. It's just amazing.

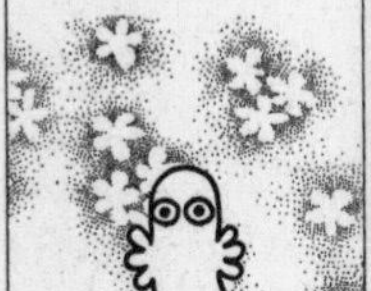

Nyoro - Matsushita style

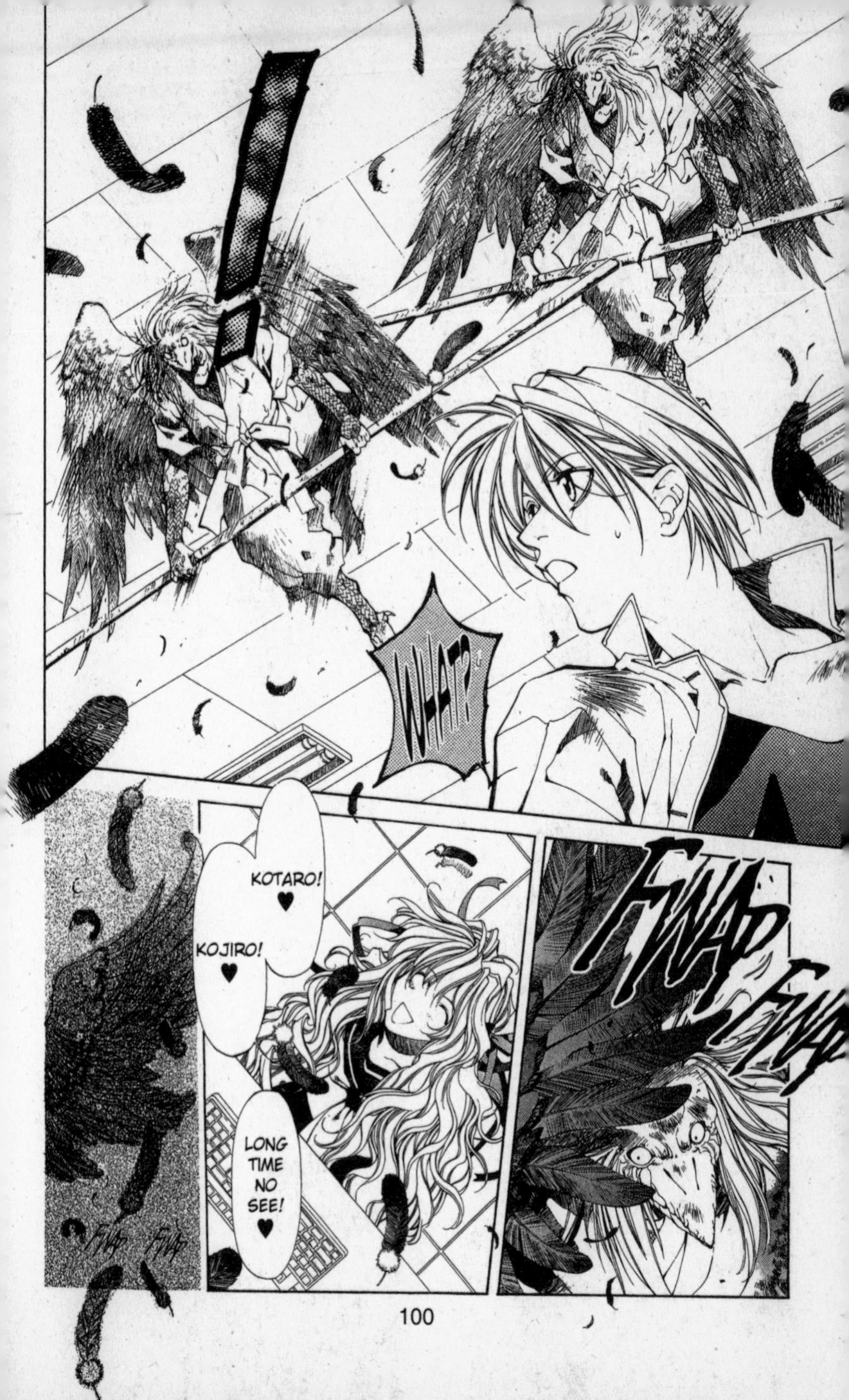
WHAT?!
FWAP FWAP
KOTARO! ♥
KOJIRO! ♥
LONG TIME NO SEE! ♥
FWAP FWAP

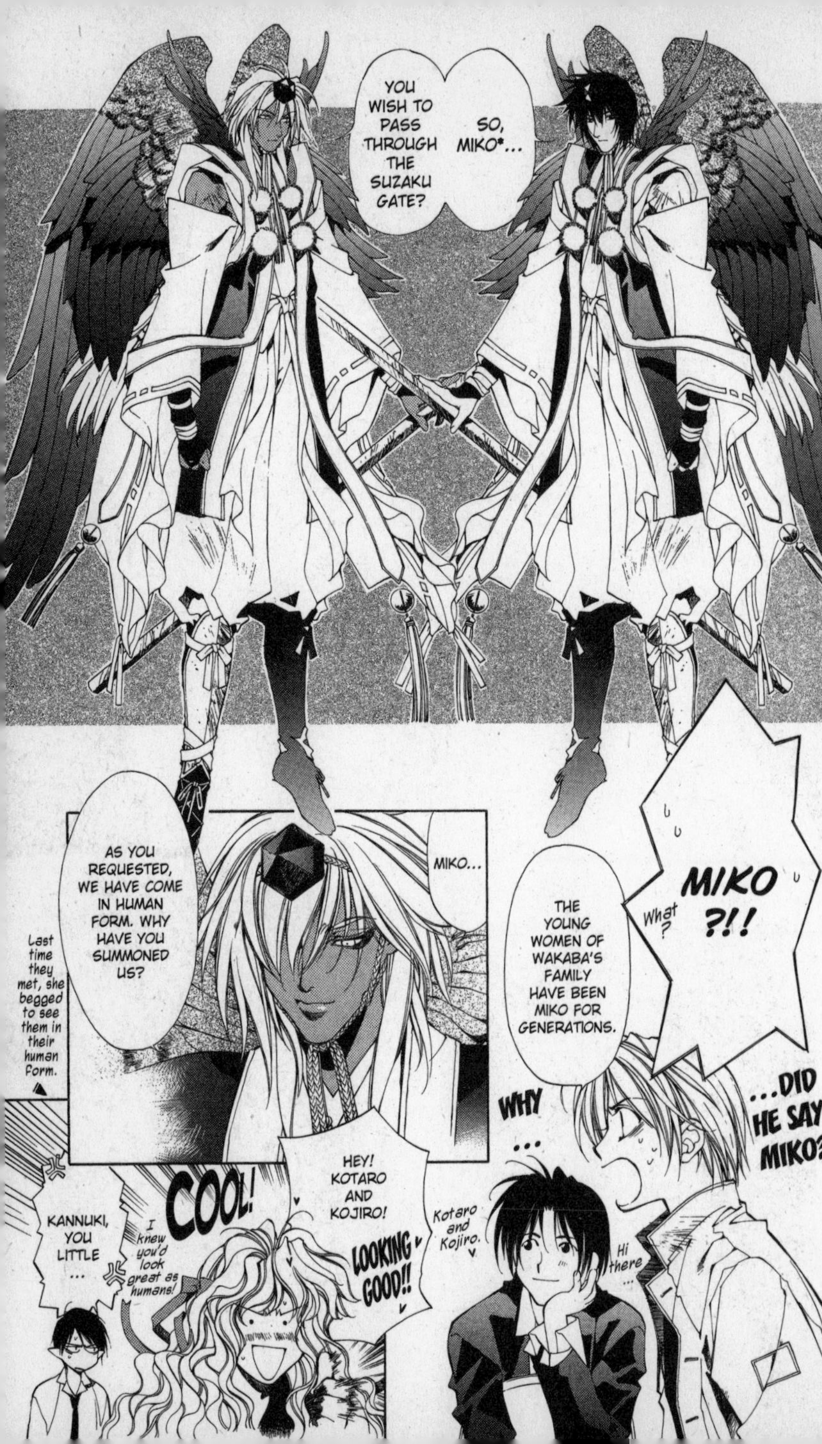
SO, MIKO*...
YOU WISH TO PASS THROUGH THE SUZAKU GATE?
MIKO ?!!
What?
THE YOUNG WOMEN OF WAKABA'S FAMILY HAVE BEEN MIKO FOR GENERATIONS.
MIKO...
AS YOU REQUESTED, WE HAVE COME IN HUMAN FORM. WHY HAVE YOU SUMMONED US?
Last time they met, she begged to see them in their human form.
WHY...
...DID HE SAY MIKO?
Hi there...
Kotaro and Kojiro.
HEY! KOTARO AND KOJIRO!
LOOKING GOOD!!
COOL!
I knew you'd look great as humans!
KANNUKI, YOU LITTLE ...

*A miko is a shrine maiden. -Ed.

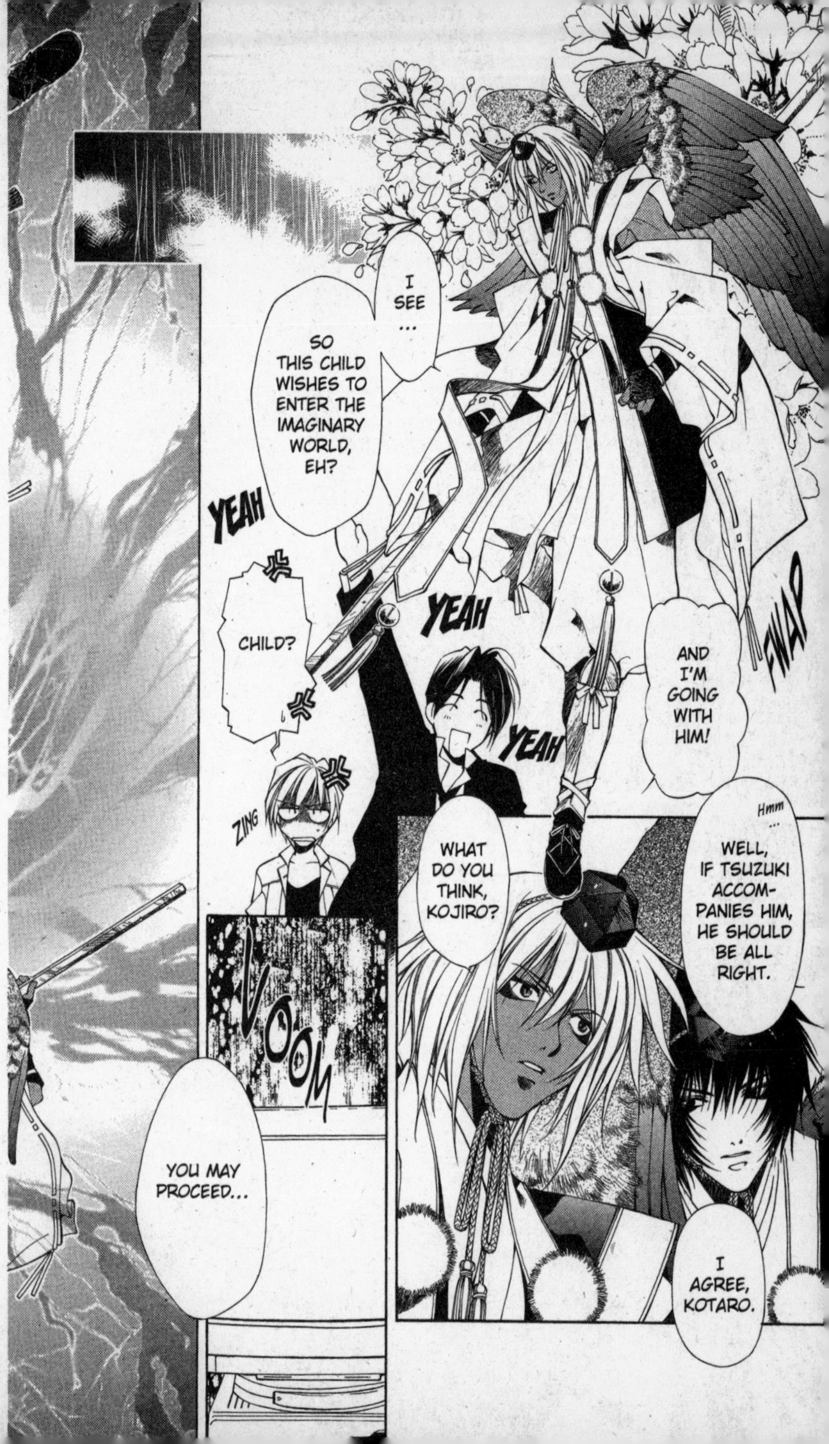
I SEE...
SO THIS CHILD WISHES TO ENTER THE IMAGINARY WORLD, EH?
FWAP
AND I'M GOING WITH HIM!
YEAH
YEAH
YEAH
CHILD?
ZING
Hmm...
WELL, IF TSUZUKI ACCOMPANIES HIM, HE SHOULD BE ALL RIGHT.
WHAT DO YOU THINK, KOJIRO?
I AGREE, KOTARO.
VOOM
YOU MAY PROCEED...

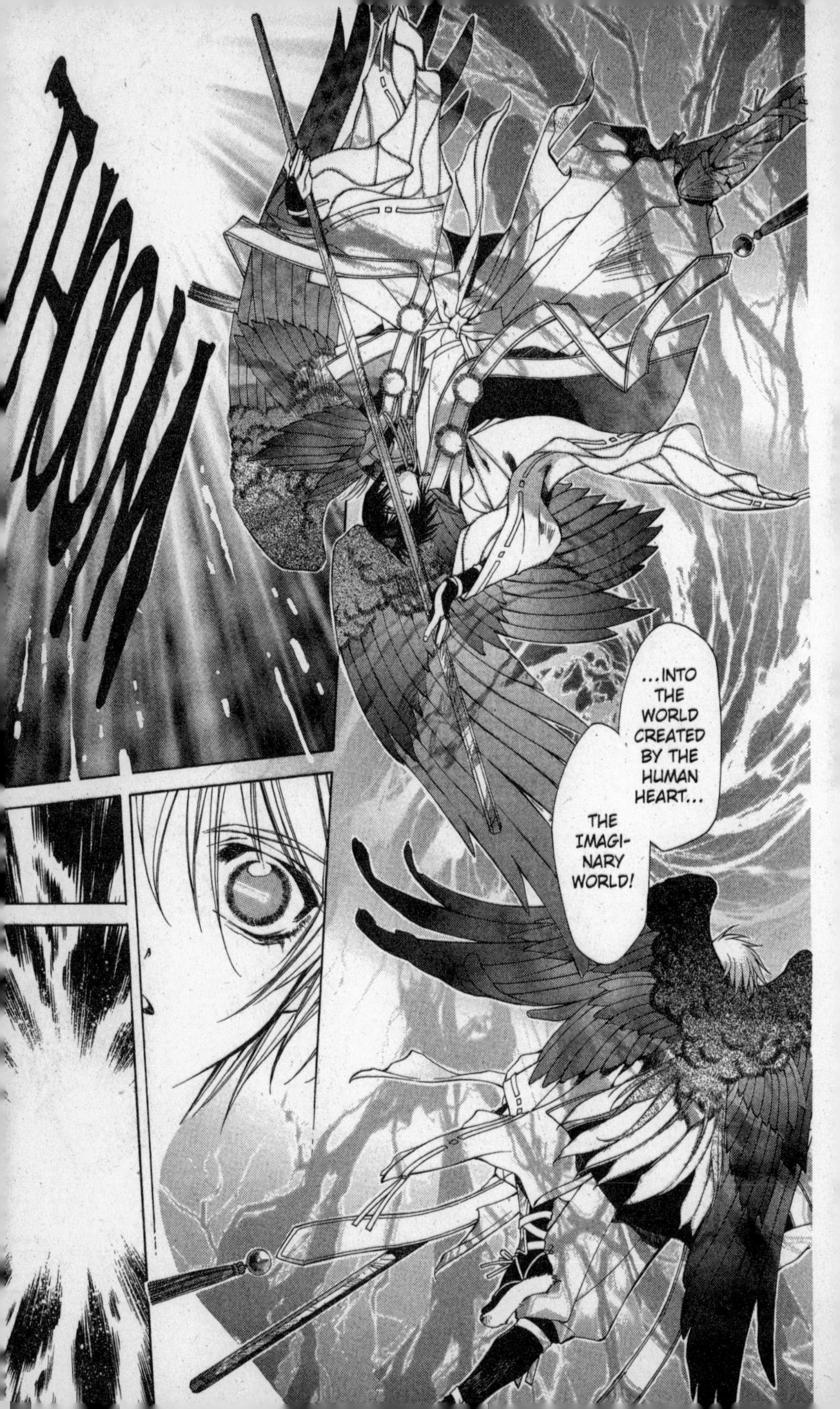
...INTO THE WORLD CREATED BY THE HUMAN HEART...
THE IMAGINARY WORLD!

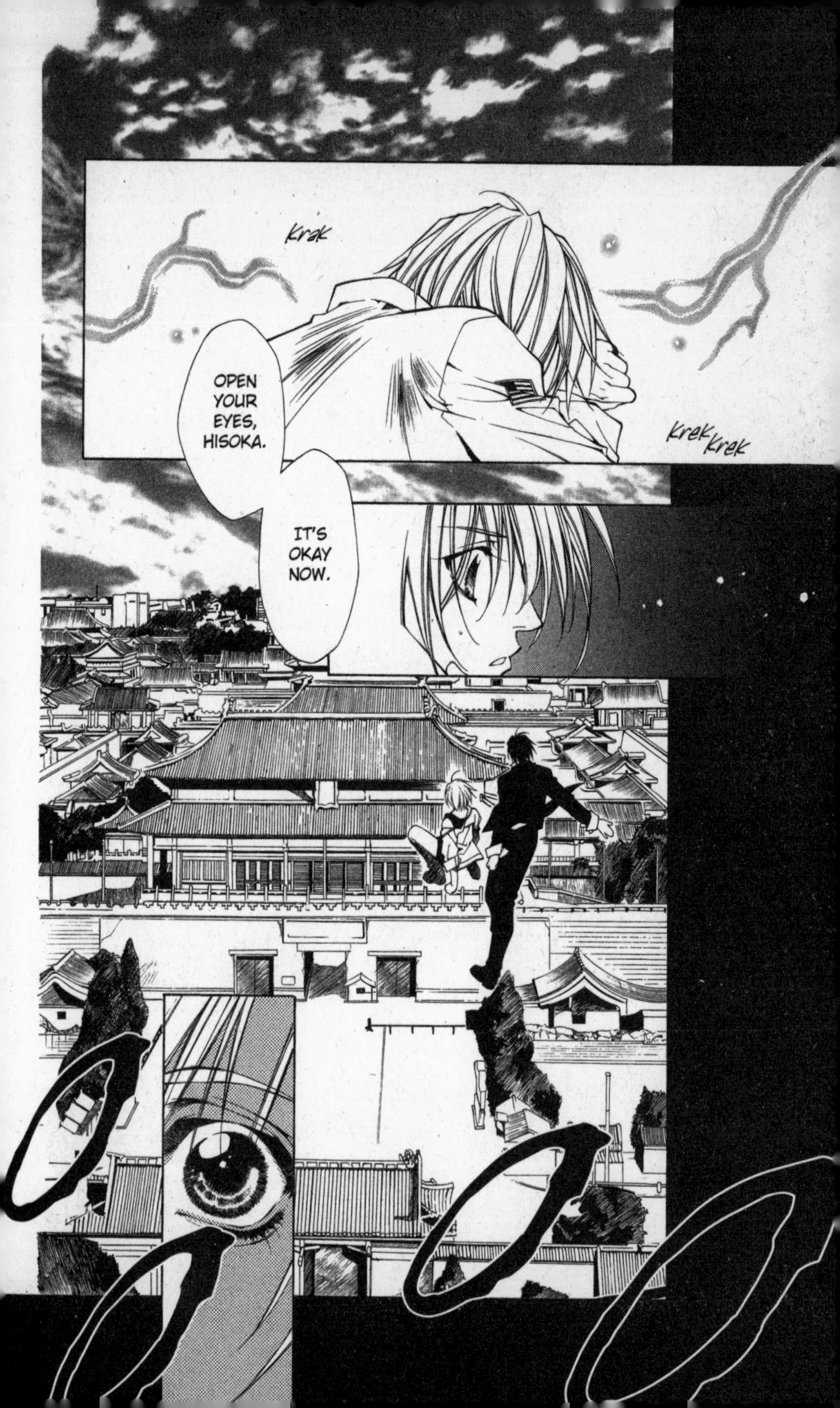
Krak
Krek Krek
OPEN YOUR EYES, HISOKA.
IT'S OKAY NOW.

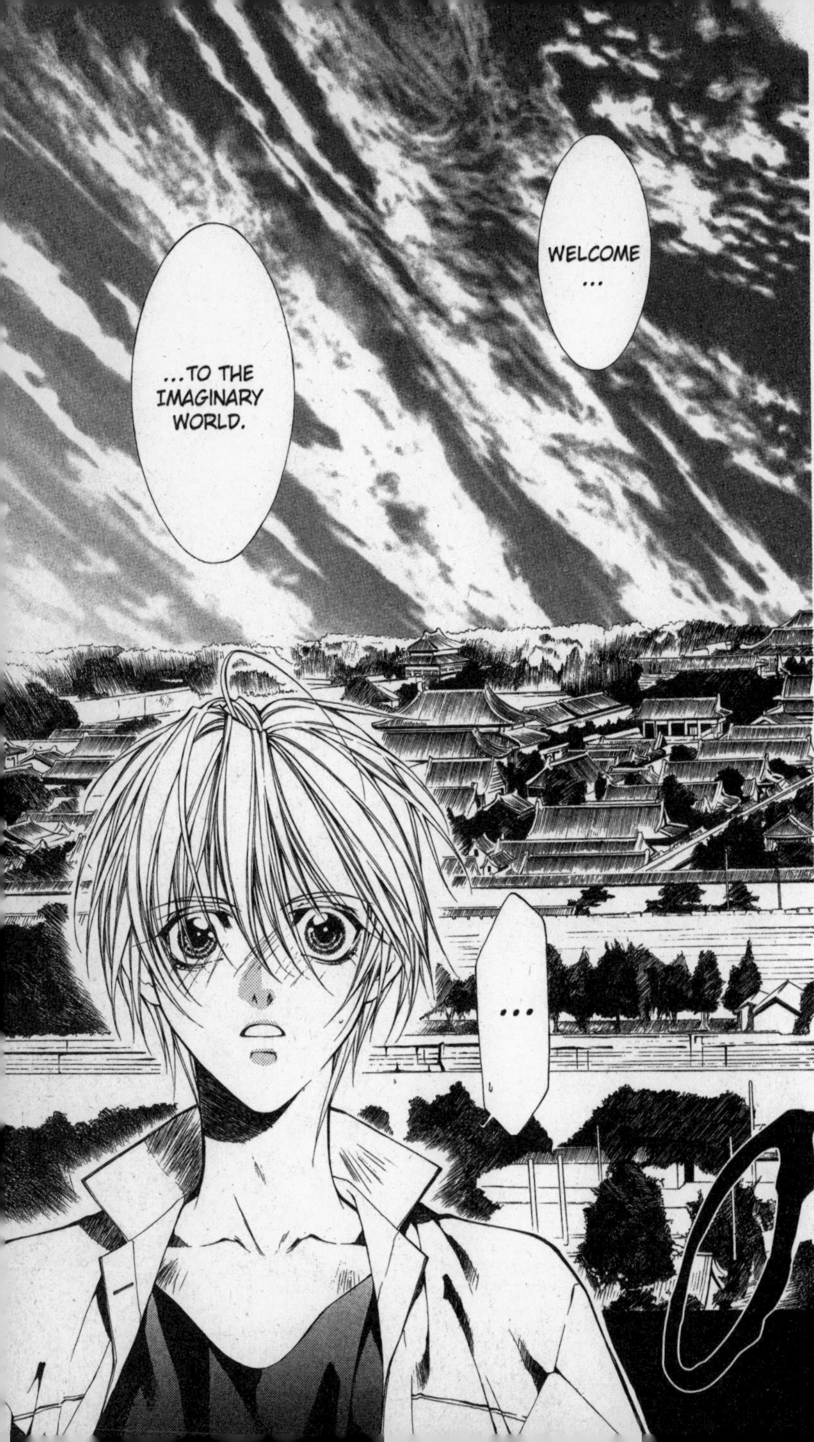
WELCOME ...
...TO THE IMAGINARY WORLD.
...

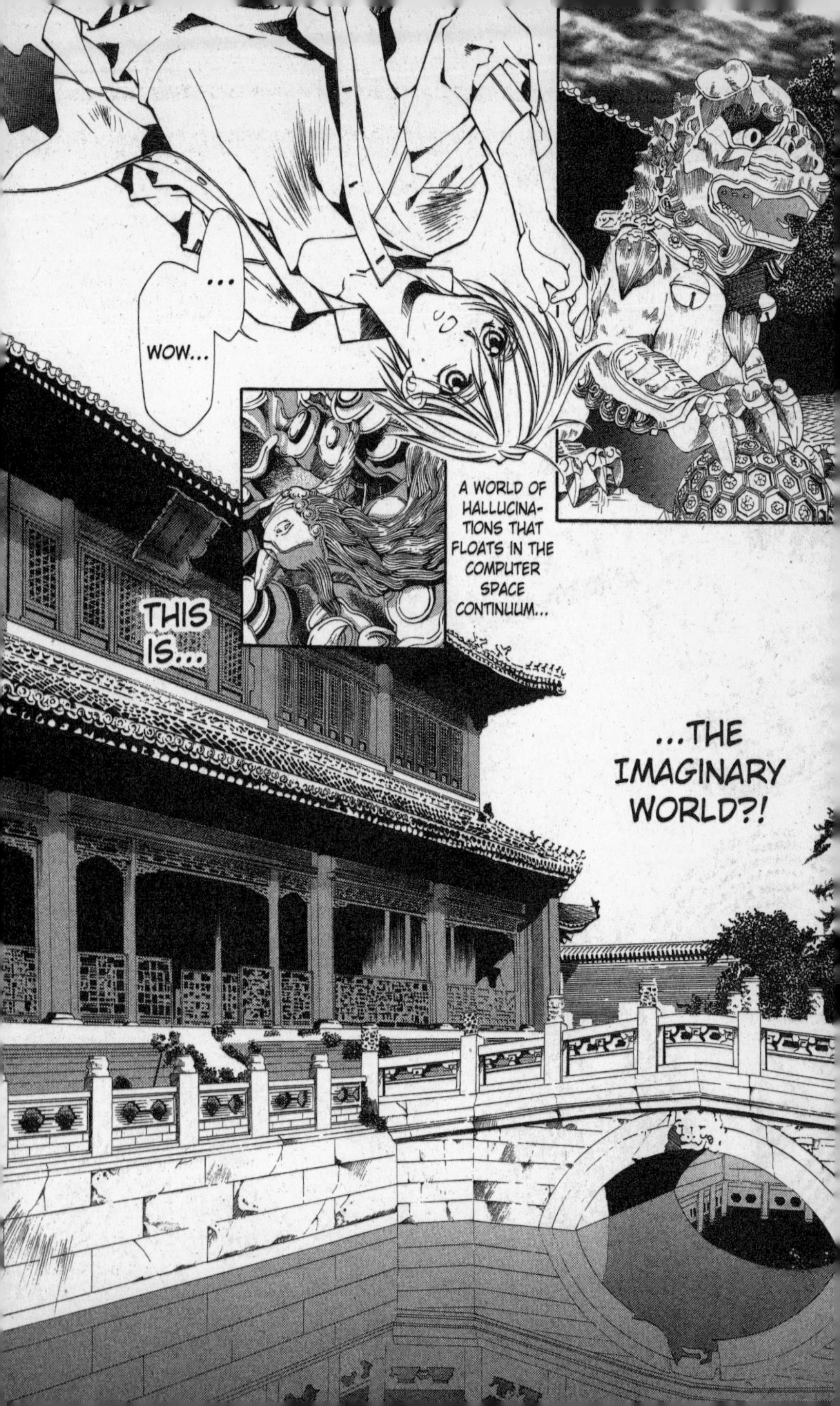
...
WOW...
A WORLD OF HALLUCINATIONS THAT FLOATS IN THE COMPUTER SPACE CONTINUUM...
THIS IS...
...THE IMAGINARY WORLD?!

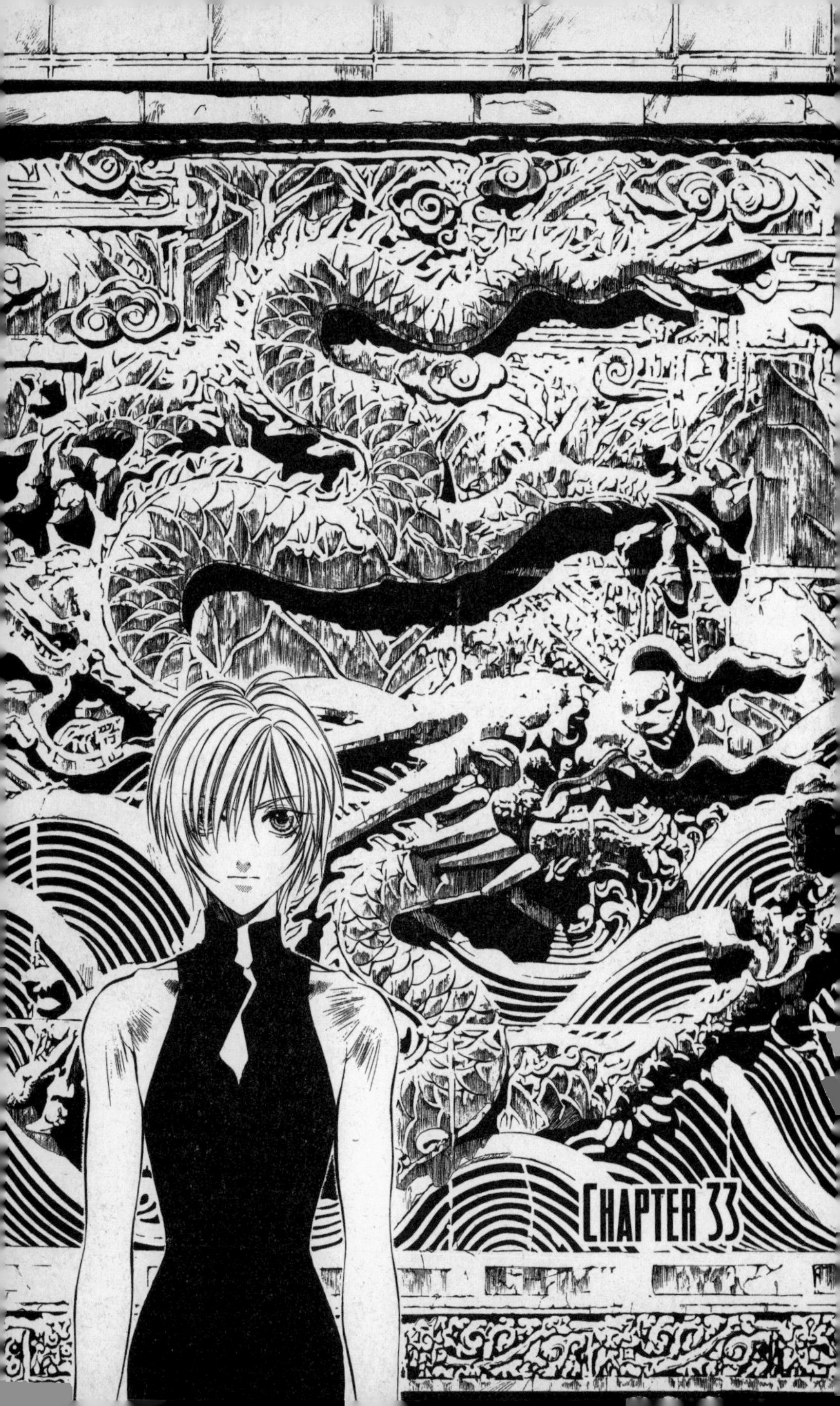
CHAPTER 33

THE IMAGINARY WORLD...

THE SHIMMERING CASTLE
THAT FLOATS IN THE COMPUTER
SPACE CONTINUUM

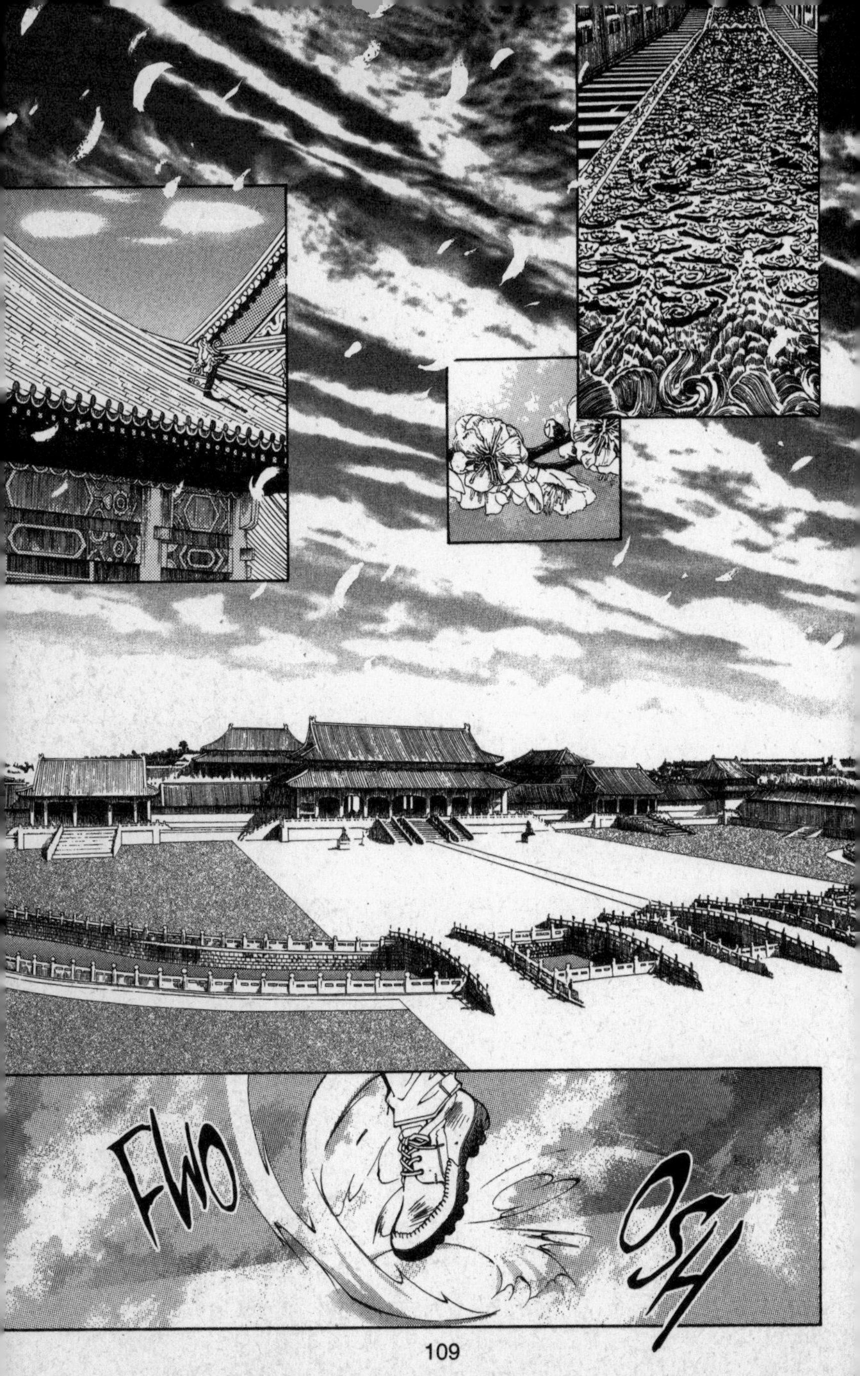
FWOOSH

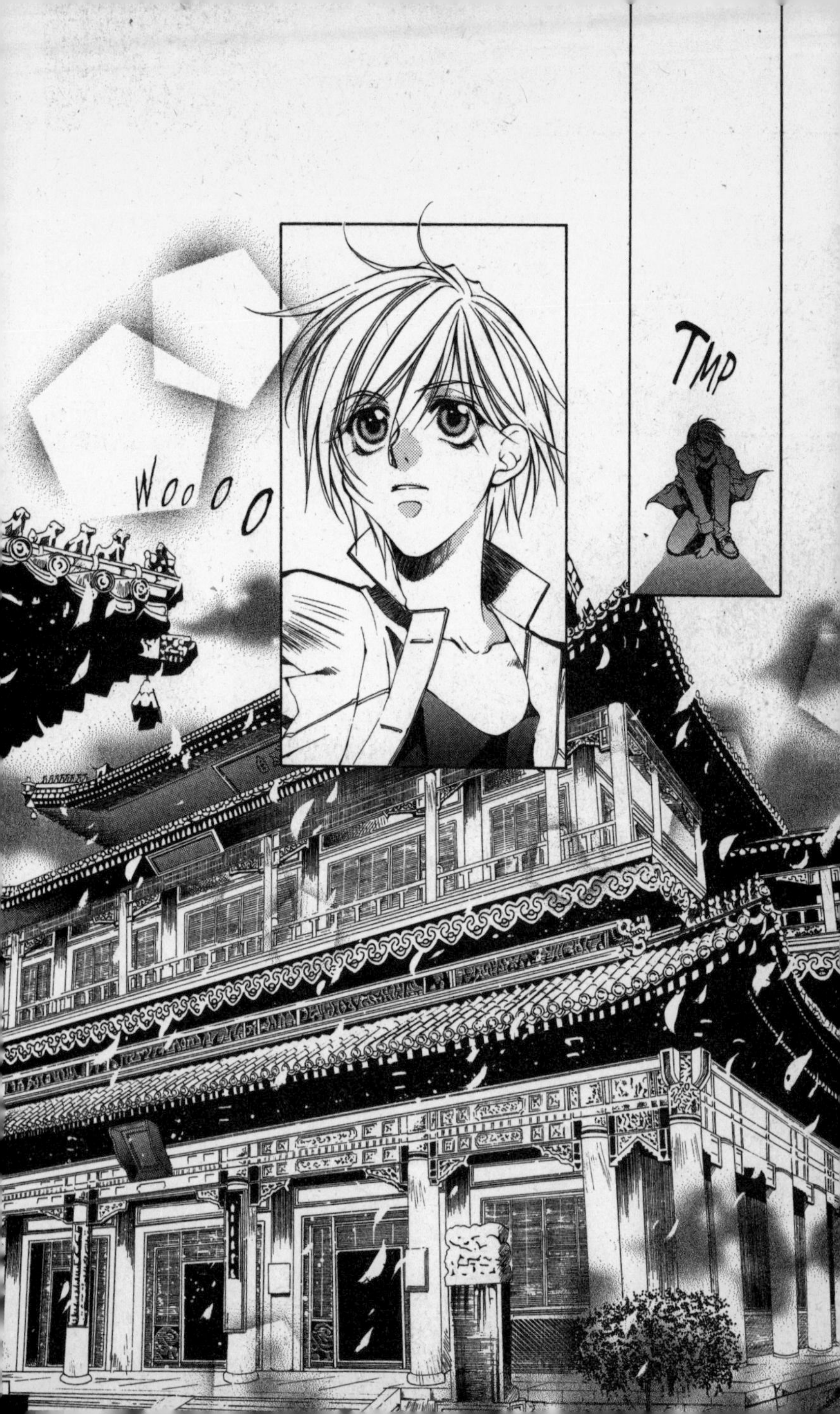
TMP
WOOOO

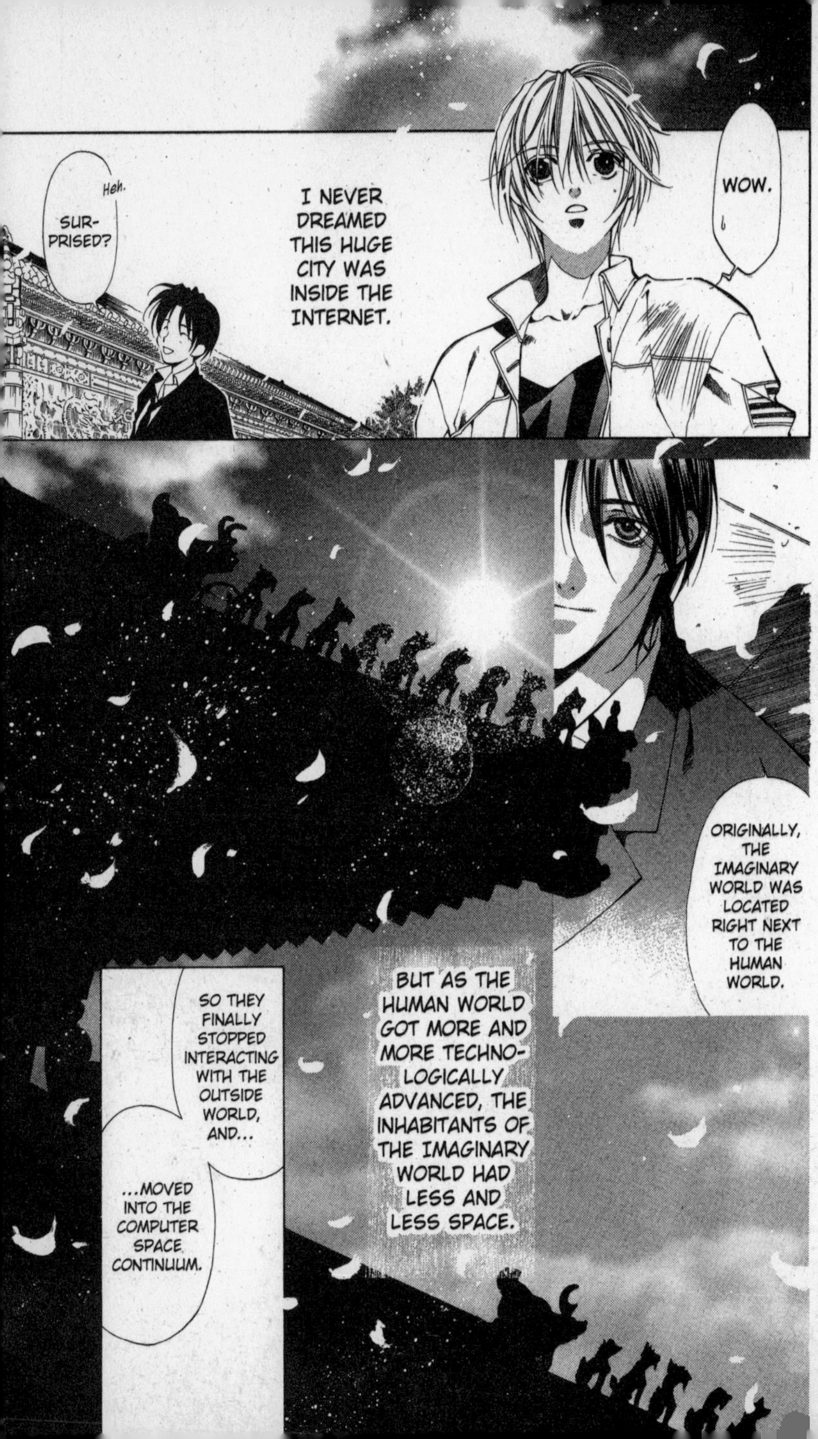
WOW.
I NEVER DREAMED THIS HUGE CITY WAS INSIDE THE INTERNET.
Heh.
SUR-PRISED?
ORIGINALLY, THE IMAGINARY WORLD WAS LOCATED RIGHT NEXT TO THE HUMAN WORLD.
BUT AS THE HUMAN WORLD GOT MORE AND MORE TECHNO-LOGICALLY ADVANCED, THE INHABITANTS OF THE IMAGINARY WORLD HAD LESS AND LESS SPACE.
SO THEY FINALLY STOPPED INTERACTING WITH THE OUTSIDE WORLD, AND...
...MOVED INTO THE COMPUTER SPACE CONTINUUM.

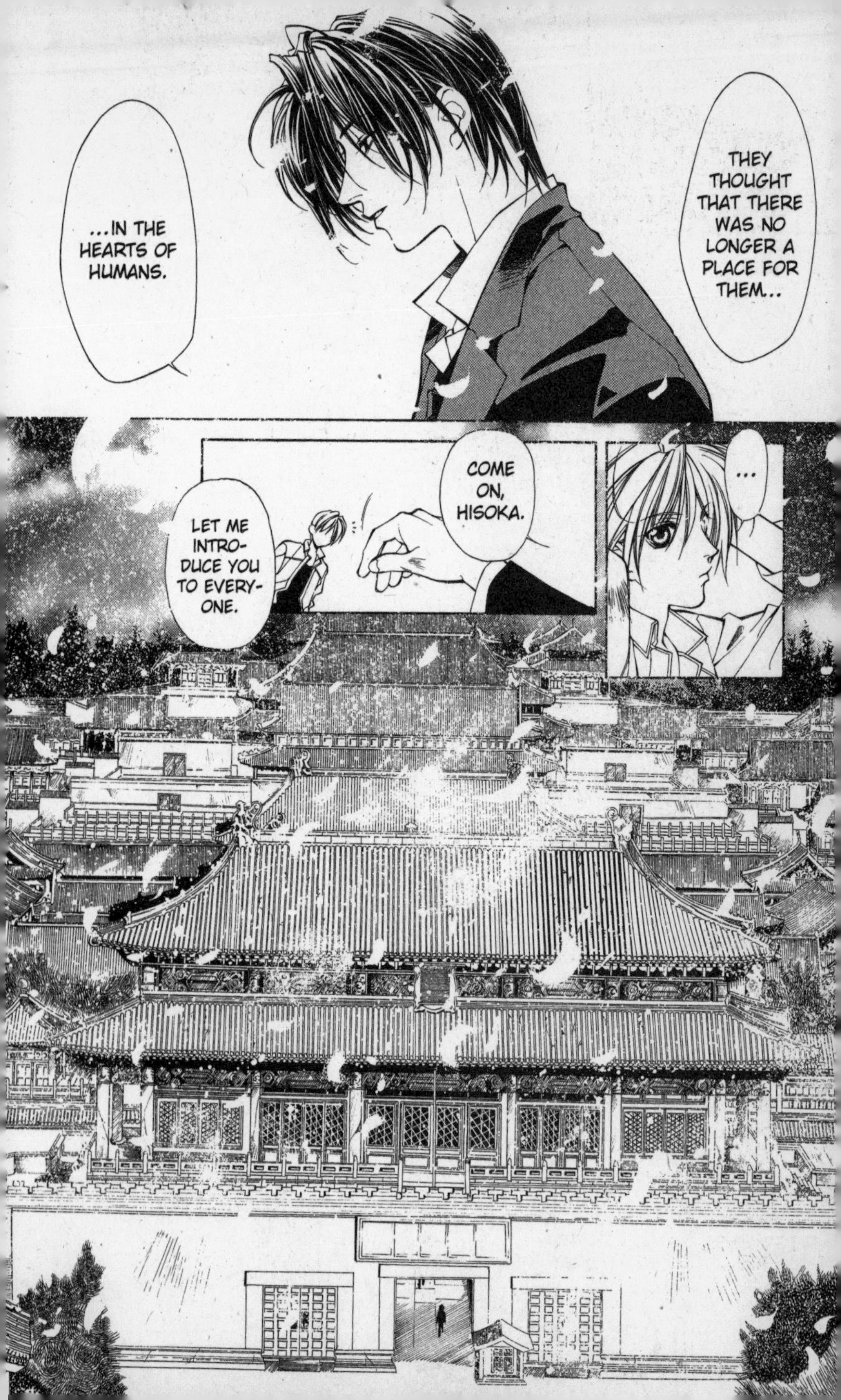
THEY THOUGHT THAT THERE WAS NO LONGER A PLACE FOR THEM...
...IN THE HEARTS OF HUMANS.
...
COME ON, HISOKA.
LET ME INTRO-DUCE YOU TO EVERY-ONE.

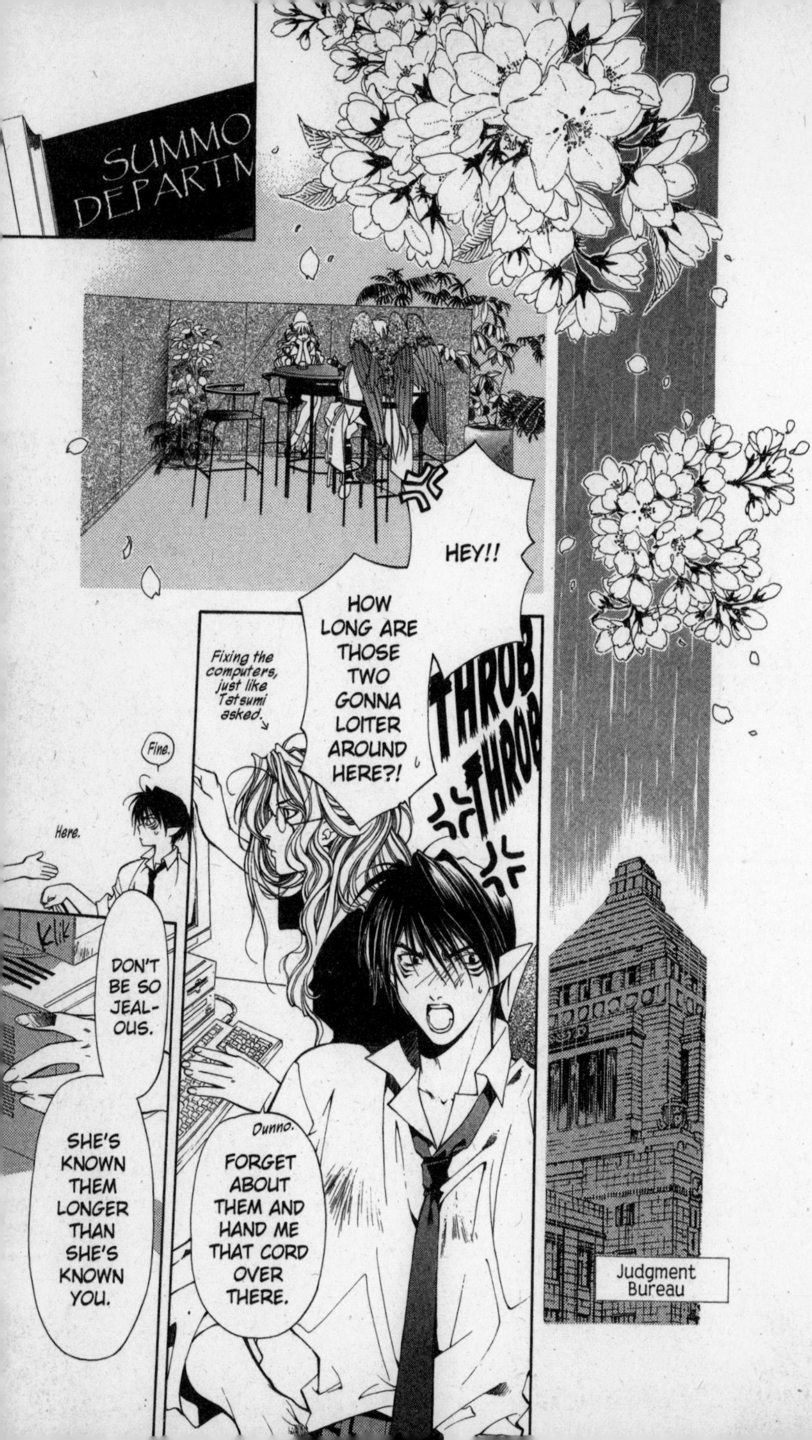

Judgment Bureau
SUMMO
DEPARTM
HEY!!
HOW LONG ARE THOSE TWO GONNA LOITER AROUND HERE?!
THROB THROB
Fixing the computers, just like Tatsumi asked.
Fine.
Here.
Klik
Dunno.
FORGET ABOUT THEM AND HAND ME THAT CORD OVER THERE.
DON'T BE SO JEAL-OUS.
SHE'S KNOWN THEM LONGER THAN SHE'S KNOWN YOU.

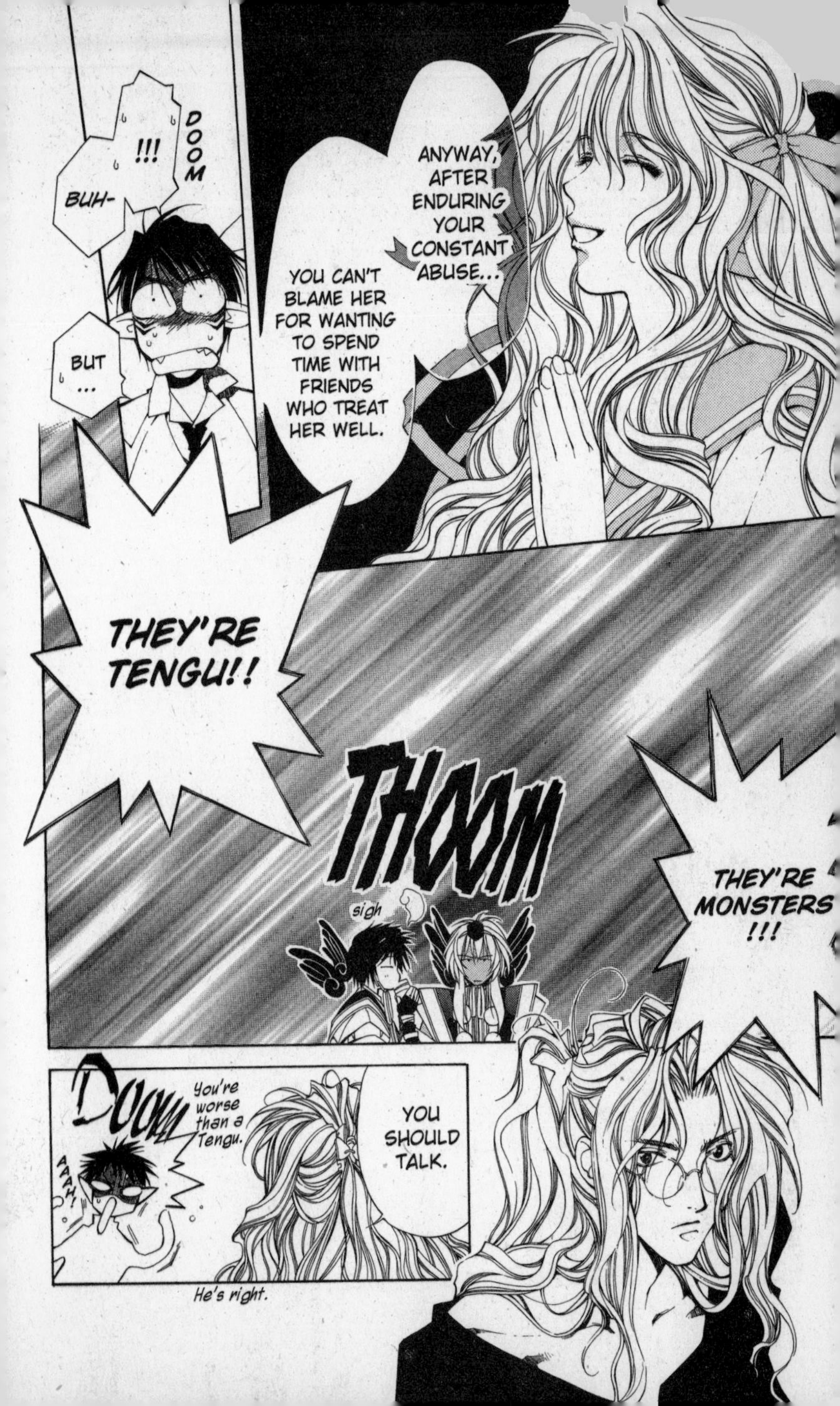
ANYWAY, AFTER ENDURING YOUR CONSTANT ABUSE...
YOU CAN'T BLAME HER FOR WANTING TO SPEND TIME WITH FRIENDS WHO TREAT HER WELL.
DOOM
!!!
BUH-
BUT ...
THEY'RE TENGU!!
THEY'RE MONSTERS !!!
THOOM
sigh
YOU SHOULD TALK.
You're worse than a Tengu.
DOOM
AAAH!
He's right.

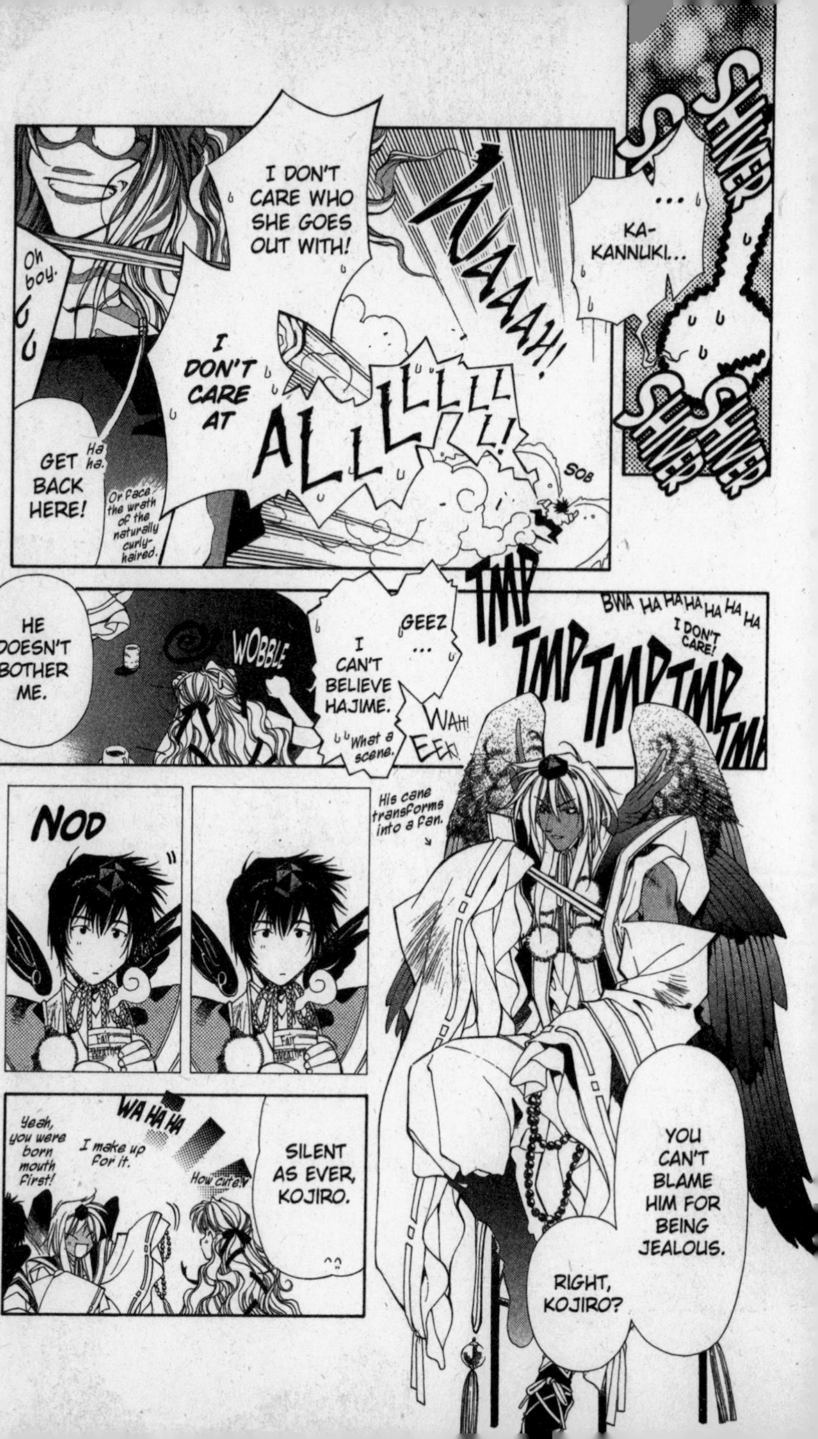
SHIVER
... KA-KANNUKI...
SHIVER SHIVER
I DON'T CARE WHO SHE GOES OUT WITH!
WAAAAH!
I DON'T CARE AT
ALLLLLLLLL!
SOB
Oh boy.
GET BACK HERE!
Ha ha.
Or face the wrath of the naturally curly-haired.
TMP TMP TMP TMP TMP TMP
BWA HA HA HA HA HA HA
I DON'T CARE!
GEEZ ...
I CAN'T BELIEVE HAJIME.
What a scene.
WAH!
EEK!
WOBBLE
HE DOESN'T BOTHER ME.
His cane transforms into a fan.
YOU CAN'T BLAME HIM FOR BEING JEALOUS.
RIGHT, KOJIRO?
NOD
SILENT AS EVER, KOJIRO.
How cute.
WA HA HA
I make up for it.
Yeah, you were born mouth first!

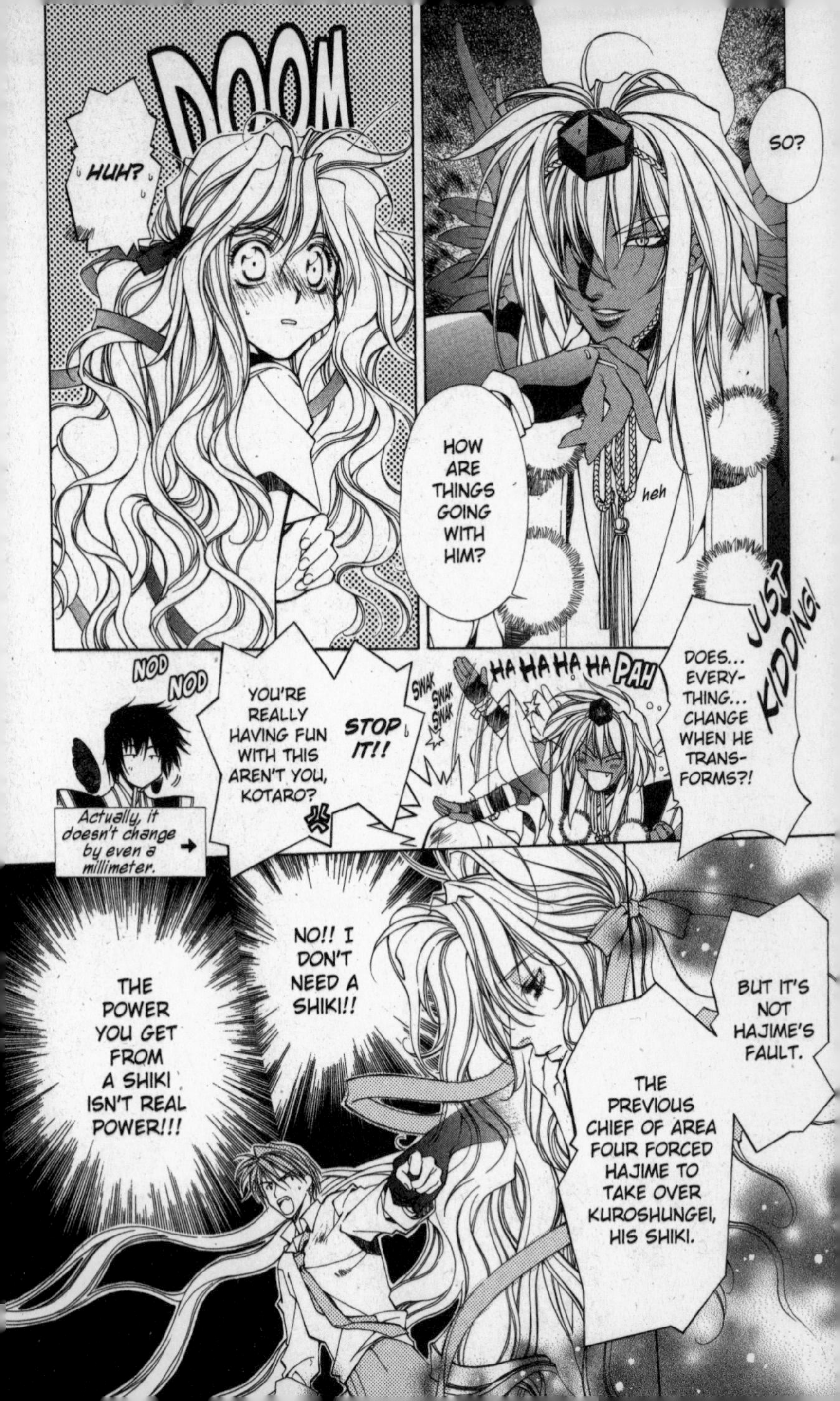
SO?
HOW ARE THINGS GOING WITH HIM?
heh
DOOM
HUH?
DOES... EVERY-THING... CHANGE WHEN HE TRANS-FORMS?!
JUST KIDDING!
HA HA HA HA HA PAH
SWAK SWAK SWAK
STOP IT!!
YOU'RE REALLY HAVING FUN WITH THIS AREN'T YOU, KOTARO?
NOD NOD
Actually, it doesn't change by even a millimeter.
BUT IT'S NOT HAJIME'S FAULT.
THE PREVIOUS CHIEF OF AREA FOUR FORCED HAJIME TO TAKE OVER KUROSHUNGEI, HIS SHIKI.
NO!! I DON'T NEED A SHIKI!!
THE POWER YOU GET FROM A SHIKI ISN'T REAL POWER!!!

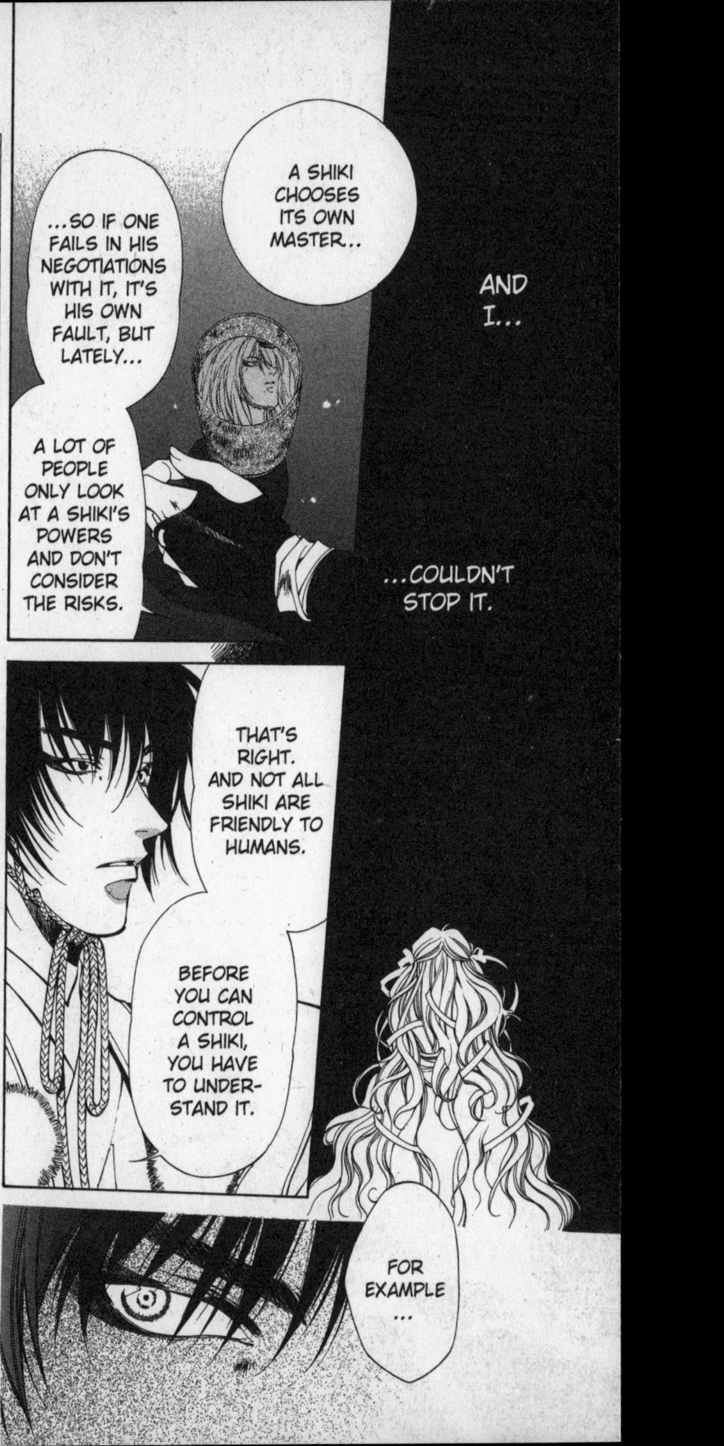
A SHIKI CHOOSES ITS OWN MASTER...
...SO IF ONE FAILS IN HIS NEGOTIATIONS WITH IT, IT'S HIS OWN FAULT, BUT LATELY...
A LOT OF PEOPLE ONLY LOOK AT A SHIKI'S POWERS AND DON'T CONSIDER THE RISKS.
AND I...
...COULDN'T STOP IT.
THAT'S RIGHT. AND NOT ALL SHIKI ARE FRIENDLY TO HUMANS.
BEFORE YOU CAN CONTROL A SHIKI, YOU HAVE TO UNDERSTAND IT.
FOR EXAMPLE ...

I'm going to write a little about the Tengu, Kotaro and Kojiro. They're twins, although they don't look alike. They have known Wakaba the miko for a long time, but they're more friends of the Kannuki family than personal friends of Wakaba's. Maybe something happened a long time ago. Maybe they challenged Wakaba's ancestors to a show of strength and lost. When you think about it that way, Kotaro and Kojiro seem kind of pathetic. (Laugh)

The Tengu have red tattoos on their eyes. (That's right, those are tattoos, and they're red, but you can't tell in black & white.) And the tattoos have a protective power. (But I don't know what it is.) Maybe when they were little, their master gave them those tattoos so they'd always be safe. I'll explain the world of the demons and Japanese Shiki gods in forthcoming volumes. By the way, demons usually wear tall geta sandals, but these two wear straw sandals.

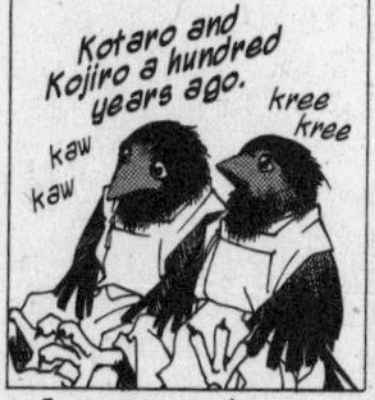
Kotaro and Kojiro a hundred years ago.
kaw kaw
kree kree

I want a crow like this.

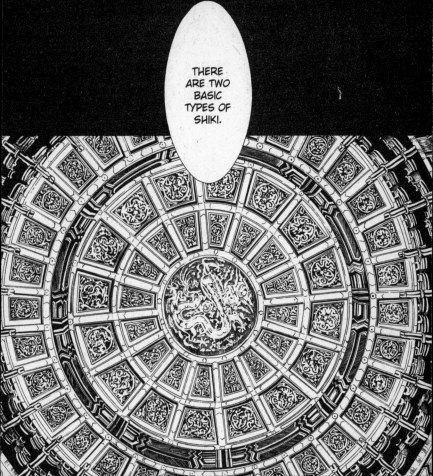

THERE
ARE TWO
BASIC
TYPES OF
SHIKI.

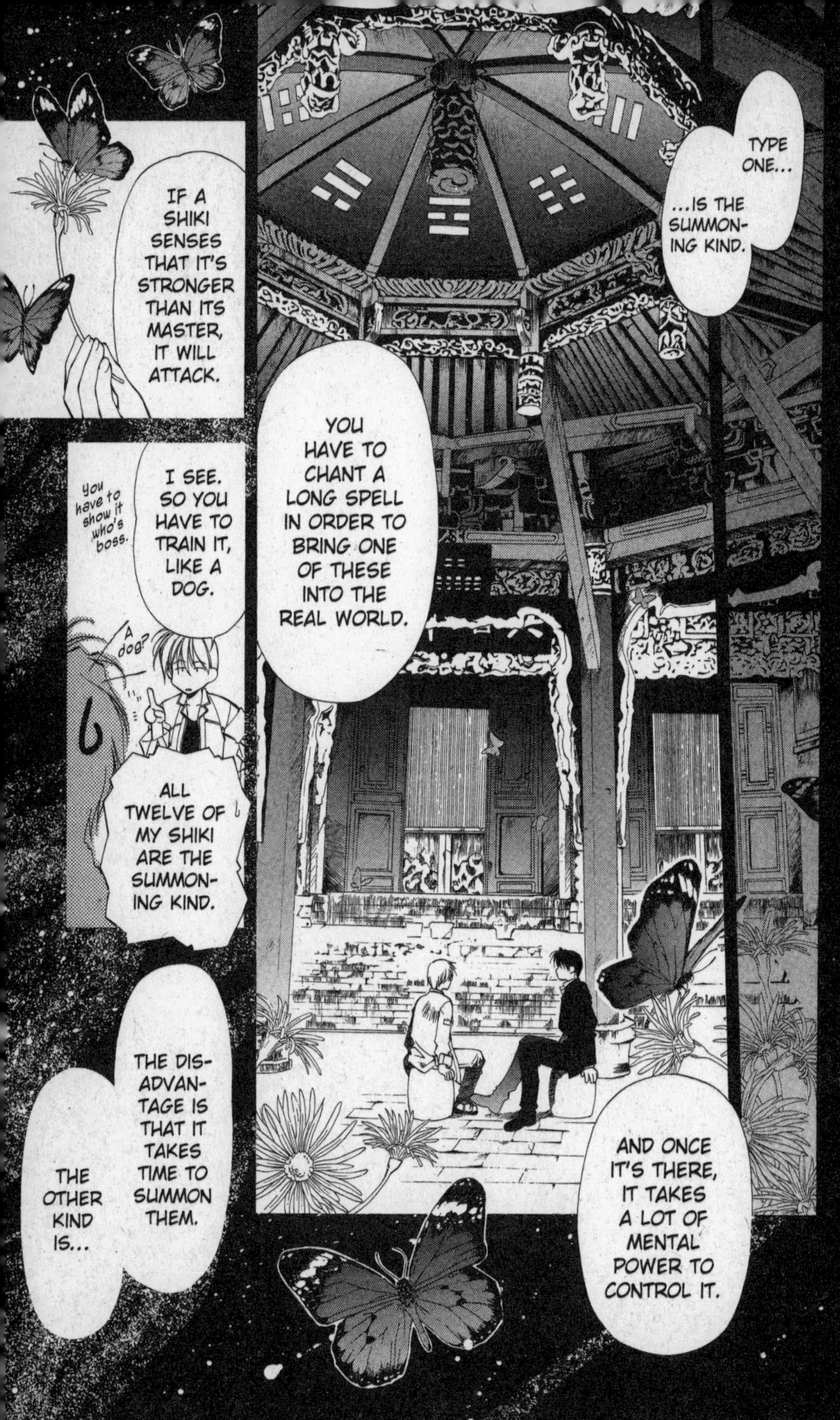
TYPE ONE...
...IS THE SUMMONING KIND.
YOU HAVE TO CHANT A LONG SPELL IN ORDER TO BRING ONE OF THESE INTO THE REAL WORLD.
AND ONCE IT'S THERE, IT TAKES A LOT OF MENTAL POWER TO CONTROL IT.
IF A SHIKI SENSES THAT IT'S STRONGER THAN ITS MASTER, IT WILL ATTACK.
I SEE. SO YOU HAVE TO TRAIN IT, LIKE A DOG.
You have to show it who's boss.
A dog?
ALL TWELVE OF MY SHIKI ARE THE SUMMONING KIND.
THE DISADVANTAGE IS THAT IT TAKES TIME TO SUMMON THEM.
THE OTHER KIND IS...

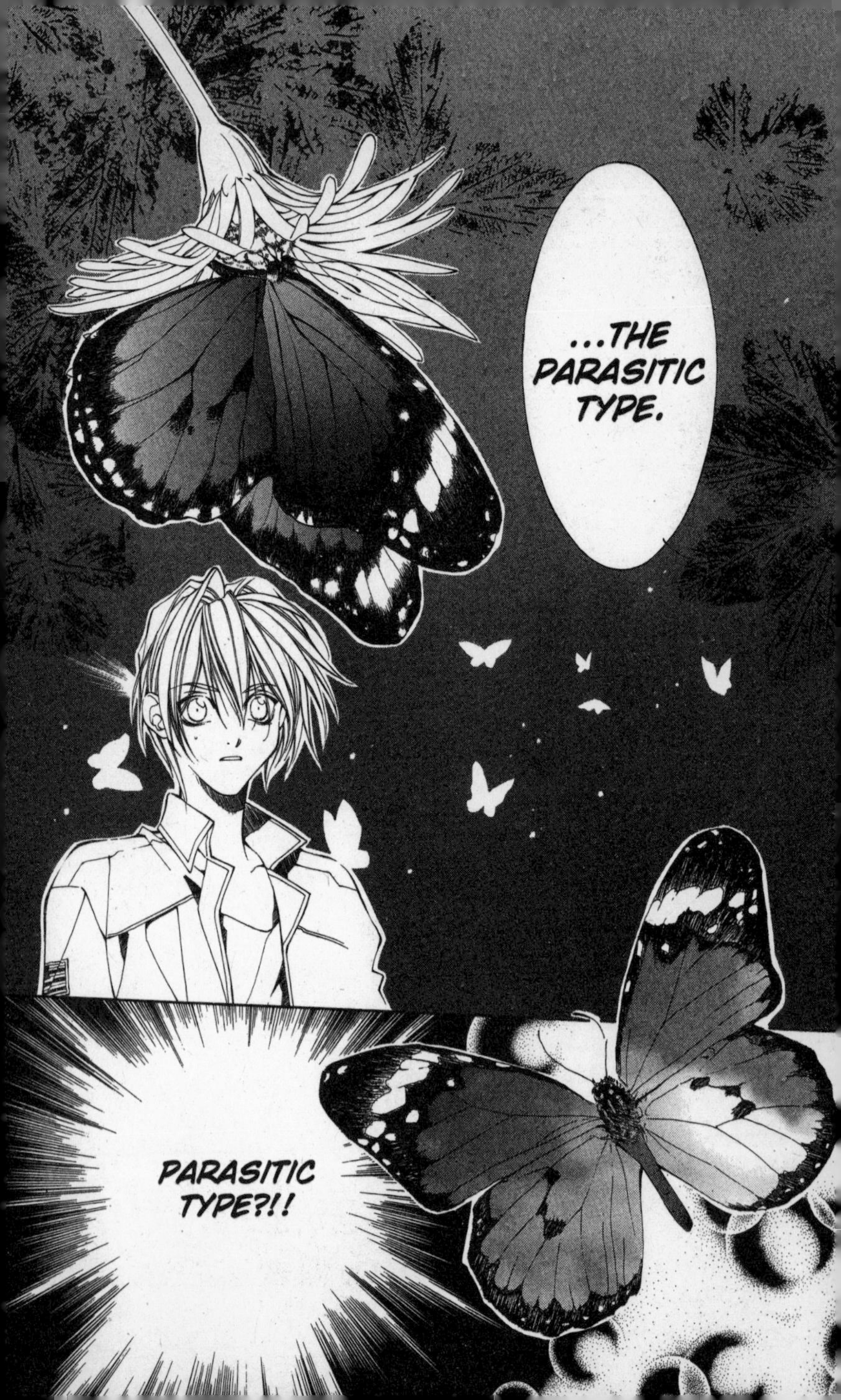
...THE PARASITIC TYPE.
PARASITIC TYPE?!!

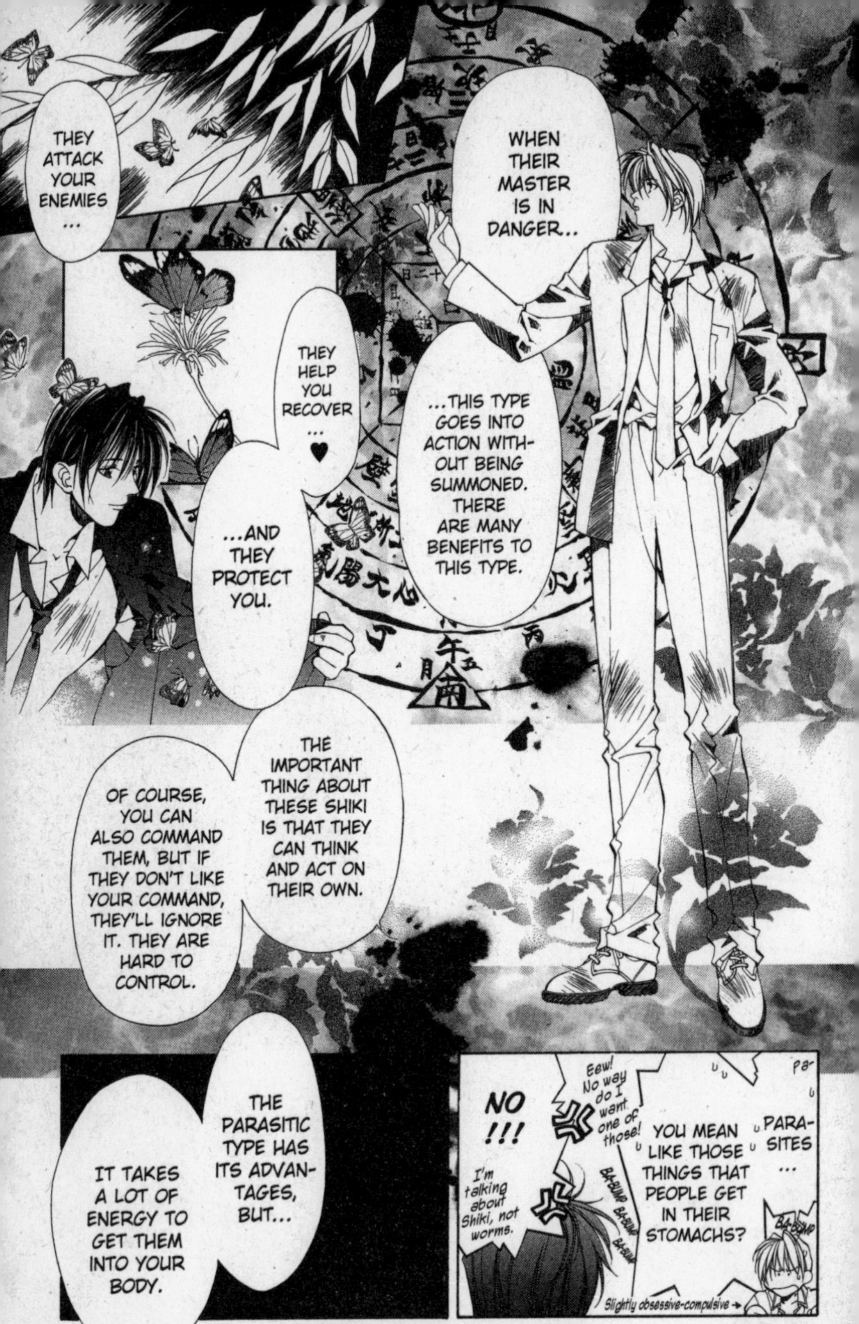
WHEN THEIR MASTER IS IN DANGER...
...THIS TYPE GOES INTO ACTION WITHOUT BEING SUMMONED. THERE ARE MANY BENEFITS TO THIS TYPE.
THEY ATTACK YOUR ENEMIES...
THEY HELP YOU RECOVER... ♥
...AND THEY PROTECT YOU.
THE IMPORTANT THING ABOUT THESE SHIKI IS THAT THEY CAN THINK AND ACT ON THEIR OWN.
OF COURSE, YOU CAN ALSO COMMAND THEM, BUT IF THEY DON'T LIKE YOUR COMMAND, THEY'LL IGNORE IT. THEY ARE HARD TO CONTROL.
Pa-
PARA-SITES...
YOU MEAN LIKE THOSE THINGS THAT PEOPLE GET IN THEIR STOMACHS?
BA-BUMP
Eew! No way do I want one of those!
NO!!!
BA-BUMP BA-BUMP BA-BUMP
I'm talking about Shiki, not worms.
Slightly obsessive-compulsive →
THE PARASITIC TYPE HAS ITS ADVANTAGES, BUT...
IT TAKES A LOT OF ENERGY TO GET THEM INTO YOUR BODY.

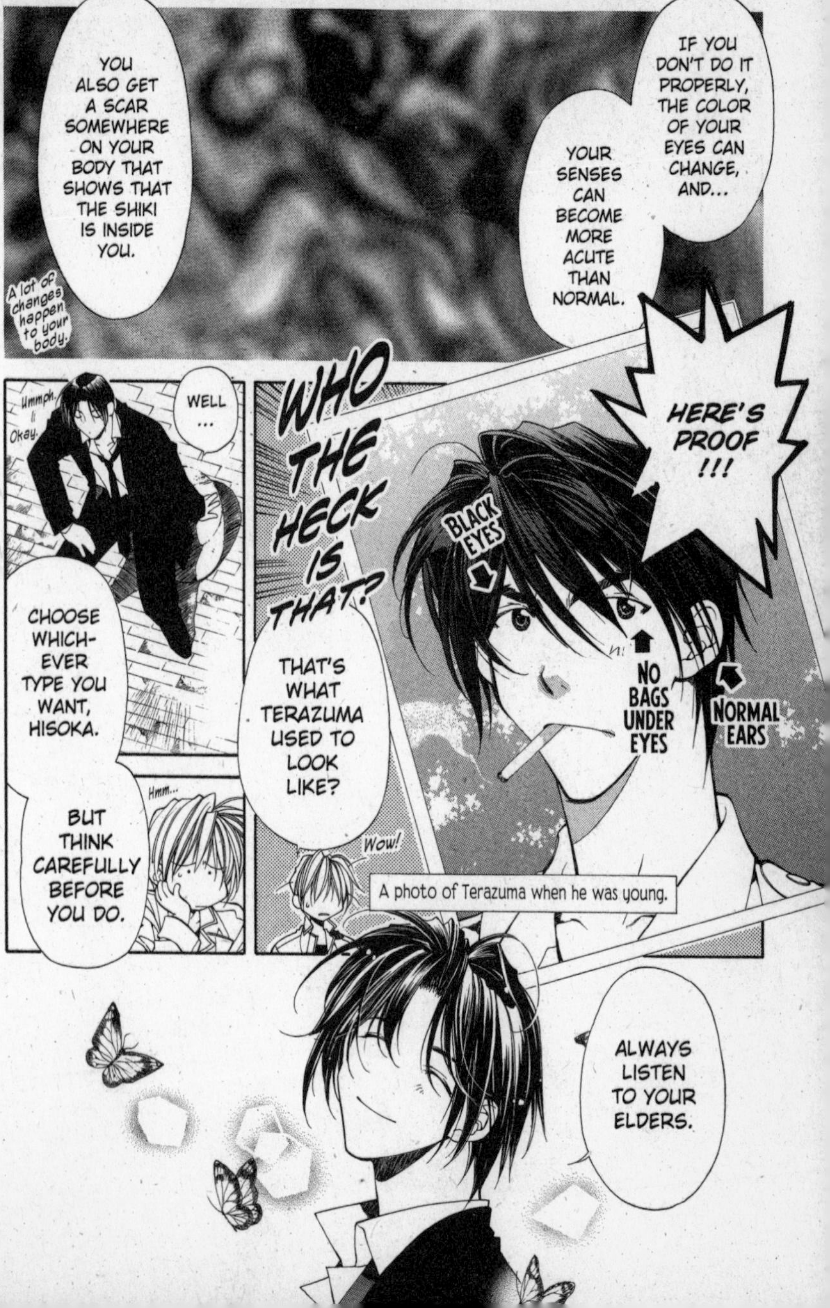
IF YOU DON'T DO IT PROPERLY, THE COLOR OF YOUR EYES CAN CHANGE, AND...
YOUR SENSES CAN BECOME MORE ACUTE THAN NORMAL.
YOU ALSO GET A SCAR SOMEWHERE ON YOUR BODY THAT SHOWS THAT THE SHIKI IS INSIDE YOU.
A lot of changes happen to your body.
HERE'S PROOF !!!
WHO THE HECK IS THAT?
BLACK EYES
NO BAGS UNDER EYES
NORMAL EARS
THAT'S WHAT TERAZUMA USED TO LOOK LIKE?
Wow!
A photo of Terazuma when he was young.
WELL ...
Ummph.
Okay.
CHOOSE WHICH-EVER TYPE YOU WANT, HISOKA.
Hmm...
BUT THINK CAREFULLY BEFORE YOU DO.
ALWAYS LISTEN TO YOUR ELDERS.

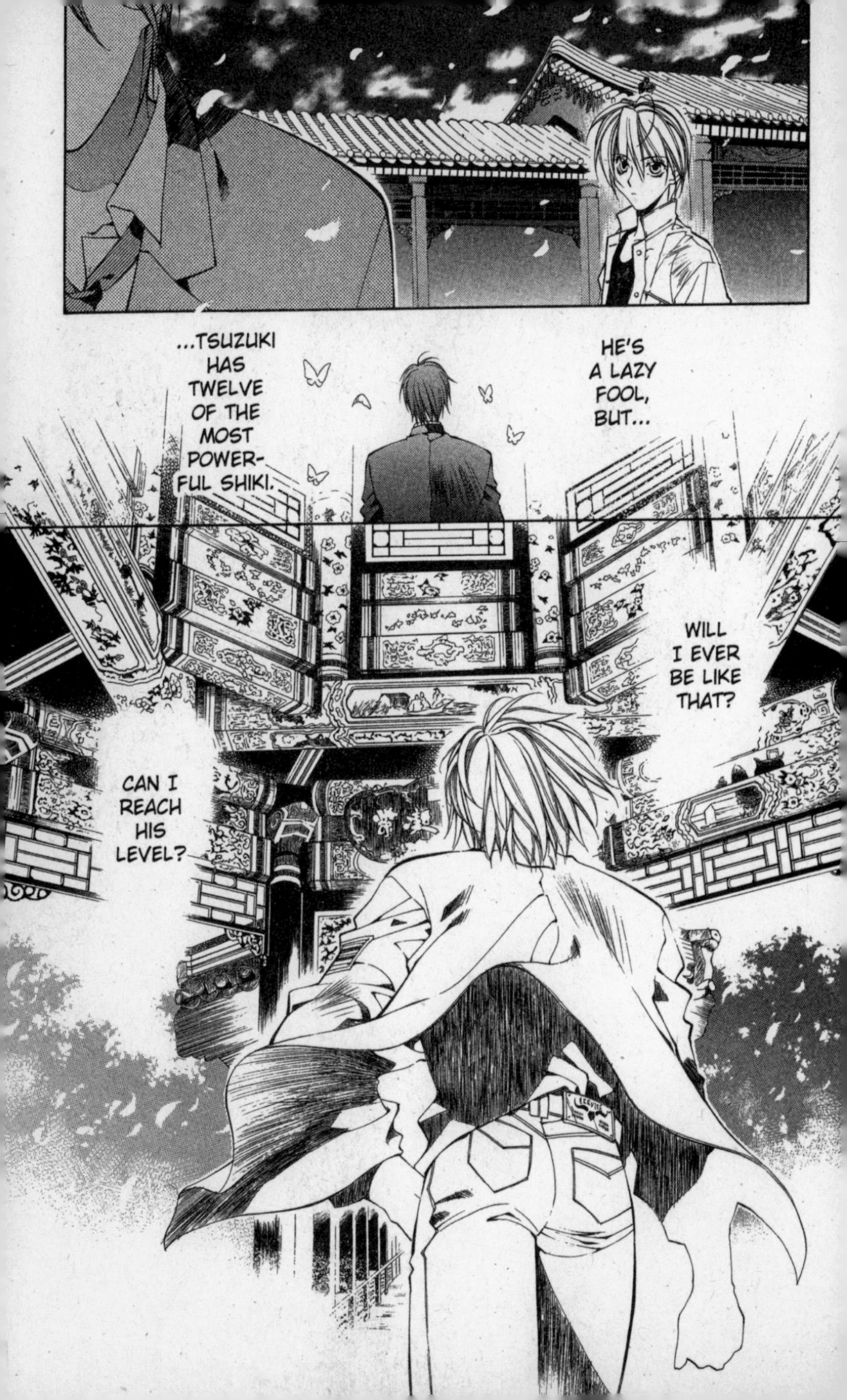
HE'S A LAZY FOOL, BUT...
...TSUZUKI HAS TWELVE OF THE MOST POWER-FUL SHIKI.
WILL I EVER BE LIKE THAT?
CAN I REACH HIS LEVEL?

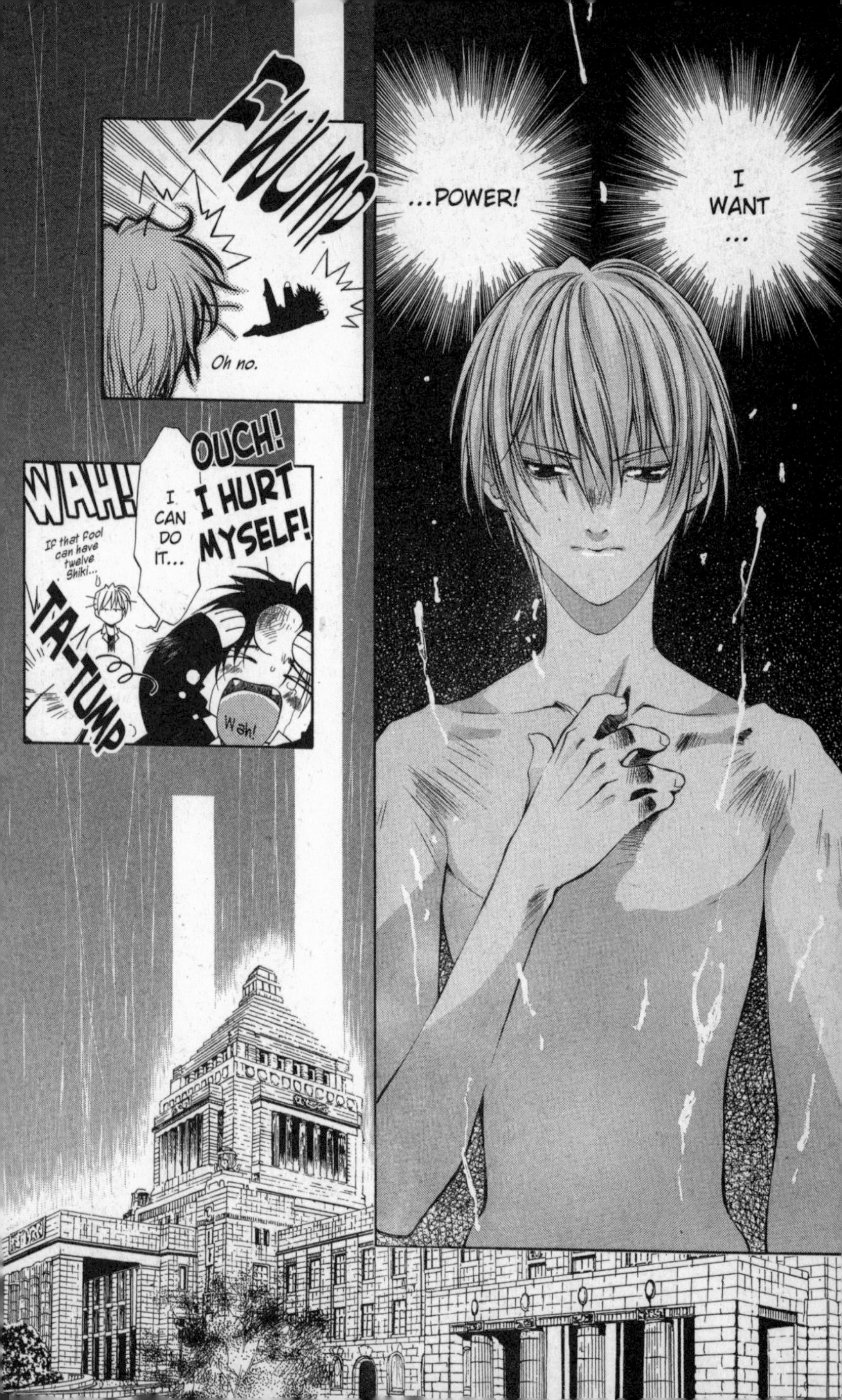
I WANT ...
...POWER!
FWUMP
Oh no.
OUCH! I HURT MYSELF!
I CAN DO IT...
WAH!
If that fool can have twelve Shiki...
TA-TUMP
Wah!

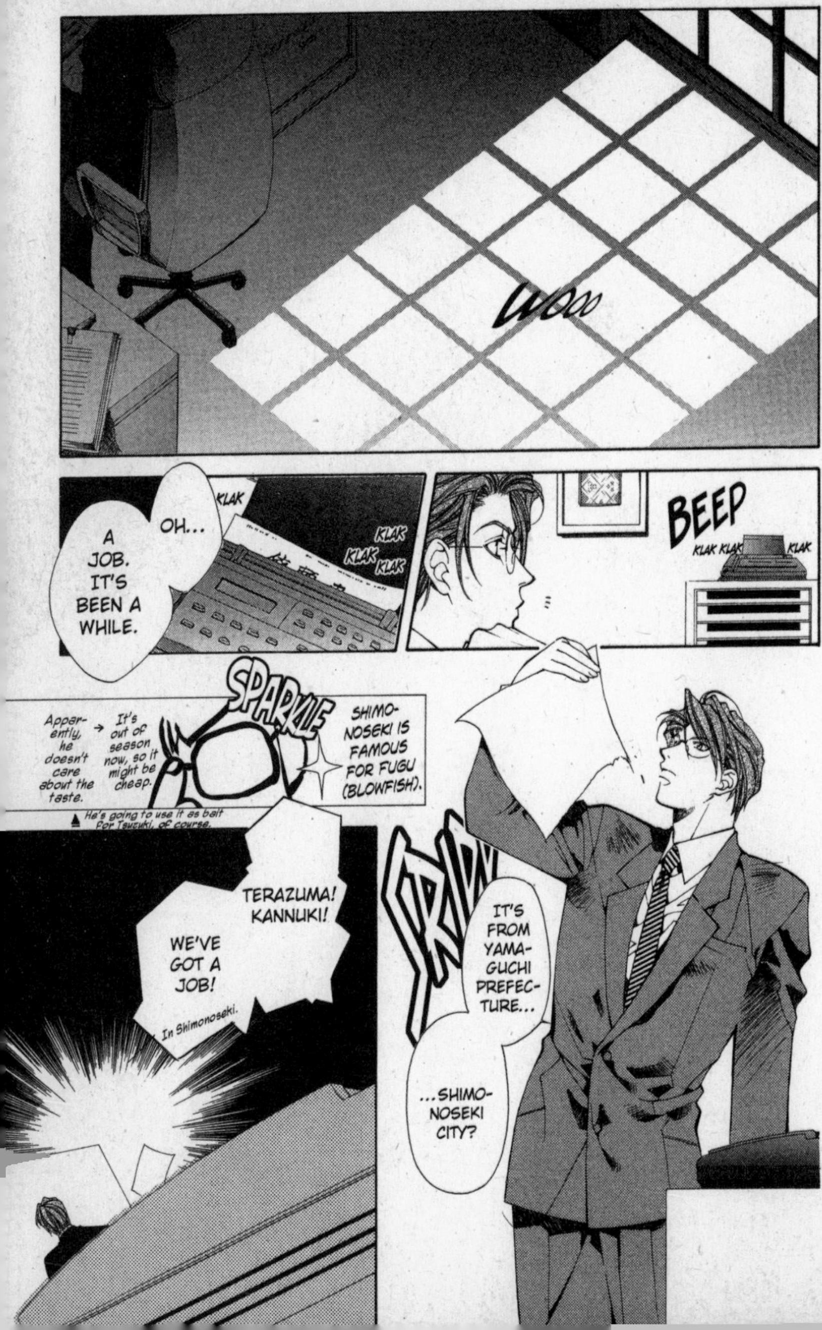
WOOO
BEEP
KLAK KLAK KLAK
KLAK
KLAK KLAK KLAK
OH...
A JOB. IT'S BEEN A WHILE.
IT'S FROM YAMAGUCHI PREFECTURE...
...SHIMONOSEKI CITY?
SHIMONOSEKI IS FAMOUS FOR FUGU (BLOWFISH).
SPARKLE
It's out of season now, so it might be cheap.
Apparently, he doesn't care about the taste.
He's going to use it as bait for Tsuzuki, of course.
TERAZUMA! KANNUKI!
WE'VE GOT A JOB!
In Shimonoseki.

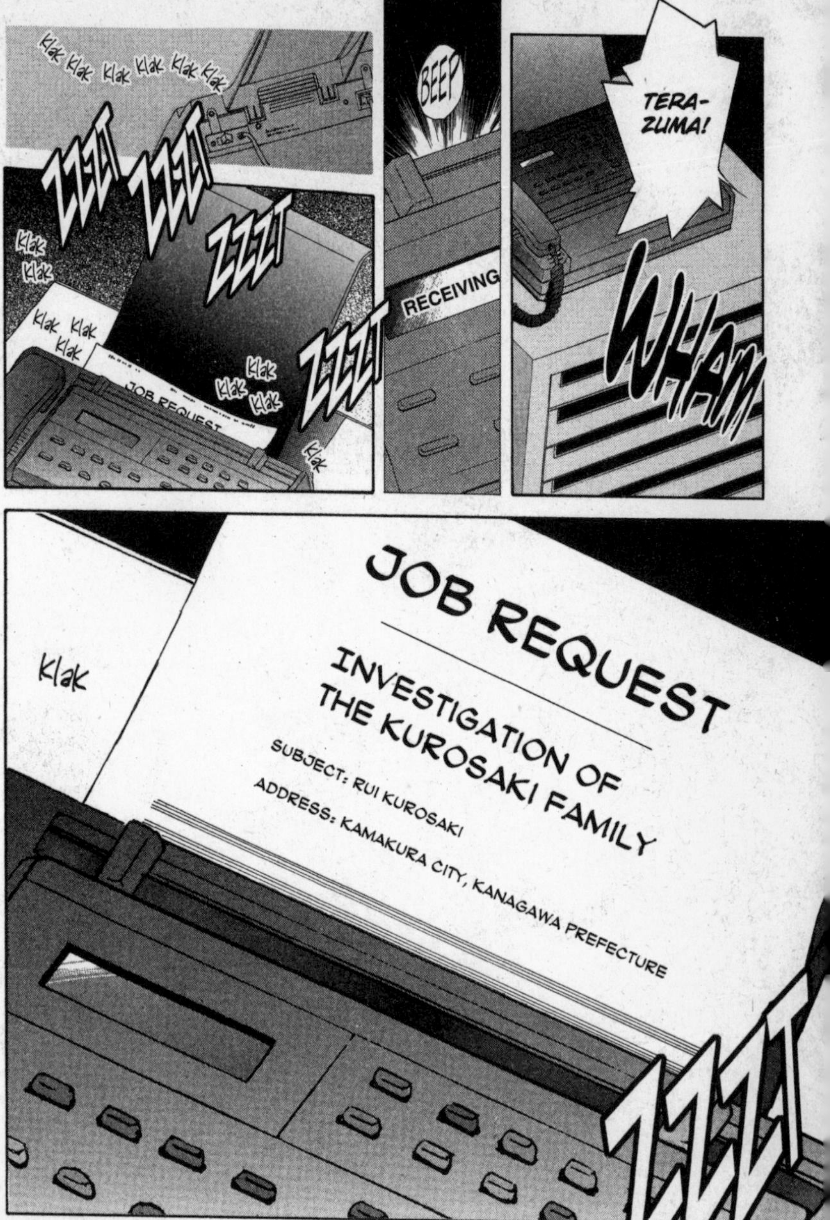
TERA-
ZUMA!
WHAM
BEEP
RECEIVING
Klak Klak Klak Klak Klak Klak
ZZZZT
ZZZZT
Klak
Klak
ZZZZT
Klak Klak
Klak
JOB REQUEST
Klak
Klak
Klak
ZZZZT
Klak
Klak
JOB REQUEST
INVESTIGATION OF
THE KUROSAKI FAMILY
SUBJECT: RUI KUROSAKI
ADDRESS: KAMAKURA CITY, KANAGAWA PREFECTURE
ZZZZT

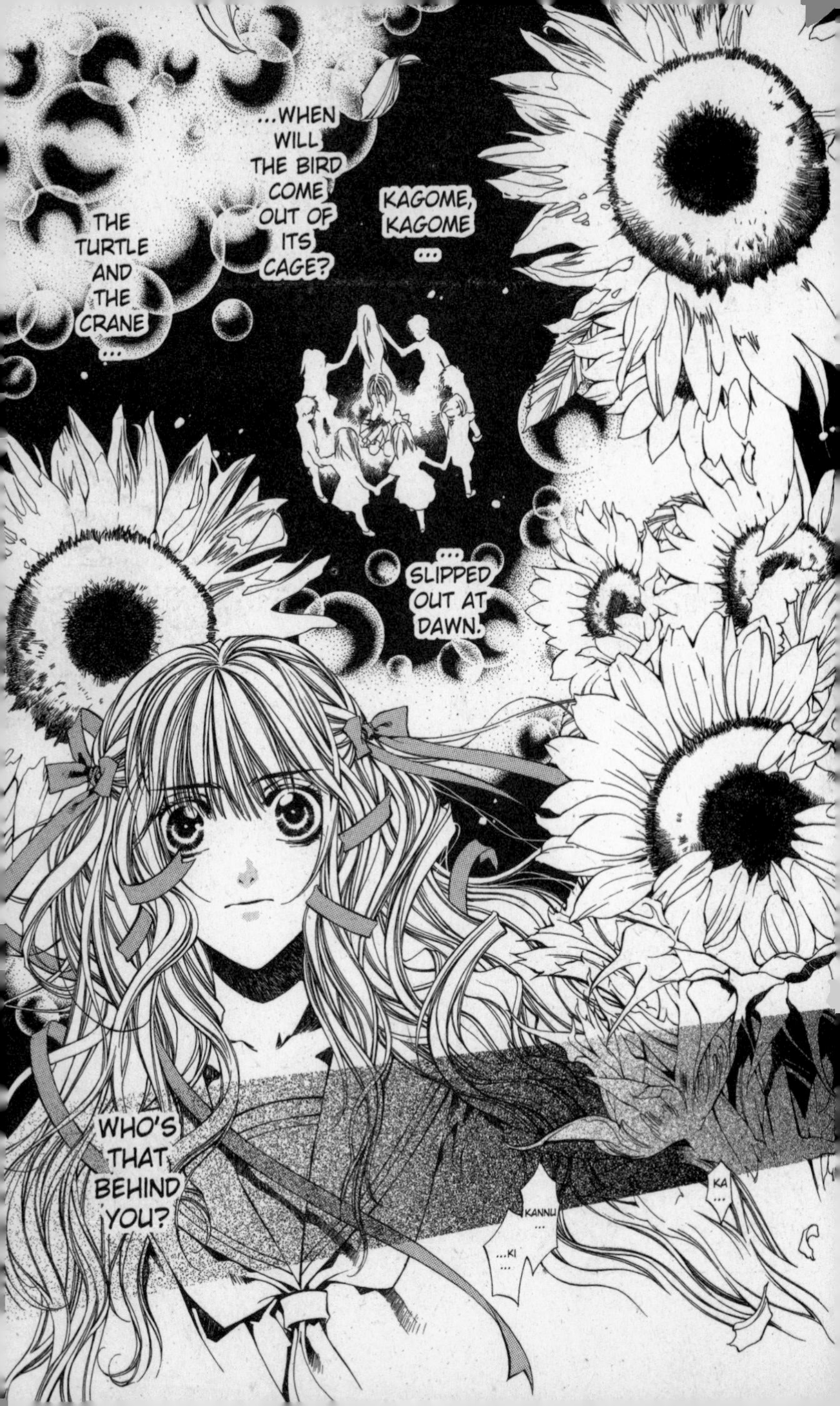
KAGOME, KAGOME ...
...WHEN WILL THE BIRD COME OUT OF ITS CAGE?
THE TURTLE AND THE CRANE ...
... SLIPPED OUT AT DAWN.
WHO'S THAT BEHIND YOU?
KA ...
KANNU ...
...KI ...

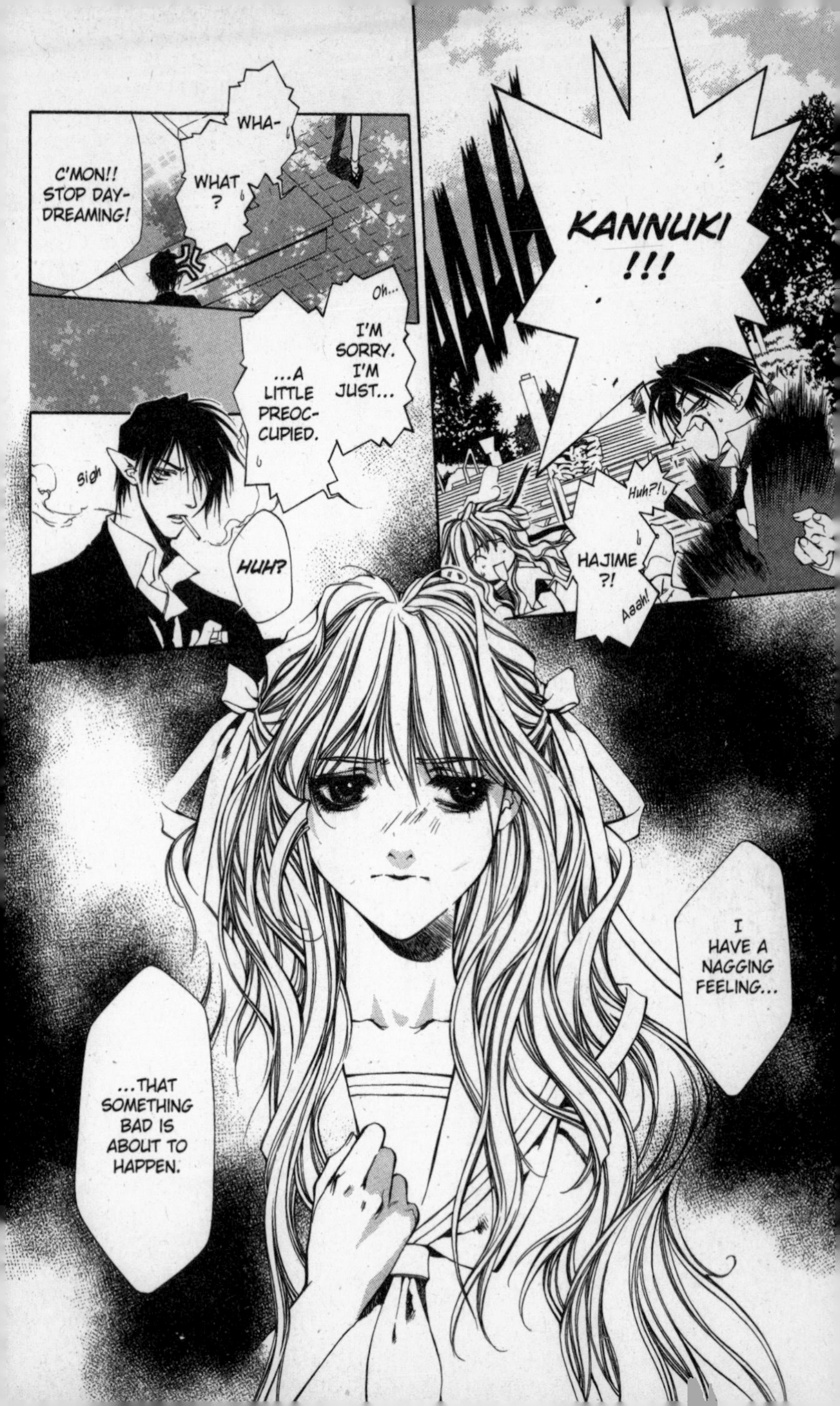
KANNUKI !!!
Huh?!
HAJIME ?!
Aaah!
WHA-
WHAT ?
C'MON!! STOP DAY-DREAMING!
Oh...
I'M SORRY. I'M JUST...
...A LITTLE PREOCCUPIED.
Sigh
HUH?
I HAVE A NAGGING FEELING...
...THAT SOMETHING BAD IS ABOUT TO HAPPEN.

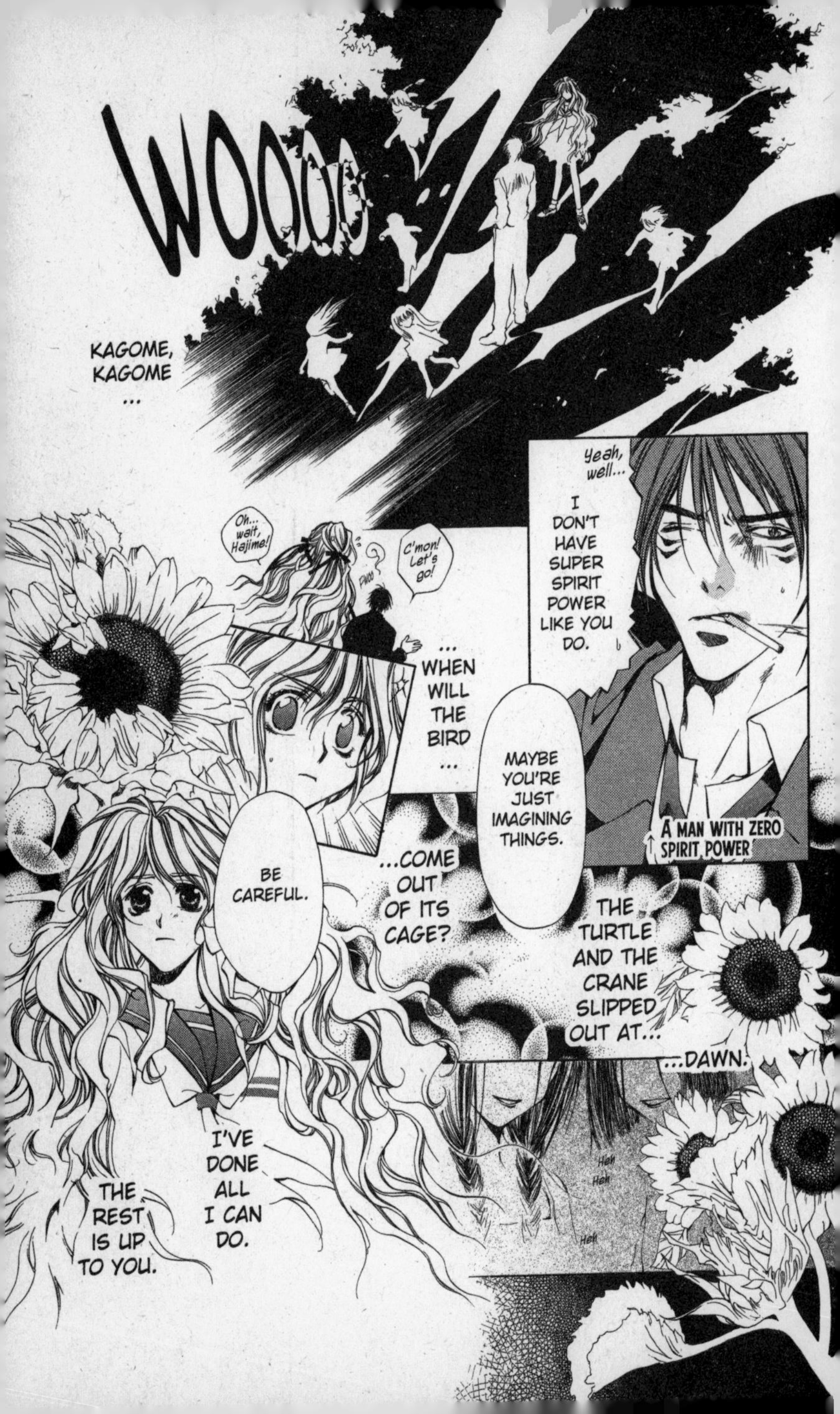
WOOOO
KAGOME, KAGOME ...
Yeah, well...
I DON'T HAVE SUPER SPIRIT POWER LIKE YOU DO.
↑ A MAN WITH ZERO SPIRIT POWER
MAYBE YOU'RE JUST IMAGINING THINGS.
C'mon! Let's go!
Oh... wait, Hajime!
... WHEN WILL THE BIRD ...
...COME OUT OF ITS CAGE?
BE CAREFUL.
THE TURTLE AND THE CRANE SLIPPED OUT AT...
...DAWN.
Heh Heh Heh
I'VE DONE ALL I CAN DO.
THE REST IS UP TO YOU.

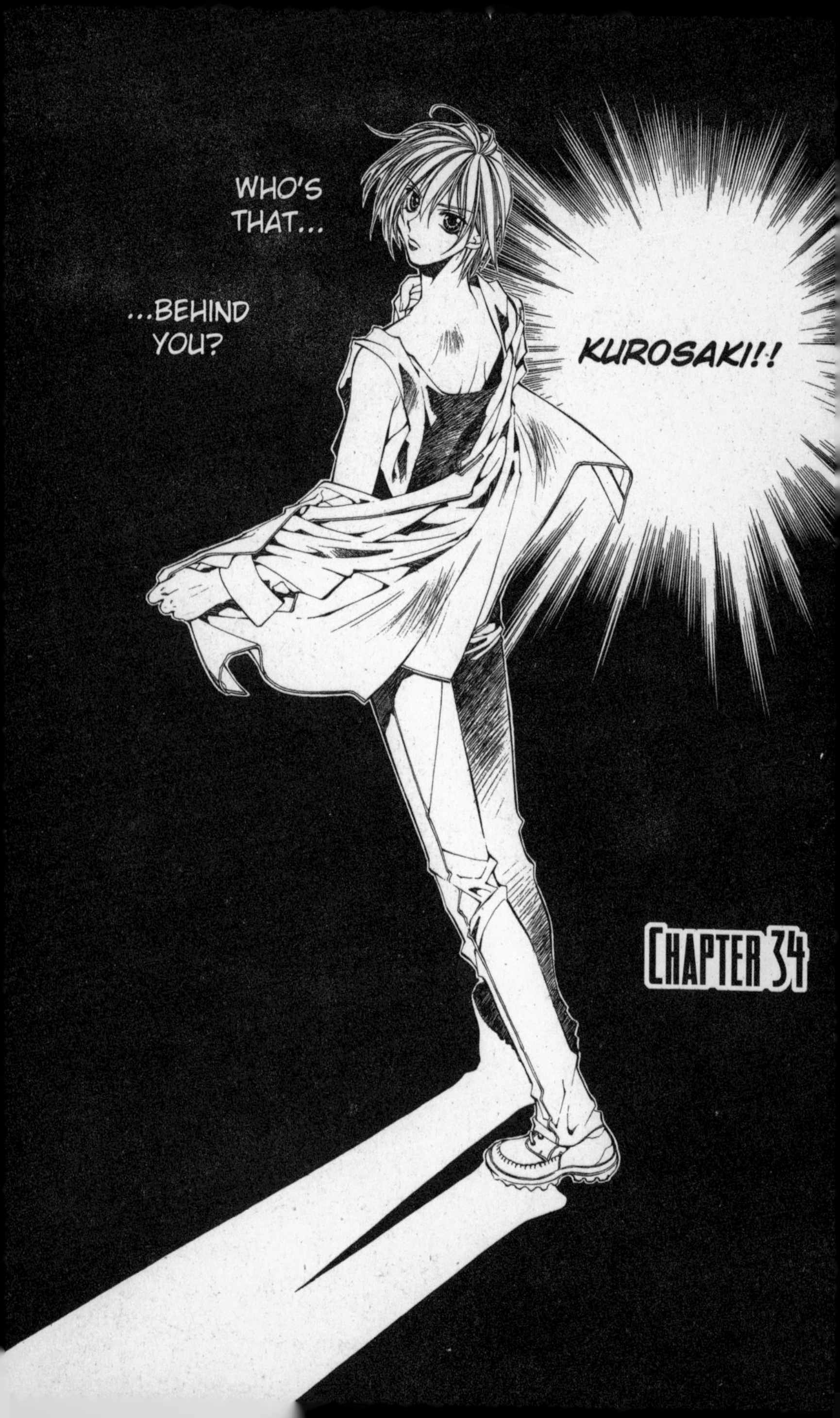
KUROSAKI!!
WHO'S THAT...
...BEHIND YOU?
CHAPTER 34

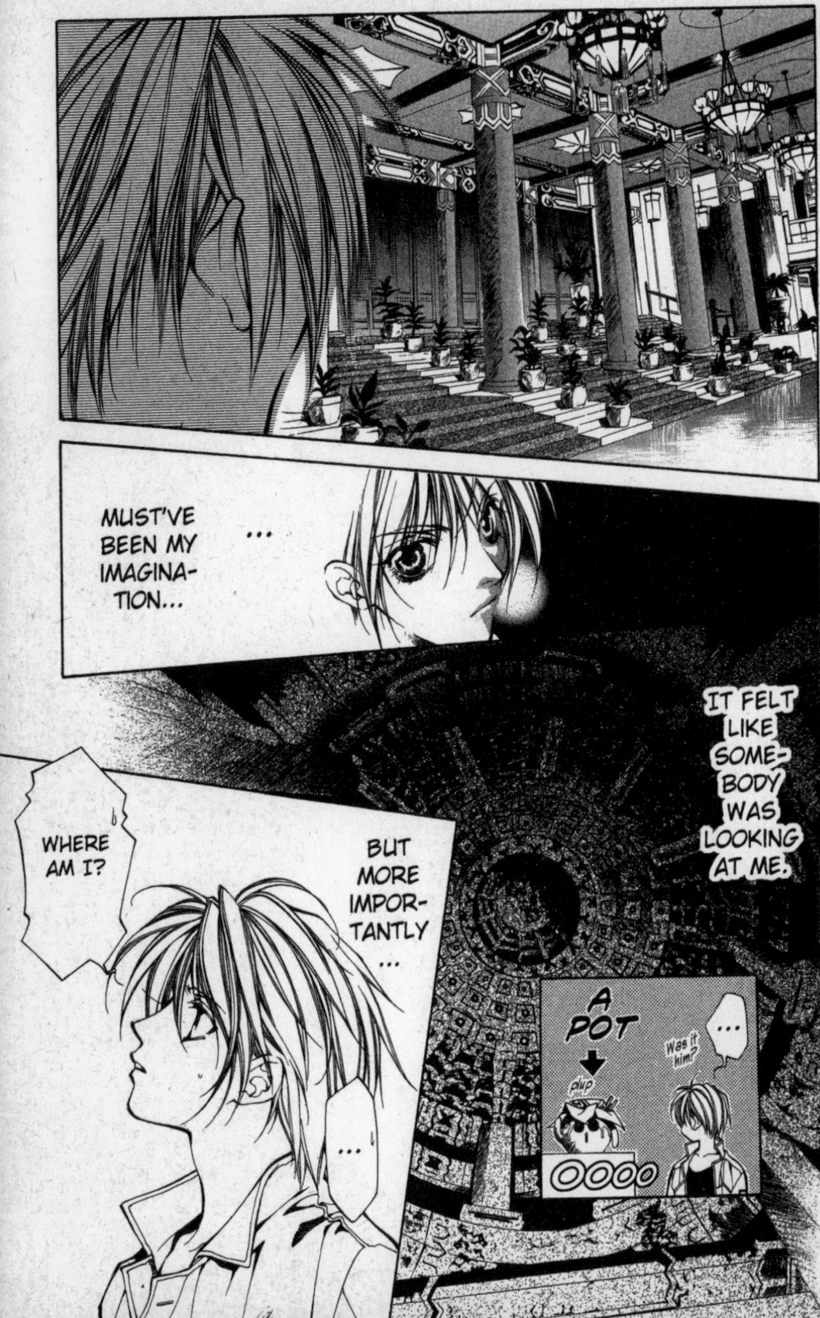
...
MUST'VE BEEN MY IMAGINATION...
IT FELT LIKE SOMEBODY WAS LOOKING AT ME.
BUT MORE IMPORTANTLY...
WHERE AM I?
...
...
Was it him?
A POT
plup
OOOO

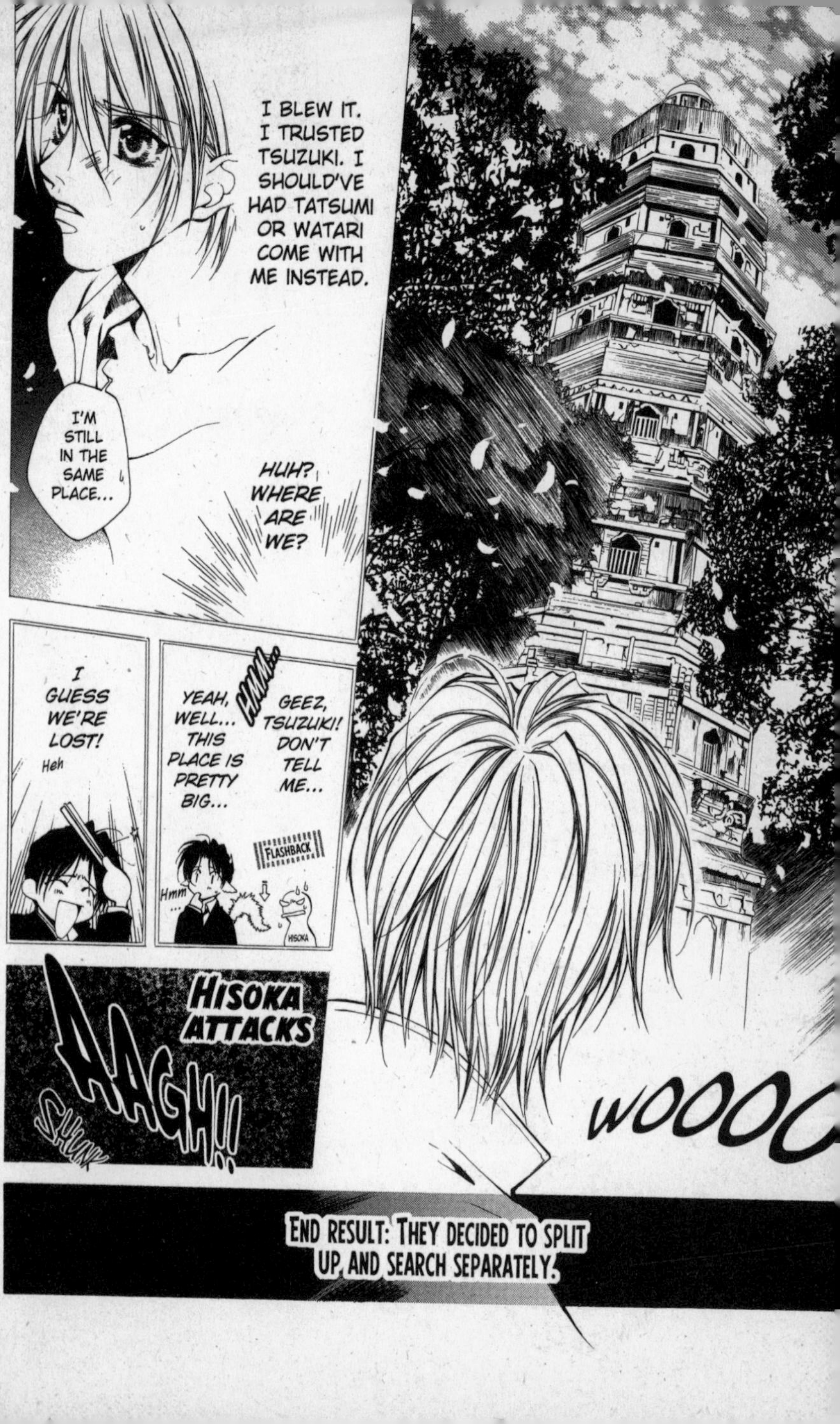
WOOO
I BLEW IT. I TRUSTED TSUZUKI. I SHOULD'VE HAD TATSUMI OR WATARI COME WITH ME INSTEAD.
I'M STILL IN THE SAME PLACE...
HUH? WHERE ARE WE?
GEEZ, TSUZUKI! DON'T TELL ME...
HMM...
YEAH, WELL... THIS PLACE IS PRETTY BIG...
FLASHBACK
Hmm
HISOKA
I GUESS WE'RE LOST!
Heh
HISOKA ATTACKS
AAGH!!
SHUK
END RESULT: THEY DECIDED TO SPLIT UP AND SEARCH SEPARATELY.

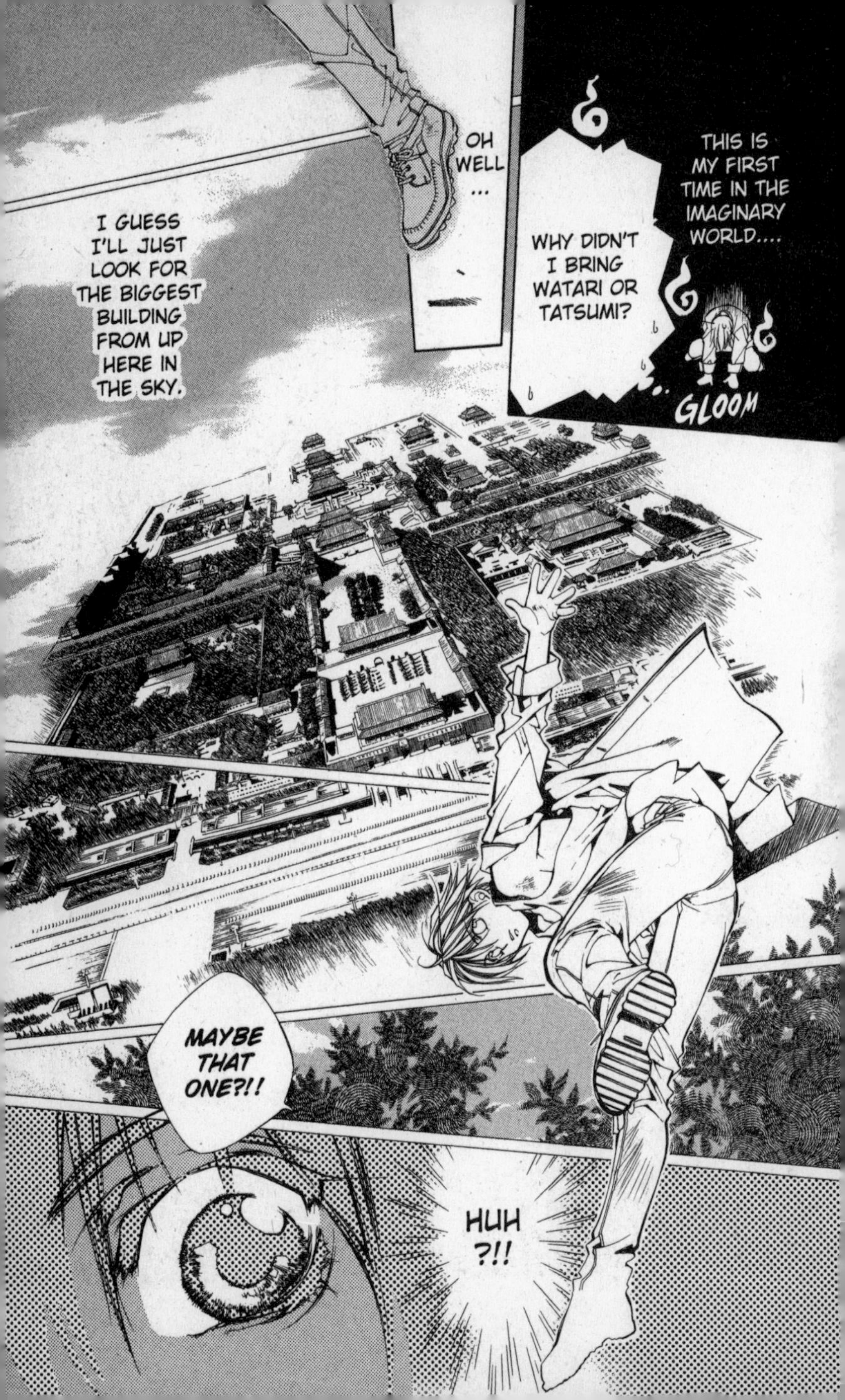
THIS IS MY FIRST TIME IN THE IMAGINARY WORLD....
WHY DIDN'T I BRING WATARI OR TATSUMI?
GLOOM
OH WELL ...
I GUESS I'LL JUST LOOK FOR THE BIGGEST BUILDING FROM UP HERE IN THE SKY.
MAYBE THAT ONE?!!
HUH ?!!

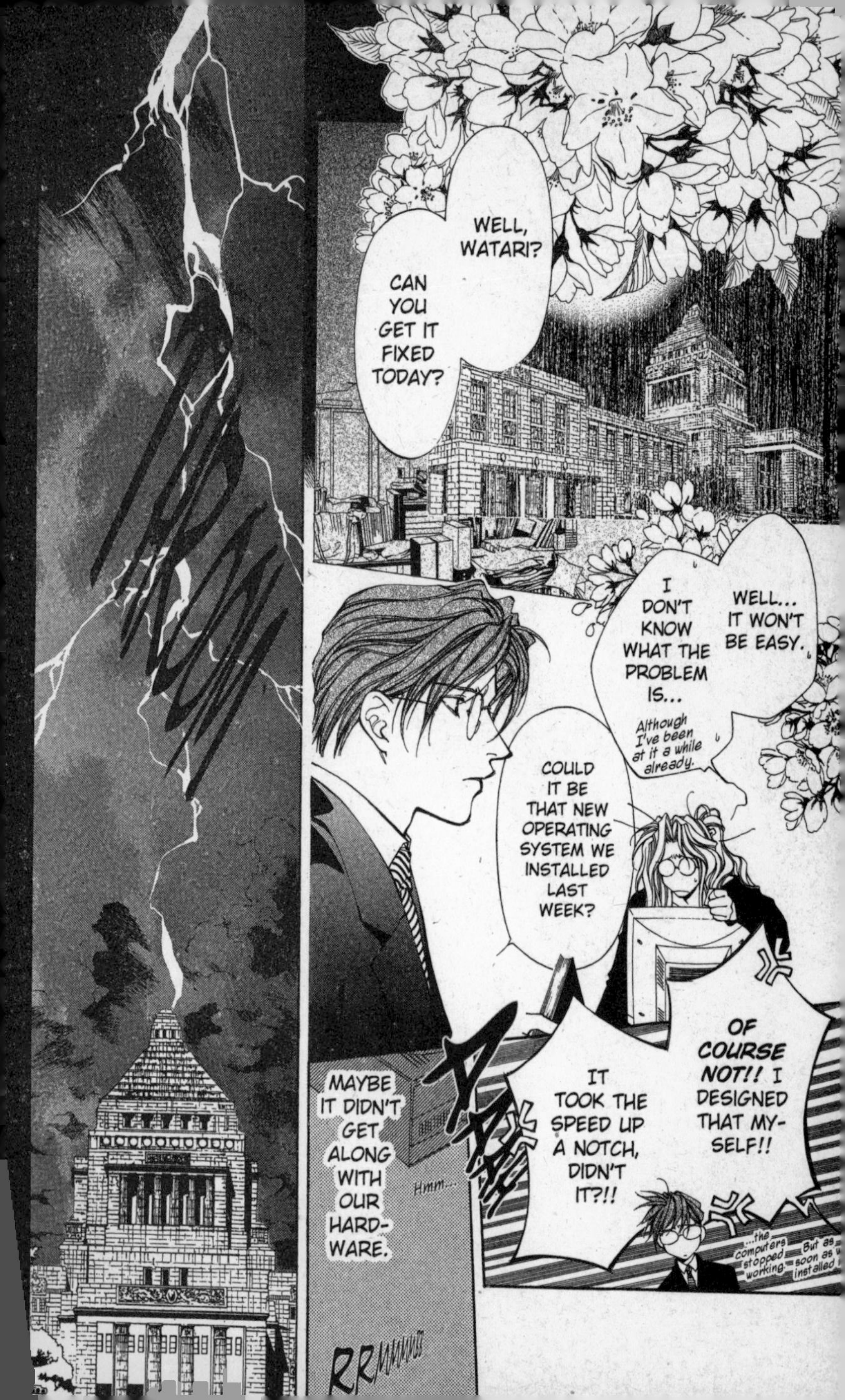
WELL, WATARI?
CAN YOU GET IT FIXED TODAY?
WELL... IT WON'T BE EASY.
I DON'T KNOW WHAT THE PROBLEM IS...
Although I've been at it a while already.
COULD IT BE THAT NEW OPERATING SYSTEM WE INSTALLED LAST WEEK?
OF COURSE NOT!! I DESIGNED THAT MY-SELF!!
IT TOOK THE SPEED UP A NOTCH, DIDN'T IT?!!
But as soon as w installed
...the computers stopped working.
MAYBE IT DIDN'T GET ALONG WITH OUR HARD-WARE.
Hmm...
RR

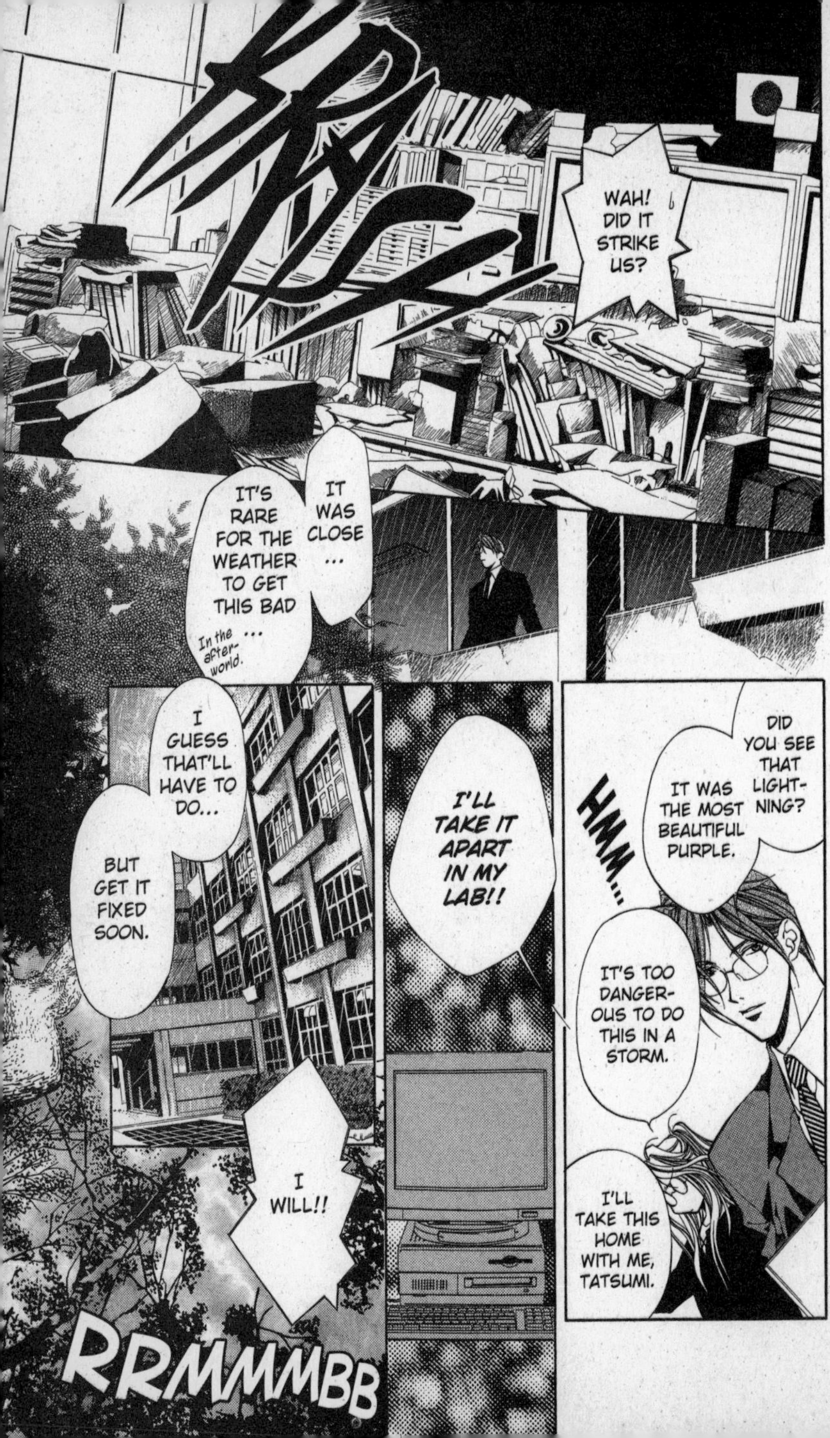
WAH! DID IT STRIKE US?
IT WAS CLOSE...
IT'S RARE FOR THE WEATHER TO GET THIS BAD...
In the after-world.
DID YOU SEE THAT LIGHT-NING?
IT WAS THE MOST BEAUTIFUL PURPLE.
HMM...
IT'S TOO DANGER-OUS TO DO THIS IN A STORM.
I'LL TAKE THIS HOME WITH ME, TATSUMI.
I'LL TAKE IT APART IN MY LAB!!
I GUESS THAT'LL HAVE TO DO...
BUT GET IT FIXED SOON.
I WILL!!
RRMMMBB

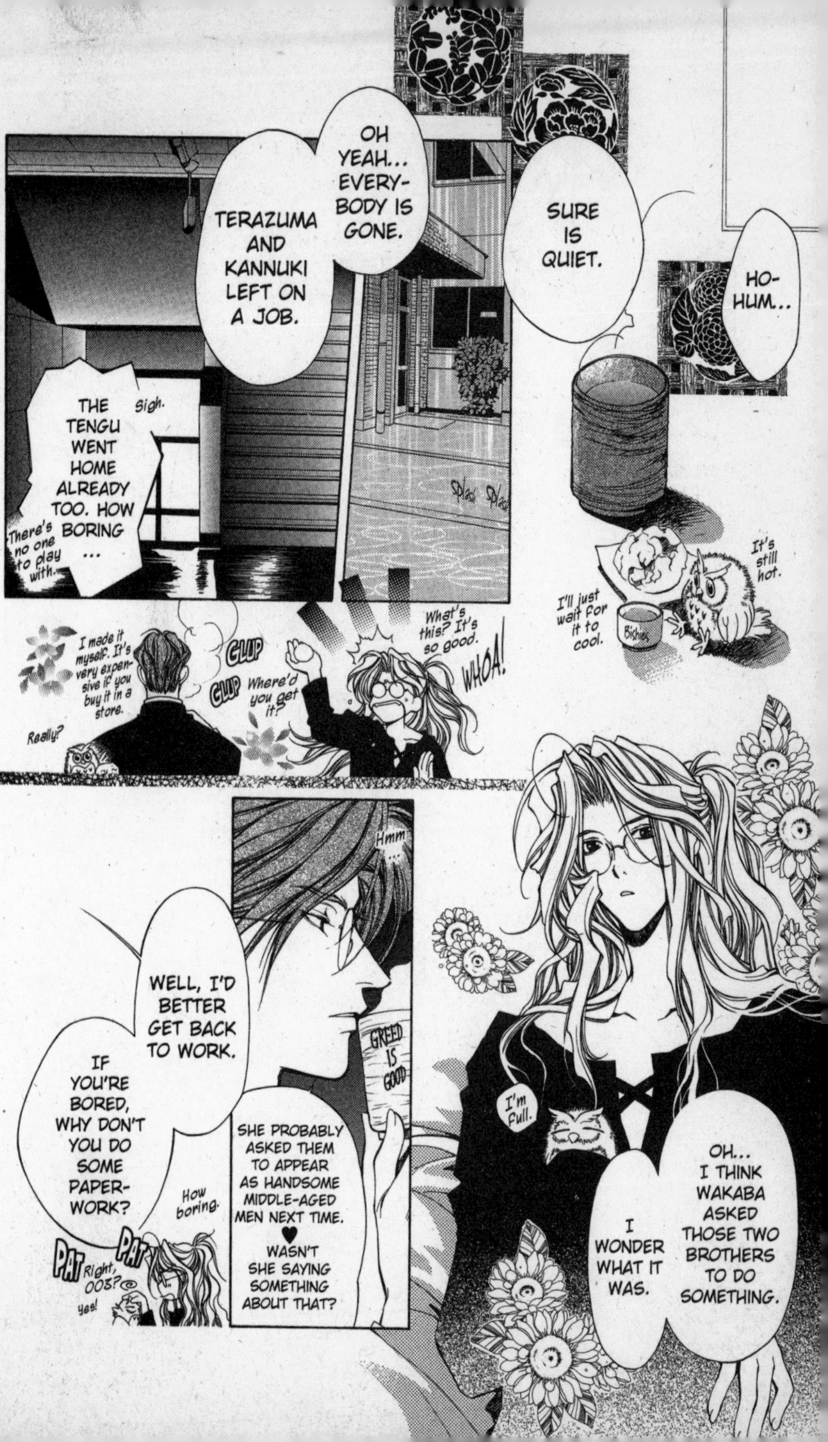
HO-HUM...
SURE IS QUIET.
OH YEAH... EVERYBODY IS GONE.
TERAZUMA AND KANNUKI LEFT ON A JOB.
Sigh.
THE TENGU WENT HOME ALREADY TOO. HOW BORING ...
There's no one to play with.
It's still hot.
I'll just wait for it to cool.
Bishies
WHOA!
What's this? It's so good.
Where'd you get it?
GLUP
GLUP
I made it myself. It's very expensive if you buy it in a store.
Really?
OH... I THINK WAKABA ASKED THOSE TWO BROTHERS TO DO SOMETHING.
I WONDER WHAT IT WAS.
I'm full.
Hmm...
SHE PROBABLY ASKED THEM TO APPEAR AS HANDSOME MIDDLE-AGED MEN NEXT TIME. ♥ WASN'T SHE SAYING SOMETHING ABOUT THAT?
GREED IS GOOD
WELL, I'D BETTER GET BACK TO WORK.
IF YOU'RE BORED, WHY DON'T YOU DO SOME PAPER-WORK?
How boring.
PAT
PAT
Right, 003?
Yes!

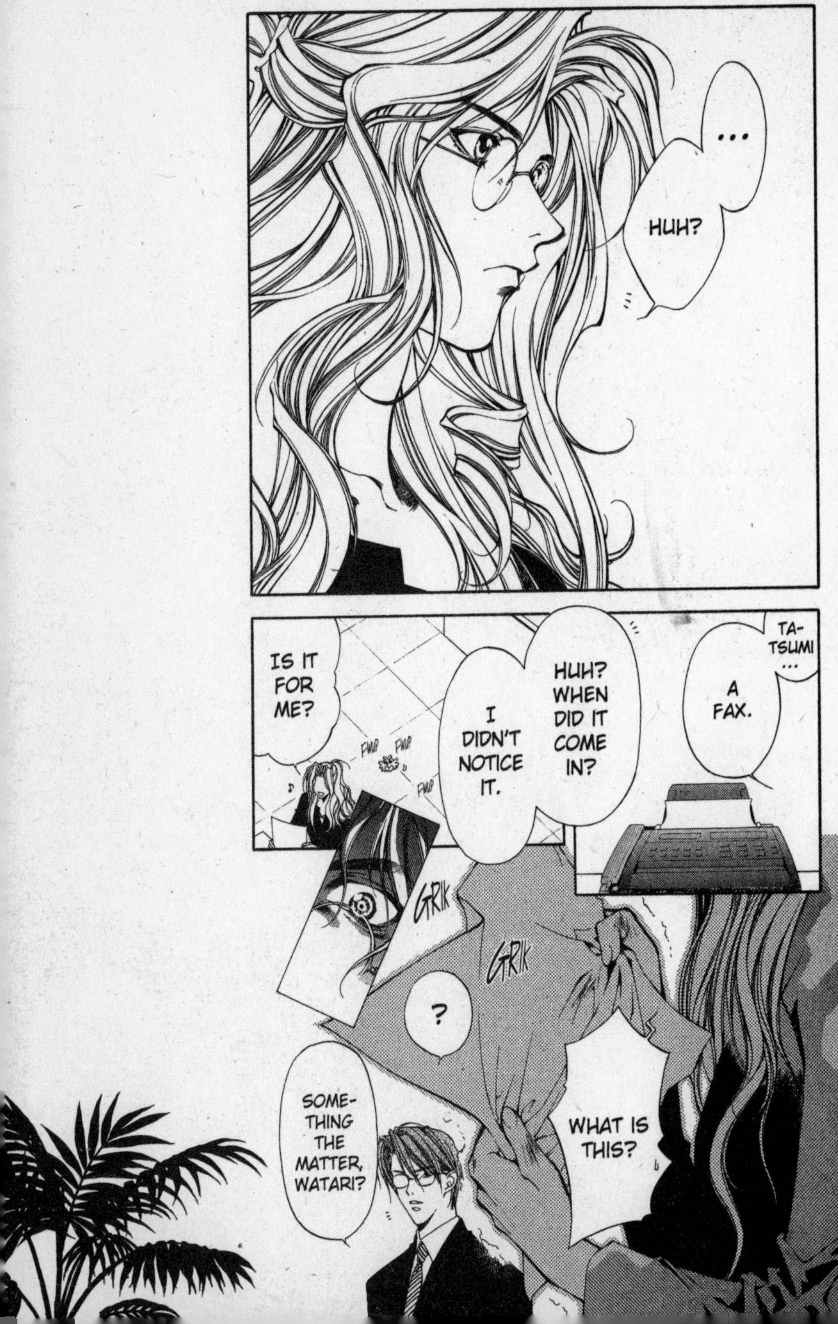
...
HUH?
TA-TSUMI...
A FAX.
HUH? WHEN DID IT COME IN?
I DIDN'T NOTICE IT.
IS IT FOR ME?
FWUP FWUP
FWUP
GRIK
GRIK
?
WHAT IS THIS?
SOME-THING THE MATTER, WATARI?

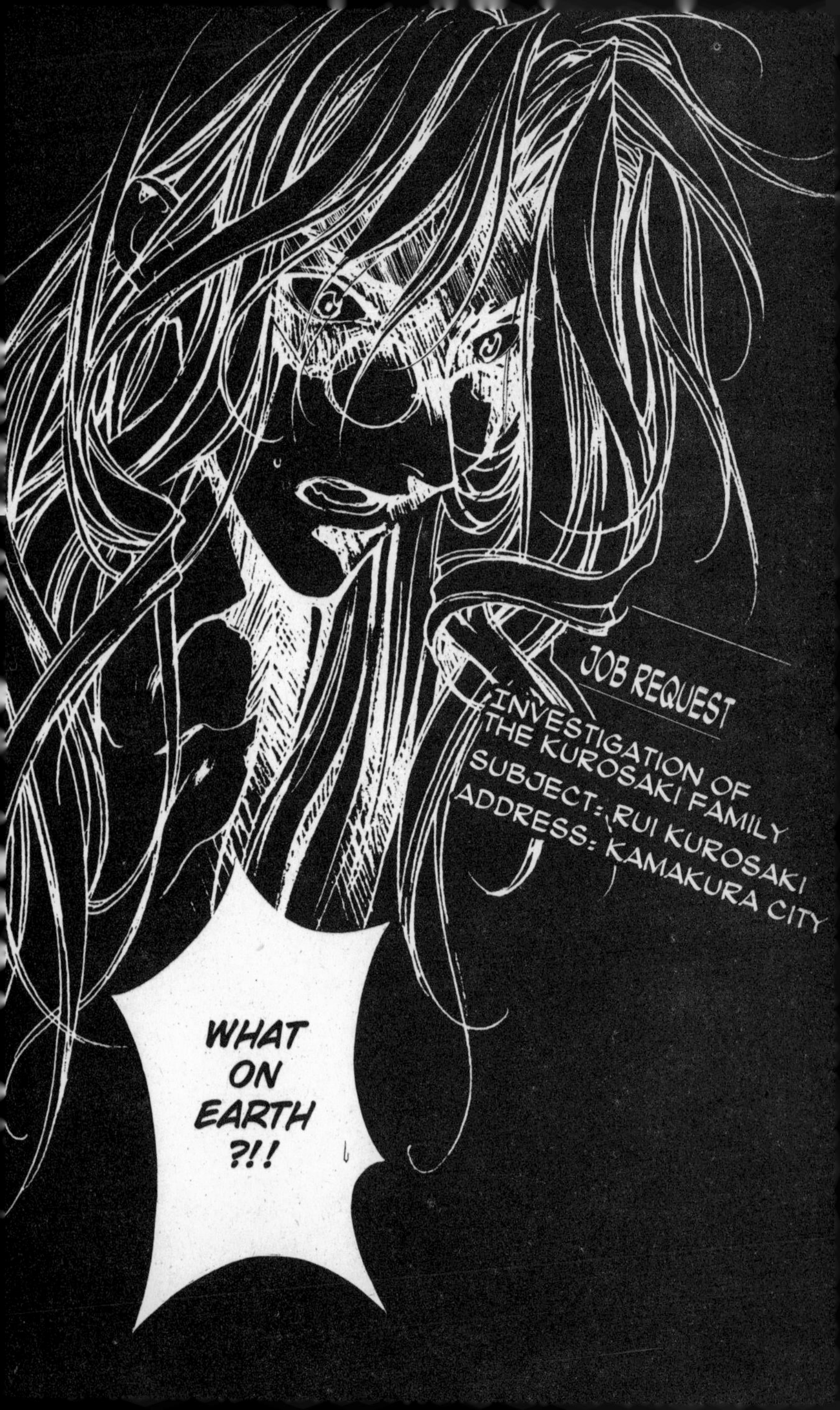
JOB REQUEST
INVESTIGATION OF THE KUROSAKI FAMILY
SUBJECT: RUI KUROSAKI
ADDRESS: KAMAKURA CITY
WHAT ON EARTH ?!!

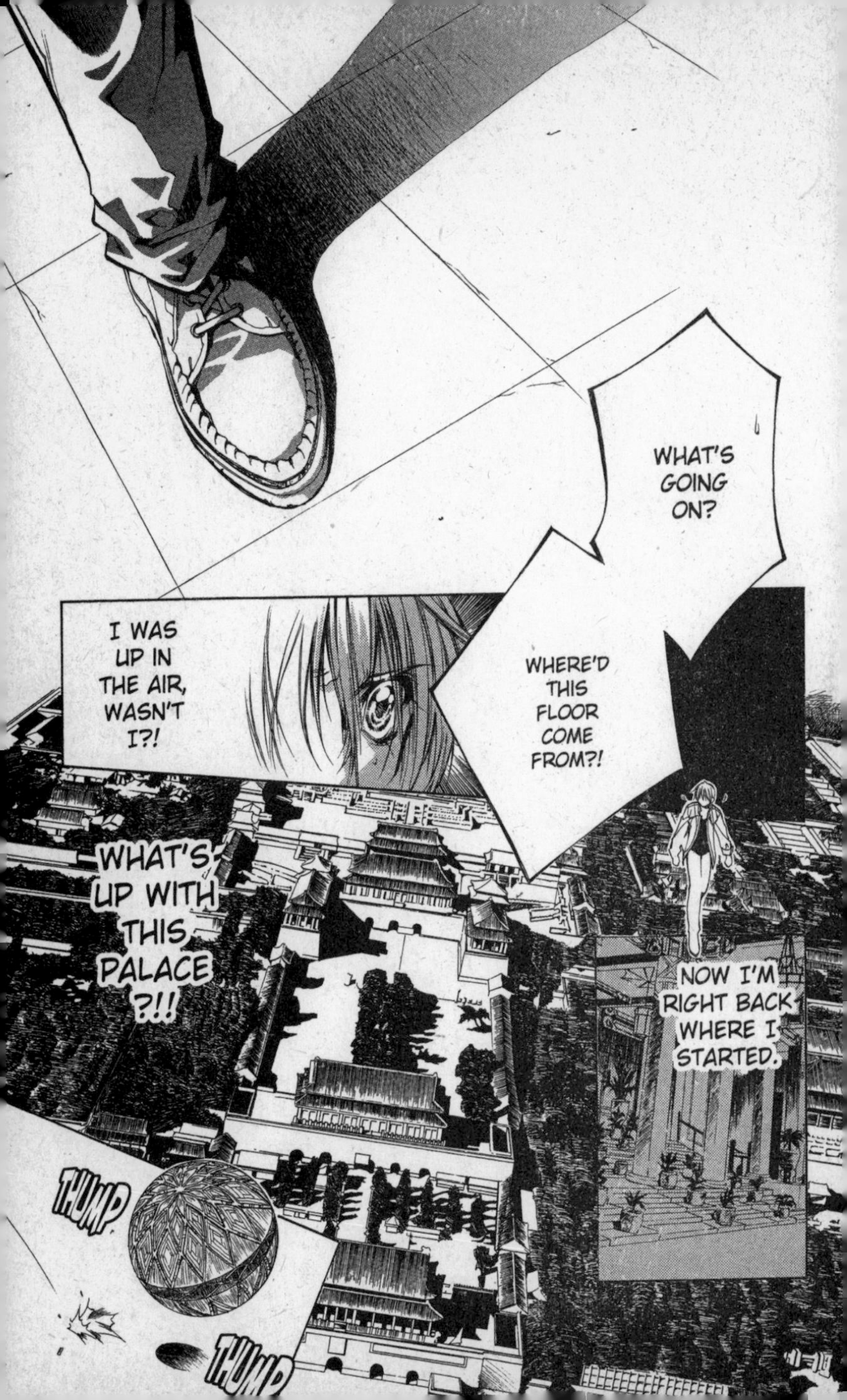
WHAT'S GOING ON?
WHERE'D THIS FLOOR COME FROM?!
I WAS UP IN THE AIR, WASN'T I?!
NOW I'M RIGHT BACK WHERE I STARTED.
WHAT'S UP WITH THIS PALACE?!!
THUMP
THUMP

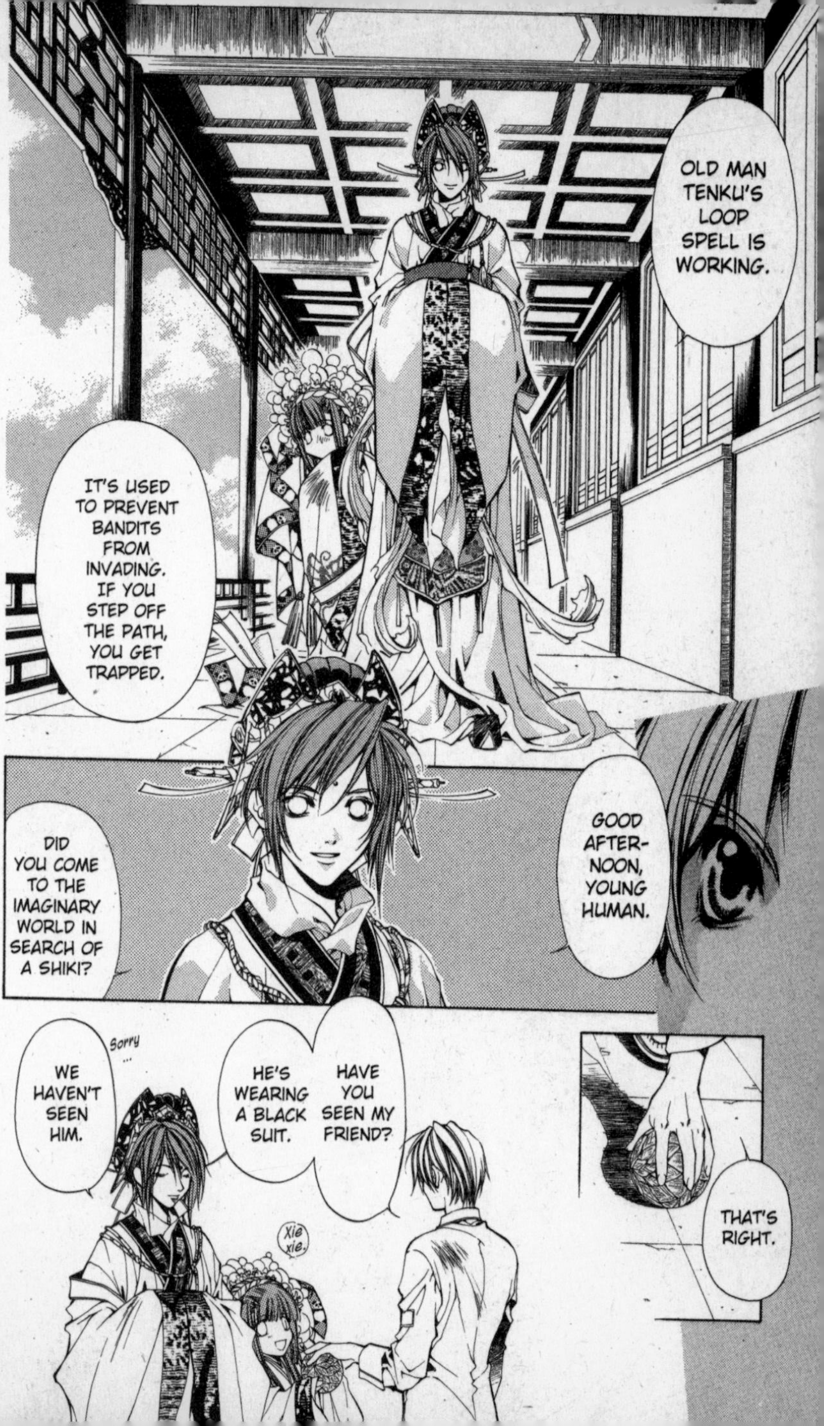
OLD MAN TENKU'S LOOP SPELL IS WORKING.
IT'S USED TO PREVENT BANDITS FROM INVADING. IF YOU STEP OFF THE PATH, YOU GET TRAPPED.
GOOD AFTERNOON, YOUNG HUMAN.
DID YOU COME TO THE IMAGINARY WORLD IN SEARCH OF A SHIKI?
THAT'S RIGHT.
HAVE YOU SEEN MY FRIEND?
HE'S WEARING A BLACK SUIT.
Sorry...
WE HAVEN'T SEEN HIM.
Xie xie.

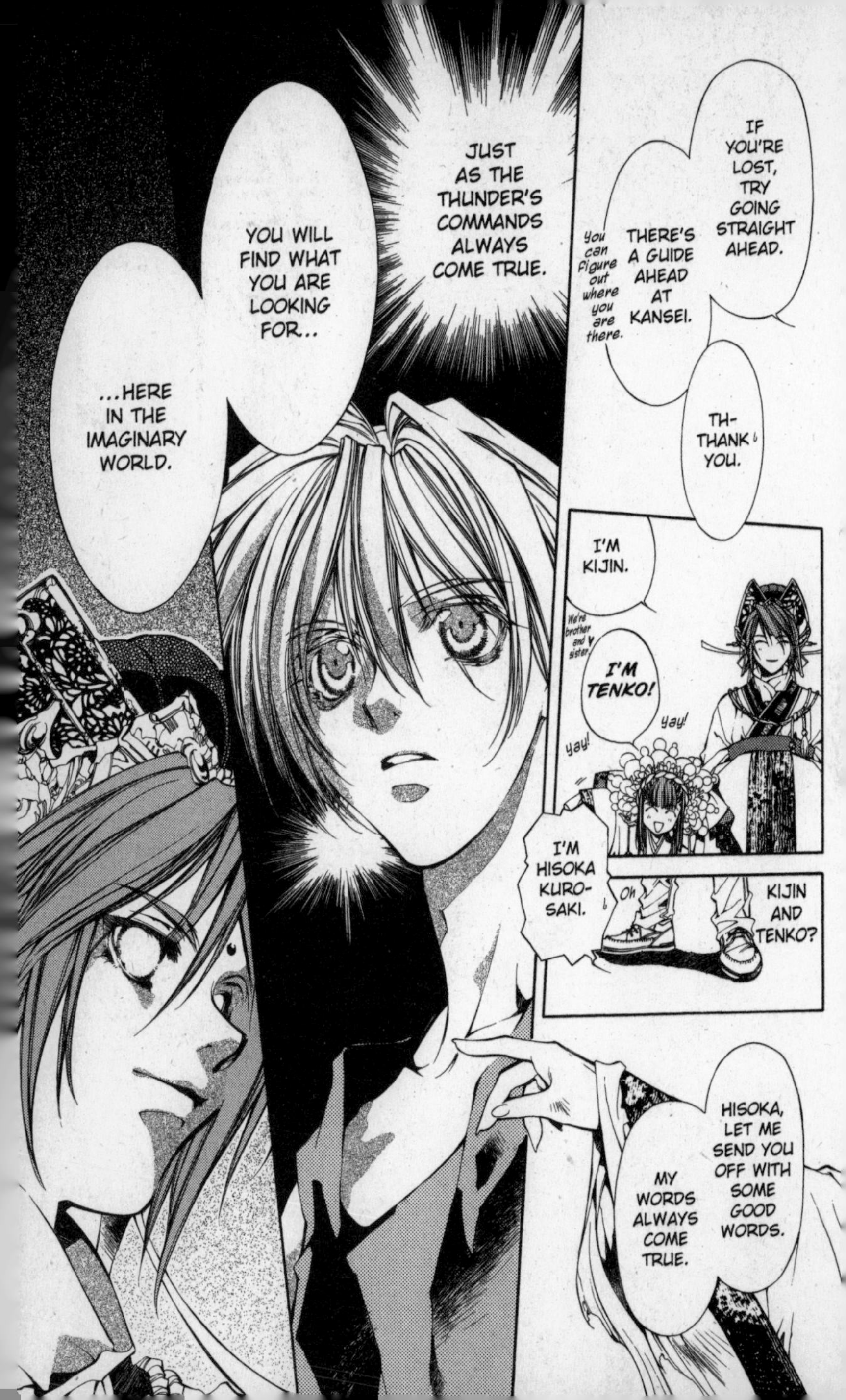
IF YOU'RE LOST, TRY GOING STRAIGHT AHEAD.
THERE'S A GUIDE AHEAD AT KANSEI.
You can figure out where you are there.
TH-THANK YOU.
I'M KIJIN.
We're brother and sister
I'M TENKO!
yay!
yay!
KIJIN AND TENKO?
Oh
I'M HISOKA KURO-SAKI.
HISOKA, LET ME SEND YOU OFF WITH SOME GOOD WORDS.
MY WORDS ALWAYS COME TRUE.
JUST AS THE THUNDER'S COMMANDS ALWAYS COME TRUE.
YOU WILL FIND WHAT YOU ARE LOOKING FOR...
...HERE IN THE IMAGINARY WORLD.

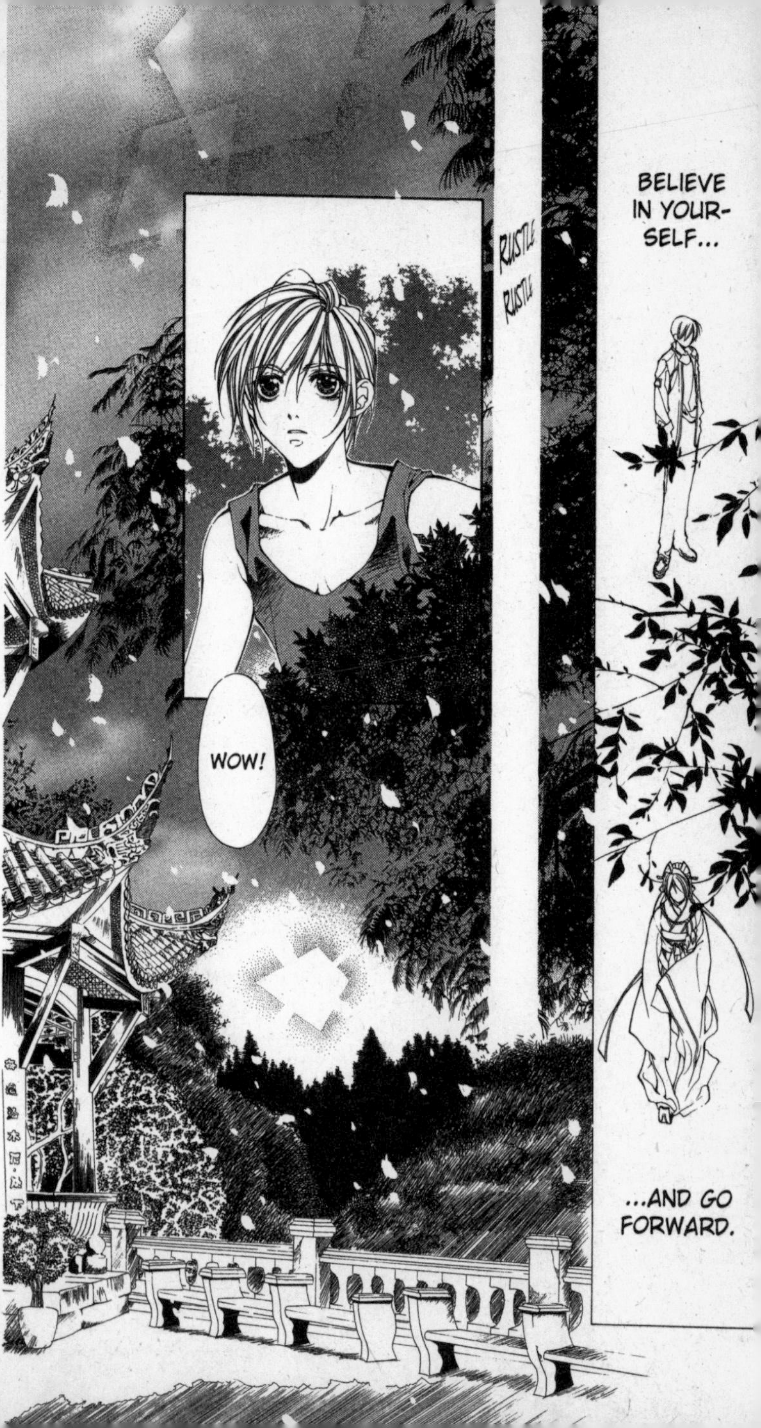
BELIEVE IN YOURSELF...
...AND GO FORWARD.
RUSTLE RUSTLE
WOW!

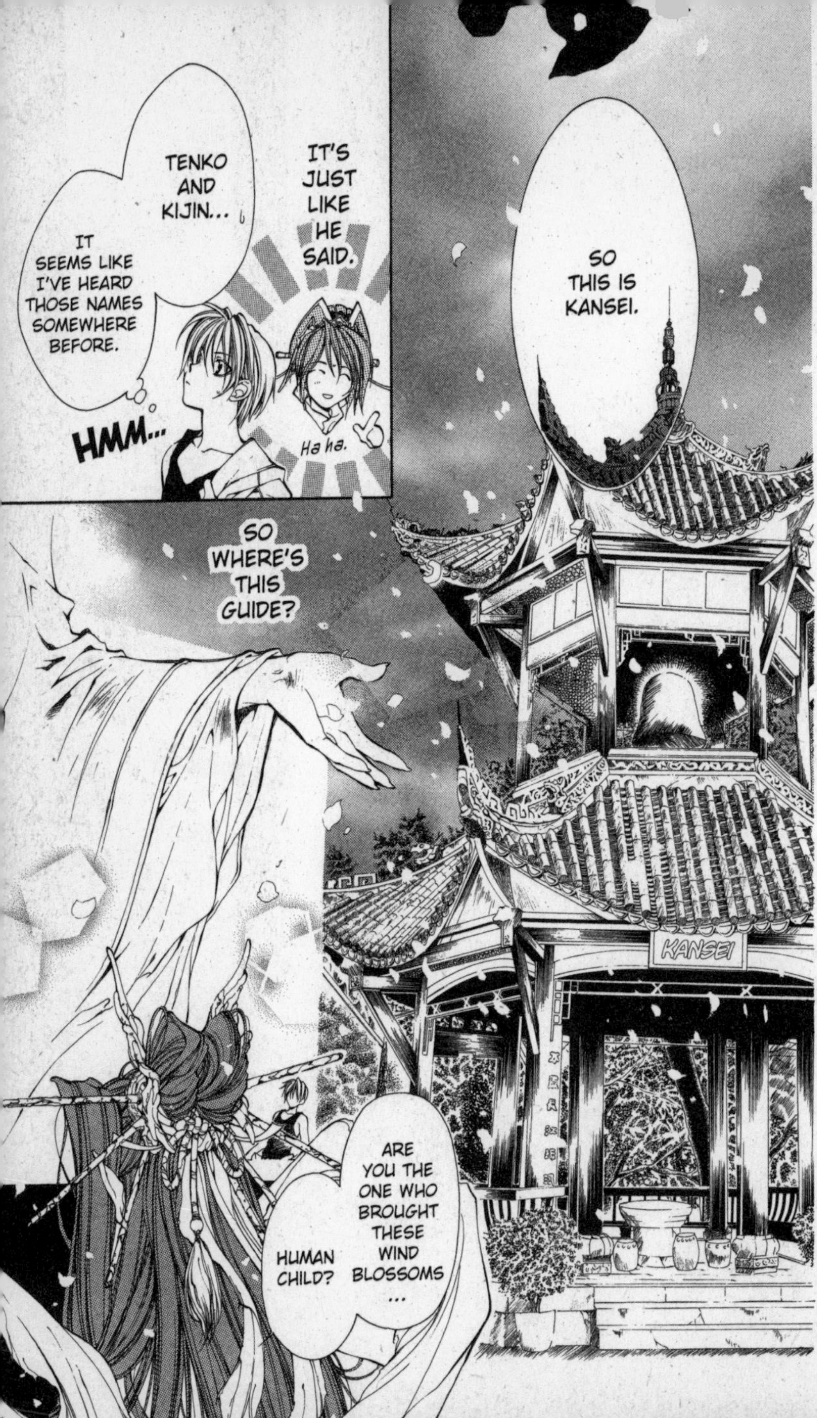
SO THIS IS KANSEI.
KANSEI
IT'S JUST LIKE HE SAID.
TENKO AND KIJIN...
IT SEEMS LIKE I'VE HEARD THOSE NAMES SOMEWHERE BEFORE.
Ha ha.
HMM...
SO WHERE'S THIS GUIDE?
ARE YOU THE ONE WHO BROUGHT THESE WIND BLOSSOMS...
HUMAN CHILD?

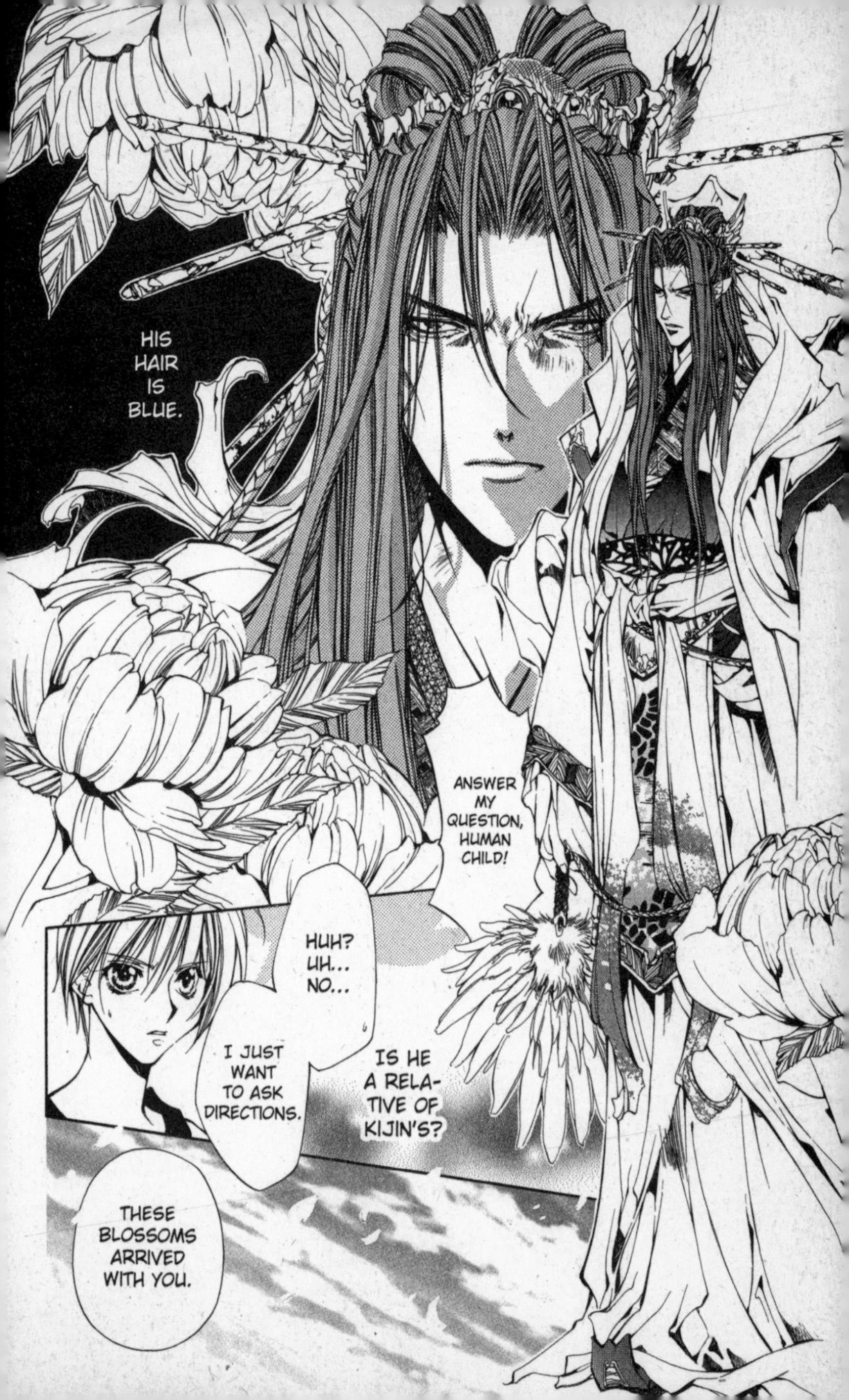
HIS HAIR IS BLUE.
ANSWER MY QUESTION, HUMAN CHILD!
HUH? UH... NO...
I JUST WANT TO ASK DIRECTIONS.
IS HE A RELA-TIVE OF KIJIN'S?
THESE BLOSSOMS ARRIVED WITH YOU.

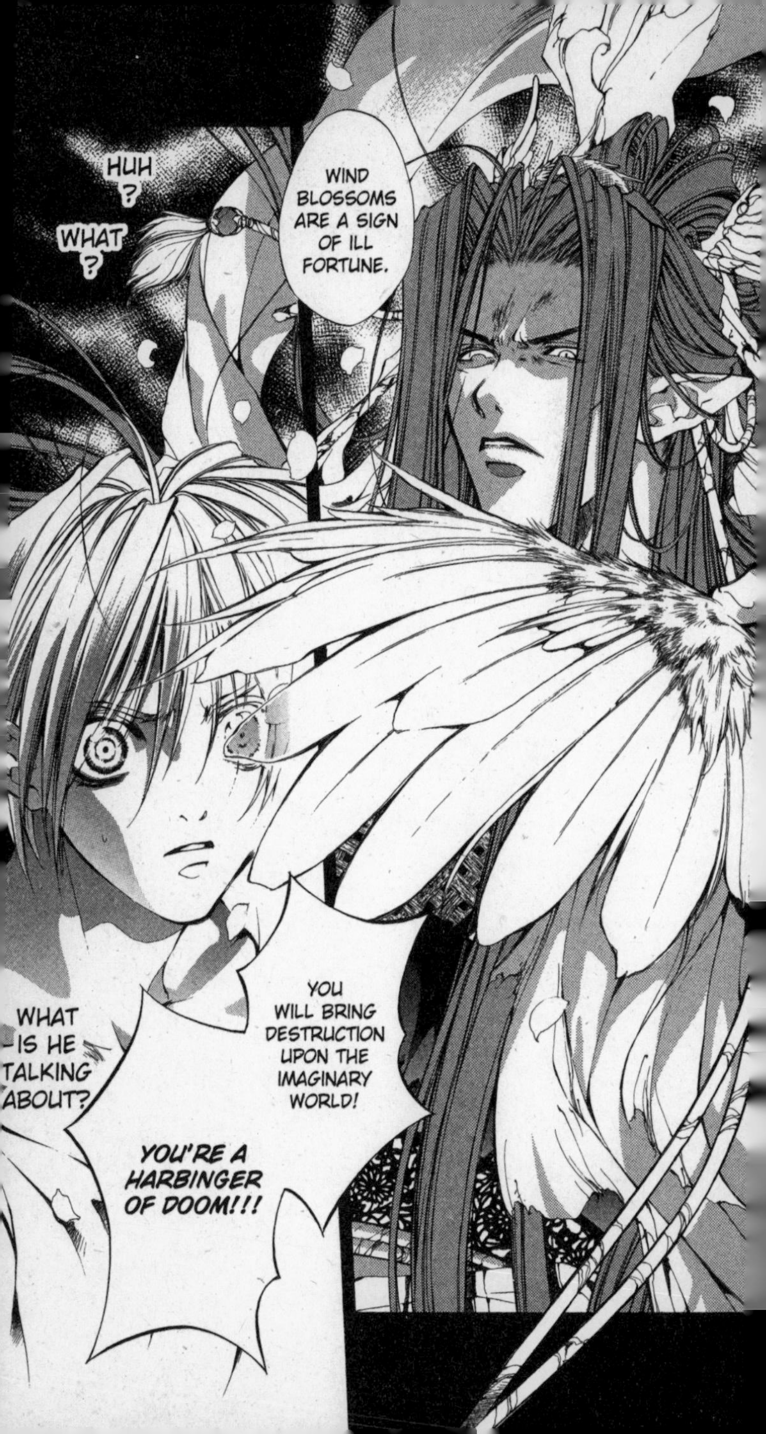
WIND BLOSSOMS ARE A SIGN OF ILL FORTUNE.
HUH?
WHAT?
YOU WILL BRING DESTRUCTION UPON THE IMAGINARY WORLD!
WHAT IS HE TALKING ABOUT?
YOU'RE A HARBINGER OF DOOM!!!

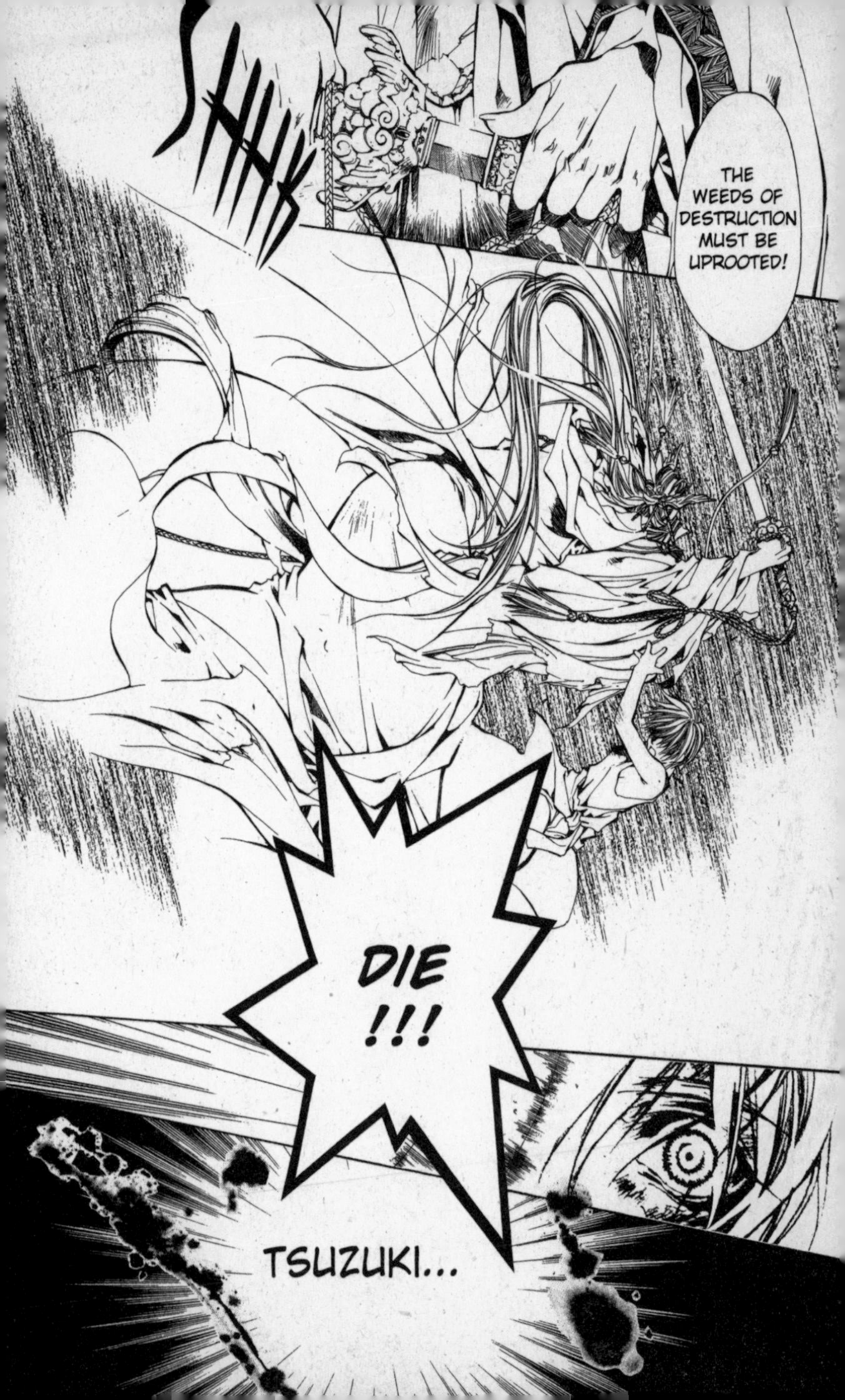
THE WEEDS OF DESTRUCTION MUST BE UPROOTED!
SHHK
DIE !!!
TSUZUKI...

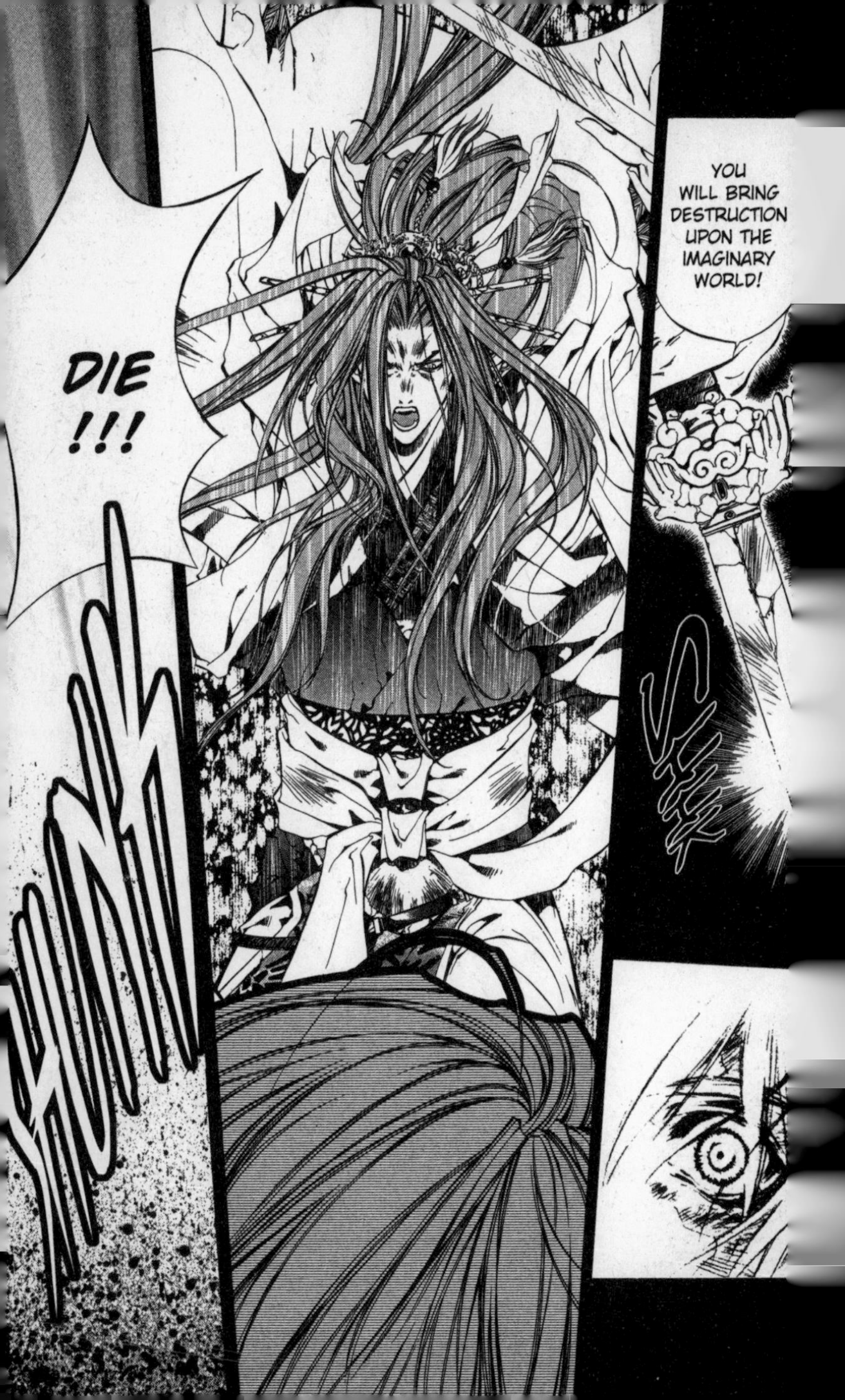
YOU WILL BRING DESTRUCTION UPON THE IMAGINARY WORLD!
DIE !!!

Chapter 35

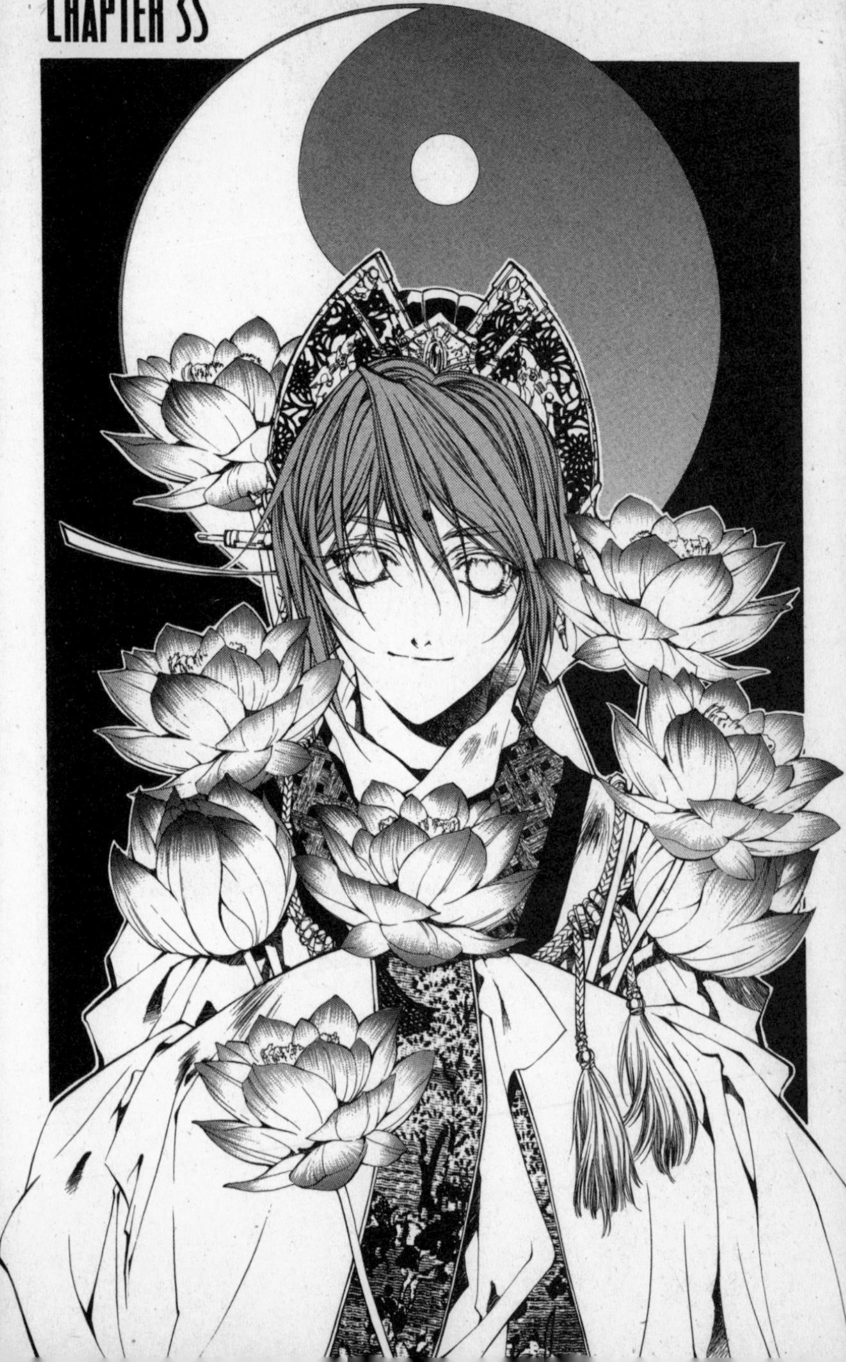

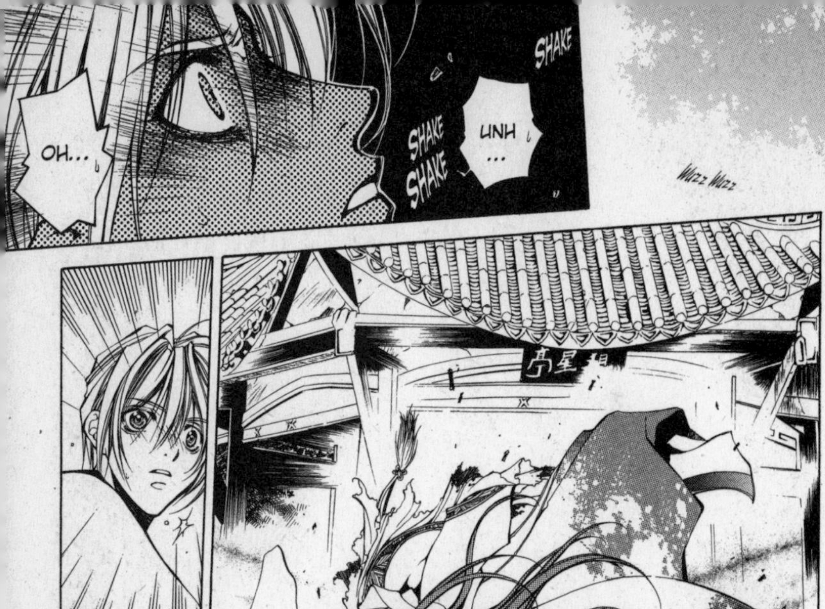
SHAKE
UNH ...
SHAKE SHAKE
OH...
Wuzz Wuzz
...
Whoa!
FWUMP
HMPH! WHAT AM I GOING TO DO WITH HIM?
HE THINKS EVERYONE IS GOING TO BRING DESTRUCTION UPON US.

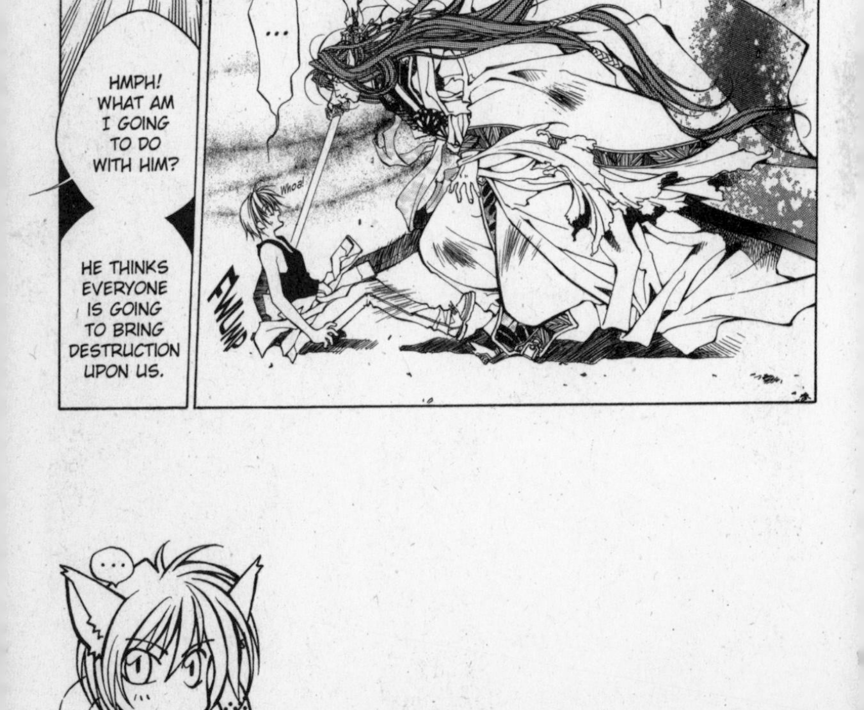
...

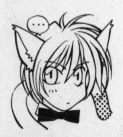

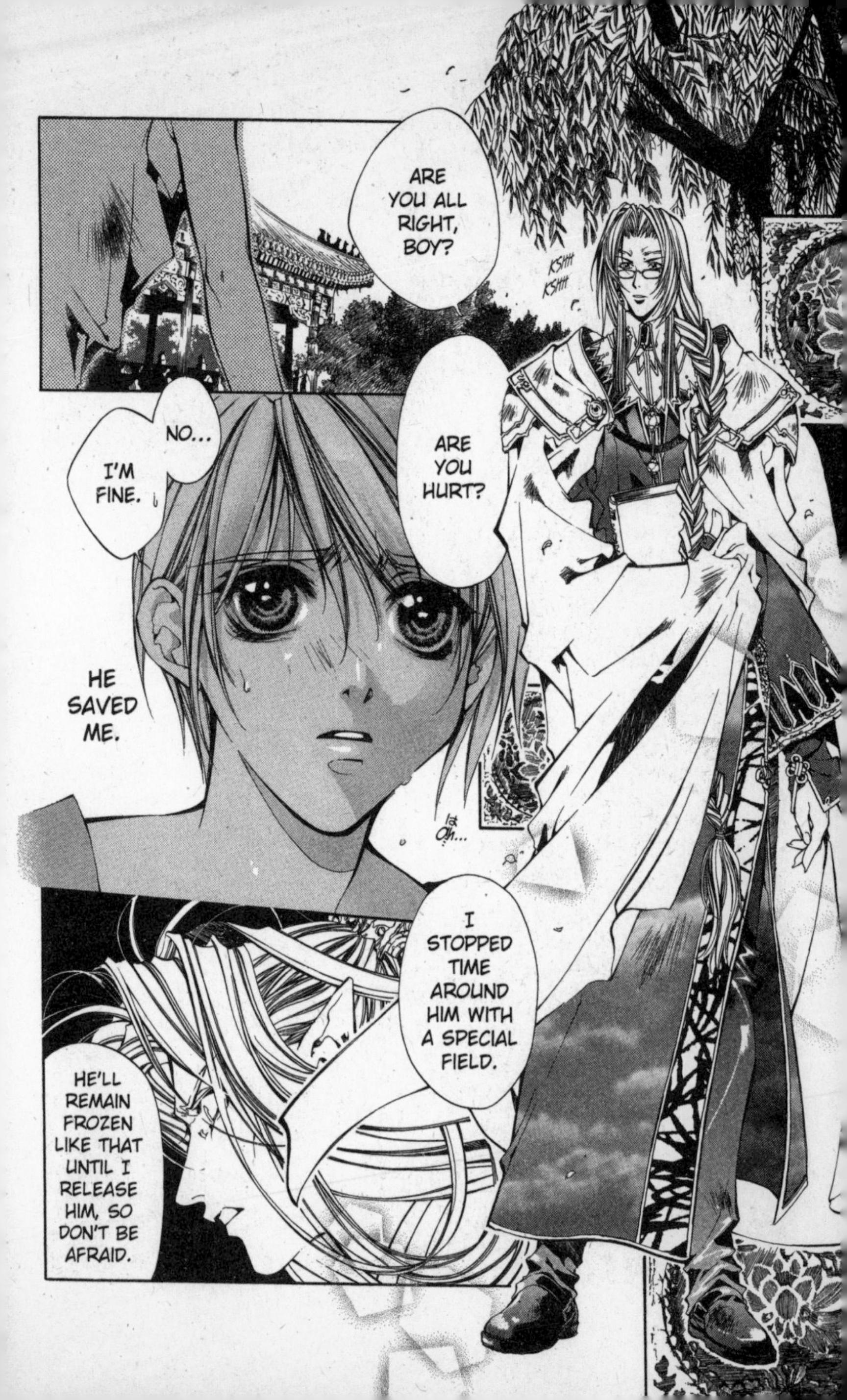
KSHH KSHH
ARE YOU ALL RIGHT, BOY?
ARE YOU HURT?
NO...
I'M FINE.
HE SAVED ME.
Oh...
I STOPPED TIME AROUND HIM WITH A SPECIAL FIELD.
HE'LL REMAIN FROZEN LIKE THAT UNTIL I RELEASE HIM, SO DON'T BE AFRAID.

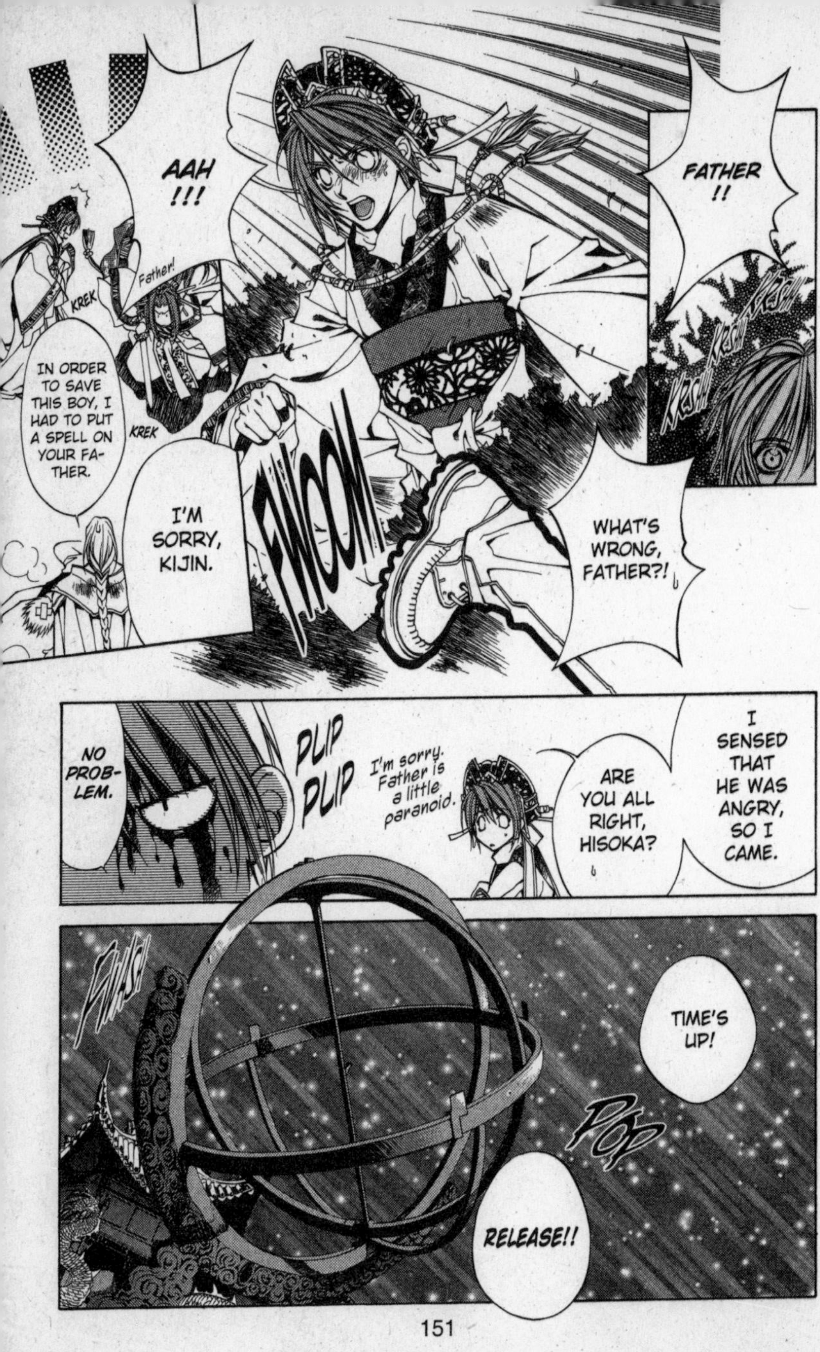
FATHER !!
KRSH KRSH KRSH
AAH !!!
WHAT'S WRONG, FATHER?!
FWOOM
Father!
KREK
IN ORDER TO SAVE THIS BOY, I HAD TO PUT A SPELL ON YOUR FATHER.
KREK
I'M SORRY, KIJIN.
I SENSED THAT HE WAS ANGRY, SO I CAME.
ARE YOU ALL RIGHT, HISOKA?
I'm sorry. Father is a little paranoid.
PLIP PLIP
NO PROBLEM.
TIME'S UP!
POP
RELEASE!!

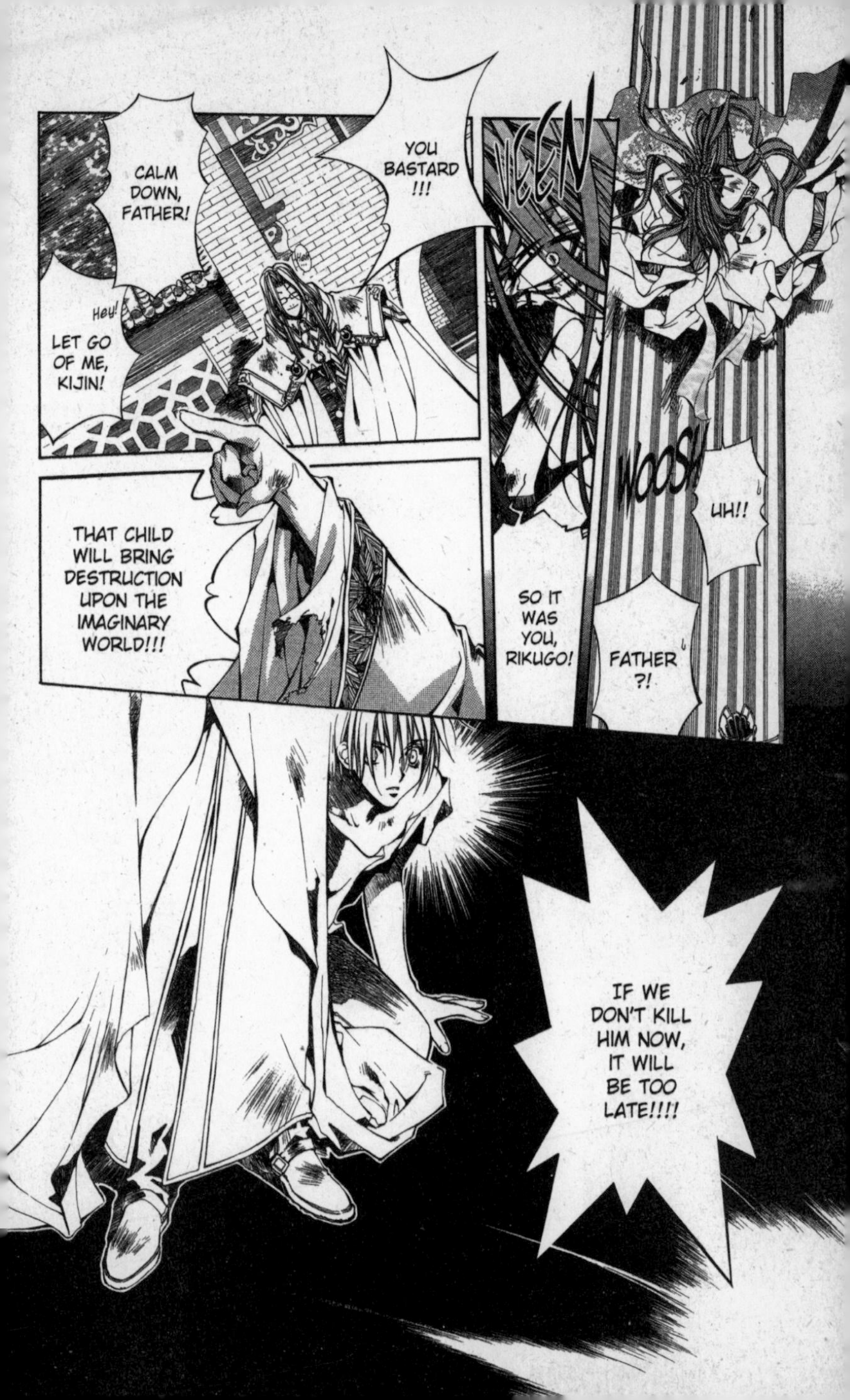
VEEN
WOOSH
UH!!
FATHER ?!
SO IT WAS YOU, RIKUGO!
YOU BASTARD !!!
CALM DOWN, FATHER!
Hey!
LET GO OF ME, KIJIN!
THAT CHILD WILL BRING DESTRUCTION UPON THE IMAGINARY WORLD!!!
IF WE DON'T KILL HIM NOW, IT WILL BE TOO LATE!!!!

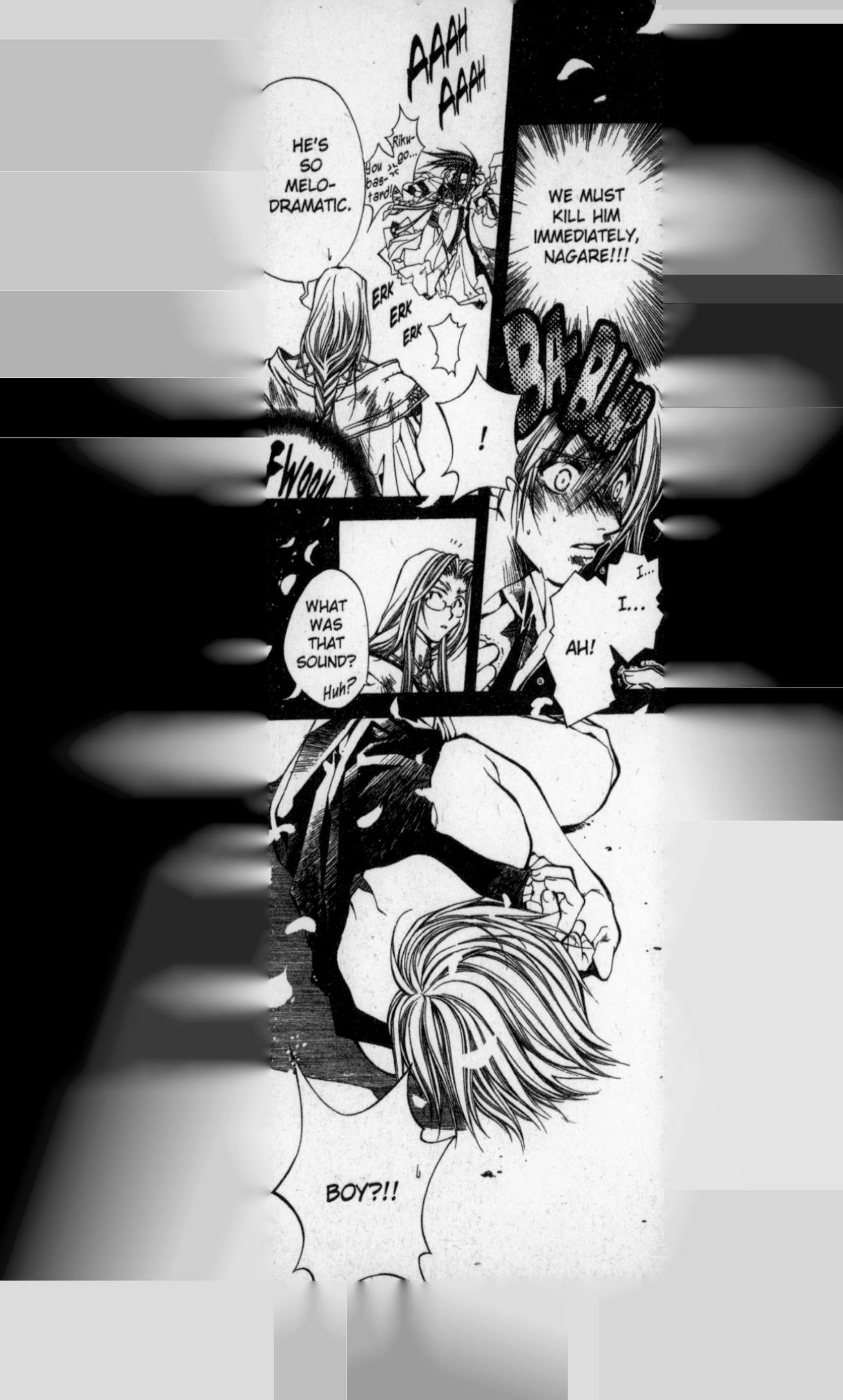
WE MUST KILL HIM IMMEDIATELY, NAGARE!!!
AAAH AAAH
Riku-go...
You bastard!!
HE'S SO MELO-DRAMATIC.
ERK ERK ERK
!
FWOOM
BA-BUM
I... I...
AH!
WHAT WAS THAT SOUND?
Huh?
BOY?!!

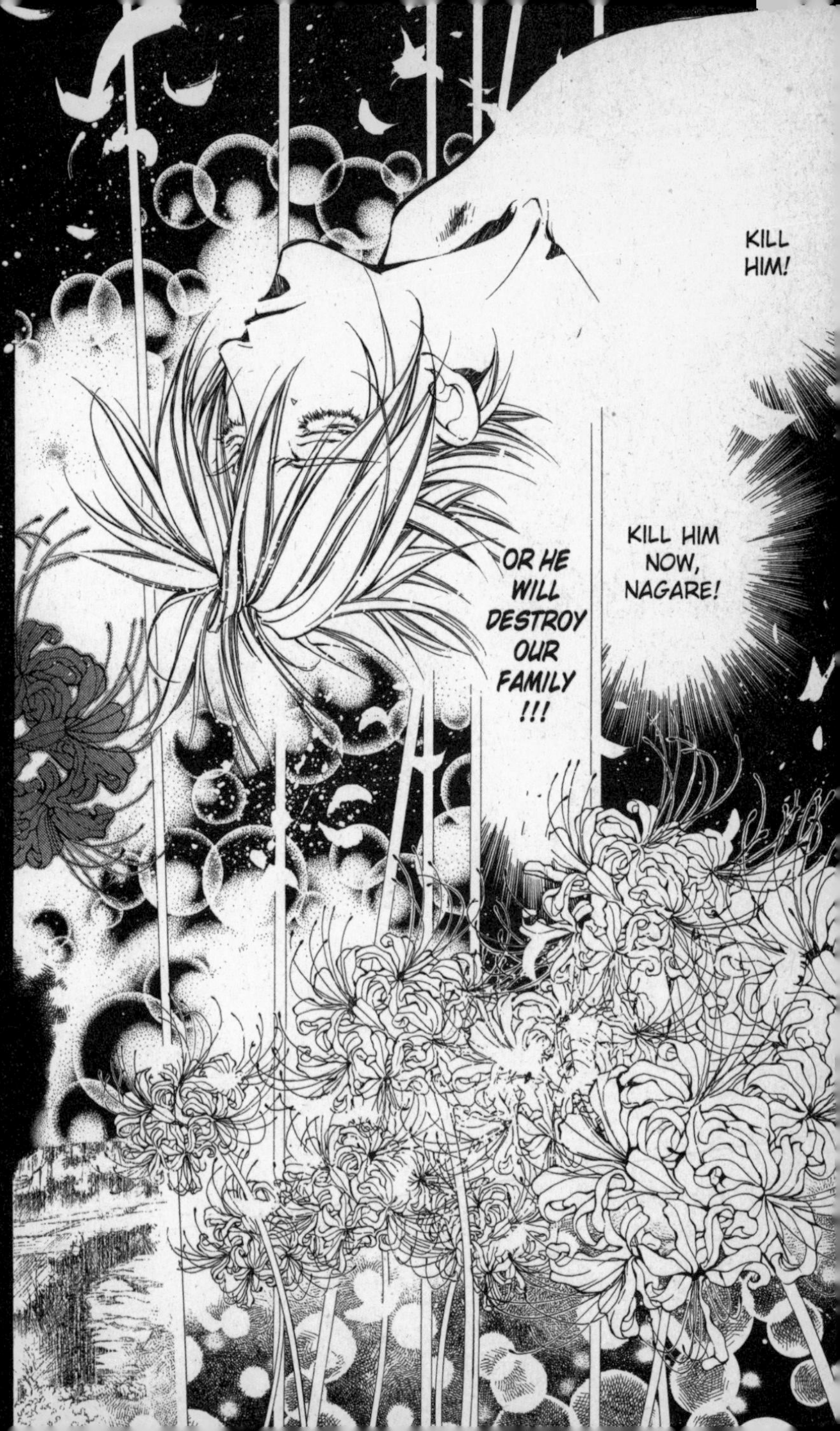
KILL HIM!
KILL HIM NOW, NAGARE!
OR HE WILL DESTROY OUR FAMILY !!!

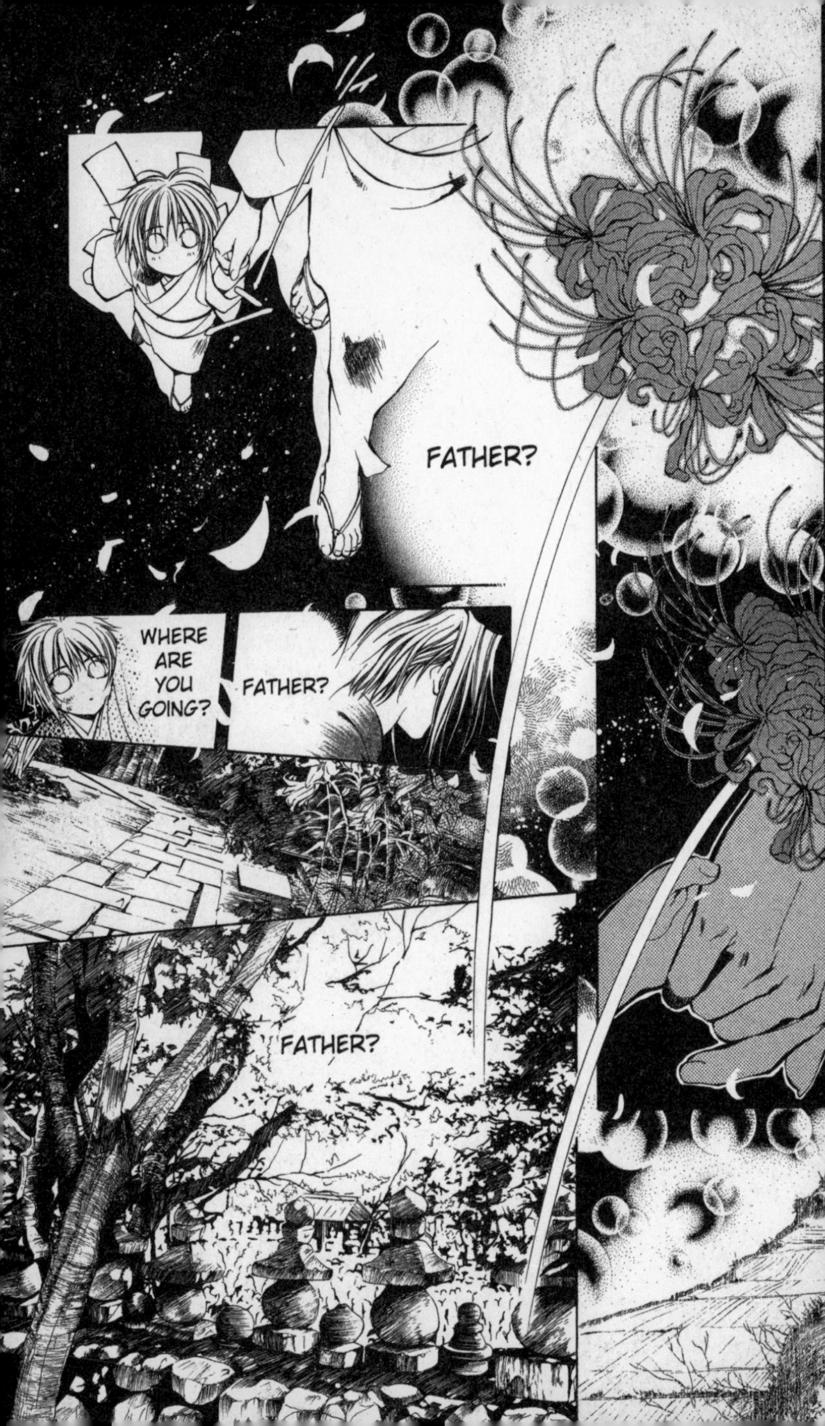
FATHER?
FATHER?
WHERE ARE YOU GOING?
FATHER?

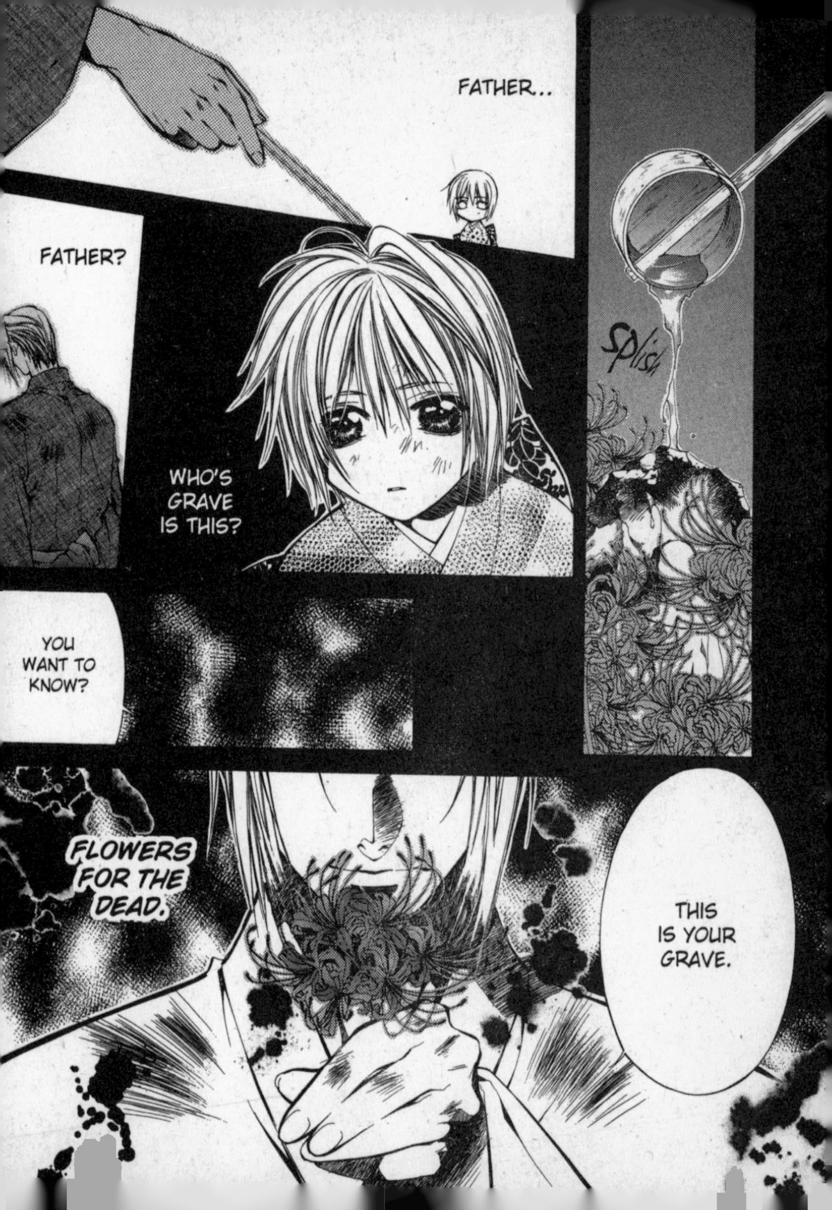
Splish
FATHER...
WHO'S GRAVE IS THIS?
FATHER?
YOU WANT TO KNOW?
THIS IS YOUR GRAVE.
FLOWERS FOR THE DEAD.

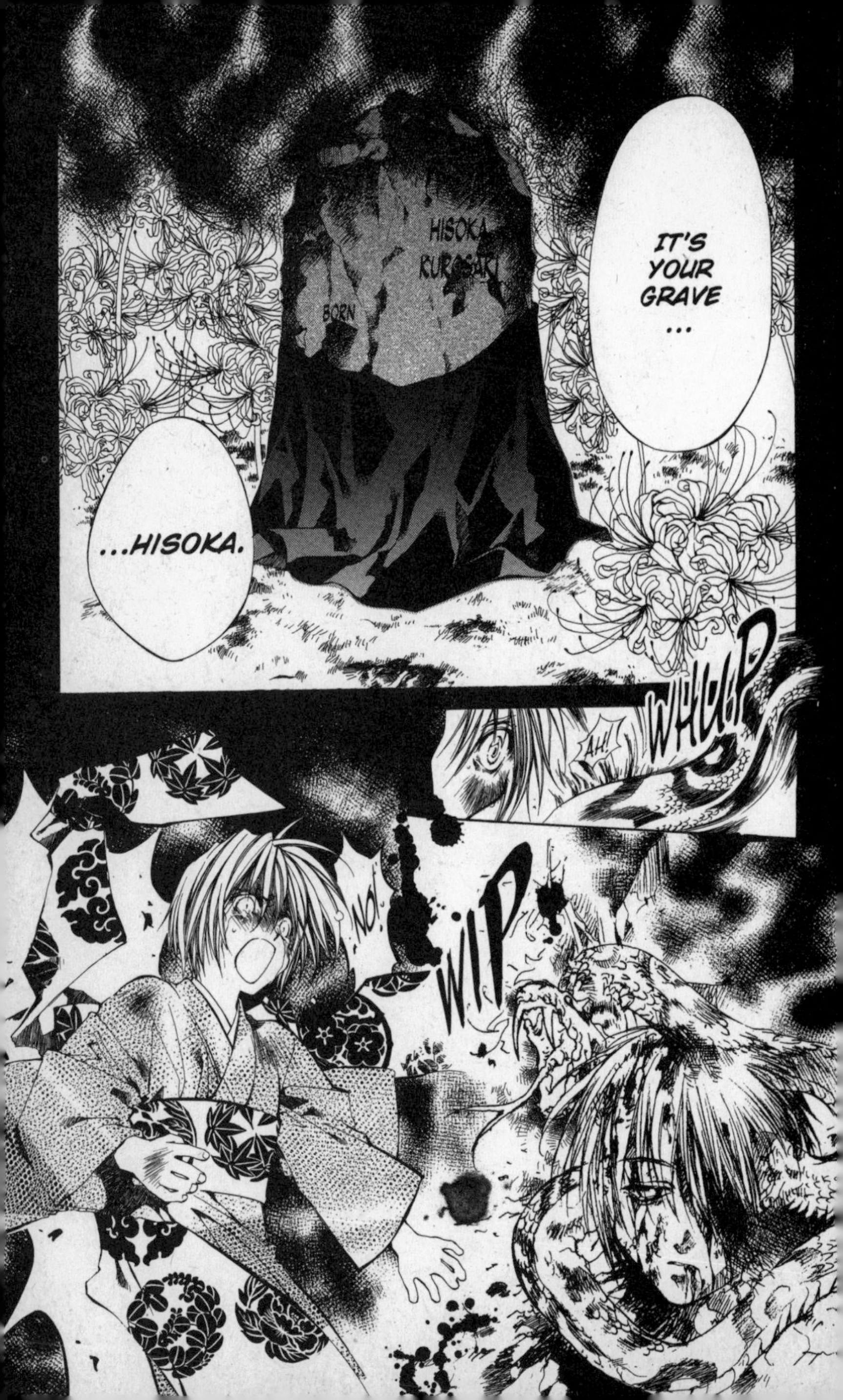
IT'S YOUR GRAVE ...
HISOKA KUROSAKI
BORN
...HISOKA.
WHUP
AH!
WIP
NO!

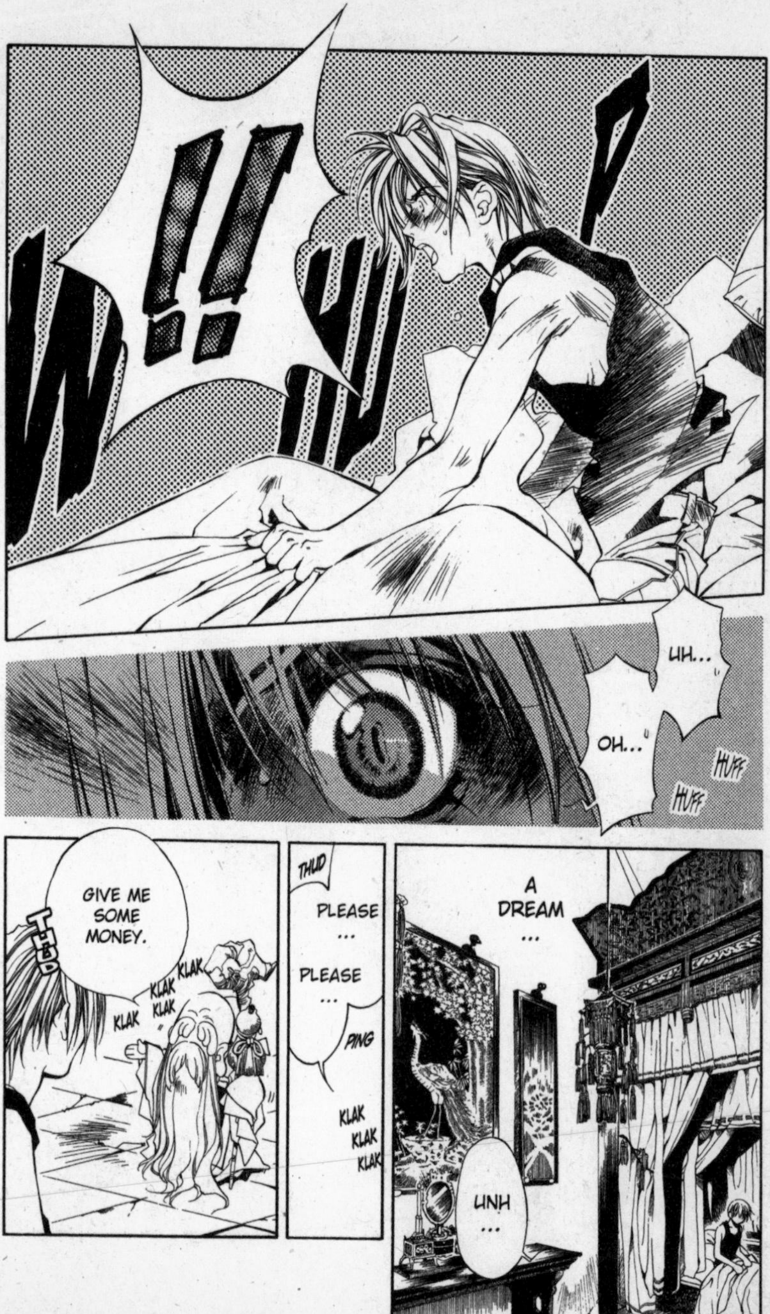
UH...
OH...
HUFF
HUFF
A DREAM ...
UNH ...
THUD
PLEASE ...
PLEASE ...
PING
KLAK
KLAK
KLAK
GIVE ME SOME MONEY.
THUD
KLAK
KLAK
KLAK
KLAK

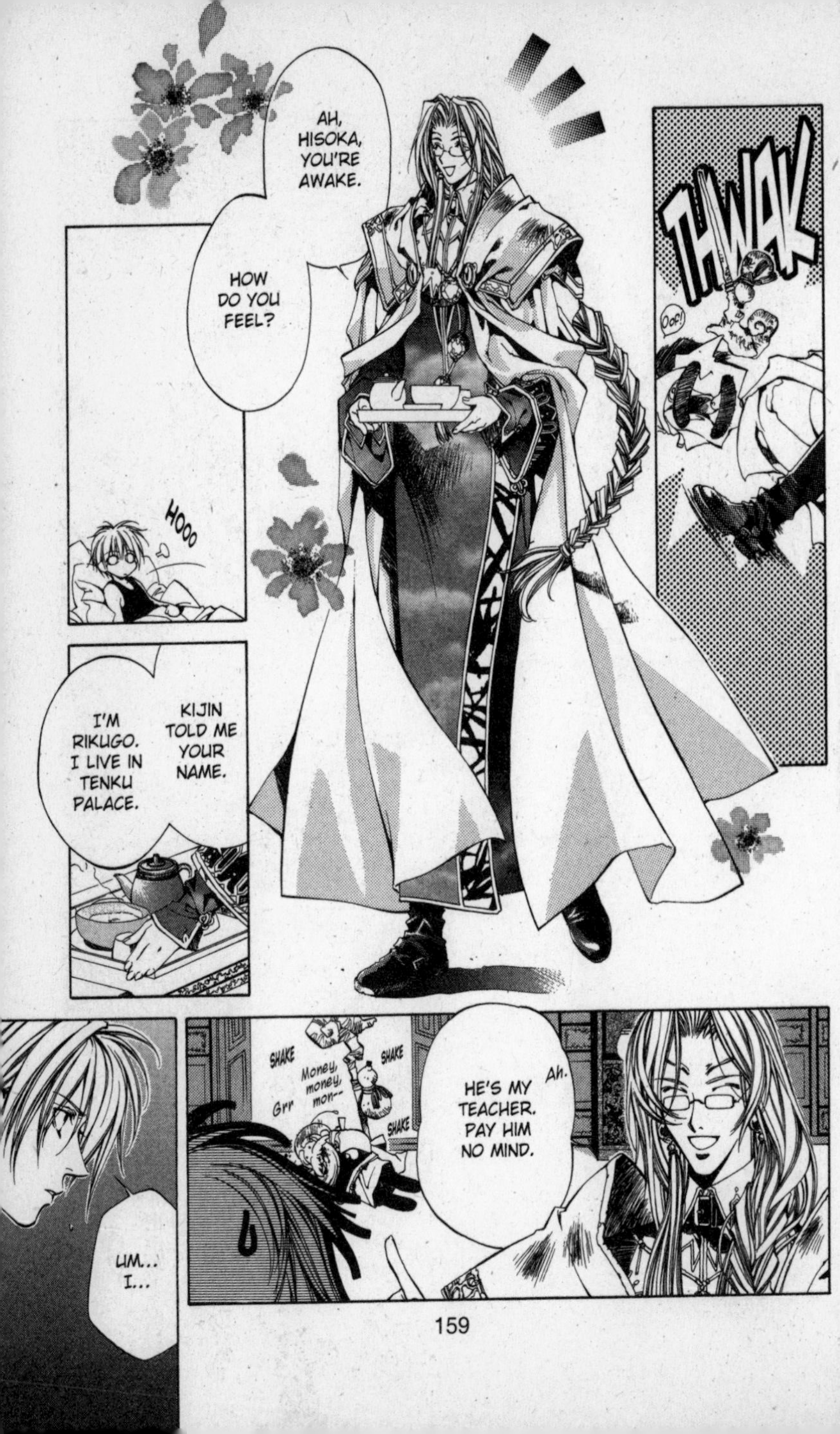
THWAK
Oof!
AH, HISOKA, YOU'RE AWAKE.
HOW DO YOU FEEL?
HOOO
KIJIN TOLD ME YOUR NAME.
I'M RIKUGO. I LIVE IN TENKU PALACE.
Ah.
HE'S MY TEACHER. PAY HIM NO MIND.
SHAKE
SHAKE
Money, money, mon--
Grr
SHAKE
UM... I...

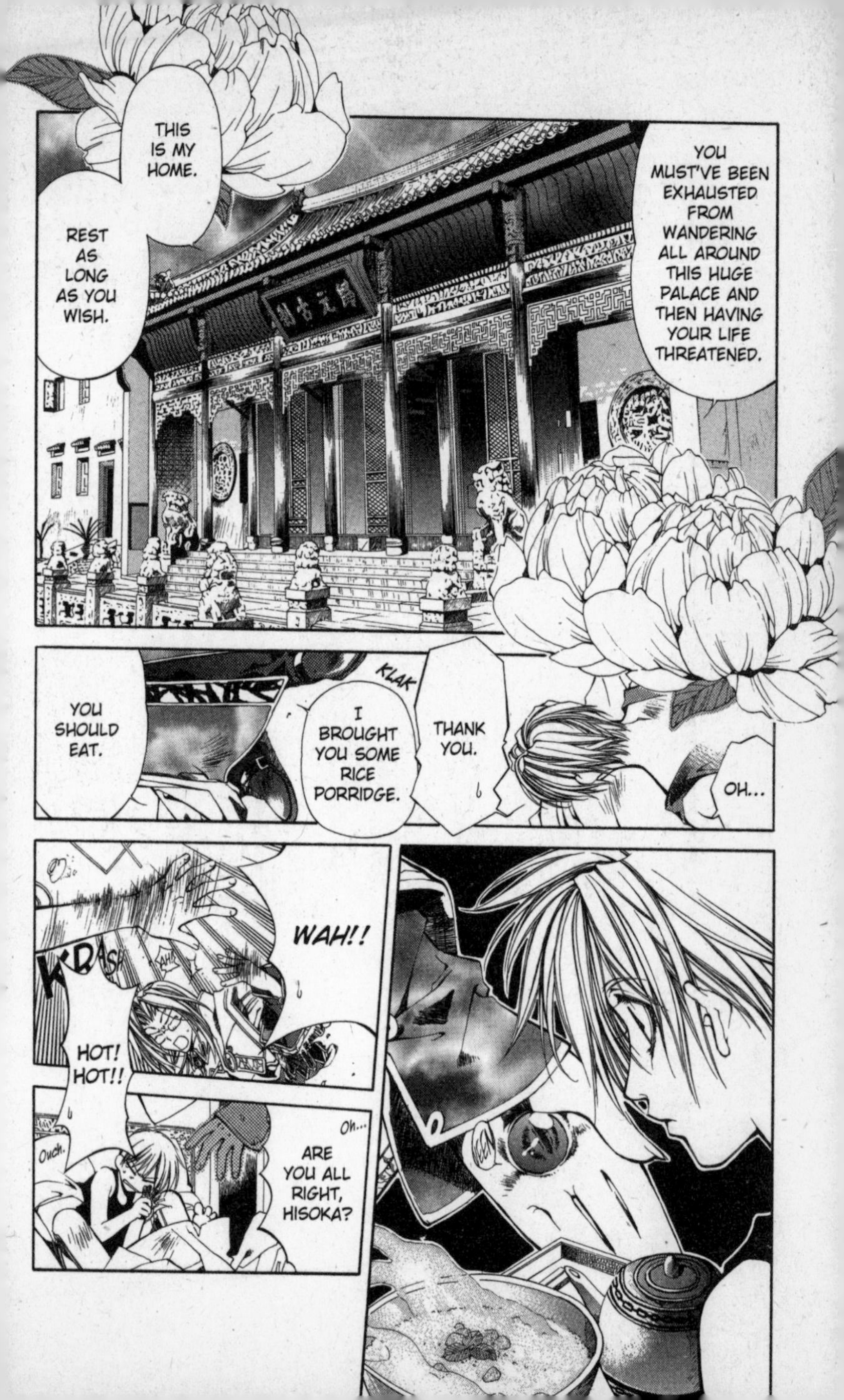
YOU MUST'VE BEEN EXHAUSTED FROM WANDERING ALL AROUND THIS HUGE PALACE AND THEN HAVING YOUR LIFE THREATENED.
THIS IS MY HOME.
REST AS LONG AS YOU WISH.
OH...
THANK YOU.
KLAK
I BROUGHT YOU SOME RICE PORRIDGE.
YOU SHOULD EAT.
WAH!!
K'DASH
HOT! HOT!!
Oh...
ARE YOU ALL RIGHT, HISOKA?
Ouch.

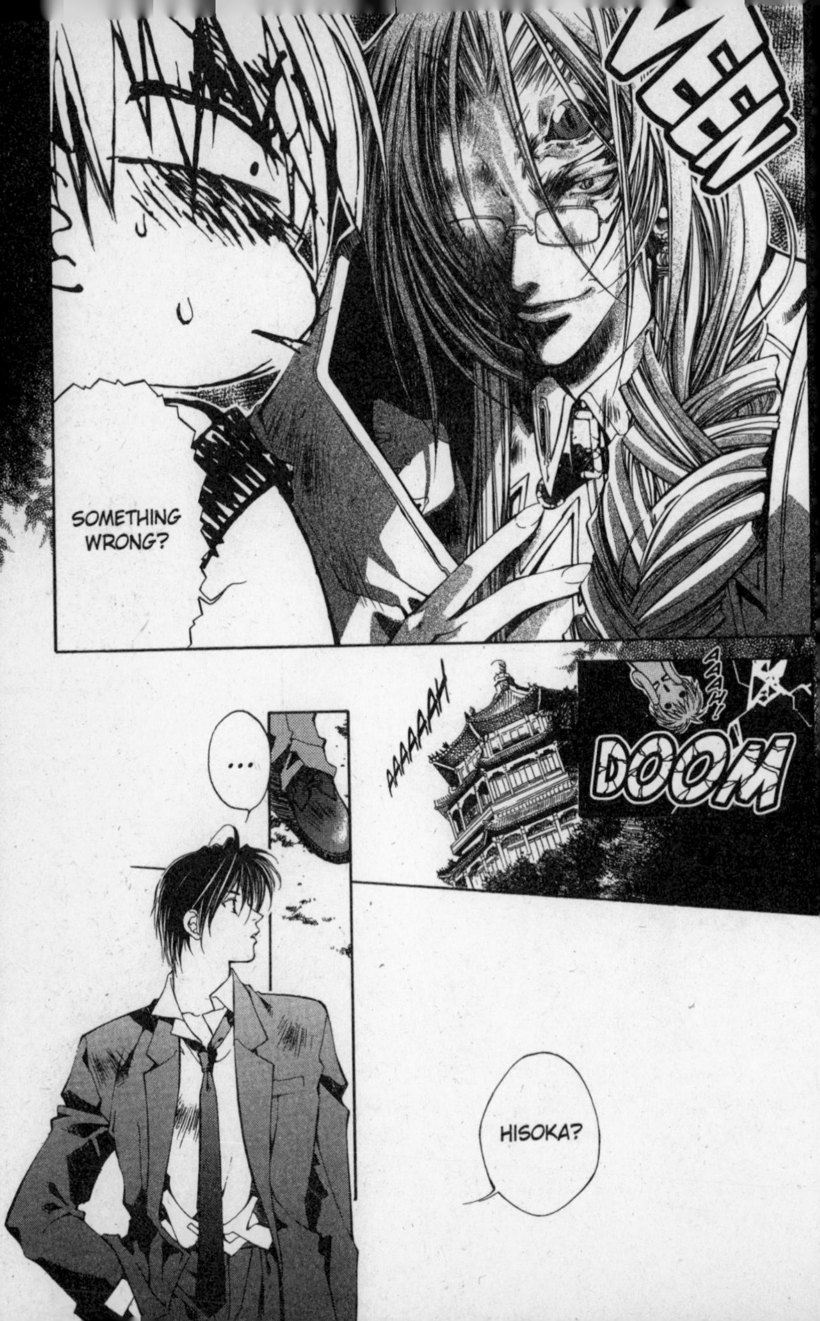
VEEN
SOMETHING WRONG?
AAAAH!
DOOM
AAAAAAH
...
HISOKA?

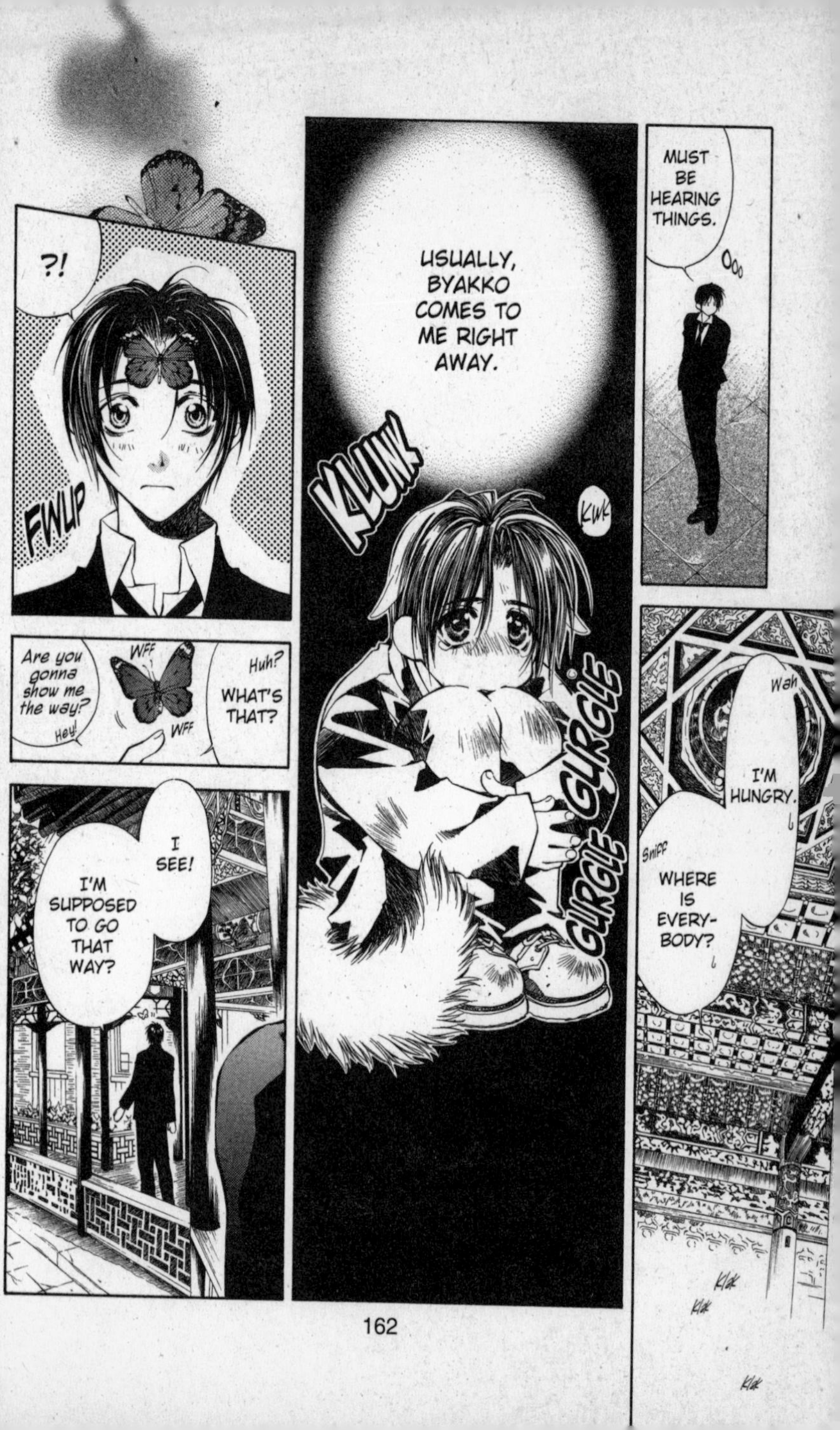
MUST BE HEARING THINGS.
Ooo
Wah
I'M HUNGRY.
Sniff
WHERE IS EVERY-BODY?
Klak
Klak
Klak
USUALLY, BYAKKO COMES TO ME RIGHT AWAY.
KLUNK
KWK
GURGLE GURGLE
?!
FWUP
Huh?
WHAT'S THAT?
WFF
Are you gonna show me the way?
Hey!
WFF
I SEE!
I'M SUPPOSED TO GO THAT WAY?

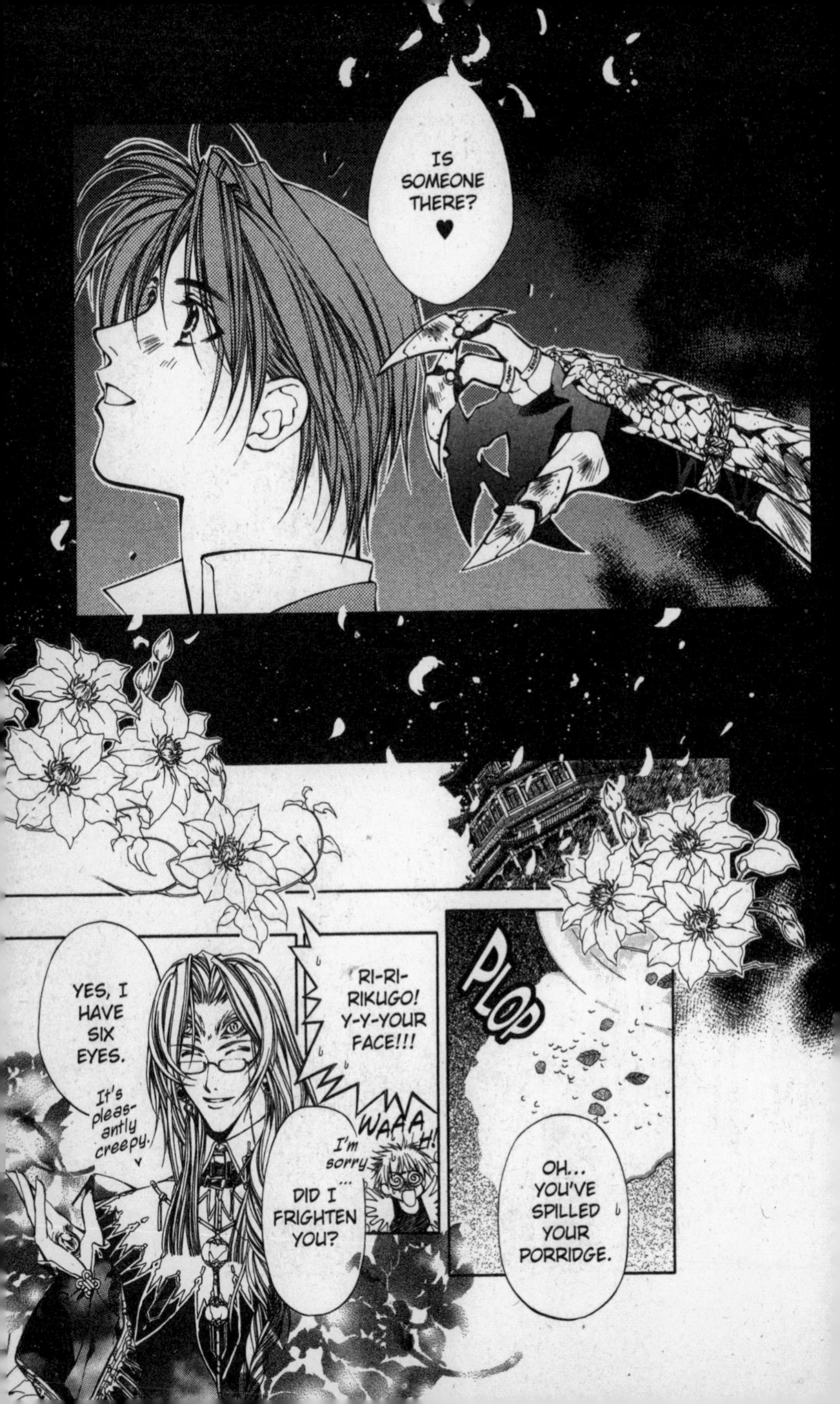
IS SOMEONE THERE? ♥
PLOP
OH... YOU'VE SPILLED YOUR PORRIDGE.
RI-RI-RIKUGO! Y-Y-YOUR FACE!!!
WAAAH!
I'm sorry...
DID I FRIGHTEN YOU?
YES, I HAVE SIX EYES.
It's pleasantly creepy.

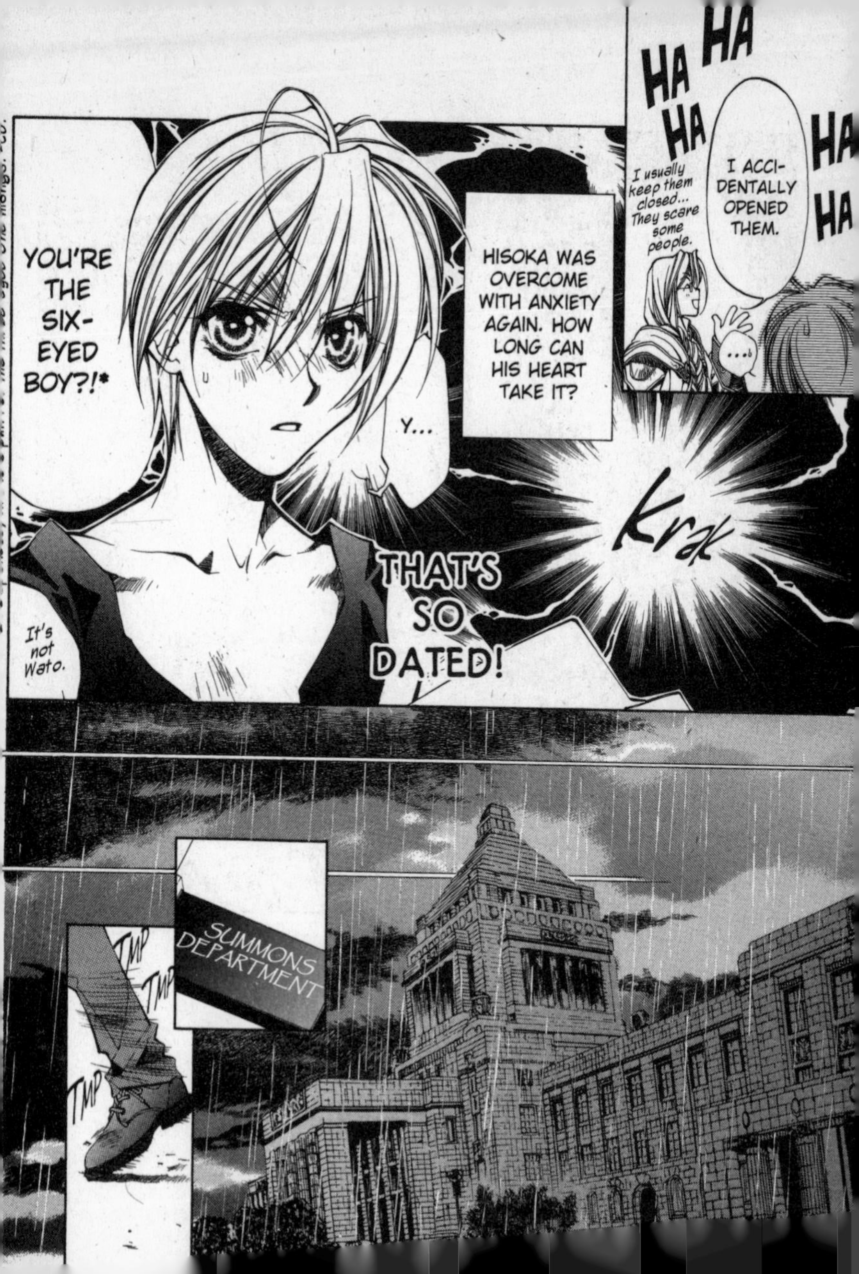
HA HA HA HA HA HA
I ACCI-DENTALLY OPENED THEM.
I usually keep them closed... They scare some people.
...
HISOKA WAS OVERCOME WITH ANXIETY AGAIN. HOW LONG CAN HIS HEART TAKE IT?
YOU'RE THE SIX-EYED BOY?!*
Y...
Krak
THAT'S SO DATED!
It's not Wato.
SUMMONS DEPARTMENT
TMP
TMP
TMP

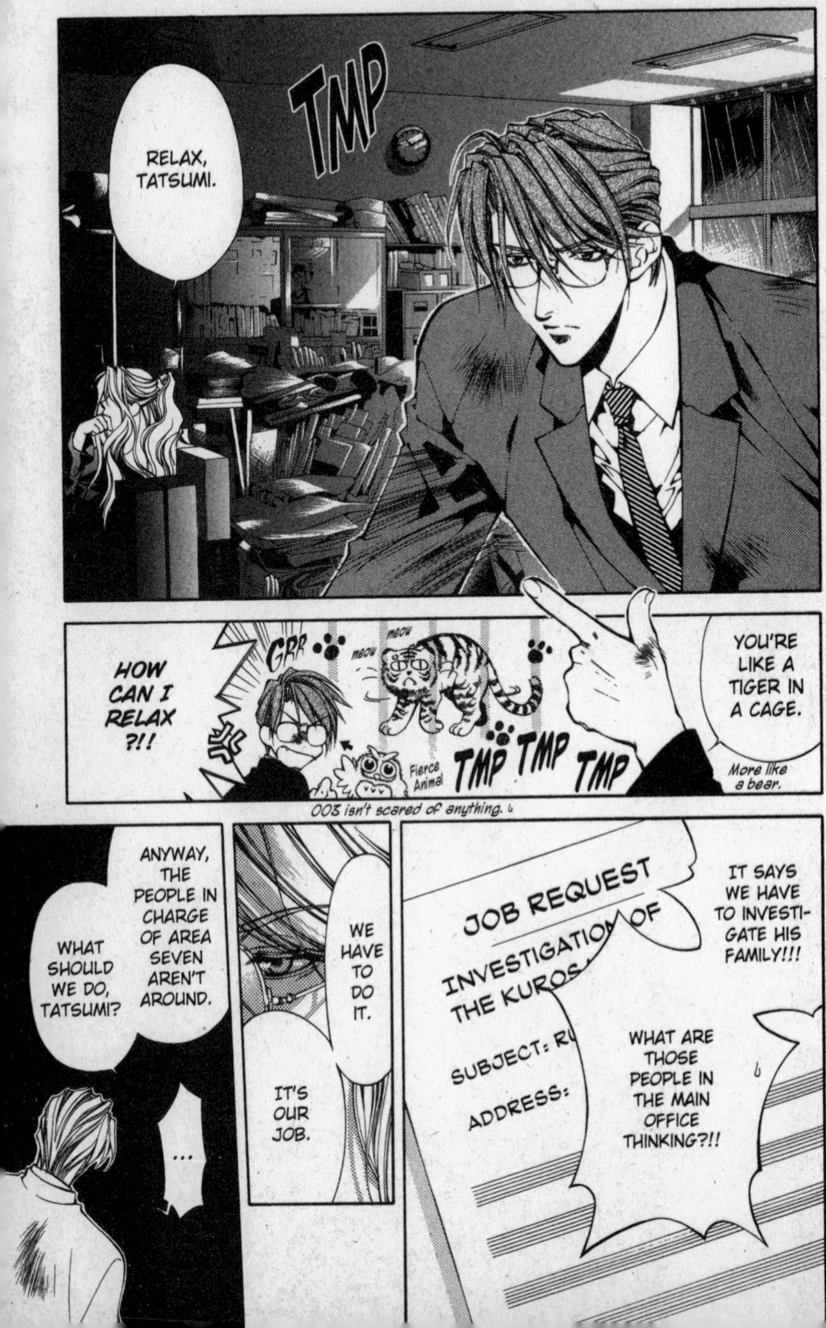
TMP
RELAX, TATSUMI.
YOU'RE LIKE A TIGER IN A CAGE.
More like a bear.
TMP TMP TMP
meow
meow
GRR
Fierce Animal
HOW CAN I RELAX ?!!
003 isn't scared of anything.
IT SAYS WE HAVE TO INVESTIGATE HIS FAMILY!!!
JOB REQUEST
INVESTIGATION OF THE KUROS
SUBJECT: R
ADDRESS:
WHAT ARE THOSE PEOPLE IN THE MAIN OFFICE THINKING?!!
WE HAVE TO DO IT.
IT'S OUR JOB.
ANYWAY, THE PEOPLE IN CHARGE OF AREA SEVEN AREN'T AROUND.
WHAT SHOULD WE DO, TATSUMI?
...

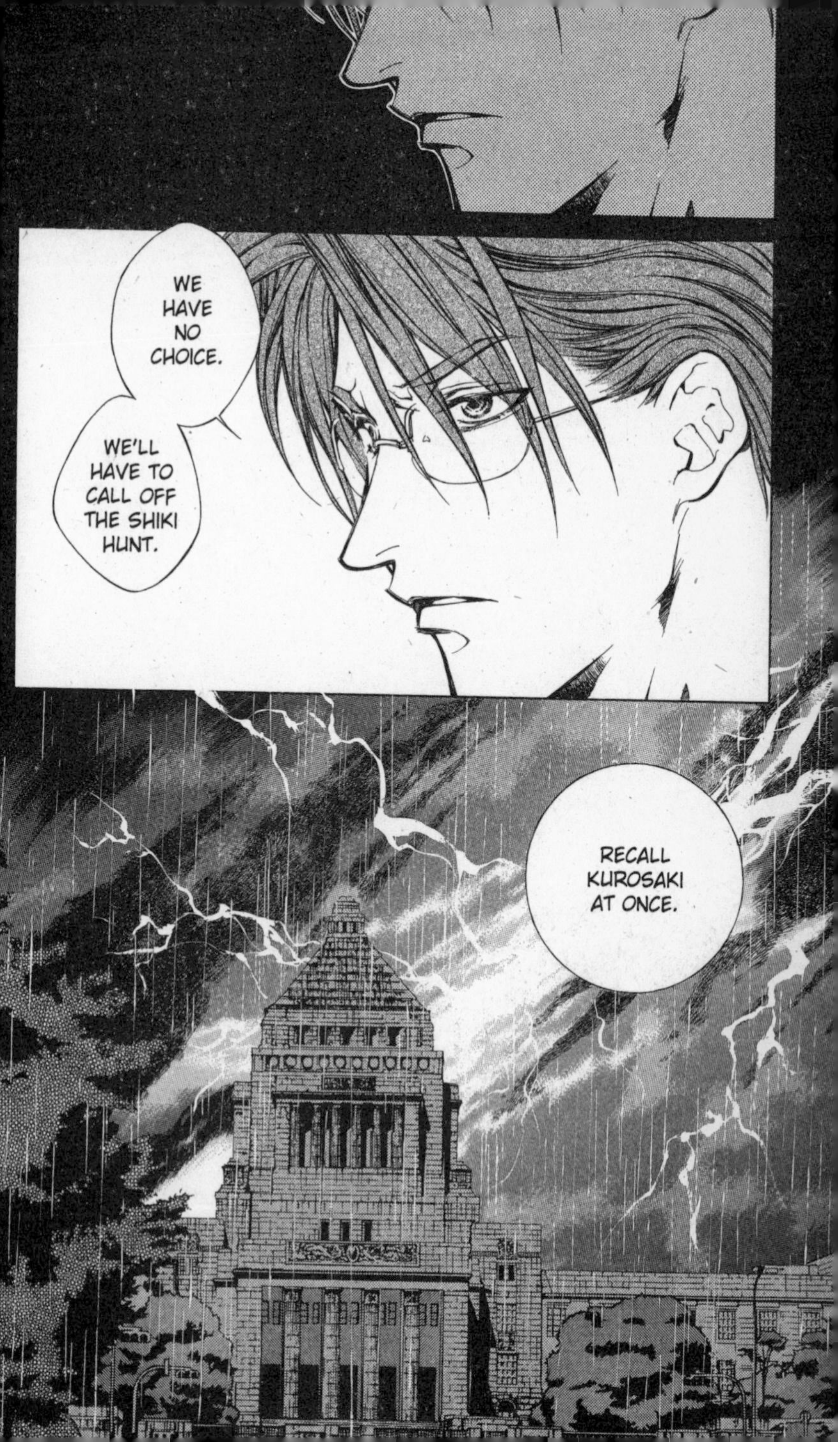
WE HAVE NO CHOICE.
WE'LL HAVE TO CALL OFF THE SHIKI HUNT.
RECALL KUROSAKI AT ONCE.

CHAPTER 36

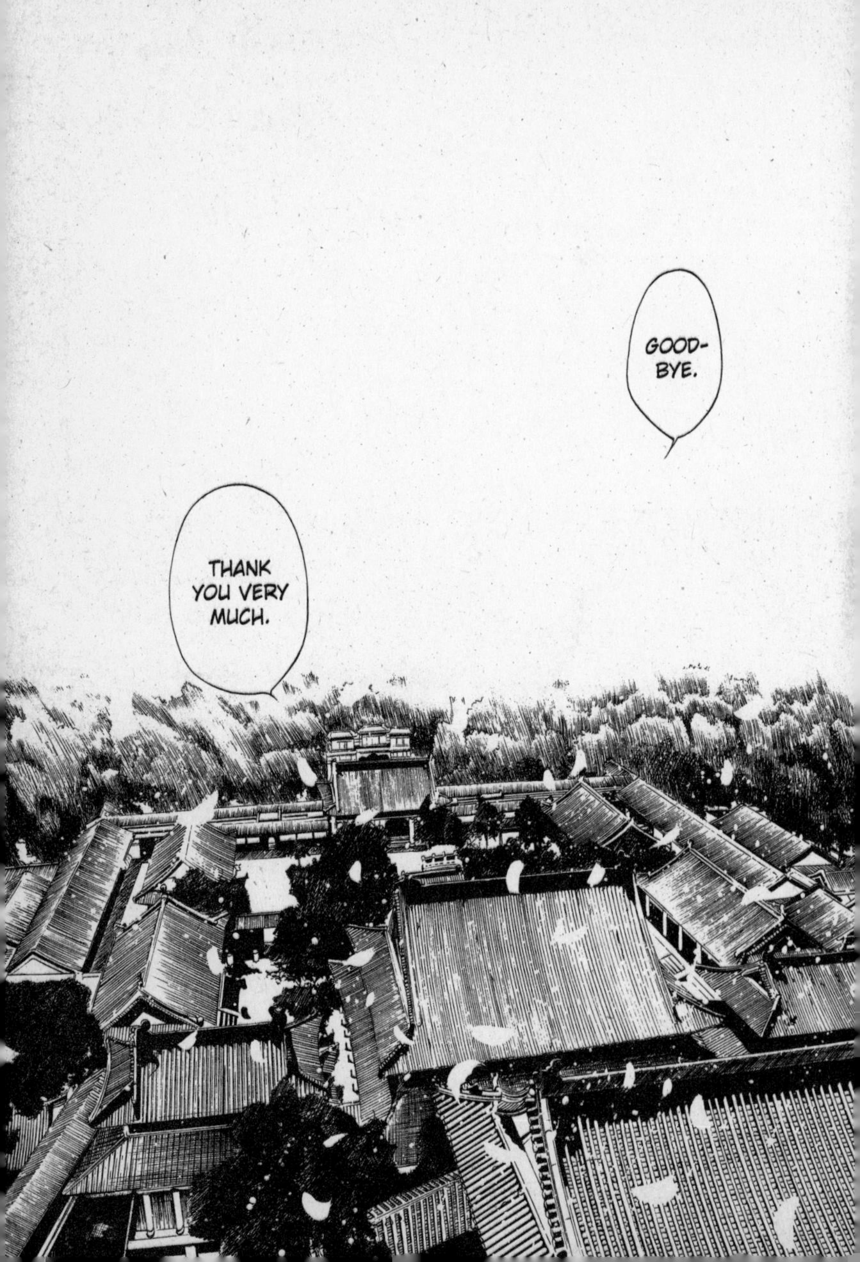
GOOD-BYE.
THANK YOU VERY MUCH.

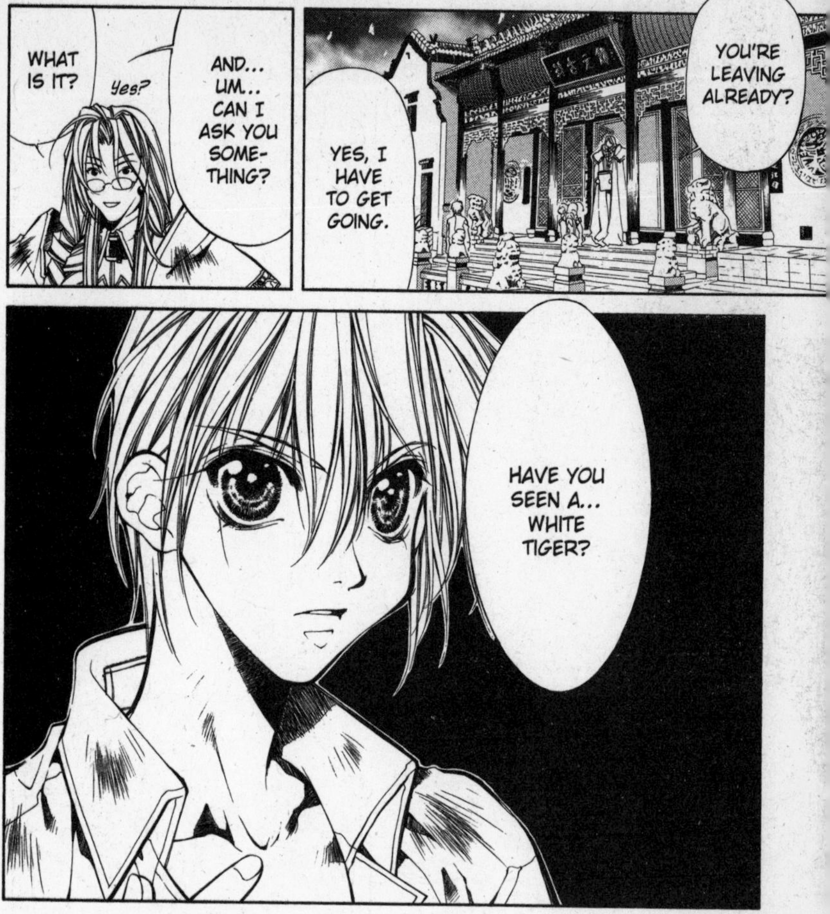
YOU'RE LEAVING ALREADY?
YES, I HAVE TO GET GOING.
AND... UM... CAN I ASK YOU SOME-THING?
Yes?
WHAT IS IT?
HAVE YOU SEEN A... WHITE TIGER?

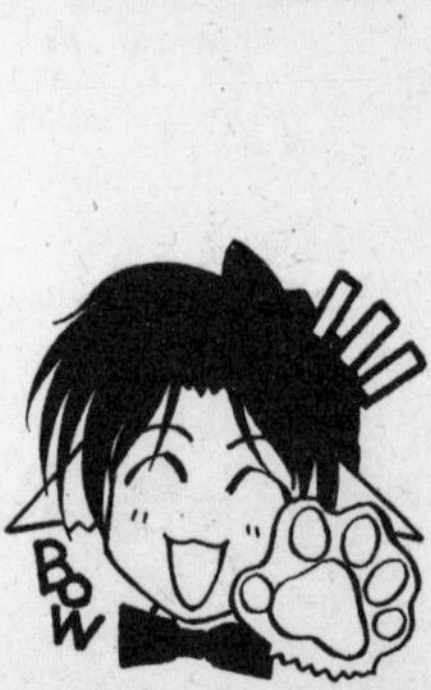
BOW

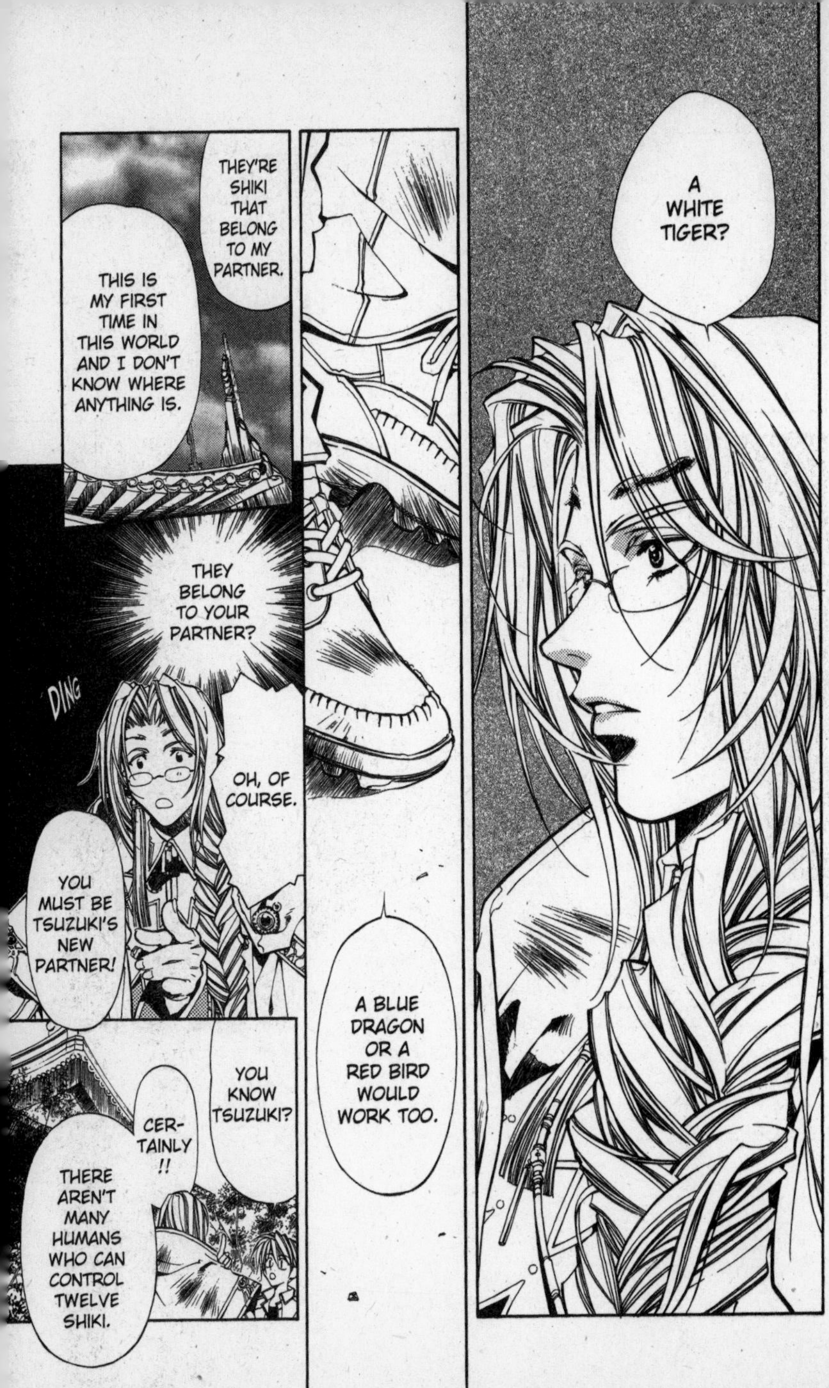
A WHITE TIGER?
A BLUE DRAGON OR A RED BIRD WOULD WORK TOO.
THEY'RE SHIKI THAT BELONG TO MY PARTNER.
THIS IS MY FIRST TIME IN THIS WORLD AND I DON'T KNOW WHERE ANYTHING IS.
THEY BELONG TO YOUR PARTNER?
DING
OH, OF COURSE.
YOU MUST BE TSUZUKI'S NEW PARTNER!
YOU KNOW TSUZUKI?
CER-TAINLY!!
THERE AREN'T MANY HUMANS WHO CAN CONTROL TWELVE SHIKI.

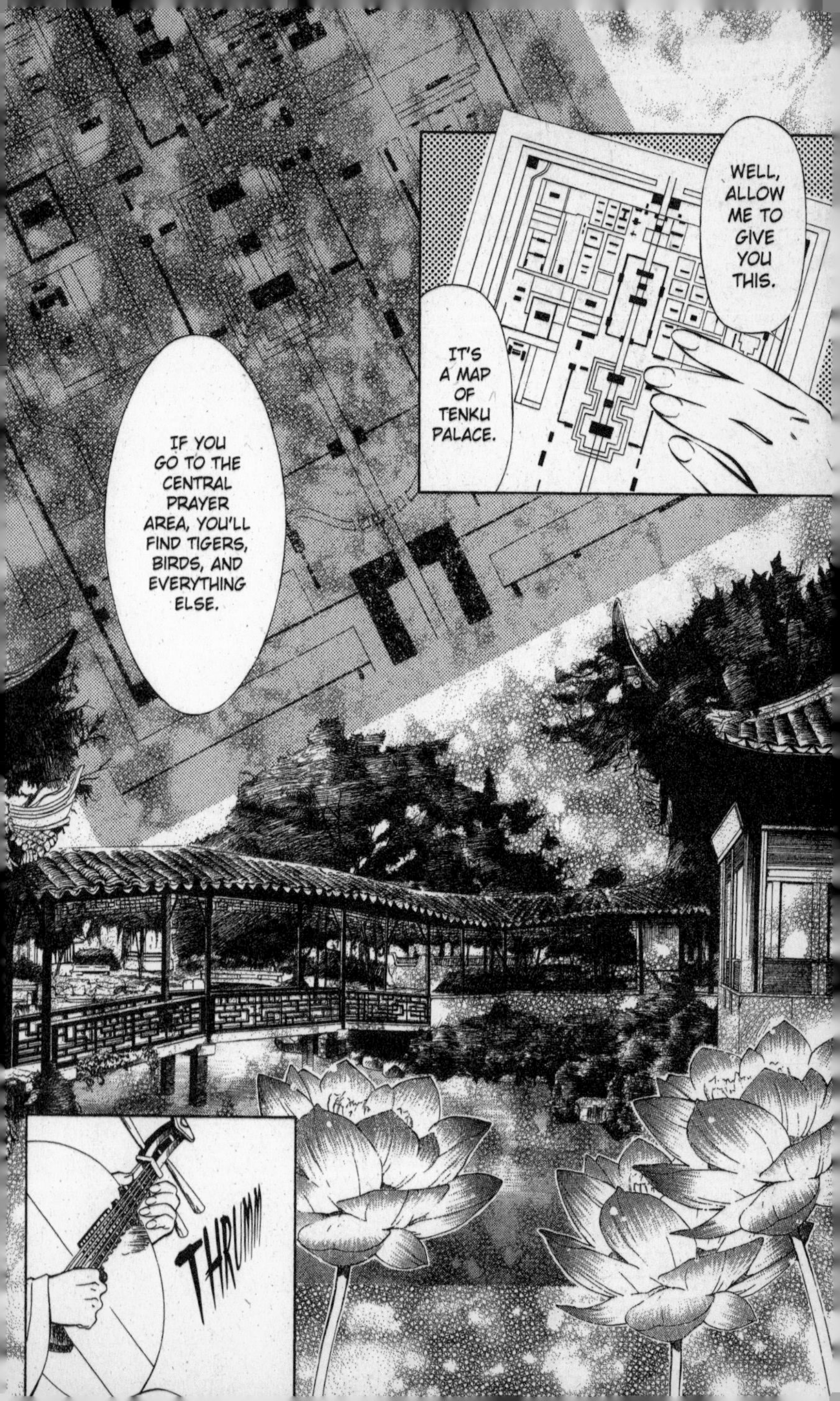
WELL, ALLOW ME TO GIVE YOU THIS.
IT'S A MAP OF TENKU PALACE.
IF YOU GO TO THE CENTRAL PRAYER AREA, YOU'LL FIND TIGERS, BIRDS, AND EVERYTHING ELSE.
THRUMM

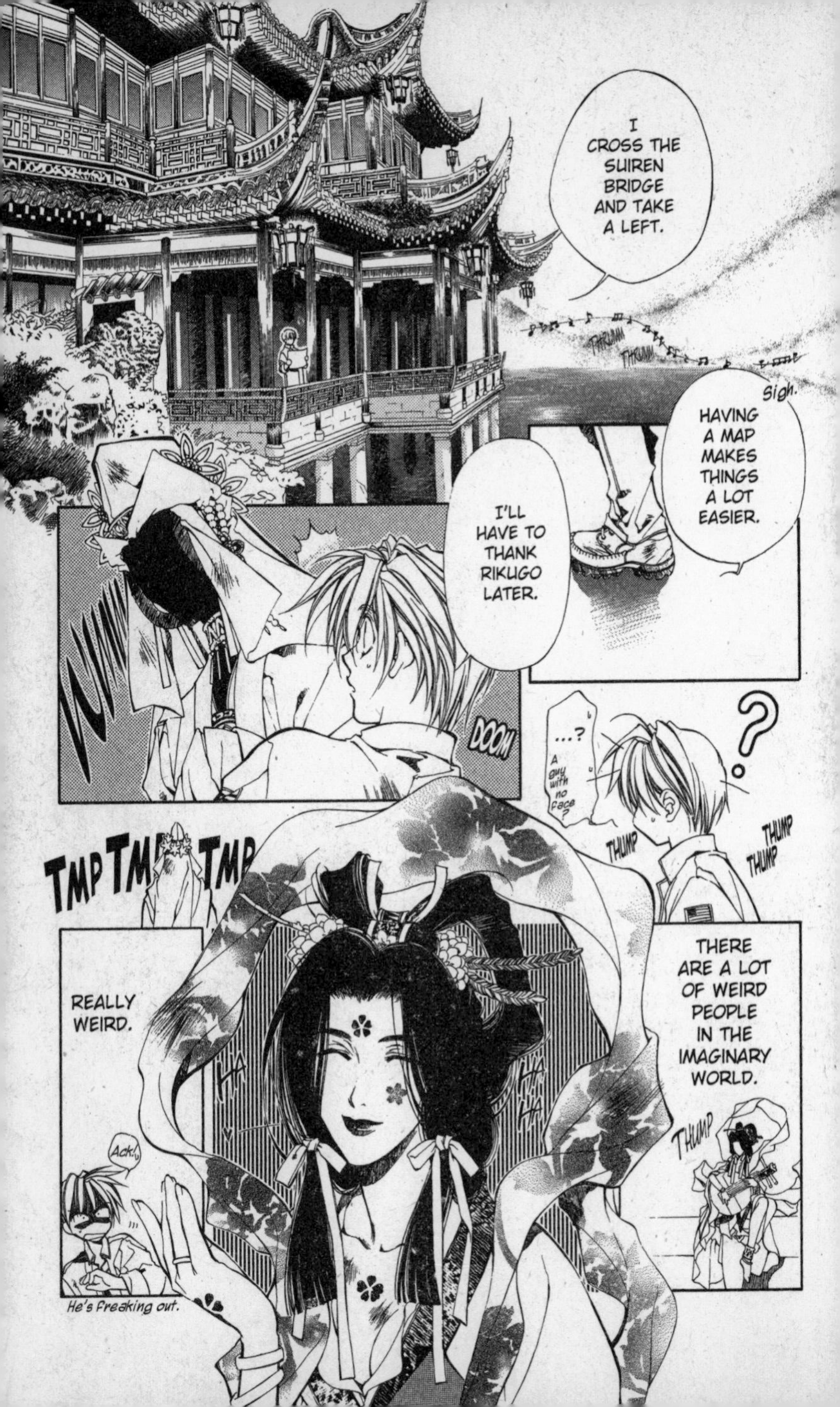
I CROSS THE SUIREN BRIDGE AND TAKE A LEFT.
THRUM THRUM
Sigh.
HAVING A MAP MAKES THINGS A LOT EASIER.
I'LL HAVE TO THANK RIKUGO LATER.
DOOM
...?
A guy with no face?
?
THUMP THUMP THUMP
TMP TMP TMP
THERE ARE A LOT OF WEIRD PEOPLE IN THE IMAGINARY WORLD.
REALLY WEIRD.
HA HA
HA HA
THUMP
Ack!
He's freaking out.

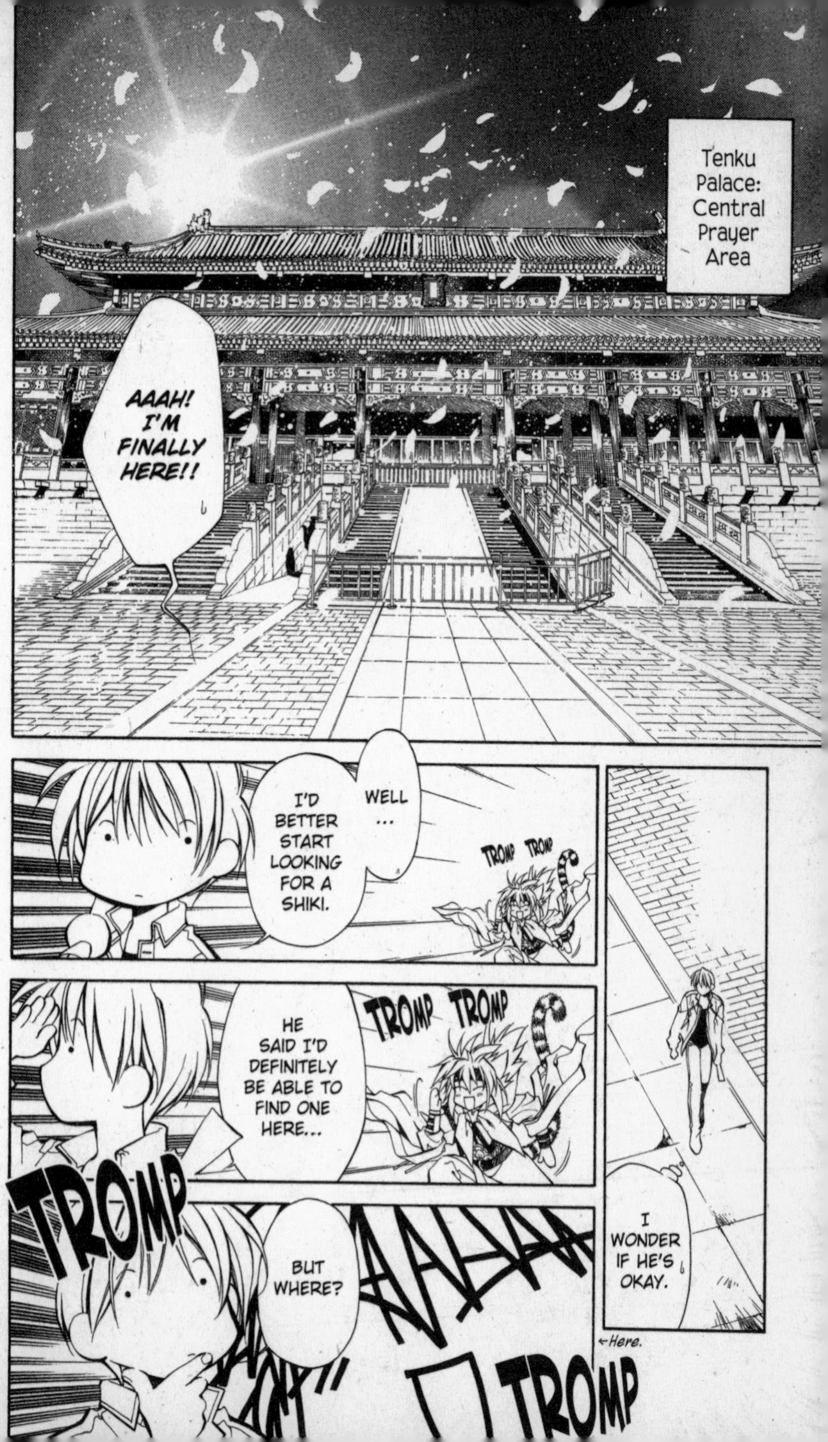
Tenku Palace: Central Prayer Area
AAAH! I'M FINALLY HERE!!
I WONDER IF HE'S OKAY.
←Here.
TROMP TROMP
WELL...
I'D BETTER START LOOKING FOR A SHIKI.
TROMP TROMP
HE SAID I'D DEFINITELY BE ABLE TO FIND ONE HERE...
TROMP
BUT WHERE?
TROMP
TROMP

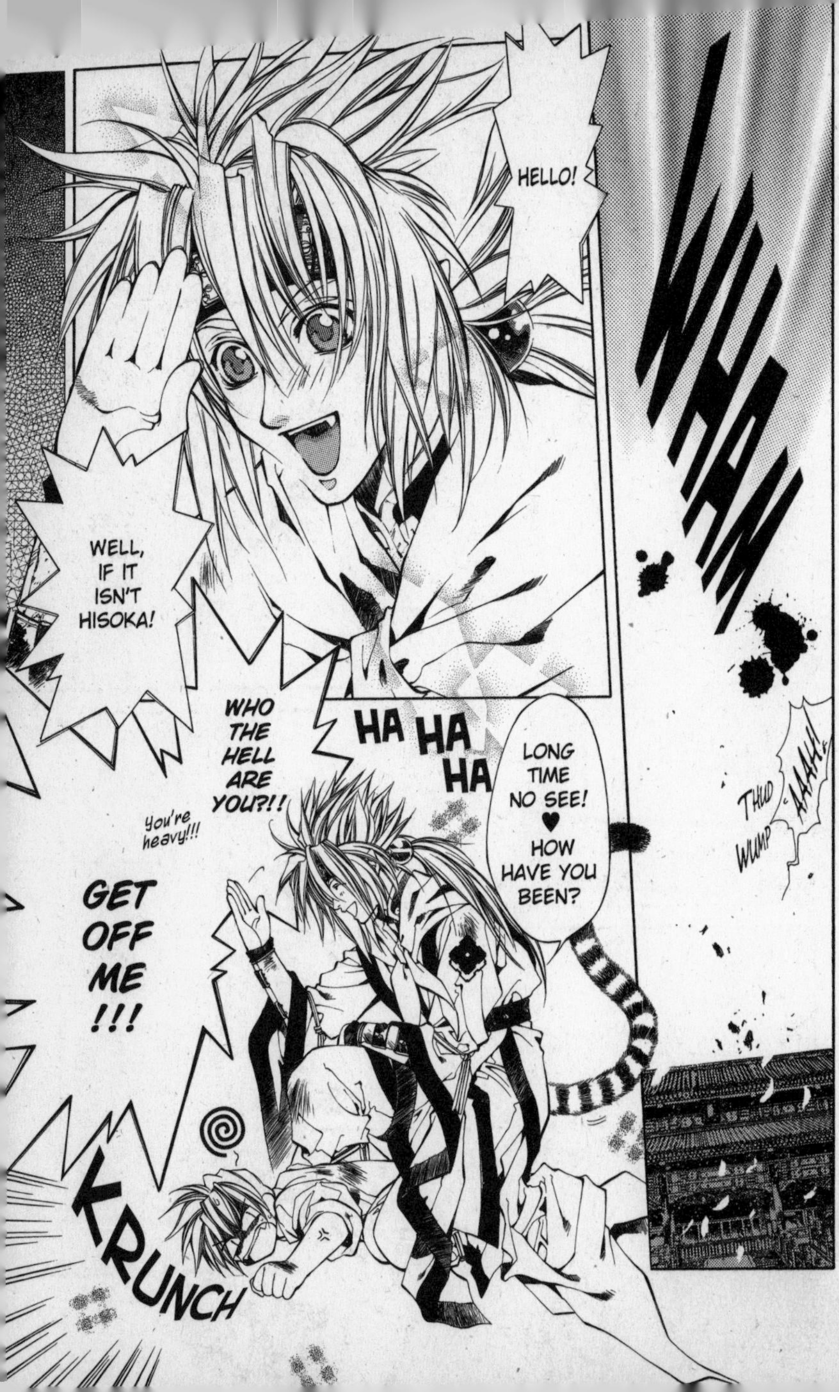
HELLO!
WELL, IF IT ISN'T HISOKA!
WHAM
THUD WUMP
AAAH!
LONG TIME NO SEE! ♥ HOW HAVE YOU BEEN?
HA HA HA
WHO THE HELL ARE YOU?!!
You're heavy!!!
GET OFF ME!!!
KRUNCH

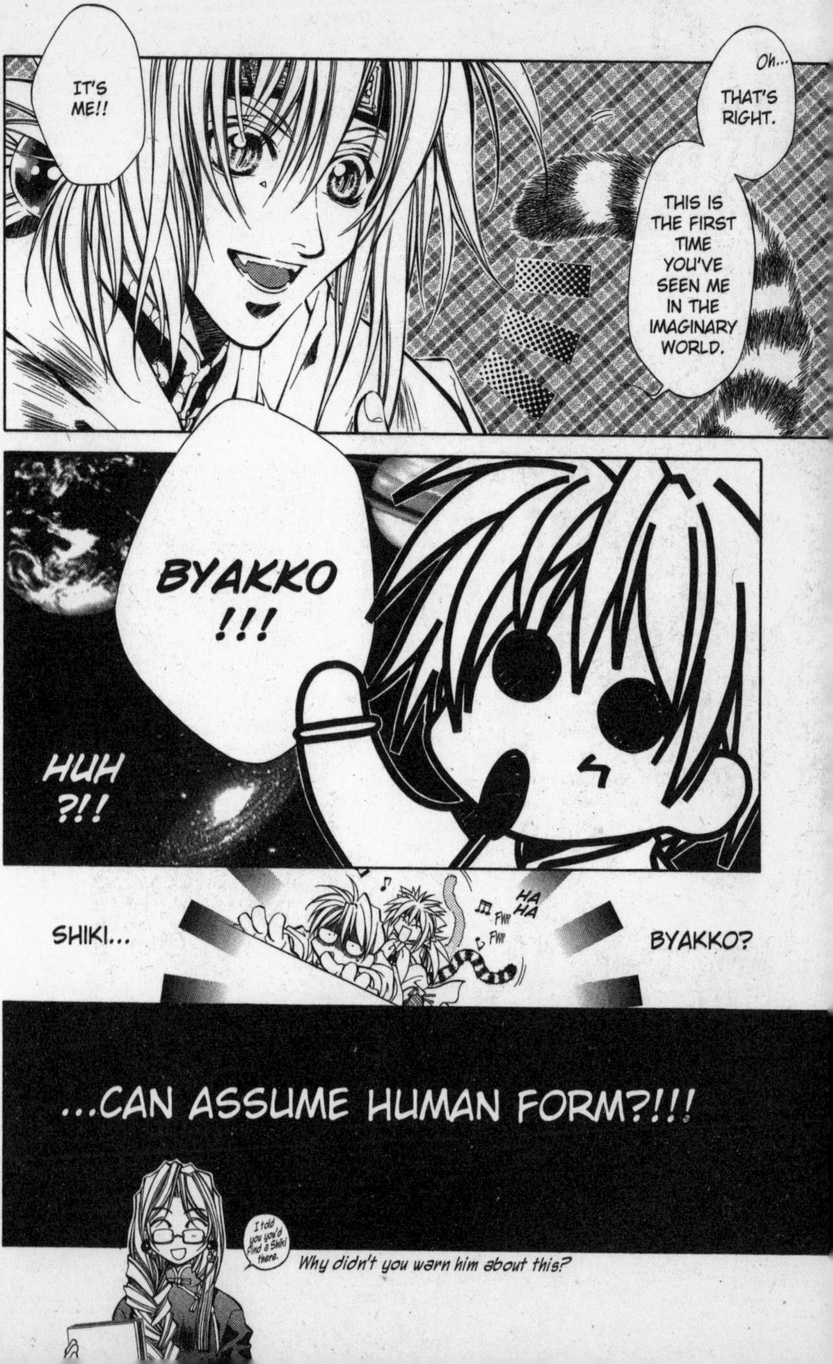
Oh...
THAT'S RIGHT.
THIS IS THE FIRST TIME YOU'VE SEEN ME IN THE IMAGINARY WORLD.
IT'S ME!!
BYAKKO !!!
HUH ?!!
HA HA
FWP
FWP
BYAKKO?
SHIKI...
...CAN ASSUME HUMAN FORM?!!!
Why didn't you warn him about this?
I told you you'd find a Shiki there.

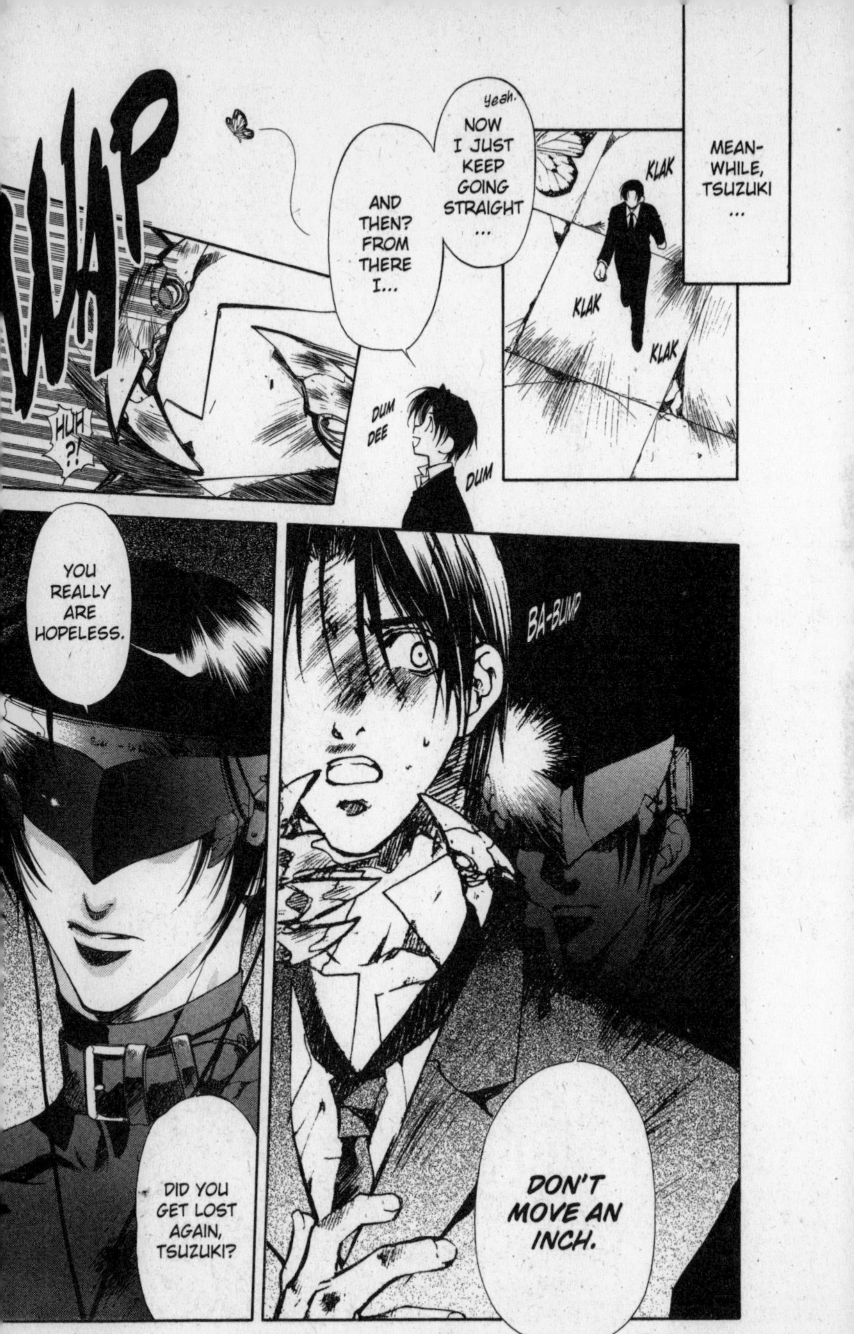
MEAN-WHILE, TSUZUKI ...
KLAK
KLAK
KLAK
yeah.
NOW I JUST KEEP GOING STRAIGHT ...
AND THEN? FROM THERE I...
DUM DEE
DUM
WAP
HUH ?!
BA-BUMP
DON'T MOVE AN INCH.
YOU REALLY ARE HOPELESS.
DID YOU GET LOST AGAIN, TSUZUKI?

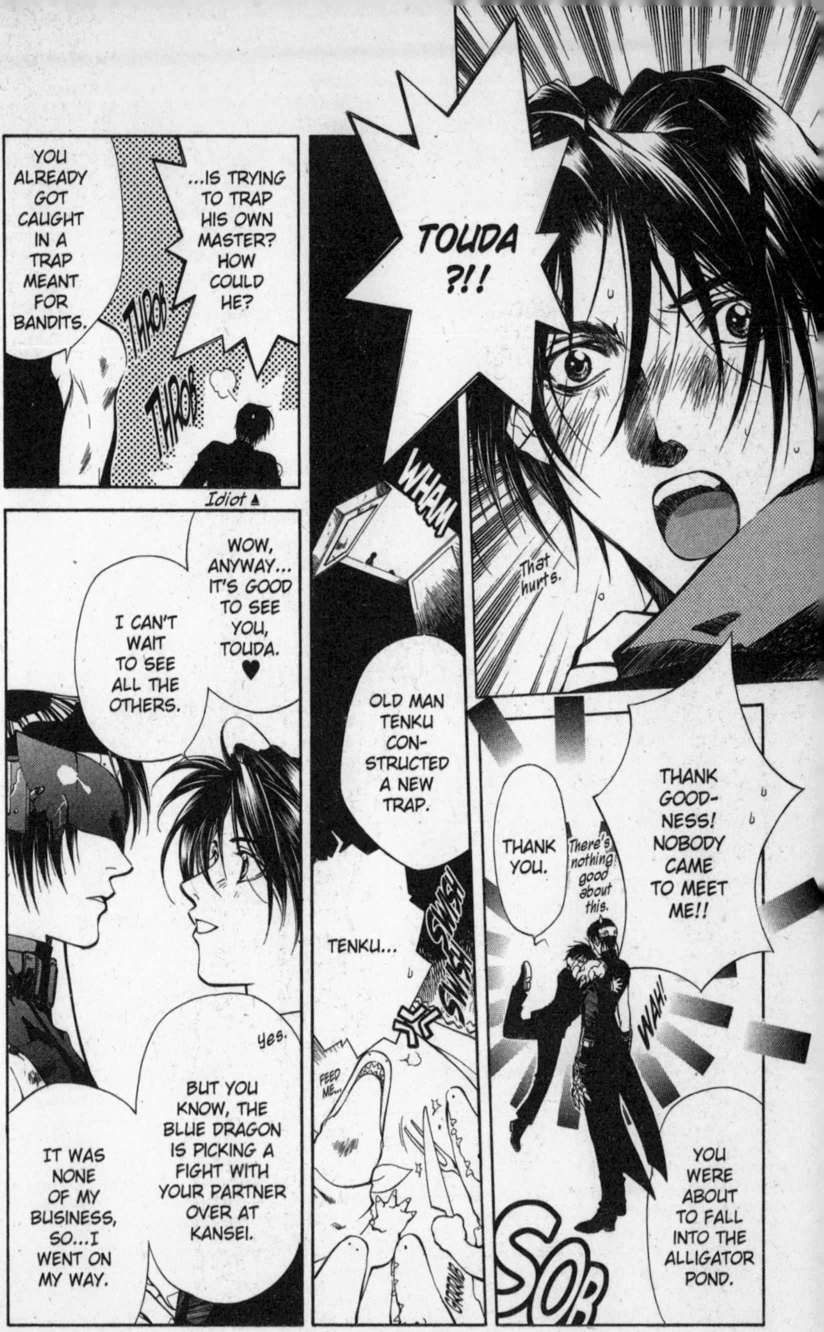
TOUDA ?!!
WHAM
That hurts.
THANK GOODNESS! NOBODY CAME TO MEET ME!!
THANK YOU.
There's nothing good about this.
WAH!
YOU WERE ABOUT TO FALL INTO THE ALLIGATOR POND.
SOB
OLD MAN TENKU CONSTRUCTED A NEW TRAP.
TENKU...
SWISH SWISH
FEED ME...
GROWL
...IS TRYING TO TRAP HIS OWN MASTER? HOW COULD HE?
YOU ALREADY GOT CAUGHT IN A TRAP MEANT FOR BANDITS.
THROB THROB
Idiot ▲
WOW, ANYWAY... IT'S GOOD TO SEE YOU, TOUDA. ♥
I CAN'T WAIT TO SEE ALL THE OTHERS.
yes.
BUT YOU KNOW, THE BLUE DRAGON IS PICKING A FIGHT WITH YOUR PARTNER OVER AT KANSEI.
IT WAS NONE OF MY BUSINESS, SO...I WENT ON MY WAY.

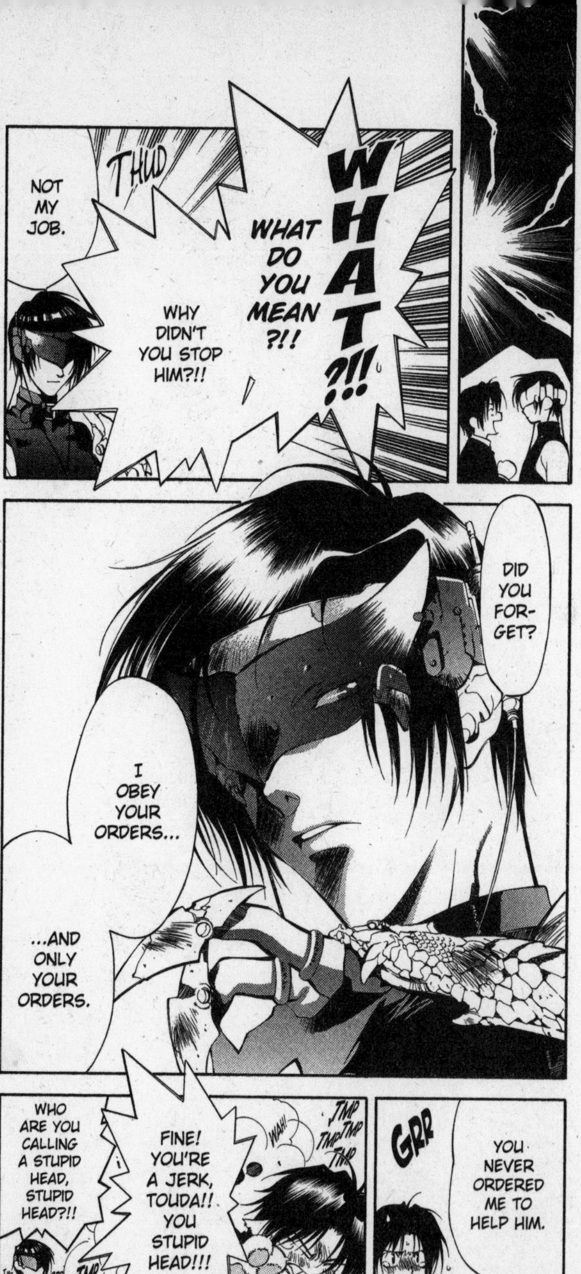
WHAT ?!!
WHAT DO YOU MEAN ?!!
THUD
NOT MY JOB.
WHY DIDN'T YOU STOP HIM?!!
DID YOU FOR-GET?
I OBEY YOUR ORDERS...
...AND ONLY YOUR ORDERS.
YOU NEVER ORDERED ME TO HELP HIM.
GRR
TMP TMP TMP TMP
WAH!
FINE! YOU'RE A JERK, TOUDA!! YOU STUPID HEAD!!!
WHO ARE YOU CALLING A STUPID HEAD, STUPID HEAD?!!
GRR
Ingrate.
TMP TMP

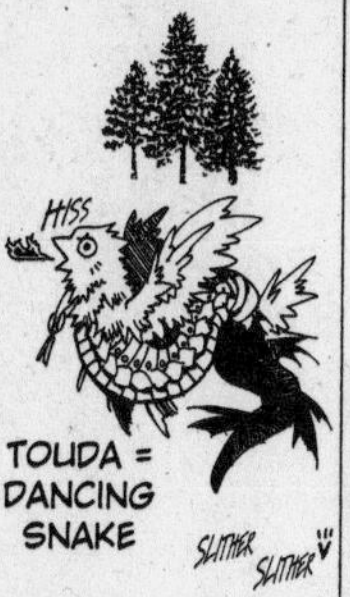
HISS
SLITHER SLITHER

TOUDA = DANCING SNAKE

When I looked it up in the Japanese kanji dictionary, that's the definition I got. (Laugh) I really like Touda. It's so nice to have a doll that does whatever you tell it to. Women want to rule and control, just like men. Of course, I don't have any interest in controlling real people, only dolls. (That might actually be a danger sign.) It's really fun to draw these servant characters. I guess I have a warped personality.

I was thinking about including some bonus pages in this volume with drawings of all twelve Shiki, but then I realized that all twelve Shiki didn't appear in the story. So I decided to do it in the next volume. I didn't have much time either. I've been really busy. Actually, I really wanted to do a lot of corrections in this volume, but there wasn't time for that either. The truth is that I just wasn't motivated. (I was too busy writing the new weekly stories.) So I'm not quite satisfied with volume 9. I'm sorry. I'll really make volume 10 something I can be proud of... I hope.

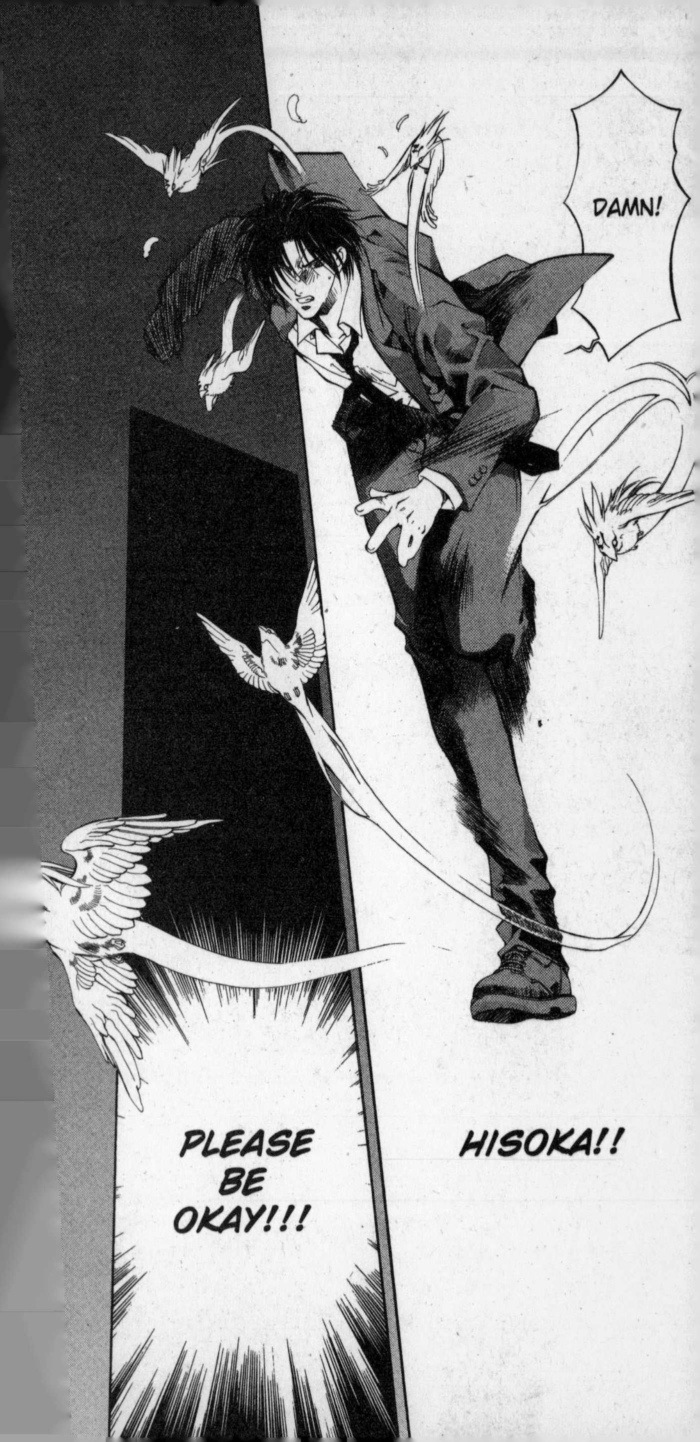
DAMN!
HISOKA!!
PLEASE BE OKAY!!!

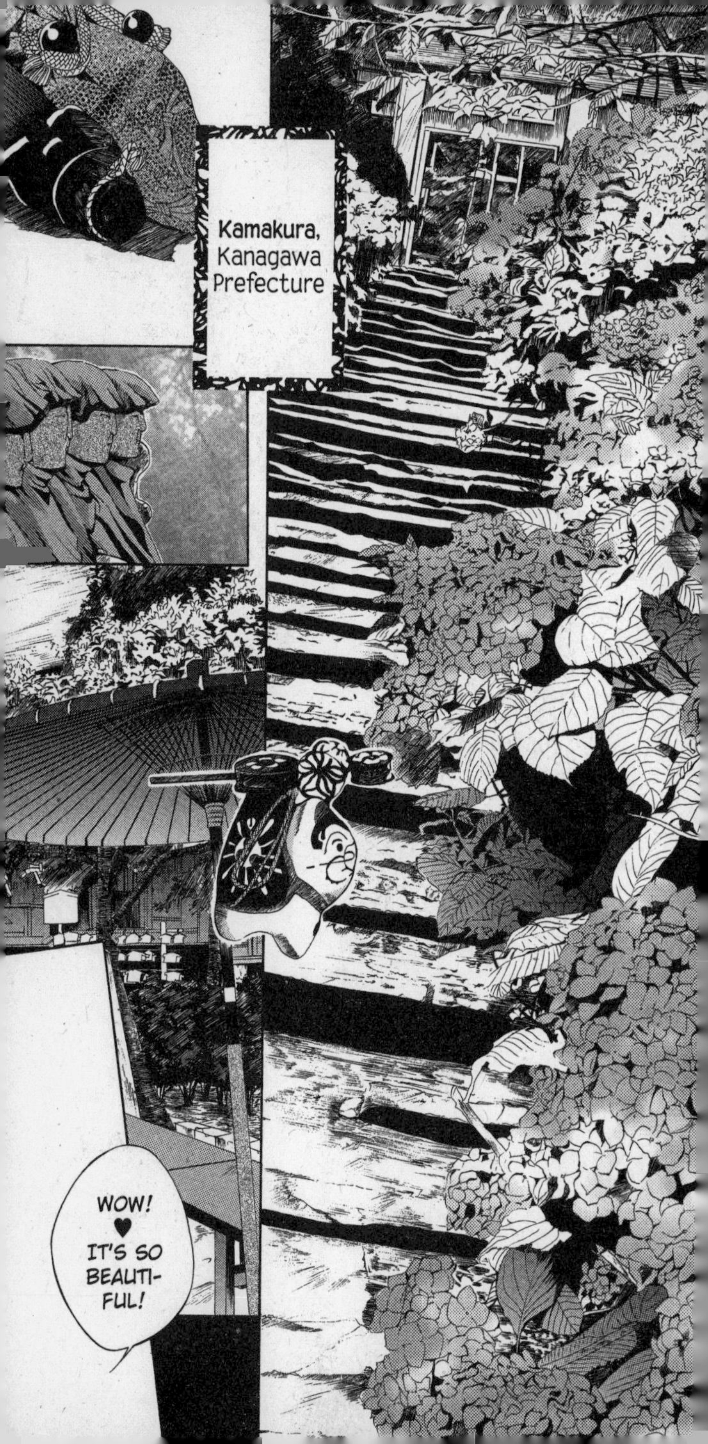
Kamakura, Kanagawa Prefecture
WOW! ♥ IT'S SO BEAUTI-FUL!

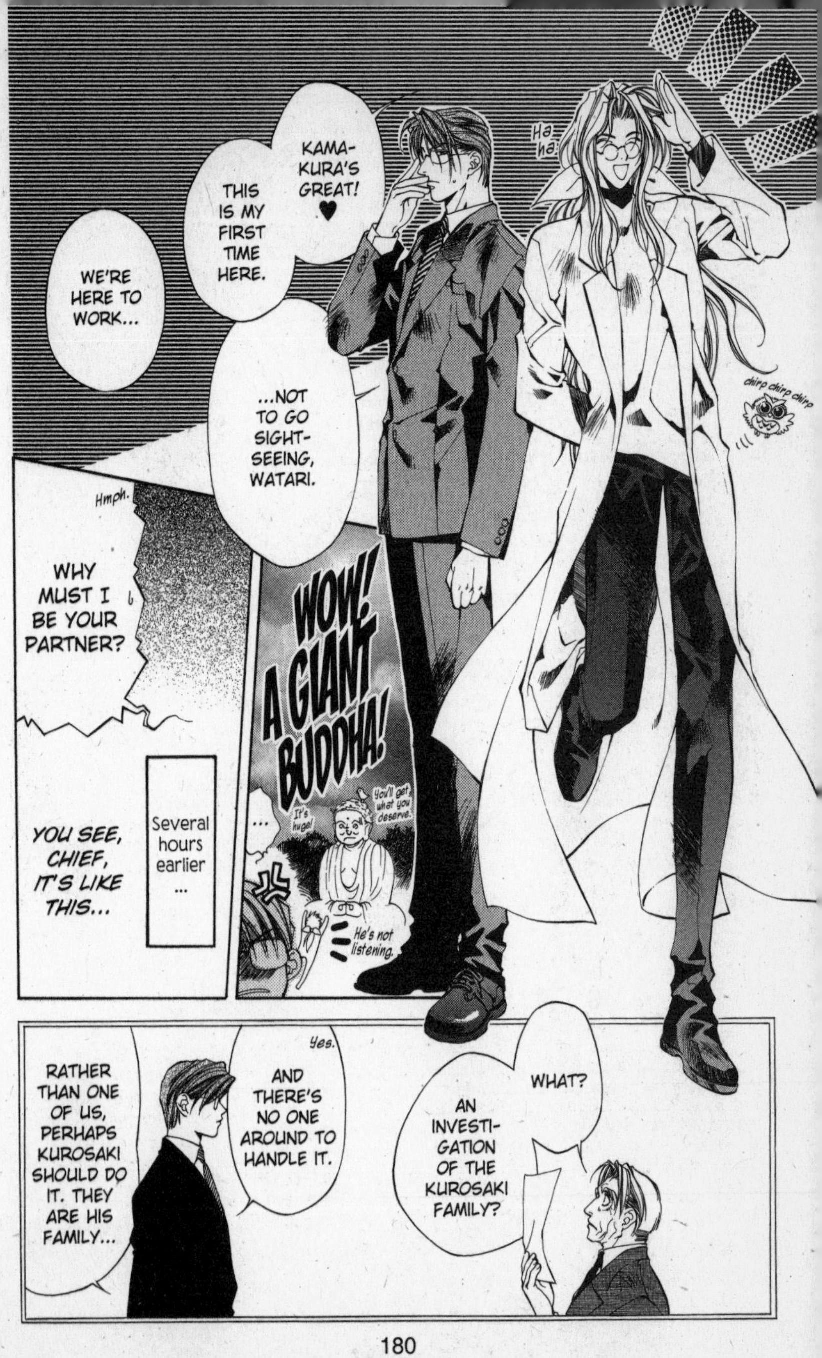
Ha ha
KAMA-KURA'S GREAT! ♥
THIS IS MY FIRST TIME HERE.
WE'RE HERE TO WORK...
...NOT TO GO SIGHT-SEEING, WATARI.
chirp chirp chirp
WOW! A GIANT BUDDHA!
It's huge!
You'll get what you deserve.
...
He's not listening.
Hmph.
WHY MUST I BE YOUR PARTNER?
Several hours earlier ...
YOU SEE, CHIEF, IT'S LIKE THIS...
WHAT?
AN INVESTI-GATION OF THE KUROSAKI FAMILY?
Yes.
AND THERE'S NO ONE AROUND TO HANDLE IT.
RATHER THAN ONE OF US, PERHAPS KUROSAKI SHOULD DO IT. THEY ARE HIS FAMILY...

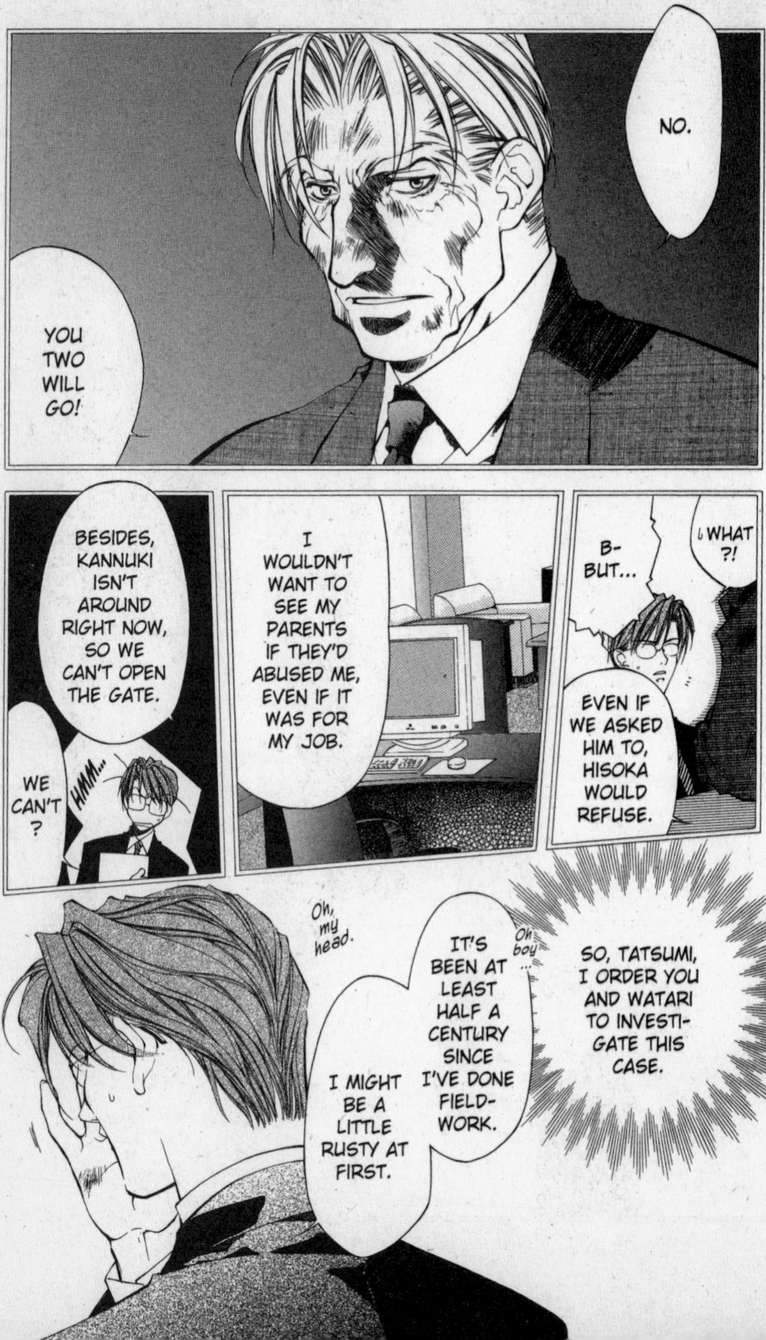
NO.
YOU TWO WILL GO!
WHAT?!
B-BUT...
EVEN IF WE ASKED HIM TO, HISOKA WOULD REFUSE.
I WOULDN'T WANT TO SEE MY PARENTS IF THEY'D ABUSED ME, EVEN IF IT WAS FOR MY JOB.
BESIDES, KANNUKI ISN'T AROUND RIGHT NOW, SO WE CAN'T OPEN THE GATE.
HMM...
WE CAN'T?
SO, TATSUMI, I ORDER YOU AND WATARI TO INVESTI-GATE THIS CASE.
Oh boy...
IT'S BEEN AT LEAST HALF A CENTURY SINCE I'VE DONE FIELD-WORK.
I MIGHT BE A LITTLE RUSTY AT FIRST.
Oh, my head.

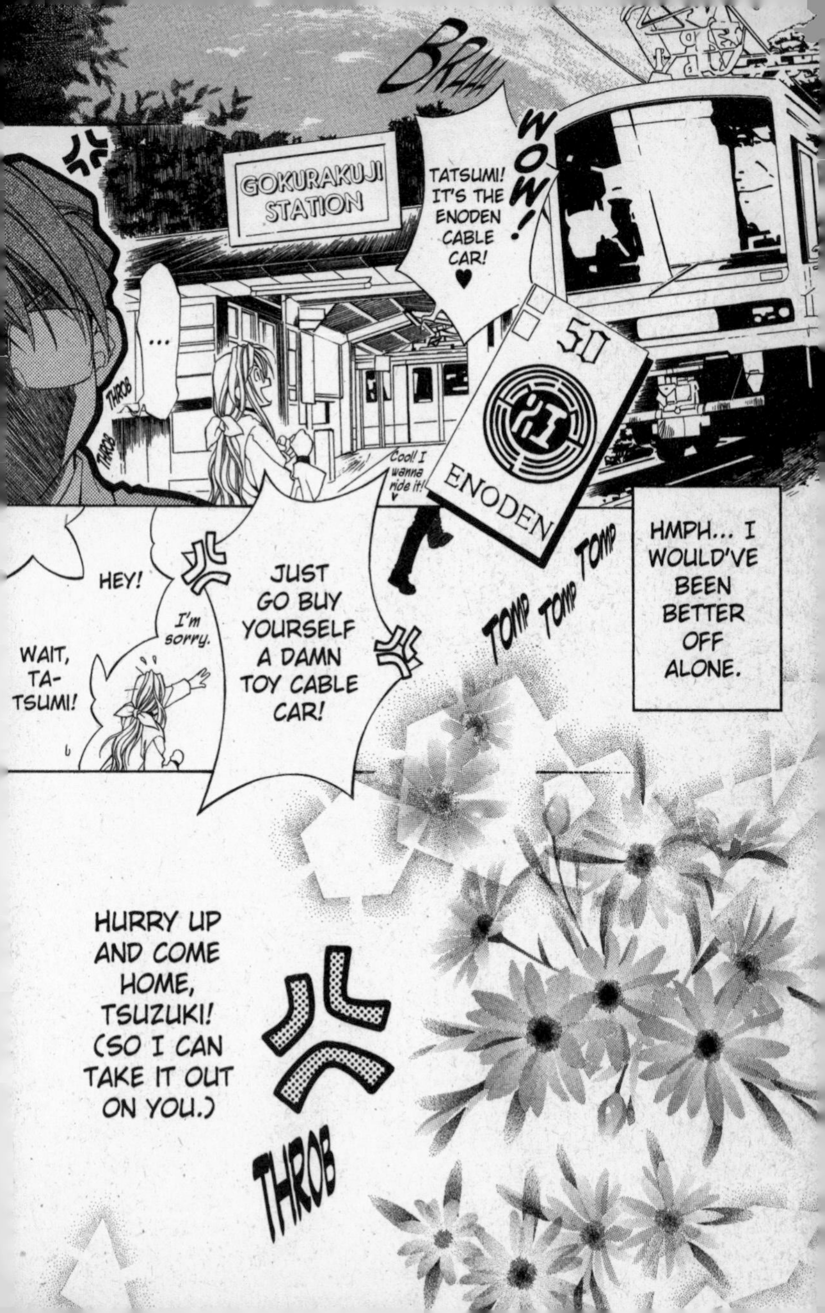
WOW!
TATSUMI! IT'S THE ENODEN CABLE CAR! ♥
GOKURAKUJI STATION
50
ENODEN
Cool! I wanna ride it! ♥
...
THROB
THROB
HMPH... I WOULD'VE BEEN BETTER OFF ALONE.
TOMP TOMP TOMP
JUST GO BUY YOURSELF A DAMN TOY CABLE CAR!
I'm sorry.
HEY!
WAIT, TA-TSUMI!
HURRY UP AND COME HOME, TSUZUKI! (SO I CAN TAKE IT OUT ON YOU.)
THROB

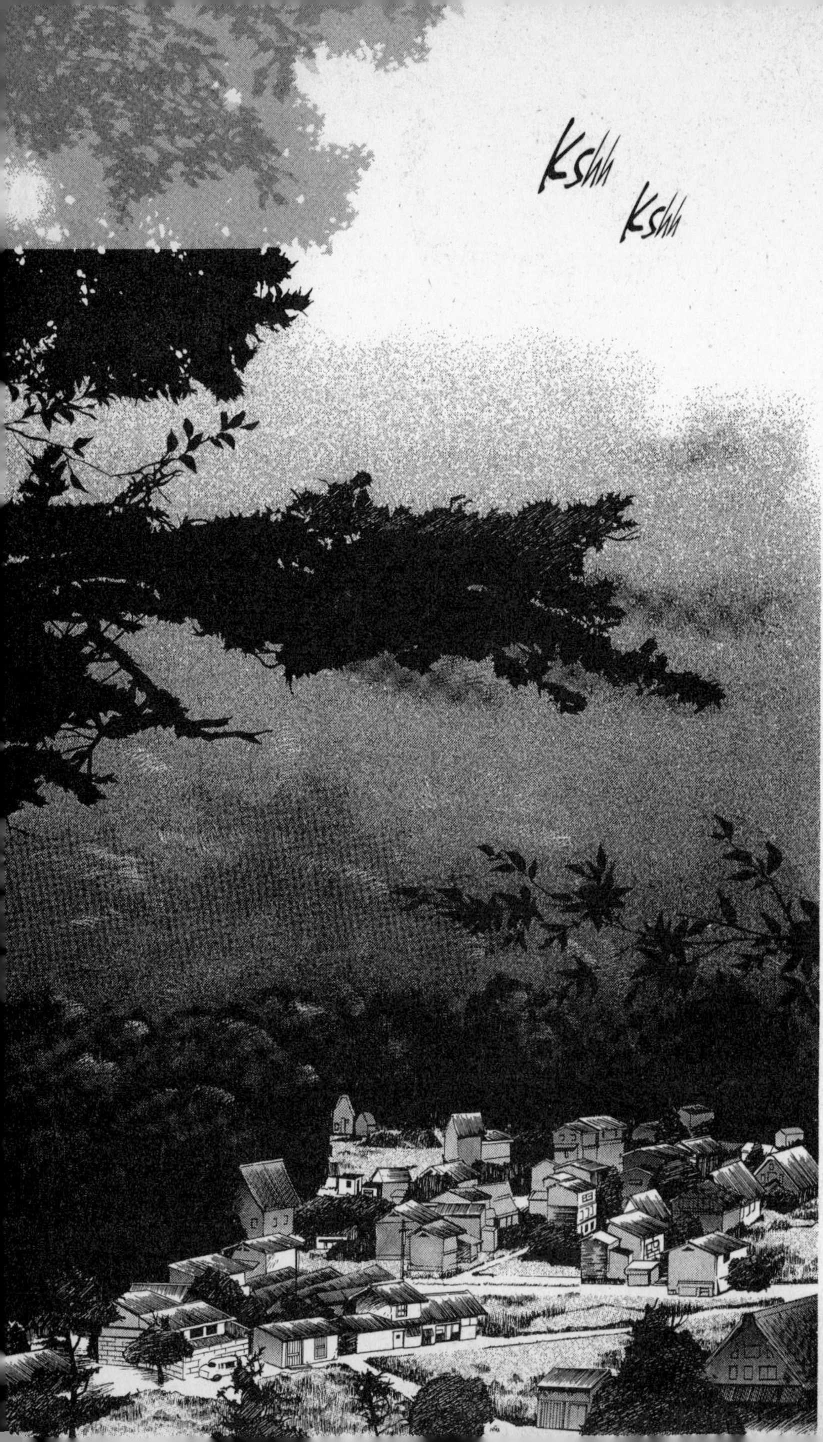
Kshh
Kshh

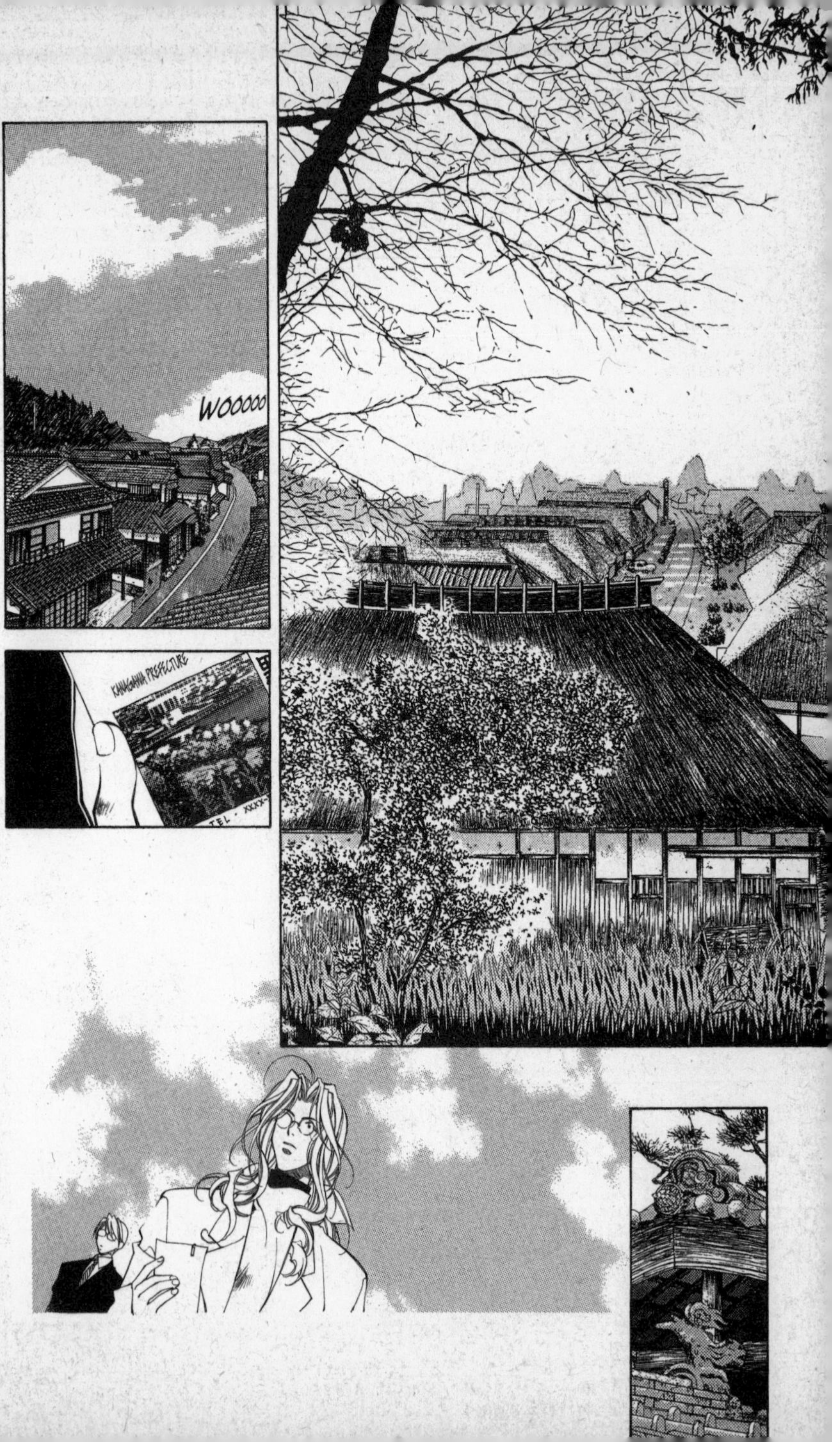
WOOOOO
KANAGAWA PREFECTURE
TEL · XXXX-

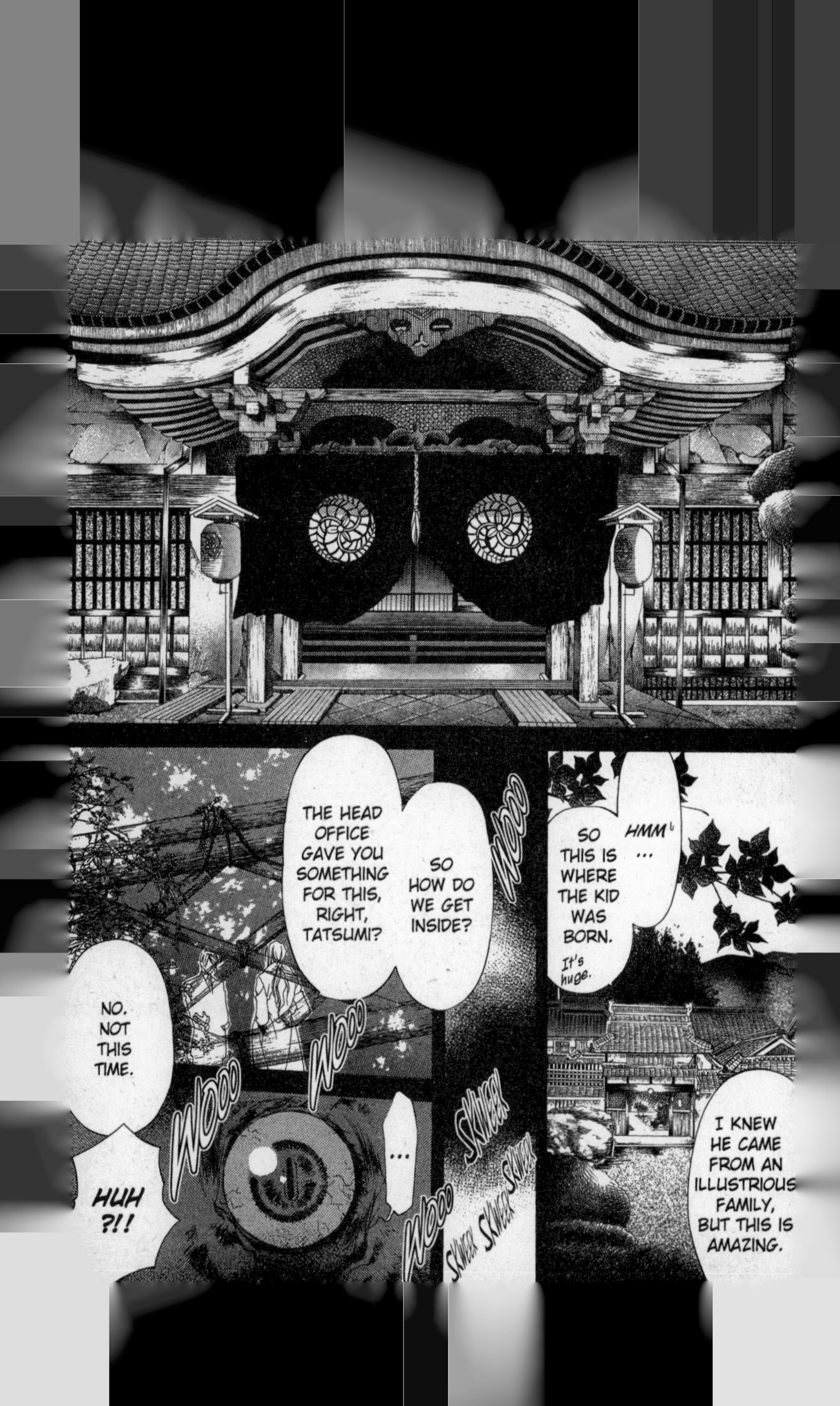
HMM ...
SO THIS IS WHERE THE KID WAS BORN.
It's huge.
I KNEW HE CAME FROM AN ILLUSTRIOUS FAMILY, BUT THIS IS AMAZING.
SO HOW DO WE GET INSIDE?
THE HEAD OFFICE GAVE YOU SOMETHING FOR THIS, RIGHT, TATSUMI?
WOOO
NO. NOT THIS TIME.
WOOO
WOOO
HUH ?!!
...
SKWEEK
WOOO
SKWEEK
SKWEEK
SKWEEK

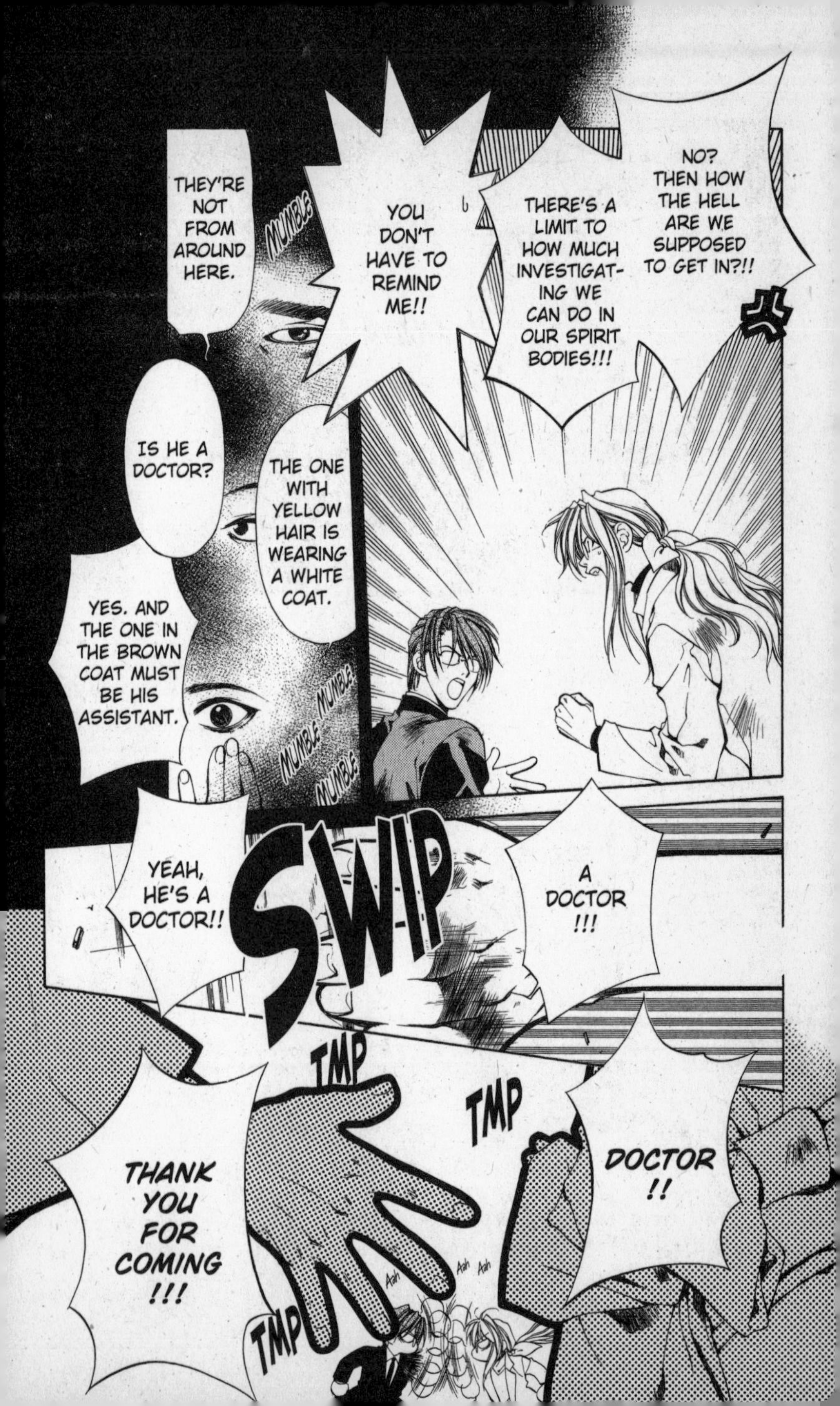

NO? THEN HOW THE HELL ARE WE SUPPOSED TO GET IN?!!
THERE'S A LIMIT TO HOW MUCH INVESTIGATING WE CAN DO IN OUR SPIRIT BODIES!!!
YOU DON'T HAVE TO REMIND ME!!
MUMBLE
THEY'RE NOT FROM AROUND HERE.
THE ONE WITH YELLOW HAIR IS WEARING A WHITE COAT.
IS HE A DOCTOR?
YES. AND THE ONE IN THE BROWN COAT MUST BE HIS ASSISTANT.
MUMBLE
MUMBLE
MUMBLE
A DOCTOR!!!
SWIP
YEAH, HE'S A DOCTOR!!
DOCTOR!!
TMP
TMP
THANK YOU FOR COMING!!!
Aah
Aah
Aah
TMP

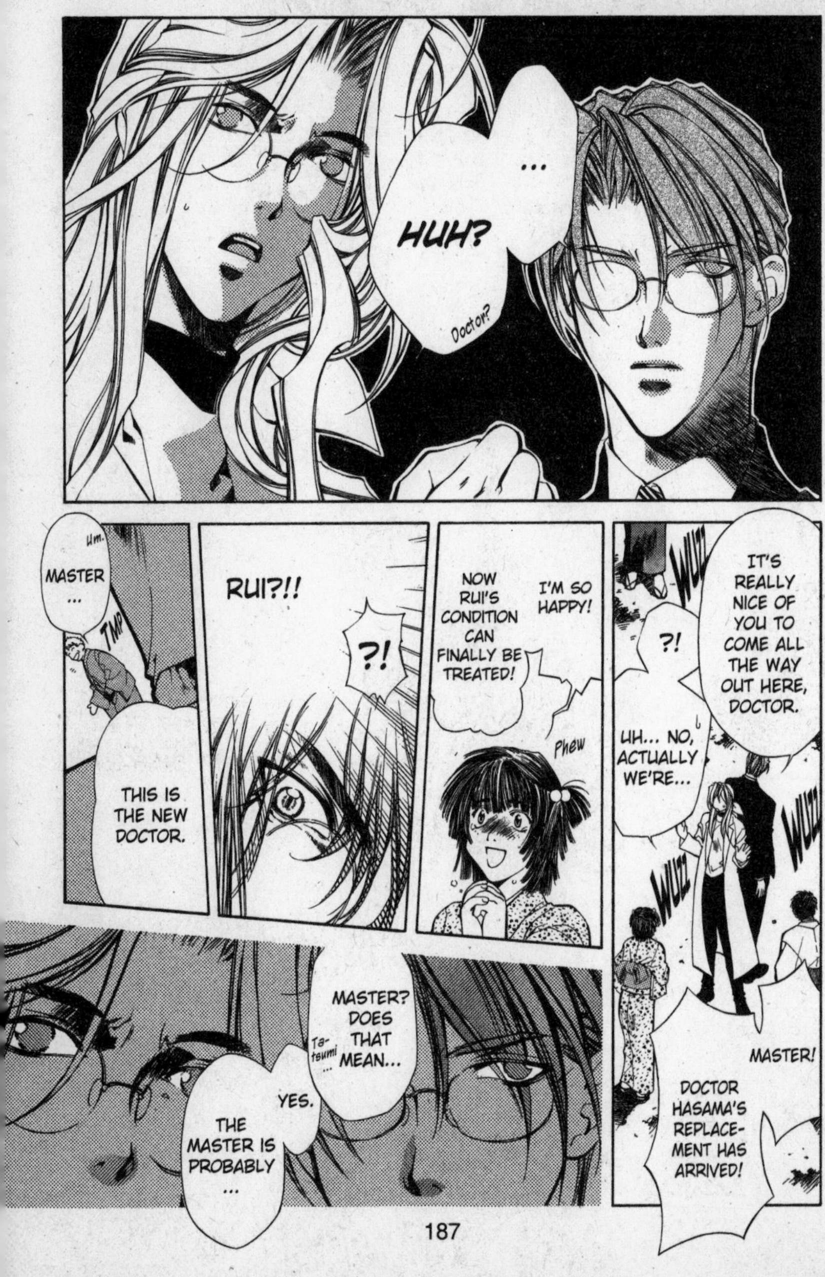
...
HUH?
Doctor?
IT'S REALLY NICE OF YOU TO COME ALL THE WAY OUT HERE, DOCTOR.
WUZZ
?!
UH... NO, ACTUALLY WE'RE...
WUZZ
WUZZ
MASTER!
DOCTOR HASAMA'S REPLACEMENT HAS ARRIVED!
I'M SO HAPPY!
NOW RUI'S CONDITION CAN FINALLY BE TREATED!
Phew
RUI?!!
?!
Um.
MASTER ...
TMP
THIS IS THE NEW DOCTOR.
MASTER? DOES THAT MEAN...
Tatsumi ...
YES.
THE MASTER IS PROBABLY ...

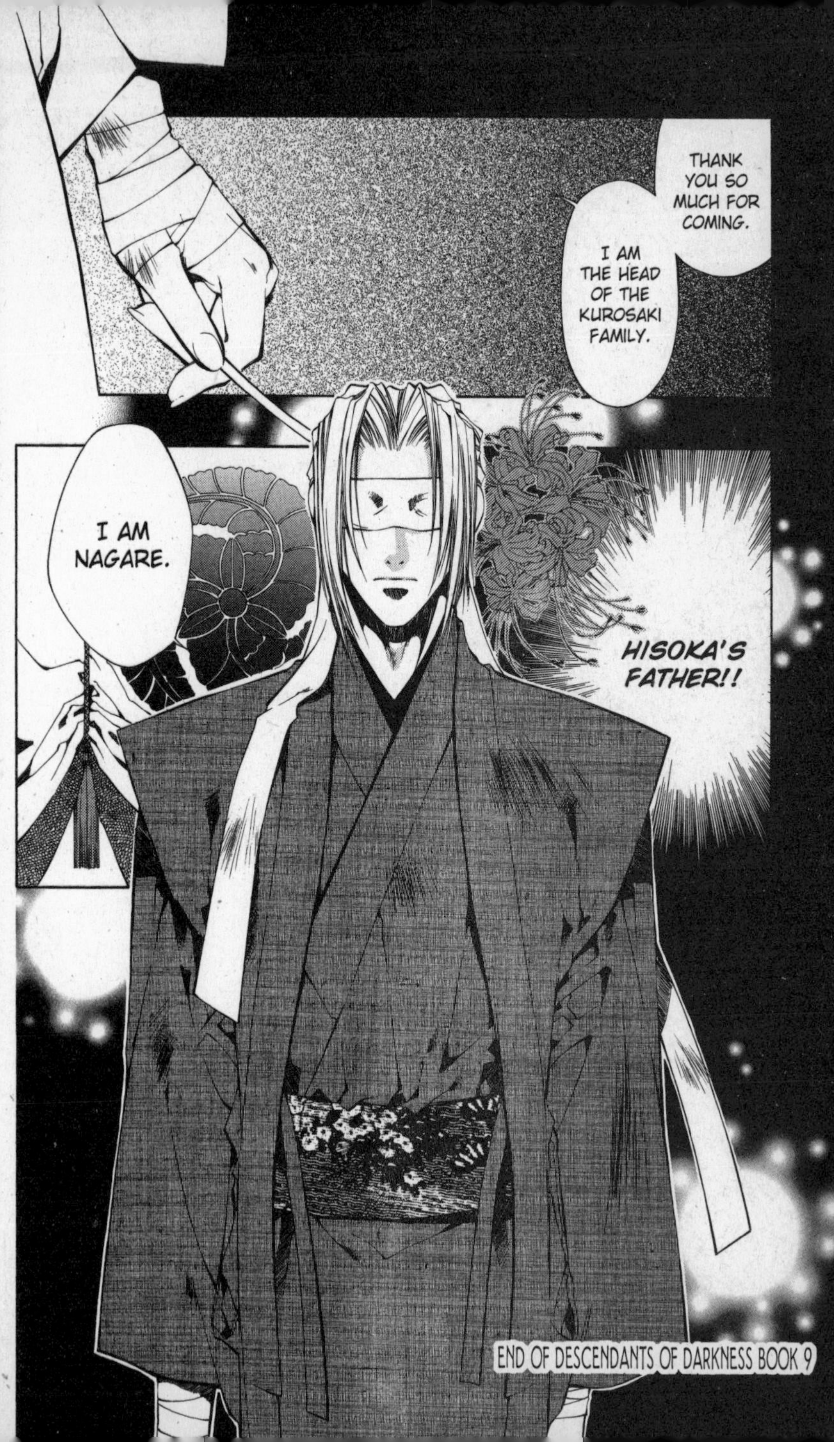
THANK YOU SO MUCH FOR COMING.
I AM THE HEAD OF THE KUROSAKI FAMILY.
I AM NAGARE.
HISOKA'S FATHER!!
END OF DESCENDANTS OF DARKNESS BOOK 9

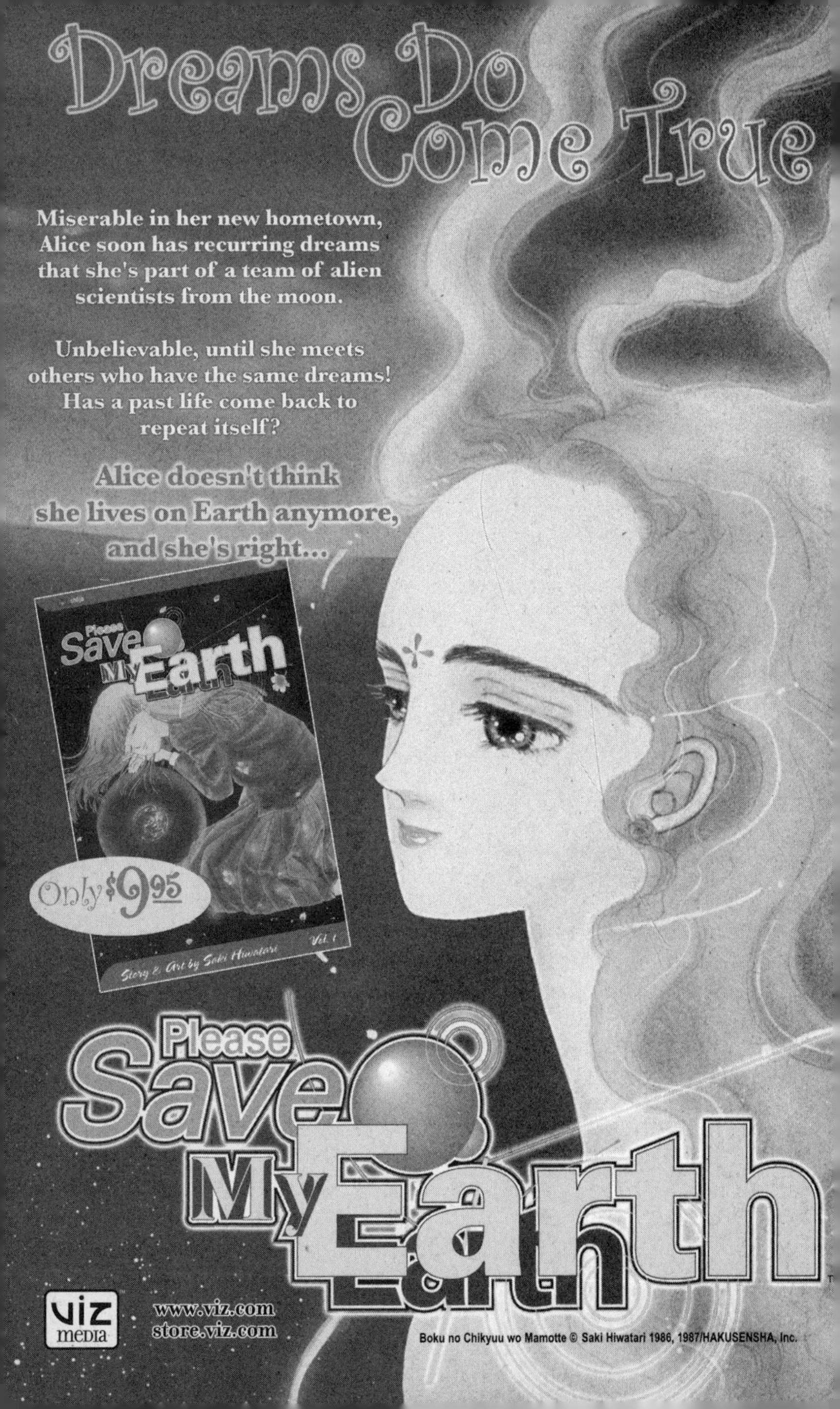
Dreams Do Come True
Miserable in her new hometown, Alice soon has recurring dreams that she's part of a team of alien scientists from the moon.
Unbelievable, until she meets others who have the same dreams! Has a past life come back to repeat itself?
Alice doesn't think she lives on Earth anymore, and she's right...
Please Save My Earth
Only $9.95
Story & Art by Saki Hiwatari
Vol. 1
Please Save My Earth
viz media
www.viz.com
store.viz.com
Boku no Chikyuu wo Mamotte © Saki Hiwatari 1986, 1987/HAKUSENSHA, Inc.

LOVE SHOJO? LET US KNOW!

☐ Please do NOT send me information about VIZ Media products, news and events, special offers, or other information.

☐ Please do NOT send me information from VIZ' trusted business partners.

Name: _____

Address: _____

City: _____ State: _____ Zip: _____

E-mail: _____

☐ Male ☐ Female Date of Birth (mm/dd/yyyy): ___ / ___ / _____ (Under 13? Parental consent required)

What race/ethnicity do you consider yourself? (check all that apply)

☐ White/Caucasian   ☐ Black/African American   ☐ Hispanic/Latino

☐ Asian/Pacific Islander ☐ Native American/Alaskan Native ☐ Other: _____

What VIZ shojo title(s) did you purchase? (indicate title(s) purchased)

_____

What other shojo titles from other publishers do you own? _____

_____

Reason for purchase: (check all that apply)

☐ Special offer   ☐ Favorite title / author / artist / genre

☐ Gift   ☐ Recommendation   ☐ Collection

☐ Read excerpt in VIZ manga sampler   ☐ Other _____

Where did you make your purchase? (please check one)

☐ Comic store   ☐ Bookstore   ☐ Mass/Grocery Store

☐ Newsstand   ☐ Video/Video Game Store

☐ Online (site:_____) ☐ Other _____

How many shojo tit **many were VIZ shojo titles?**
(please check one from

SHOJO MANGA

- ☐ None
- ☐ 1 – 4
- ☐ 5 – 10
- ☐ 11+

- ☐ 1 – 4
- ☐ 5 – 10
- ☐ 11+

What do you like most about shojo graphic novels? (check all that apply)

- ☐ Romance
- ☐ Drama / conflict
- ☐ Fantasy
- ☐ Comedy
- ☐ Real-life storylines
- ☐ Relatable characters
- ☐ Other ______________________________

Do you purchase every volume of your favorite shojo series?

- ☐ Yes! Gotta have 'em as my own
- ☐ No. Please explain: ______________________________

Who are your favorite shojo authors / artists? ______________________________

____

What shojo titles would like you translated and sold in English? ______________________________

____

THANK YOU! Please send the completed form to:

NJW Research
ATTN: VIZ Media Shojo Survey
42 Catharine Street
Poughkeepsie, NY 12601

Your privacy is very important to us. All information provided will be used for internal purposes only and will not be sold or otherwise divulged.